BODILY CITATIONS

GENDER, THEORY, AND RELIGION

GENDER, THEORY, AND RELIGION
Amy Hollywood, Editor

The Gender, Theory, and Religion series provides a forum for interdisciplinary scholarship at the intersection of the study of gender, sexuality, and religion.

BODILY
CITATIONS

RELIGION AND JUDITH BUTLER

Edited by

Ellen T. Armour

and

Susan M. St. Ville

COLUMBIA UNIVERSITY PRESS   NEW YORK

COLUMBIA UNIVERSITY PRESS

Publishers Since 1893

New York, Chichester, West Sussex

Copyright © 2006 Columbia University Press

Library of Congress Cataloging-in-Publication Data

Bodily Citations : religion and Judith Butler / edited by Ellen T. Armour and Susan M. St. Ville.

    p.   cm.

Includes bibliographical references and index.

ISBN 0-231-13406-1 (cloth : alk. paper) — ISBN 0-231-13407-x (pbk. : alk. paper) — ISBN 0-231-50864-6

    1. Religions. 2. Butler, Judith. 3. Feminist theory. 4. Sex role—Religious aspects.

    5. Gender identity. I. Armour, Ellen T., 1959– II. St. Ville, Susan M., 1963–

BL410.B63 2006

202.082--dc22

2005034516

∞ Casebound editions of Columbia University Press books are printed on permanent and durable acid-free paper.

Printed in the United States of America

c 10 9 8 7 6 5 4 3 2 1

p 10 9 8 7 6 5 4 3 2 1

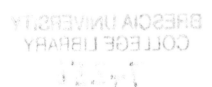

CONTENTS

PREFACE AND ACKNOWLEDGMENTS

THOUGH NOW CONSIDERABLY expanded, this volume originated from a set of sessions sponsored by the Feminist Theory and Religious Reflection Group at the 1997 national meeting of the American Academy of Religion in San Francisco. The group took advantage of the meeting's location to invite feminist and queer theorist Judith Butler, professor of rhetoric and comparative literature at the University of California in Berkeley, to respond to a set of papers by scholars of religion in various fields using her work. Professor Butler graciously agreed, and two dynamic sessions with a combined audience of several hundred took place. The response to those sessions and the important place that Professor Butler's work continues to occupy in women's studies, queer theory, and disciplines that engage those fields (including religion) inspired us to produce this anthology.[1] While we expect this book will find an audience among scholars in religion who are already interested in Butler, we also hope to attract scholars of religion who are not familiar with—or may even be skeptical about—her work. In addition, we hope that the book will appeal to scholars of feminist and queer theory who may be unaware of—or even skeptical about—religious studies. A word or two, then, to entice both kinds of readers into the volume.

THE TROUBLE WITH GENDER (AND BEYOND)

Though not her first book, the publication of *Gender Trouble: Feminism and the Subversion of Identity* in 1990 brought Judith Butler to prominence.[2] *Gender Trouble* broke new ground in feminist theory and became a founding text in the emerging field of queer theory with its assertion that gender produces sex. Masculinity and femininity, Butler argued, are bodily performances based on the demands of our heterosexual and phallocentric economy, not expressions of the body's inner nature. In monographs that followed, *Bodies That Matter* (1993), *Excitable Speech* (1997), and *The Psychic Life of Power* (1997), Butler refined and expanded upon *Gender Trouble* by developing more detailed accounts of the mechanisms through which identities are produced and resisted while attending to the political contexts in which they function.[3] In recent years Butler has turned her attention to kinship structures (*Antigone's Claim: Kinship Between Life and Death*, 2000) and international politics (*Contingency, Hegemony, Universality*, 2000, co-written with Slavoj Žižek and Ernesto Laclau), including America's responses to September 11 (in *Precarious Life: The Powers of Mourning and Violence*, 2004).[4] Her latest book, *Undoing Gender* (2004), returns once again to the fraught terrain of sexuality and gender nearly twenty-five years after *Gender Trouble*.[5] Her investigations into all these arenas continue to explore and expose the interplay of psychic, linguistic, and political forces.

The essays in *Bodily Citations* focus on Judith Butler's performative theory of gender, the aspect of her work that continues to exercise the greatest influence on academia. We have provided in "Judith Butler—in Theory" an account of the contours of this theory and its significance for the study of religion; what follows here positions this volume in relation to critical questions raised about Butler's theory. Even those who have never read a word of *Gender Trouble* may be aware of the brief firestorms of controversy that have erupted around Butler in the public press in recent years. A review of Butler's major works written by Martha Nussbaum for the *New Republic* (February 22, 1999) is a case in point.[6] Although in our judgment Nussbaum's review has been rightly critiqued as unnecessarily vicious and irresponsible, it seems to us important to address.[7] Doing so provides a useful entrée into critical questions about Butler's work that are raised and, in some cases, addressed in *Bodily Citations*. Nussbaum accuses Butler (as have others before) of substituting the doing of supposedly subversive things with words for genuine feminist political engagement. Elevating language to center stage distorts reality and troubles structures foundational to political activism, she argues. Stable identities (including that of being a woman) and the ability to act freely—both notions challenged by Butler's work—seem to be basic requirements for any kind of politics, feminist or otherwise. Engaging with

Butler, Nussbaum claims, results inevitably in a paralyzing quietism that eviscerates feminist politics.

The questions Nussbaum raises echo what seem to be lingering—if uninformed—suspicions about not only Butler's work but certain kinds of theory on which it depends. What does theory of the type Butler engages (psychoanalytic, deconstructive, poststructuralist) offer those who struggle with hardscrabble political realities? Butler, like the theorists on whom she draws, has been accused of resorting to jargon-laden prose that some deride as camouflage for weak ideas. Are the insights to be gained from submerging oneself in what is purported to be, at least, inscrutable prose and convoluted ideas (or convoluted prose about inscrutable ideas) worth the intellectual labor?

The introduction to Butler's work that follows will, we trust, effectively put to rest suspicions based on misunderstanding or misreading of this theorist. Many of the essays will shed new light on those questions that need serious consideration. Indeed, examining the uses to which religionists put Butler's work strikes us as an excellent location for responding to these questions and suspicions. Though itself frequently subject to oversimplification in the popular media and the secular imagination (the religious imagination, too, for that matter), religion is an aspect of culture that has its moments of high theory *and* its hardscrabble realities. Those of us who have taken it up as an academic pursuit are perhaps especially attuned to the complexities of religious ideas and their materializations in religious texts and practices of various sorts engaged in by perfectly ordinary people to ordinary and extraordinary effect. Even those who go about their lives paying little or no attention to religious matters cannot avoid their effects. For good and for ill, religious traces persist even within the West's putatively secular culture—overtly as a source of conflict (as in the so-called culture wars) but also covertly (as the unacknowledged root of certain cultural traditions). Religion, like gender and sexuality (and often with them), is a site where language, materiality, theory, and politics all come together in complex ways.

PUTTING BUTLER TO WORK

In addition to deepening and broadening our understanding of the import of Butler's work, *Bodily Citations* offers a distinctive approach to the study of religion by applying a common theoretical lens to a set of issues that emerge from diverse religious sites. The introduction to this volume describes the essays in more detail. We take a moment here to provide readers who are unfamiliar with the academic study of religion with a map that situates each essay in relationship to that field.

This volume deploys a rather broad understanding of the study of religion. While most of the authors of these essays hold PhDs in religious studies, two are trained in other fields. Dance and performance studies scholar Rebecca Schneider turns to religious ritual and the embodied practice of female performance artists to refine challenges to Butler's views on the body, knowledge, and agency. Anthropologist Saba Mahmood draws on her research on an urban women's mosque movement in Cairo to argue for greater nuance in theorizing agency. Religious studies scholar Amy Hollywood continues in this vein by arguing that a deeper consideration of religious ritual and ritual theory could strengthen Butler's account of performativity.

The remaining essays in this volume are drawn from subfields generally representative of religious studies (biblical studies, theology, ethics, and the history of religions). Theologians and ethicists working out of Christian traditions use Butler's work to craft creative responses to contemporary challenges. Claudia Schippert begins to articulate a queer religious ethics modeled on womanist ethics, a model that allows her to build on Butler's work on normativity. Karen Trimble Alliaume appropriates Butler's theory of performativity to renew and reframe debates over the Roman Catholic Church's insistence that the ordained must be, like Jesus, physically male. Christina Hutchins uses Butler's work to analyze the rather complex subject position of "*the* lesbian minister."

Scholars in biblical studies and the history of religions use Butler's work to read sometimes troubling sacred texts. Biblical scholars Teresa Hornsby and Ken Stone draw on Butler to craft approaches to the Bible that are able to contest its use against those deemed "other" because of gender or sexuality. Hornsby inquires after the strategies that sustain and undercut feminist approaches to biblical studies and proposes her own reading of the nameless prostitute in Luke's gospel. Stone offers a queer reading of the creation stories in Genesis, traditionally cited in support of heterosexuality's normative status, exposing textual ambiguities that undercut that usage and open up other possibilities. Butler's work allows Susanne Mrozik, a scholar of Buddhism, to uncover resistances to normative associations between masculine embodiment and virtue in the Indian Buddhist story of Rūpāvatī.

That scholars in religious studies are open to engaging Butler's work reflects a characteristic of the study of religion in general. Aptly described as interdisciplinary, scholars of religion in all of its subfields frequently apply methods and theories drawn from various disciplines in the humanities and/or social sciences. However, we have asked the contributors to this volume to do more than simply apply Butler's theories to their own scholarly projects. Tat-siong Benny Liew, in his response to *Queer Commentary and the Hebrew Bible*, calls for biblical scholars not just to use queer theory but also to "interrogate, or even transform queer theory. . . . After all, what would entice a Judith Butler or a Michael Warner to read our work if we are just demonstrating over and over again the 'correctness' of their formulations?" (185–86). We could not agree more and would extend his admonition to include all scholars of religion who use any theory—particularly those theories that have developed in order to attend to marginalized others. Each of these essays was selected because its author "speaks back" to Butler. That is, in addition to deploying Butler to good effect in analyzing various aspects of religion, these scholars also raise questions about, pose challenges to, extend and/or deepen Butler's own work from the perspective of the study of religion. We are grateful that Professor Butler has, in fact, not only been enticed to read the essays contained herein but has written a response to the volume as a whole. Appropriately, for the moment at least, the last word belongs to her.

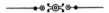

Some material in Karen Trimble Alliaume's essay appeared in earlier form in "The Risks of Repeating Ourselves: Reading Feminist/Womanist Figures of Jesus" *Cross Currents* (Summer 1998) 48, no. 2 (http://www.crosscurrents. org/alliaume.htm).

"Performativity, Citationality, Ritualization," by Amy Hollywood, is reprinted by permission from *History of Religions* 42, no. 2 (2002): 93–116, originally published by University of Chicago Press.

"Unconforming Becomings: The Significance of Whitehead's Novelty and Butler's Subversion for the Repetitions of Lesbian Identity and the Expansion of the Future," by Christina Hutchins, is reprinted by permission of *Process and Difference: Between Cosmological and Poststructuralist Postmodernisms*, ed. Catherine Keller and Anne Daniell (New York: State University of New York Press, 2002). Copyright © 2002 State University of New York. All rights reserved.

Saba Mahmood's essay is based on material that first appeared in *Politics of Piety: The Islamic Revival and the Feminist Subject* (Princeton University Press, 2005). We thank Princeton University Press for permission to use this material.

A portion of Rebecca Schneider's essay appeared in "Taking the Blind in Hand," *Contemporary Theatre Review* 10, no. 3 (2000): 23-38, and is used here by permission from Routledge Press. The journal's Web site may be accessed at http://www.tandf.co.uk.

Ken Stone, "The Garden of Eden and the Heterosexual Contract," is from *Take Back the Word: A Queer Reading of the Bible*, ed. Robert E. Goss and Mona West (Cleveland: Pilgrim, 2000), 57–70. Copyright © 2000 by the Pilgrim Press. Revised by permission.

Funds provided by the R. A. Webb Professorship at Rhodes College helped make this project possible. The editors are grateful to Rhodes College for its support.

NOTES

1. For a sample of the monographs and anthologies by scholars of religion that use Butler's work, see the bibliography at the end of this volume. Note that they come from most subfields of religious studies including theology, ethics, history of religions, and biblical studies.

2. Judith Butler, *Gender Trouble: Feminism and the Subversion of Identity* (GT). For complete references to books authored by Butler (either alone or with others), see the bibliography at the end of this volume. All citations of these texts in the essays that comprise this volume will be referenced in abbreviated form using the abbreviations given in the bibliography.

3. Judith Butler, *Bodies That Matter: On the Discursive Limits of "Sex"* (BTM); *Excitable Speech: A Politics of the Performative* (ES); *The Psychic Life of Power: Theories in Subjection* (PLP).

4. Judith Butler, *Antigone's Claim: Kinship Between Life and Death* (AC); Judith Butler, Ernesto Laclau, and Slavoj Žižek, *Contingency, Hegemony, Universality: Contemporary Dialogues on the Left* (CHU); *Precarious Life: The Powers of Mourning and Violence* (PL).

5. Judith Butler, *Undoing Gender* (UG).

6. Martha Nussbaum, "The Professor of Parody," *New Republic* 220, no. 8 (February 22, 1999): 37–45.

7. Warren Hedges, Gayatri Chakravorty Spivak, Seyla Benhabib et al., "Martha Nussbaum and Her Critics: An Exchange," *New Republic* 220, no. 16 (April 19, 1999): 43–45.

INTRODUCTION

O
UR PREFATORY ACCOUNT of Butler's work has begun to indicate, we trust, its rich and varied potential as a resource for
scholars of religion. Indeed, the essays gathered here reflect
in their complexity the many directions this intersection can take. Multiple
themes run through and overlap in these pieces. For heuristic purposes we
have grouped these essays into three sections representing the main topics
of textual interpretation, agency and religious subjectivity, and prospective
theoretical directions. The essays, however, refract each other in varied ways
and so, in Butlerian fashion, could be grouped and regrouped to provoke still
further avenues of inquiry.

TEXTUAL BODIES

We begin with three articles that draw on Butler to interpret religious
texts, in each case finding unexpected meanings in works that have been
influential in both Eastern and Western religious traditions. Susanne Mrozik,
a scholar of Buddhism, reviews the Sanskrit tale of Rūpāvatī, a narrative that
in its unfolding offers teaching on what is required to attain a virtuous state.

Mrozik finds useful analytical resources in Butler's theories of the materialization of bodies via the citational process as well as in the production of the abject. Appropriating these insights for her own purposes, she critically reassesses the formation of "virtuous bodies" as these are exemplified by the Buddha and his precursor the Boddhisatva. Mrozik's creative reappropriation works to uncover unexpected depths in Butler's views as she extends them to fit Buddhist contexts, allowing her to produce interpretations that challenge normative assumptions in Buddhism that routinely equate the ideal of virtue exclusively with the male body.

As Mrozik reminds us, the attainment of Buddhahood evolves through a process of birth and rebirth. The story of Rūpāvatī outlines three successive lifetimes of the founder of Buddhism. The tale is particularly useful for Mrozik because it offers multiple accounts of sexed bodies and their alterations. To point to only a few, the Buddha first appears in this story in the form of a woman, Rūpāvatī (Beautiful Woman). In the course of the narrative Rūpāvatī, in an act of generosity, mutilates her body by cutting off her breasts to feed a starving mother. Her breasts are eventually restored only to be lost again when she is reborn as a Beautiful Man (Rūpāvata), and as successive male Boddhisatvas, in the end attaining Buddhahood. While traditional readings have interpreted Rūpāvatī's excision of her breasts as a moment when her body becomes male (thus in line with the ideal that equates virtue with the male body), Mrozik sees in this mutilation an embracing of the abject and the emergence in Rūpāvatī's altered form of alternatively sexed beings. With this reading in place, the way is opened for a proliferation in interpretations of the Buddha as, in Mrozik's terms, "omnibodied" and for a more fluid reconceptualization of the Buddhist community as well.

Authors Ken Stone and Teresa Hornsby draw on Butler's writings to interpret the Hebrew Bible and New Testament respectively. Stone focuses his attention on the two creation accounts found in Genesis. Noting the tendency of queer critics to concentrate on undermining biblical passages that explicitly condemn homosexuality, Stone takes a different tack. He argues rather for the importance of calling into question those texts like the creation stories that, while silent on homosexuality, exert force by working to establish and secure the norms of binary sexual difference and compulsory heterosexuality. His review of the priestly account in which God creates humans in the divine image as male and female demonstrates the ways the text has prompted biblical interpreters as disparate as Karl Barth and Phyllis Trible to find a divine sanction in sexual dimorphism. When Stone turns to the Yahwist account, however, he follows Butler's interpretive lead to locate instabilities and ambiguities in the text that call into question the totalizing reach of the Scriptures' assumed heteronormativity. In this passage, where God first creates a single human being who only later is divided into two, Stone suggests questions of sex and gender are more ambiguous than most interpreters have acknowledged. Stone finds, for example, in the undefined sex of the initial human creature a space where alternative models of subjectivity might proliferate. His reexamination of these central scriptural passages leads Stone finally to a consideration of the task of queer biblical interpretation and the transformative effects that are opened, in this case for gay male readers who continue to engage and be shaped by these texts.

In "The Annoying Woman: Biblical Scholarship After Judith Butler," Teresa Hornsby considers the ways in which Butler's insights raise the stakes for feminist biblical interpretation. Butler's observation that even our most subversive actions emerge from the web of cultural discourses and so are prone to unwittingly perpetuate its ideologies leads Hornsby to question what remains possible for feminist biblical interpretation. She explores this question through a consideration of Luke 7:36–50 in which an unnamed woman anoints the feet of Jesus. While Hornsby is drawn to the powerful physical and erotic overtones of this story, she observes that traditional interpretations routinely cast the woman as a prostitute or as otherwise guilty of sexual transgression or excess. Further, feminist scholars have been no more effective in finding positive value in this figure. More commonly, they have critiqued Luke for undermining the anointing woman by casting her as silent, nameless, and subservient. In so doing, Hornsby charges, feminists reinforce reigning assumptions that equate silence with powerlessness, overlooking the force of the woman's physical actions and the possibility that a more radical meaning might be found in her seemingly subordinate stance.

To chart a different course, Hornsby uses interpretive tools exemplified in Butler's reading of the classic Antigone story. Like Antigone, she suggests, the anointing woman can be viewed as a liminal figure who because of her very anonymity cannot easily be placed in the social structure. Butler cautions against the desire to fill in the outlines of such an undefined figure and in so doing to seek a representative model for behavior. Rather she recognizes the lack of definition as opening a space for the generation of unexpected possibilities.

For Hornsby, viewing the silence of the anointing woman in this way draws attention more fully to her actions, particularly to the erotic physicality or desire that plays between the woman and Jesus. Where earlier interpretations skirt this aspect, or note it only to quickly condemn or restrain it, Hornsby is able to call it to the fore. She demonstrates how this desire works in the text to give the lie to the stability of social and sexual standards that have heretofore held place. Still, Hornsby ends with a cautionary reminder that her own reading, too, functions as a performance that is subject to unexpected appropriations. Though her reading cannot then effect a full-scale revolution, its disruption of norms makes a beginning.

EMBODYING IDENTITIES

The four papers comprising the middle section of the collection use Butler in different ways to ponder questions of agency. In "Disturbingly Catholic: Thinking the Inordinate Body" Karen Trimble Alliaume critically analyzes orthodox Catholic teachings against women's ordination as well as feminist responses or challenges to the magisterium. She finds Butler useful as she untangles the "web of symbolism" that links Jesus's corporeal body to the constitution of the corporate body of Christ that is the Church and does so in such a way that women, precisely because of their bodies, are excluded from leadership roles. Tracing how "gender matters" in the formation of Roman Catholic women, Alliaume suggests that Butler helps us to see the full extent of the violence inflicted on women through the Church's teachings. She observes that at its deepest levels Christianity is structured according to a "logic of imitation" wherein Christ stands as the model believers must mimic in order to be saved. And yet, given Catholicism's official insistence on gender complementarity, this is an imitation from which women will always fall short.

In her article Alliaume details how this logic of imitation marks the magisterium's teaching that priests must be male because only men can adequately resemble the male Christ. Still further, she contends that feminist challenges to this teaching unwittingly continue to employ its underlying logic when they advocate copying the humanity of Christ. Following Butler, Alliaume then turns to imagine the possibilities that open when the relationships between Christ, believers, and the church are rethought according to a logic of citationality. Such an emphasis shifts attention from the figure of Jesus, which is rooted in the past, to the ongoing communal process of seeking to both follow and reembody the living Christ. It is sustained by the recognition that it is through these citations that Jesus's body, as well as the bodies of believers, is continually materialized. As with all performative processes, Alliaume observes, the re-citation of Christ would be marked by an openness to multiple and unexpected redeployments—in this case to the multiple ways in which Jesus could be re-presented by Church leaders to the faithful. Such an openness, she suggests, offers renewed pathways for women's agency within Catholicism.

Christina K. Hutchins writes "Unconforming Becomings" in the context of debates over the inclusion of gays and lesbians in Christian church communities. As she notes, these often contentious discussions have brought concreteness to issues of identity politics more often discussed in the abstract. As a minister in the United Church of Christ and as a lesbian, Hutchins is well aware of the immediacy of these questions. She frames her article with reflections on the ambivalence she feels when asked to speak as a representative of gay members of her church. Hutchins traces this discomfort to the fact that such efforts at inclusion tend to assume an essentialist understanding of gay identity that, however defined or understood, is inherently reductive and inevitably reinforces a binary opposition between homosexuals and heterosexuals. She is thus led to explore the alternative models of subjectivity proposed in Alfred North Whitehead's process metaphysics and Judith Butler's theory of performativity. While there are important differences between these thinkers, Hutchins finds in both a vision of the subject that both honors engagement with concrete experiences and emphasizes openness to change and renewal. These more fluid models of identity, she asserts, avoid or deconstruct the binarisms of essentialism that fund the logic of exclusion. Furthermore, both theorists locate the subject's agency in what Butler terms its capacity for "subversive resignification." Significantly, both characterize this tendency of the subject toward the unexpected in positive terms as a movement toward or capacity for pleasure.

With these models of subjectivity in hand, Hutchins proceeds to articulate the implications they hold for a theologically disclosive politics of inclusion. While it is important to maintain identity categories (e.g., lesbian) so that visibility is secured, she argues that it is equally important to highlight the instabilities of all identities. By giving full and public recognition to the incompleteness in their midst, religious institutions become part of the movement that enables structural transformation. Hutchins moves beyond Butler (though with Whitehead) to claim that this dynamic process evidences the presence of a holy and creative love. She concludes with the suggestion that the process leaves believers with dual directives of responsibility and hope. Responsibility resides in the call to remain attentive to possibilities for change in the face of an unexpected future. Hope in turn is found in the excess that lies always beyond what is actualized.

Claudia Schippert finds in Butler's writings a valuable resource as she begins to envision the shape a queer ethics might take. Against those critics who have discounted Butler's usefulness for ethics because she deconstructs the voluntarist subject, Schippert argues that performativity provides an alternative form of agency that can fund the moral decision making of those who are rendered invisible by the dominant culture. In particular she highlights suggestions in Butler's texts that the realm of the abject holds open such possibilities. To build on those suggestions, Schippert conducts a rereading of Katie Cannon's womanist ethics through a Butlerian lens. She finds in Cannon's description of the moral wisdom of African American women a realization of the radical promise that might reside in a realm that both exceeds and forms the "constitutive outside" of the dominant culture. Suggesting that a queer ethics can be developed along parallel lines, Schippert offers the phrase "taking on the abject" to describe its character. As the dynamic constitutive of queer moral agency, "taking on" connotes both embracing that which is excluded and countering that which is normative. Such agents, and this ethics, Schippert imagines will function according to "a different geometry," one more akin to that evidenced in black holes where what is invisible exerts decisive influence.

Anthropologist Saba Mahmood takes up the question of agency in the context of her study of a contemporary women's mosque movement that is part of the Islamic revival in Egypt. Movements such as this—in which women intentionally engage in practices from study to prayer to veiling in order to cultivate more modest and pious selves—have most often been dismissed by Western feminists as examples of the repressive reach of religious conservatism. To Mahmood, however, such critiques reveal more about liberal conceptions of freedom and agency that have predominated in feminist theory than they do about the subjectivity forged by the women of the mosques. She turns to Butler's performative subject as a model that is better able to honor the historical specificity of this movement. At the same time, her ethnographic research rooted in Islamic women's descriptions of their desires, practices, and goals sheds a critical light, revealing blind spots and gaps in Butler's theory. She notes, for example, that in her writings Butler tends to develop the concept of agency primarily in the context of supporting resistance against social norms (e.g., her reading of drag's significance). Yet Butler neglects to articulate other ways beyond conformity or conflict in which subjects come to inhabit social structures. Mahmood deepens her critique of Butler by suggesting that the gaps in her theory result in part from Butler's tendency to conceptualize performativity in terms of signification. She sketches a broader notion of performativity informed by ritual theorists and Aristotelian notions of habitus, which she contends is better able to capture the nuances of the bodily practices and disciplines of the women in the mosque movement that enable the cultivation of a particular subjectivity.

Mahmood's analysis carries implications for contemporary feminist theorists as well as a broad range of scholars of religion. Recognizing that our conceptual formations have been decisively shaped by a progressive political agenda leads to important questions: what is elided from view by these formations, and what forms of implicit and explicit violence are wrought as a result on those whose lives are not shaped in accord with Western political ideals? Mahmood's article serves as a call to keep feminist political and analytical work open to challenges arising from the multitude of socially specific sites. As she observes, this call is of particular importance in this historical moment when religious difference takes such a prominent and problematic place in international affairs.

THEORIZING BODIES

We conclude with two pieces more directly concerned with theoretical questions posed to Butler, particularly as these center on the controversial relationship between the discursive and material realms. Rebecca Schneider's training as a scholar of performance studies allows her a unique perspective from which to reflect on the status of language and the body in Butler's theory of performativity. She does so through a close reading of Butler's 1997 *Qui Parle* article "'How Can I Deny That These Hands and This Body Are Mine?'" and a passage in *Excitable Speech* in which Butler interprets a traditional folk parable.

In the *Qui Parle* article Butler takes up Descartes' reflections on doubt, writing, and the body in order to answer critics who charge that her own work dissolves the material body. Butler argues convincingly in the article that she, like Descartes, has not done away with the body but rather continually finds its trace in and through her writing. Yet Schneider continues her inquiry to ask about the status of the body Butler has retrieved. She notes that while Butler's article claims to examine the dynamic of writing and reading, her focus is primarily on writing. As a result, the body Butler finds remains elusive, the specter of the hand that writes but that remains always at a distance.

To Schneider Butler's concentration leaves aside other modes in which the body is known and encountered in language. These modes are represented by the act of reading wherein Butler herself suggests those who take up a text are "compelled" to reperform its language. To explore these occluded possibilities, Schneider turns to a brief passage in which Butler comments on a folk tale retold by Toni Morrison as a parable about writing and reading. In the tale a group of children attempt to trick an elderly blind woman by asking her whether a bird they are holding is alive or dead. The woman responds, "I do not know—what I do know is it is in your hands." Following Morrison's reading, which portrays the woman as a writer, Butler interprets her response as highlighting the blindness of writing, the fact that once written the writer (and her body) stand at a remove from the text (itself a body) and its fate. When Schneider takes this parable into her own hands, however, she finds an alternative interpretation, one that evokes the existence of a form of "tactile knowing" using the text. Here the writer's body moves through the spoken word to touch the children, evoking and underscoring the significance of their own bodily, in-handed response.

This evocation of another relationship of the body to language as well as another form of knowledge, Schneider suggests, can also be seen in the work of performance artists who seek to challenge and break down the timeworn distinction between theater, with its disembodied spectator, and the more participatory practice of ritual. Such an understanding of body and language, which is indebted to yet moves beyond Butler, holds promise for religious studies, not only in its reflections on ritual as a mode of knowledge but also in considering more fully the embodied character of religious texts.

Amy Hollywood likewise attends to Butler's attempts to answer those who accuse her of granting excessive power to language. She observes that Butler's response hinges on her claim that language is performative and as such materializes rather than eliminates the body. Further, Butler suggests that it is through ritualized bodily practices as well as speech acts that subjects come to be. Still, Hollywood notes, critics remain unconvinced in part because these rituals, when theorized at all by Butler, tend to be construed along the lines of the theory of performative linguistic utterances she has adopted from J. L. Austin. Thus, her treatment seems to return the body to the realm of language. Hollywood seeks to provide a fuller account of ritual and bodily practices that could clarify Butler's theory of performativity and reduce its vulnerability to the charge of inadequately accounting for the material.

To accomplish this task, Hollywood reviews the understanding of ritual found in Austin and Derrida, two main influences on Butler's thought. For Austin, rituals stand as prime examples of what distinguishes performative speech from ordinary constative speech. While constatives mean what they say via the sign's similarity to the signified independent of context and speaker, rituals do not. The power of the ritual is context dependent, Austin argues; it resides in its ability to recite conventions and in the speaker who performs and authorizes it. Derrida challenges Austin's attempt to distinguish between constative and performative language on these grounds. As structuralism claims, language is a system of signs arbitrarily connected to what they signify by convention. Thus all language is performative. So-called constative language's ability to mean what it says is, like all rituals, dependent on iterability and ultimately lies outside the control of the speaker. The resemblance between ritual and language goes the other way as well. The arbitrariness of language extends to all rituals, Derrida argues. Thus, strictly determining the external context that authorizes a ritual is ultimately impossible. Rather, performatives constitute or generate their own contexts in the process of enactment.

Hollywood draws on Derrida to outline a view of ritualization that places bodily practices at the heart of the reiterative process. Derrida's account of performativity enables a more nuanced theory of the bodily actions of ritual practice that can address problems in Butler's thought. Thinking ritual and language together would allow Butler to develop her claim that the body is materialized in language in such a way that the two are neither strictly separate nor reducible to each other. Such a move would provide theoretical ballast to her ongoing insistence that the force of the performative resides in the body and constitutes it as a potential site of resistance. Hollywood's reflections also extend and deepen theories of ritual offered by religious studies scholars such as Talal Asad and Catherine Bell. To acknowledge the arbitrariness that shapes the intersection of language and the body as affecting belief and practice underscores the potential inherent in ritual to "misfire" and thus contribute to the development of new and unexpected religious subjects.

BODILY CITATIONS

JUDITH BUTLER—IN THEORY

ELLEN T. ARMOUR AND SUSAN M. ST. VILLE

C AN OR SHOULD "women" be the subject of feminism? This is the question that launches Judith Butler's landmark text, *Gender Trouble: Feminism and the Subversion of Identity* (1990). In asking and answering it, Butler refracted a decade of debate within feminist theory over its proper subject. Critiques from women of color, postcolonial theorists, and lesbian and gay theorists had exposed the limitations of feminism's subject. The "woman" on whose behalf theorists theorized and activists organized was bounded in ways that excluded many of those whom feminism claimed to support. Questions about feminism's proper subject were exacerbated by the influx of French poststructuralist and psychoanalytic theories into the American academy in that same decade, an event that also marks the horizon of *Gender Trouble's* appearance. These theories challenged concepts at the root of identity politics by raising questions about representation, identity, and politics as usual. While some feminists saw in these new intellectual currents potential for deepening understanding of and ability to respond effectively to conditions of oppression—including those perpetuated by women against one another—others saw only trouble on the horizon. Gender was indeed in trouble, it seemed; but where would that trouble lead? What stakes, dangers, and possibilities did that trouble portend—theoretically and politically?

Butler took up the challenge of pursuing those questions. Trouble led her into and through the latest trends in French theory as well as feminist research in the humanities, social and natural sciences. Out of that mix she instantiated an important shift in feminist theory, one whose effects continue to resonate within that field and those that intersect with it. More than identifying distinct truths about gender, Butler invites us into a mode of inquiry or process of thought, the character of which is captured well by the word *trouble*. Integral to it is a constant and thoroughgoing questioning of received assumptions—a "troubling" that allows new possibilities for thought and action to emerge. In order to grasp the mode of inquiry her writings embody, we will follow her thought in action and trace the disruptions and reappropriations by which it moves.

It is perhaps easiest to perceive Butler's contribution to feminist theory by focusing on her review and revision of the sex/gender debate, a central feature of contemporary gender theory. The theoretical arm of feminism's second wave in the United States adopted early on the distinction between sex (male or female) and gender (masculine or feminine), a move frequently traced back to the influence of Simone de Beauvoir and Robert Stoller.[1] Both wanted to counter biological determinism; that is, the commonly held view that feminine and masculine social roles and behavior follow as a natural consequence from the biological differences between female and male bodies. Thus both distinguished between the male and female sexes, understood to be bodily givens, and masculine and feminine gender roles, understood as socially constructed or matters of custom rather than nature. In *The Second Sex* Beauvoir's analysis of "women's situation" put descriptive flesh on her claim that "one is not born a woman, but, rather, becomes one," which many in the English-speaking world (including Butler) read (or misread, according to Toril Moi) as demonstrating the normative power of gender.[2]

Once acknowledged, the sex/gender distinction served a certain purpose for those invested in opening new opportunities for men and women. As socially constructed, the reigning expectations of masculinity and femininity are putatively open to revision. Expectations for behavior appropriate to men and women can change and shift in multiple directions. Theoretically, biological males could take on feminine roles (becoming house husbands, for example) while biological females could take on masculine roles (becoming powerful businesspeople, for example). In short, bodies need not dictate or limit what is possible socially.

For later Anglophone feminist theorists the distinction between naturally given sexes and socially constructed genders came to have its own commonsense appeal. Yet eventually this assumption too came under interrogation as thinkers began to ask about the "natural" quality of the distinction between the sexes.[3] In various ways different thinkers showed that the natural realm itself never comes to us in an uninterpreted or transparent form. What may seem to be a natural division of the sexes into male and female is itself the product of a specific history. Further, these interpretations themselves serve distinct ends, benefiting some regimes of thought more than, or to the exclusion of, others. Some theorists concluded that sex was as socially constructed as gender and thus itself open to new and different interpretive configurations. Rather than the stable foundation upon which cultures constructed expectations for gendered subjects, sex itself appeared to be subject to variations in different cultural contexts.

For those who accepted the pervasiveness of the constructed character of the gendered/sexed subject, the challenge became how to think and talk about construction. Since societal norms established the constraints for gendered/sexed identities, they must play some role in the process by which individuals took up those identities. On the other hand, feminism's political aim of changing normative constraints required an agent that could resist them. The challenge became developing a theory of gender that could allow for the work of both.

Performativity

Resolving this particular dilemma is central to Butler's project in *Gender Trouble*. As Butler saw it, theorists began to stumble as they sought to solve the question of who or what does the constructing. On the one hand, some insisted that if there is nothing beyond construction, the realm of social discourse or language itself must be the constructing agent. This view left no room for human agency and thus appeared to foreclose on possibilities for resistance and/or change. If subjectivity is wholly and seamlessly shaped by the working of discourse, then the subject's fate and possibilities for action are as determined by the social order as they previously were believed to be by biology. On the other hand, different theorists placed construction in the hands of the individual subject, who forges a sexed/gendered self by choosing (more or less) freely among the options made available within its social context. While this view secures a form of human agency, it does so by presupposing a subject that retains an identity outside the realm of social discourse. Noting that these debates were roughly analogous to those within modern philosophy over whether the human being possessed a genuinely free will, Butler diagnosed the controversy as symptomatic of liberal humanism's recapitulation, the very understanding of subjectivity that earlier feminist theorists like Carol Gilligan and Nancy Chodorow had exposed as infused with masculinist assumptions.

Moving beyond the sway of liberalism requires a theory of subject construction that grounds the very possibility of agency within an understanding of the human being as culturally formed and bound. Formulating such a theory, Butler asserts, requires a certain suspicion toward grammar and the language it is said to order. Asking who or what guides construction gets us off to the wrong start. That question relies on a view of language that presupposes a clear distinction between the subject who speaks, the words spoken, and the object acted upon. Butler turns away from this view of language as descriptive of reality to philosopher J. L. Austin's understanding of performative language.

Performative language is technically language that "does what it says" or produces the reality it names. For example, within the context of a wedding ceremony, the statement "I now pronounce you husband and wife" moves two people from the state of single adults to that of a married couple. One might assume that the power to bring about the result resides in the will and discretion of the speaker—in this case, that of the judge or clergyperson. Butler, however, appeals to poststructuralist theorists, especially Derrida, to offer an alternative account of the power of performatives. This view locates the power in the working of language, specifically in the process of the linguistic utterance. So, "I now pronounce you husband and wife" works because the statement invokes and reiterates a social norm. It is the action itself, the citation of the convention or norm (within a certain ritual context) that is the center of power, not the judge or minister who utters the words.

Viewing performativity as a citational process accounts for the productive and regulative affects of norms as well as their failures. Norms are able to compel a citation because they establish the guidelines for what is socially acceptable and workable. In this case, the formula "I now pronounce you husband and wife" defines the boundary between the unmarried and married states. To fail to cite or invoke the formula (or others akin to it) is to fail to achieve the desired state. At the same time, however, the power of the norms is itself citational. The formula produces a husband and wife where once stood a man and a woman because it re-cites its previous use. With each reiteration, the force of the norm is further consolidated. Without reiteration the norm cannot be said to have power in any meaningful sense. In this way the citational process produces (that is, gives body or weight to) the norms it invokes. Before their citation norms have only a provisional or potential status; it is in and through their invocation that they gain a concrete or actual embodiment/existence.

According to Butler, however, the process of citation disguises or conceals the dependence of norms on the process of reiteration. While social norms are historical and so potentially revisable, they gain the appearance of fixed or eternal givens by their repeated reiteration in and by the subjects who take them on. Because of this appearance the norms are less likely to be questioned—it seems unthinkable and too risky to forsake them.

Gender as Performative

What results from understanding the construction of the gendered/ sexed subject as a performative process? An example from current events may help contextualize the significance of Butler's contribution. Whether or not "practicing homosexuals" should be ordained and their unions blessed are matters over which mainline denominations have threatened to split.[4] Gay marriage erupted as a major political issue (not coincidentally, given the Republican Party's desire to ensure a large turnout of their religious base) as the 2004 presidential election season shifted into high gear. The way debates over homosexuality are often framed reveals much about current cultural assumptions concerning the links between sex, gender, and desire. Those who are opposed to gay rights decry homosexuality as a "lifestyle choice." To counter that view some gay rights advocates argue that being gay is a matter of nature, not choice, a view that also seems to fund scientific research into the so-called gay gene. The rhetoric of these debates suggests a common-sense understanding of the relationship between sex, gender, and desire that runs as follows: gender (acting masculine or feminine) is an expression of our bodies (male or female). That is, males (naturally) act masculine while females (naturally) act feminine. Sexual desires are thought to be expressions of bodily nature as well. Males (naturally) act masculine and desire women; females (naturally) act feminine and desire men. Desiring otherwise calls into question the match between one's gender and one's sex. Our culture tends to equate homosexuality in men with effeminacy and in women with masculinity (though things were rather different in the ancient world).[5]

Butler turns this linear understanding of the relationship of sex, gender, and desire on its head. Critically appropriating feminist theory, psychoanalytic theory, and the work of Michel Foucault, she argues that, rather than *being* an expression of (immutable) sex, gender *produces* sex. Masculinity and femininity are learned bodily performances that masquerade as natural by invoking bodily markers (primary and secondary sex characteristics) as their signature and guarantee. Our binary sex/gender system arises not from nature but from a social system of compulsory heterosexuality that requires desire to channel itself via these subjectivities. Desire is not the (natural) expression of sex or gender, rather it is prescribed by the larger social context. Butler cites Foucault's work (among others) on the history and theory of sexuality to remind us that biological sex is often ambiguous at all bodily levels (the genetic, the genital, and the morphological). That variability is sometimes violently policed through physical and emotional disciplines that render life outside the norms unbearable or impossible. Feminism, Butler argues, needs to reconfigure its subject to take the reality of this genealogy into account.

Psychoanalytic theory—especially that of Jacques Lacan—is of particular importance to Butler's account of the process by which we become normatively sexed/gendered subjects. According to Lacan's versions of the Oedipus and castration complexes, becoming a subject is a process of conscious and unconscious negotiation with one's own desires, needs, and losses as well as others' expectations, all within a context governed by cultural norms.[6] To become a sexed/gendered subject is to take up a position in relation to language within a linguistic and sexual economy whose center of value is the phallus. The phallus does not exist per se; it is, rather, the imaginary object around which desire circulates. But the sexual and linguistic positions available to us are defined in its terms: either we (believe we) "have" the phallus (a masculine subject position) or we (believe we) "are" the phallus (a feminine subject position). The circuit of desire is motivated by the impossible aim of possessing the phallus; each position desires the other because it offers what it longs to have. The circuit of desire is thus heterosexual.

Because these norms define the viable forms of subjectivity within a culture, subjection to them is necessary to recognition and acceptance as a subject. Louis Althusser's concept of interpellation comes into play here. Althusser describes the process of subjectification as structured by call and response. His paradigmatic example is the experience of being hailed by a policeman. One hears, "hey, you!" and turns around. In turning around, one is constituted/constitutes oneself as the one called, as always already guilty. The process of taking up gendered/sexed subject positions has an analogous call and response structure, according to Butler. This performative process begins immediately as the baby is identified and so "named" as either a boy or a girl. The process is ongoing and reiterative. Time and again the developing subject is compelled to "cite" or take on as its own the behavior and identity suited to its designated sex. True to the pattern, with each citation the subjectivity of the person is affirmed and the preeminence of the norms of heterosexuality is strengthened.

For Butler the performative process is not purely theoretical or intellectual. She insists that it has real material effects. As she notes, in the designation of the baby as either a boy or a girl the morphological interpretation that guides both society's expectations for the child and the subject's sense of its own physical boundaries and possibilities is shaped. This morphological perception in turn dictates the practices that constantly mark and remark the body into an identifiable physical form. In this way the social norms come to reside in and find a concrete manifestation in the body of the social subject. Thus, as Butler clarifies in *Bodies That Matter* (1993), the performative process is a process of materialization. Each subject carries the traces of its own history of bodily and emotional investment; indeed, the bodily ego is the mark of the (always tenuous) accomplishment of gendered/ sexed subjectivity.

Further, Butler specifies that the performative process is not only reiterative and material but also exclusionary. If social norms define the realm of intelligible and viable subjectivity, they also mark the boundaries beyond which lie the unintelligible and unacceptable. In this netherworld, which Butler describes as that of the abject, reside those who do not adequately cite the social norms. Included here would be those whose morphology is neither identifiably male nor female as well as those whose desires do not conform to heterosexual dictates. The abject exist in a paradoxical state. Although granted no standing or even acknowledgment (and so subject to mistreatment), they are also socially necessary in that they form the "constitutive outside" against which the accepted subject may be understood and defined.

Changing the System

So far our description of Butler's theory of gender has focused on its account of our current sexual regime (how gendered/sexed subjects come to be, why they take the particular forms they do, and where they fit on the cultural map). Recall, however, that Butler shares the political aim of many gender theorists: to promote change in the current sex/gender system. Crucial to realizing that aim are the fissures she has exposed that trouble the system's coherence and mastery. First, the system is cultural and discursive all the way down; the relationship between bodies and the genders that are materialized in and through them is ultimately contingent, not necessary. Second, the materialization of sexed/gendered identities is not static or discrete but is rather a citational process. The appearance of seemingly heteronormative constructs in gay and lesbian life renders this process visible. As Butler writes, "gay is to straight not as copy is to original, but as copy is to copy" (GT, p. 31). Following Derrida, Butler argues that to perform is to re-cite but to recite is not necessarily to repeat. Citations *can* be faithful reiterations, but iteration is made possible only by the space between the copy and the copy. No repetition is exactly the same. It is precisely this space that opens up the possibility for subversion and change.

Butler turns to drag performances as the primary example of gender gone astray. Drag performances subvert the sex/gender system by exposing the contingency of the relationship between biological sex and gender. That certain men can act persuasively hyperfeminine undoes the system's power to compel normative repetitions. Drag performances expose gender as itself performative; that is, as constructed of stylizations that invoke the body as their signature and guarantee. That guarantee is, however, illusory.

Responses to *Gender Trouble*

The emerging discipline of queer theory saw in Butler's work fruitful theoretical ground for articulating the proliferation of marginalized sexual identities as "queer"; that is, as forged out of creative expropriations of raw materials given by culture.[7] Gay activist organizations like ACT-UP and Queer Nation appropriated Butler's theory as a resource for formulating political strategy. The reviews among feminist theorists were somewhat mixed. Though lauded by some, others were skeptical about the ultimate value of *Gender Trouble* to feminist theory.[8] Many recognized in Butler's argument a groundbreaking advance in overcoming the impasses that had beset the field. Here was a theory whose account of the interplay between self and society explained the staying power of gender roles but also pointed toward an opening for political change. The very mechanism of identity formation and consolidation—performativity—was itself the potential agent for change. The groundwork for change lay within the citationality of the gender norms themselves; if gender is as gender does, gender can be undone.

Others, however, saw problems in Butler's formulation of the trouble with gender; problems that, in their view, called into question its usefulness as a tool for feminist analysis and feminist politics. Some read Butler's reliance on drag to support her claims regarding gender's performativity as replacing the old feminist slogan "the personal is political" with "the parodic is political," an approach to politics that they found naive and ineffectual.[9] Others applauded Butler for exposing compulsory heterosexuality as an unthought ground of feminism, but criticized her for leaving uninterrogated race's effects within a heterosexist framework.[10] Ironically, Butler's attempt to overcome feminism's bondage to liberal humanism also registered with many as a failure. Some read performativity as synonymous with performance; that is, as affirming that we choose our gender virtually as freely and easily as we choose our clothes. Gender identities would then be as easily cast off as yesterday's jeans or a theatrical costume. Others read Butler as undoing agency altogether. If there is no subject outside of language, no doer beneath the deed, and our only options are to repeat faithfully or to parody, real political change is impossible.

Since *Gender Trouble*

In her work since *Gender Trouble* Butler has clarified, deepened, extended, and in some cases revised her theoretical positions in response to her critics and to events around her.[11] *Bodies That Matter* followed three years after *Gender Trouble* and contains several essays that are clearly aimed at responding to her critics. Included are explorations of the mutual "imbrication" of sex, race, gender, and class, a refinement of her understanding of drag's subversive potential (and its limits), and deeper explorations into the constitutive features of sexual subjectivities. Since that volume Butler has continued to deepen and broaden the theoretical perspectives developed in these two books. *Excitable Speech* and *The Psychic Life of Power*, both published in 1997, continue to think through the connections between language, subjectivity, and culture exposed by *Gender Trouble* and refined by *Bodies That Matter*. The essays in *Excitable Speech* are prompted by particular events on the political scene that are marked by sex, race, and/or gender. Butler's analyses of attempts to regulate hate speech, obscenity, and pornography, and of the Clinton era's "don't ask, don't tell" policy regarding gays in the military, probe beneath the surface of these controversies for what they say about language and its effects. Clearly, words wound, but in what sense? What other violences are done in the attempt to temper their wounding power, as in the case of hate speech? In each case she investigates the consequences—intentional or unintentional—of the rhetoric invoked by the key participants in these debates. Butler exposes the differential treatment accorded certain kinds of speech (art produced by gays and lesbians, a cross burned in a black family's yard, pornography) by government officials and political activists and advocates alike. Her analyses caution against taking comfort in legal remedies for such problems by warning of the unintended consequences of legislation and court decisions based on it. Legal remedies presumptively reinscribe discursive structures of sovereignty of the subject whose word *is* his deed, who knows what he says and says what he means, whose actions match his intentions, and who wields power directly. As satisfying as it can be to hold some "one" responsible, such remedies do nothing to intervene in and are often complicit with racism, sexism, and heterosexism, the very evils that the proponents of these remedies seek to eradicate.

If *Excitable Speech* starts at the surface of political life, *The Psychic Life of Power* starts well beneath it. This book returns to and reframes the question of political agency that lay at the heart of *Gender Trouble*. Butler attempts to describe the fundamental structure of subjection that undergirds life in community. The two senses of subjection, subject formation and submission to authority, are linked, Butler argues. One does not take place without the other. But describing who or what is subjected eludes us once we come to understand subjectivity as the *result* of this process rather than its precondition. The title aptly names the project Butler has in view here: outlining the dimensions of a chiasmic process that founds both the subject (through submission to the powers that be) and its ability to resist (those same powers that be). Rather than the preexisting foundation of political agency, what we usually think of as the inner core of subjectivity comes into being through subjection. Butler posits agency as located in a physically, psychically, and socially vulnerable subject. Its vulnerabilities arise from its bodily and social dependencies, which create a web of passionate attachments to the others whom it needs (including but not limited to family). Autonomy is necessary for psychic and sometimes physical survival, but also threatens the subject insofar as it rends that network of attachments. This is the peril and the promise of subjectivity. We act not in spite of vulnerability, passionate attachment, threat, and loss but because of and through them.

Since 1997 Butler has continued to pursue the intersection of politics and theory in academic contexts and in more popular venues. She has written several pieces on queer theory and politics, including thoughtful essays on the questions of gay marriage, transsexuality, intersexed people, and antigay violence.[12] With Ernesto Laclau and Slavoj Žižek she has written a volume that embodies their common concerns for providing theoretical underpinnings for a viable leftist politics, *Contingency, Hegemony, Universality: Contemporary Dialogues on the Left*. In addition to continuing her academic work, Butler has taken on an increasingly visible role as a public intellectual; she has authored several essays in venues such as the *Nation* and the *New York Times*. A recent book, *Precarious Life*, is a collection of essays using theoretical insights gleaned over the years to critically evaluate political attitudes and actions since the events of September 11, 2001. *Undoing Gender* (2004) finds Butler returning to gender, sex, and politics via questions of life and death, violence and violation, this time with greater attention to the variety of sexual identifications (transsexual, intersexed, transgendered) that populate that terrain.[13]

Why Should Religionists Care?

From the account we have given of the paths Butler's work has taken, readers should be able to see the grounds for a possible alliance between that work and the various strands of scholarship on religion that involve analysis of gender, sex, and sexuality. Philosopher Alan Schrift has argued recently for the importance of Butler's work on subjectivity not just for feminist and queer theories but for philosophy as a whole.[14] We would make the same argument on behalf of religious studies, and thus we hope the essays appearing here will prompt many of you to explore Butler's work on your own. Her ongoing investigations into the relationships between bodies, language, and cultural norms in identity construction should interest religionists, given the role of bodily practices (including linguistic ones) in the production of religious identities. Her exposure of the lingering and deleterious effects of models of divine sovereignty in our current political context should also speak to scholars of Western religious traditions. Furthermore, a number of her recent essays touch on disturbing features of the uses made of religion in political contexts, from the Bush administration's antiterrorism policies and actions to academia.[15] We are not advocating only that religionists learn from Butler, however; it is our conviction (given concrete form by the essays in this volume) that scholars of religion offer Butler rich resources. We hope this volume will be only the latest stage in a fruitful ongoing conversation.

NOTES

1. Simone de Beauvoir, *The Second Sex*, trans. E. M. Parshley (New York: Vintage Press, 1973); Robert Stoller, *Presentations of Gender* (New Haven: Yale University Press, 1985).

2. Beauvoir, p. 301; cited in GT, p. 8. For Moi's critique, see Toril Moi, *What Is a Woman? And Other Essays* (Oxford: Oxford University Press, 1999).

3. The list of journal articles, anthologies, and monographs that Butler cites early in *Gender Trouble* is a useful index to the various dimensions of research in these areas just prior to *Gender Trouble*'s emergence. See GT, p. 151, n. 9. For more recent analyses, see, e.g., Anne Fausto-Sterling, *Sexing the Body: Gender Politics and the Construction of Sexuality* (New York: Basic, 2000); Suzanne J. Kessler, *Lessons from the Intersexed* (Piscataway, NJ: Rutgers University Press, 1998); and JoAnne Meyerowitz, *How Sex Changed: A History of Transsexuality in the United States* (Cambridge: Harvard University Press, 2002).

4. For an assessment of the various Protestant denominations' positions on this matter from a perspective informed by Butler's work and other aspects of feminist theory, see Mary McClintock Fulkerson, "Gender—Being It or Doing It? The Church, Homosexuality, and the Politics of Identity," *Que(e)rying Religion: A Critical Anthology*, ed. Gary David Comstock and Susan E. Henking (New York: Continuum, 1997); and "Church Documents on Human Sexuality and the Authority of Scripture," *Interpretation* 49, no. 1 (January 1995): 46–59.

5. Our modern notion of sexual identity has no precise correlate in the ancient world, as a number of scholars have argued. Thus, while ancient Greeks and Romans, for example, associated certain sexual practices/positions (males who are penetrated, females who penetrate) with gender transgression, they did not expect to see such practices reflected in one's bearing, taste, or dress. Moreover, they associated male same-sex bonds with virility and warned men against the effeminizing effects of too much sex with women. Scholarly works in religion on these topics include Dale Martin, *The Corinthian Body* (New Haven: Yale University Press, 1995) and Bernadette Brooten, *Love Between Women: Early Christian Responses to Homoeroticism* (Chicago: University of Chicago Press, 1996). Ken Stone's essay in this volume provides a helpful list of references to a larger body of scholarship on sexuality in the ancient world.

6. For an introduction to Lacan from a feminist perspective, see the introductory essays by Juliet Mitchell and Jacqueline Rose, editors of *Feminine Sexuality:*

Jacques Lacan and the école freudienne, trans. Jacqueline Rose (New York: Norton, 1982).

7. In particular see "More Gender Trouble: *Feminism Meets Queer Theory*," a special double issue of *Differences: A Journal of Feminist Cultural Studies* 6, nos. 2 and 3 (Summer-Fall 1994), especially Butler's introduction, "Against Proper Objects."

8. For an early thoughtful review of *Gender Trouble*, see Susan Bordo, "Postmodern Subjects, Postmodern Bodies," *Feminist Studies* 18, no. 1 (1992): 159–76. For a particularly important critical dialogue between Butler and other major feminist theorists, see Benhabib, Butler, Cornell, and Fraser, *Feminist Contentions: A Philosophical Exchange* (FC). Analyses of the issues involved (or overlooked) include Amanda Anderson, "Debatable Performances: Restaging Contentious Feminisms," in *Social Text* 54 (Spring 1998): 1–24; and Fiona Webster, "The Politics of Sex and Gender: Benhabib and Butler Debate Subjectivity," *Hypatia* 15, no. 1 (Winter 2000): 1–22. Butler's work has also been taken up by the emerging field of disability studies. For a survey, see "Critical Divides: Judith Butler's Body Theory and the Question of Disability," *NWSA Journal* 14, no. 3 (Fall 2002): 58–67.

9. For thoughtful versions of this critique, see Bordo, "Postmodern Subjects"; and Benhabib et al., F. C. Penelope Deutscher attempts to both defuse and account for this critique in her *Yielding Gender: Feminism, Deconstruction, and the History of Philosophy* (New York: Routledge, 1997), pp. 11–33.

10. On this issue see, in particular, Lisa M. Walker, "How to Recognize a Lesbian: The Cultural Politics of Looking Like What You Are," *Signs* 18, no. 4 (Summer 1993): 866–1071.

11. For Butler's own perspective on that project, see her preface to the tenth-anniversary edition, "Preface 1999," GT (1999), pp. vii–xxvi.

12. A number of these essays, originally published elsewhere, have been revised or reprinted in Butler's latest book, UG. See also her AC.

13. Butler's latest book, *Giving an Account of Oneself* (GAO), was not available at the time of this writing.

14. Alan D. Schrift, "Judith Butler: Une Nouvelle Existentialiste?" *Philosophy Today* 45, no. 1 (Spring 2001): 12–24.

15. See, e.g., "The Charge of Anti-Semitism: Jews, Israel, and the Risks of Public Critique" in PL, a response to Harvard University president Lawrence Summers's charge that academics court charges of anti-Semitism by criticizing Israel. See also her contribution to Daniel Boyarin, Daniel Itzkovitz, Ann Pellegrini, eds., *Queer Theory and the Jewish Question*, in which she reflects on popular responses to her self-presentation on a recent visit to Germany.

TEXTUAL BODIES

1. MATERIALIZATIONS OF VIRTUE: Buddhist Discourses on Bodies

SUSANNE MROZIK

Introduction: Using Butler to Read Buddhist Literature

In *Bodies That Matter* Judith Butler investigates the regulatory practices that both produce and destabilize normative heterosexuality. I draw on Butler's work to explicate and contest normative representations of body ideals in premodern South Asian Buddhist literature. Butler argues that sex, like gender, is socially constructed. In place of a concept of construction, however, she proposes that of materialization, because concepts of construction leave untheorized the materiality of sex.[1] Sexed bodies are materialized through the compulsory performance of gender norms that train, shape, and form the very contours of a person's body (BTM, pp. 54, 17). "Gender norms," Butler maintains, "operate by requiring the embodiment of certain ideals of femininity and masculinity" (BTM, pp. 231–32). These regulatory ideals are "not the product of a choice, but the forcible citation of a norm, one whose complex historicity is indissociable from relations of discipline, regulation, punishment" (BTM, p. 232). The repetitive nature of gender performance makes sex appear stable and natural (BTM, p. 10). It is precisely this stability and naturalness of sex that Butler contests.

While Butler's work is focused specifically on contesting heterosexual ideals and exclusions in Western cultures, her ideas are equally suggestive for challenging traditional representations of body ideals in Buddhism. Given the temporal, cultural, and conceptual distances between Butler's sources and my own, this chapter is not intended as a direct application of Butler's theories to a premodern South Asian Buddhist context. Rather I read Butler selectively in order to explore the possibilities for a resignification of body ideals in Buddhist traditions—ideals that are in some respects quite different from those Butler contests. My paper is an example of what Butler calls an "unanticipated reappropriation of a given work in areas for which it was never consciously intended" (BTM, p. 19).

My concern in this paper is what gives or denies value to bodies. What makes some bodies "matter" and others not? For Butler the key issue is sexual identity. Buddhism has a long history as a pan-Asian movement and has incredible internal diversity. A central concern in evaluating bodies in South Asian Buddhist literature is the association of morality with a range of physical conditions that include, but are not limited to, sex and sexual identity.[2] For instance, virtue is commonly associated with beauty, a fair complexion, health, and high caste. The close relationship Buddhists posit between body and morality means that bodies rarely appear as morally neutral in Buddhist literature. To the contrary, bodies are valued—albeit not systematically or consistently—on a continuum from abject to virtuous.

The Buddhist literature I discuss concerns the materialization of very particular kinds of virtuous bodies, namely those of a Buddha and Bodhisattva. A Buddha is a fully awakened, i.e., liberated being, representing the highest ideal in Buddhist traditions. A Bodhisattva is a nascent Buddha, a being who has dedicated him- or herself to becoming a Buddha.[3] One of the reasons why I find Butler good to think with is because she illumines a process of subject formation that enables me to see a similar process at work in the formation of a Bodhisattva or Buddha. Butler argues that normative heterosexual subject positions "depend on and are articulated through a region of abjected identifications" (BTM, p. 112). Let me first explain Butler's concept of abjection and then explain how I use this concept to think through the Buddhist material.

Butler argues that heterosexist gender norms compel the materialization of determinate types of bodies—heterosexual male and female bodies—and preclude the materialization of bodies that "do not appear properly gendered," i.e., homosexual bodies (BTM, p. 8). She calls these improperly gendered bodies "abject bodies." The abject is the "constitutive outside" of the normatively sexed subject *without which that subject could not exist*:

> The abject designates here precisely those "unlivable" and "uninhabitable" zones of
> social life which are nevertheless densely populated by those who do not enjoy the
> status of the subject, but whose living under the sign of the "unlivable" is required

to circumscribe the domain of the subject. This zone of uninhabitability will constitute the defining limit of the subject's domain; it will constitute that site of dreaded identification against which—and by virtue of which—the domain of the subject will circumscribe its own claim to autonomy and to life.

(BTM, p. 3)

Thus, Butler argues that the abject is at once the "constitutive outside" of the subject and also "inside" the subject in that it functions as the subject's "founding repudiation" (BTM, p. 3). In her critical reading of the psychoanalytic theorist Jacques Lacan, Butler demonstrates that the subject assumes a sexed position (i.e., gender) through a dual process of *identification with* and *repudiation of* an abject homosexuality. Significantly, Butler claims that repudiation of an abject homosexuality is necessary only if "on some level an identification has already taken place, an identification that is made and disavowed" (BTM, p. 113). Therefore sex is both "produced and destabilized" (BTM, p. 10) by the reiteration of heterosexist norms since these depend on abjected identifications—identifications that might be affirmed rather than disavowed. Pheng Cheah writes: "Since these hegemonic norms form bodily boundaries through exclusion, Butler suggests that the instabilities of reiteration offer the possibility of counterhegemonic rematerializations through the resignification of those alternative ideals of sex previously repressed as abject bodies deprived of symbolic value."[4] In other words, if sex is not natural, but is rather the material effect of the performance of inherently unstable heterosexist gender norms, then new kinds of bodies, formerly excluded from the domain of the social, may attain cultural legitimacy.

Identification with an abject body image is also a critical aspect of the process of materializing a Bodhisattva or Buddha.[5] Because of the distance between Butler's and my sources, I have defined and employed the concept of abjection differently than Butler. In the first instance, Buddhists believe in rebirth. Therefore the materialization of a Bodhisattva or Buddha is a process that occurs over multiple lifetimes. Further, Butler describes a psychological process that is at least in part subconscious. Identification with an abject body image in the context of Buddhism is a conscious and intentional performance. Finally, abjection is defined and evaluated differently in my sources. In certain circumstances abjection is even valorized. In such circumstances identification with an abject body image is affirmed and not disavowed, because such identification is individually and communally liberative. There are, in fact, two different discourses on abjection and bodies in general in my sources. These two discourses, the conventional and ascetic, are both critical to the formation of a Bodhisattva or Buddha. Although I appropriate Butler's concept of abjection in unexpected ways, I use the concept, as she does, to denaturalize the normative representations of body ideals. I am particularly interested in challenging the assumption in my sources that male sex is a marker of superior virtue. I do so not by demonstrating the presence of female virtuous bodies but instead by challenging the very notion that there are only two sexes (male and female) in these sources. To that end I explore the counterhegemonic materializations of virtuous bodies marked by non-normative, that is, indeterminate and alterior sexes. I use the term *indeterminate sex* to characterize bodies that blur the boundaries between male and female sexes. I use the term *alterior sex* to characterize bodies constituted by a sex that is radically other to both male and female sexes. I hope to demonstrate the way in which engagement with Butler's work provides significant critical resources for revisioning what virtue looks like.

My paper focuses on a premodern South Asian Sanskrit Buddhist narrative, "The Story of Beautiful Woman," found in an anthology of Sanskrit Buddhist stories.[6] The story displays concepts associated with two different Buddhist traditions, Hīnayāna and Mahāyāna, without invoking such sectarian labels, suggesting a degree of fluidity between these traditions. The story does not reflect engagement with tantric Buddhist ideas—an important point since tantra offers significantly different representations of gender.[7] I have chosen this story both because its views on bodies reflect broader South Asian Buddhist perspectives and because it provides a particularly complex exploration of sex. The subject of this narrative is a common one in Buddhist literature, namely, the past lives of Śākyamuni Buddha, the historical founder of Buddhism who is believed to have lived in Nepal and India between the sixth and fifth centuries b.c.e. Because Buddhists believe in rebirth, the Buddha's life begins long before he became a Buddha.[8] It begins in the remote past when, in the course of countless lifetimes, the Buddha to be, referred to as the Bodhisattva, cultivates the virtues requisite for Buddhahood. "The Story of Beautiful Woman" recounts three successive lifetimes of the Bodhisattva. In these three lifetimes the Bodhisattva cultivates the virtue of generosity by feeding the Bodhisattva's own body to starving humans and animals.

Narratives of bodily mutilation and sacrifice on the part of the Bodhisattva are common fare in Buddhist literature,[9] but this narrative is unusual in that the initial bodily mutilation is performed by a *female* Bodhisattva, that is, a female past incarnation of the future Śākyamuni Buddha. (Śākyamuni Buddha is traditionally represented in art and literature as male.) The female Bodhisattva, called Beautiful Woman (Rūpāvatī), cuts off her breasts to feed a starving human mother about to eat her live newborn son. I interpret Beautiful Woman's bodily mutilation as a conscious and intentional identification with an abject body, an identification that is not disavowed but rather is performed in order to materialize a virtuous bodied being. Beautiful Woman's long-term goal in performing this act of bodily mutilation is to become a Buddha. Ostensibly her immediate goal is to acquire a male body. Male sex is commonly regarded as a marker of superior moral development. Many Buddhist traditions consider male sex a prerequisite for attaining Buddhahood.[10] Hence its acquisition marks significant progress in a Bodhisattva's path to Buddhahood.[11] Yet I shall question whether Beautiful Woman really produces a male body or, more precisely, whether she produces only one kind of sexed body. Reading against the sexist discourse of the narrative, I shall argue that a. Beautiful Woman's bodily mutilation produces non-normatively sexed *but virtuous* Bodhisattvas, b. the Buddha is not male in this narrative, but a radically alterior being, and c. the narrative offers a vision of the Buddha as omnibodied, omnisexed, and omnigendered.[12] Embodiment is not static, but fluid. Virtue therefore has multiple and counterhegemonic forms.

The Story of Beautiful Woman

Ironically, the construction of virtuous Bodhisattva and Buddha bodies begins with a deconstruction of these bodies—literally, a series of dismemberments.[13] The story describes three successive lifetimes of the Bodhisattva, in each of which s/he engages in bodily mutilation or sacrifice. These extraordinary acts of generosity materialize ever more virtuous Bodhisattva bodies and ultimately the virtuous body of a Buddha. My essay focuses primarily on the Buddha's lifetime as Beautiful Woman because her story displays the most complex representations of sex. Her story is as follows:

Beautiful Woman lives in a time of famine. As she is walking about one day, she comes upon a starving human mother about to eat her live newborn son. Beautiful Woman does not have time to rush home and get food because the mother is at the point of death. Beautiful Woman reflects that she has experienced countless forms of suffering throughout her many lifetimes. Again and again wherever and however she has been reborn—whether in the many hells or other horrific realms of the Buddhist cosmos, whether as animal or human—repeatedly her hands, feet, ears, noses, various body parts—large and small—have been cut off. She reflects further that she has experienced such torture, along with unspecified other forms of torment, to no avail. In all her many lifetimes her suffering has brought her no benefit. She resolves now to gain some benefit for herself by *intentionally* mutilating her body. She benefits by beginning to cultivate generosity, which is a requisite virtue for Buddhahood. She asks the starving mother for a knife, cuts off her two breasts, and "satisfies the woman with her own flesh and blood."[14] She then extracts a promise from the mother that she will refrain from eating her son until Beautiful Woman has a chance to bring some more food. Bleeding profusely, Beautiful Woman goes home to her husband. She tells him what happened and then asks him to prepare food for the starving mother.

Her husband, however, tells *her* to prepare the food, and, instead, he performs a declaration of truth (*satyavacana*). Such declarations are a common feature of Sanskrit literature—Buddhist or no—and reflect the South Asian belief that words of truth have the power to alter reality. The truth Beautiful Woman's husband declares is that no one has ever seen or heard before of a deed as marvelous as that performed by Beautiful Woman. Beautiful Woman's husband requests that both her breasts reappear through the power of this declaration of truth. They do, and, presumably, Beautiful Woman goes off to the kitchen.

Immediately the narrative shifts to the realms of the Buddhist cosmos inhabited by numerous gods. Gods live long and pleasurable lives, but their lives are not eternal. Eventually they die and are reborn, usually, in less advantageous states. The only way to avoid the endless cycle of birth and rebirth is to attain liberation. The king of gods, Śakra, is worried that Beautiful Woman has earned so much merit by her act of generosity that when she dies she will be reborn as Śakra and the present Śakra might die and be reborn as something else sooner than he had bargained for. Disguising his divine identity, Śakra pays Beautiful Woman a visit to find out if she is as good as she looks. In order to determine her frame of mind before, during, and after the time she cut off her breasts he asks her a series of questions. Specifically, he wants to know if she felt any regret. An ideal donor derives pleasure from her or his gift—never regret.[15] Beautiful Woman assures Śakra that she did not feel regret and that her motive in performing this great sacrifice was to become a Buddha so that she could help others to attain liberation. At this point in the narrative Beautiful Woman makes her own declaration of truth: "By this truth, by this declaration of truth may my female sex faculty (*indriya*) disappear and may a male sex faculty (*indriya*) appear."[16] The sex faculty (*indriya*) is the faculty or power that "determines masculine and feminine primary and secondary sexual characteristics, as well as gender-role behavior."[17] According to Buddhism there are separate *indriyas*, or faculties, that govern eyes, ears, nose, tongue, body, mind, male and female sex, and life or vitality. The male sex faculty (*puruṣa indriya*) and the female sex faculty (*strī indriya*) control both physical appearance and conduct—what we would define as sex and gender.[18] Beautiful Woman's declaration of truth has the desired effect. The grammatically feminine Beautiful Woman (Rūpāvatī) becomes the grammatically male Beautiful Man (Rūpāvata). To boot, Beautiful Man gets appointed king of the region because of his great merit. When Beautiful Man dies he is reborn in a wealthy merchant family as a male Bodhisattva named Moonlight whose body at birth emits a great radiance. Moonlight gives his entire body to a flock of starving birds who eat him to the bone. Moonlight is then reborn as a male Bodhisattva named Brahmalight. Brahmalight is born into an even more prestigious family (brahmins, or priests) than that of Moonlight, and his body also emits greater radiance than Moonlight's.[19] Brahmalight offers his body to a starving tigress and is also eaten to the bone. The story now comes to a close. The Buddha praises generosity since it enabled him to progress toward Buddhahood. He exhorts all present to practice generosity as well.

Conventional Discourse on Bodies: Virtuous Bodies and Abject Bodies

There is much to be learned from this story. I shall begin by discussing the different discourses on bodies—conventional and ascetic—manifest in this story. Note that conventional and ascetic discourses are both present in one story. This is the case in general in South Asian Buddhist literature, although some literature may emphasize one form of discourse more than the other. This discussion of conventional and ascetic discourses will further the analysis of "The Story of Beautiful Woman" and also provide the reader with information relevant to South Asian Buddhist representations of bodies in general.

Clearly, the generous deeds of Beautiful Woman, Moonlight, and Brahmalight have increasingly beneficial, i.e., virtuous material effects. Virtue is embodied in terms of sex, kingship, family, caste, and bodily radiance. The single most important feature of a conventional discourse on bodies is that such discourse foregrounds bodily differences, defining bodies as more or less abject or virtuous. Most Buddhists, not just Bodhisattvas in narrative literature, were concerned with producing virtuous bodies and preventing the materialization of abject bodies. How are virtuous and abject bodies defined? How are they produced?

Buddhists, including the Bodhisattvas of our story, produce virtuous bodies by earning religious merit. Buddhists believe in karma. Living beings earn a combination of "good karma," called "merit," and "bad karma," called "sin," in accordance with their deeds. Since Buddhists also believe in reincarnation, the karmic consequences of meritorious and sinful deeds can affect one's present or future lifetimes. Buddhists are especially concerned with earning enough merit to attain a favorable rebirth in their next lifetime. A key feature of a favorable rebirth is a virtuous body.[20] Bodies are marked by a range of physical conditions including, first of all, species. One might be reborn as a human, a god, an animal, a variety of demonic beings, or as one of the unfortunate inhabitants of the numerous Buddhist hells. Buddhists believe that only human beings can become a Buddha, so at some point on the path to Buddhahood a Bodhisattva must attain a human rebirth. Beautiful Woman, Moonlight, and Brahmalight are all humans.

The features of ideal human bodies reiterate general South Asian cultural norms, not specific to Buddhism, of, in Butler's words, "what counts as a valued and valuable body" (BTM, p. 22). Ideal human bodies are marked by features such as physical beauty, fair complexion, good health, longevity, the absence of physical or mental disability, preferably—but not always—male sex, and high caste or family status.[21] I call such ideal human bodies "virtuous bodies" because of the close relationship between body and morality in Buddhist tradition.[22] Virtuous bodies are presumed to be the karmic effects of merit and serve as visible markers of a person's past virtue. Even more significantly, virtuous bodies indicate a person's *present capacity for virtue*. For example, one scholar, writing about Theravāda Buddhism in modern Sri Lanka, notes that the most attractive monks are considered to be the ones with the greatest reputations for virtue. Such monks are literally said to have the "color" or "look" or "complexion" of merit (*pin pāta*): slightly heavy set, with smooth and full faces, and with vital and light brown skin tone.[23] Body and morality are so closely related that a description of a person's features may serve as commentary on his or her moral character. This relationship underscores Butler's argument that "the very contours of the body are sites that vacillate between the psychic and the material" (BTM, p. 66; see also pp. 17, 22, 55, 59, 234). In the Buddhist context the contours of the body vacillate between the *moral* and the material. Thus Buddhist literature is replete with descriptions of beings who are disfigured by sin or reek with the stench of their immoral conduct. Conversely, other beings are perfumed or adorned with their virtues.[24]

As Butler argues, the constitutive constraints that produce the domain of "bodies that matter" also produce the domain of those that do not—that is, abject bodies. The threat of being reborn in abject material form encourages normative ethical behavior in Buddhist cultures. A striking feature of Buddhist literature is the sheer number and variety of bodies marked as abject, including—but hardly limited to—non-normatively sexed bodies. For instance, one medieval Indian monastic text warns that unrestrained sexual desire has the following karmic consequences: you will be reborn in hell or in a variety of demonic forms; if you are reborn as a human you will be one-eyed, lame, tongueless, deformed, blind from birth, deaf, or insensible; if you are reborn as an animal you will be a dog, swine, camel, donkey, monkey, elephant, horse, cow, tiger, moth, or fly.[25] The same text warns that if the male head of a household prevents his son, daughter, or wife from being ordained as a monk or nun (and commits a few other crimes as well), he will be reborn blind from birth, retarded, tongueless, as an outcaste (*caṇḍāla*), permanent servant, woman, dog, swine, ass, camel, or venomous snake. He will also be reborn as a *ṣaṇḍaka* or a *paṇḍaka*.[26]

Ṣaṇḍakas (also known as *ṣaṇḍhas* or *ṣaṇḍhakas*) and *paṇḍakas* are two of a number of terms found in different genres of South Asian literature, including medical literature, that refer to non-normatively sexed humans.[27] These terms designate a wide range of sexual practices, sexual dysfunctions, and anomalous anatomies. According to two scholars, non-normatively sexed persons include "individuals whom we might view as gay men, lesbians, bisexuals, and transvestites; the impotent; those with sexual dysfunctions other than impotence; those with sexual paraphilias or unconventional sexual behavior; and the sexually anomalous, anatomically or physiologically (for example, hermaphrodites)."[28] Non-normatively sexed persons are those who in diverse ways do not conform to normative expectations of masculine or feminine anatomy or physiology, gender roles, and sexual behavior.[29] They are also people who blur the distinctions between male and female sex.[30] Further, according to South Asian literature, non-normative sex is a matter of biology rather than social conditioning.[31] Clearly South Asian concepts of non-normative sex (at least in the premodern context) are in some respects different from the concepts of homosexuality or queerness that mark bodies as abject in Butler's sources.[32] For instance, a congenitally impotent man would be classified as a *paṇḍaka*,[33] yet to a modern Western audience this indicates nothing about his sexual orientation.

Like all abject bodies in Buddhist literature, non-normatively sexed bodies are considered the material effects of past sin. Additionally, if virtuous bodies indicate a person's present capacity for virtue, abject bodies indicate that this capacity is, at best, limited. For instance, some physical conditions prohibit one from ordaining as a monk or nun. Those prohibited from ordination include: "dwarfs, those missing a limb, the blind, the deaf, those with boils, or leprosy"[34] as well as those who are not normatively sexed. One influential scholastic text maintains that certain kinds of beings are utterly incapable of moral agency. These include anyone who is not a god or a human being, humans who are non-normatively sexed, and humans who are born in a continent to the north of the known world called Uttarakuru.[35] These unfortunate beings lack the capacity to maintain moral discipline; interestingly, they also lack the capacity to abandon such discipline. For reasons never fully explained, moral agency requires the capacity for both discipline and its opposite. The text states that neither discipline nor undiscipline can arise in the bodies of these beings because their "bodies are similar to soil saturated with salt" in which neither wheat nor bad herbs can grow.[36] Given the fact that the nature of one's body can enable or disable moral action, much of Buddhist practice centers on materializing a virtuous body in future rebirths. Practicing generosity is one of the more common techniques for earning merit. Generally this entails ritualized donations to the monastic community. A Bodhisattva, however, earns merit by practicing a higher form of generosity; s/he gives away her or his own flesh and blood.

Although a wide range of physical conditions mark virtuous bodies, "The Story of Beautiful Woman" is especially concerned with sex. The transition from a female Bodhisattva to a male Bodhisattva apparently marks significant progress toward Buddhahood, reflecting a common South Asian Buddhist belief that it takes more merit to produce male sex than female sex. That is not to say that female bodies are always considered morally inferior to male bodies, since sex is but one of a range of bodily conditions that mark virtuous bodies. For instance, a physically or mentally disabled man may have less ability and/or opportunity to earn merit than a woman in full possession of physical and mental health. Nevertheless, male sex is frequently regarded as a marker of superior moral development—and not just in narrative literature. For instance, some Buddhist scriptures claim that if a woman performs a prescribed ritual she will be reborn as a man. Some Buddhists believe that certain Buddhist paradises, or "pure lands," were devoid of women. The association of virtue with male sex has wide resonance in Buddhist traditions. For Beautiful Woman the materialization of male sex would appear to be a particularly pressing concern, since she wants to become a Buddha. Before we can interrogate the material effects of Beautiful Woman's generosity, we need to examine in greater detail the nature and implications of her bodily mutilation. I shall do so in light of Butler's concept of abjection. Discussion of bodily mutilation and sacrifice brings us to a different kind of discourse on bodies, namely, an ascetic discourse. In contrast to conventional discourse, ascetic discourse valorizes abjection because identification with an abject body image produces virtuous/liberated bodied beings.[37]

Ascetic Discourse on Bodies: Abjection as Soteriological Tool

An ascetic discourse on bodies defines both bodies and abjection differently from a conventional discourse. Whereas the conventional discourse foregrounds bodily differences, the ascetic discourse negates bodily differences because it defines *all* bodies, whether beautiful or ugly, whether healthy or sick, whether able-bodied or disabled, whether high- or low-caste, as abject. Abjection in the context of an ascetic discourse means specifically that all bodies are intrinsically foul, impermanent, and without enduring essence or worth.[38] For instance, ascetic discourse commonly represents the body as a container of foul substances such as urine, excrement, blood, phlegm, snot, and pus.[39] The body is likened to an open wound, a painted chamber pot, a bag of skin or excrement; it oozes with filth and stinks like raw meat.[40] Not surprisingly, the intended effect of such discourse is detachment from the conventionally valued body. But the ultimate aim is not to repudiate the body per se but to eradicate all desires. As Butler notes, it is the body that "mobilizes psychic action from the start" (BTM, p. 67). Buddhist ascetics try to eliminate or lessen the power of desire by cultivating an abject body image.

Why is desire so problematic? According to Buddhists desire is the source of all suffering. Buddhists define desire (literally, thirst, or *tṛṣṇā*) broadly as the desire or craving for sense pleasures and for life itself.[41] Buddhists believe that all reality is in a constant state of flux and change.[42] Everything is impermanent. Desire is problematic because no one has complete control over their lives. No matter how good an experience may be, it is not permanent. Relationships end, loved ones die, our own bodies fall ill, and we too face the inevitability of death. Suffering arises because we constantly try to hold on to pleasurable experiences and put off unpleasurable experiences. Many Buddhists define liberation as the elimination of all desire or craving. The liberated person is able to accept the impermanence of experiences and embrace each moment with joy rather than with disappointment, pain, anxiety, and so forth when particular expectations or wishes have not been met.

But note: the very fact that some people strive for liberation indicates that not all desires are bad. Beautiful Woman's desire to become a Buddha is a beneficial rather than harmful desire. Her desire is beneficial because its purpose is not primarily self-gratification, as is the case with most desires; its purpose is to become a Buddha so that she can help others end their suffering. When Buddhists speak about the necessity of eradicating desire, they mean desire in its negative sense as craving or thirst for personal gratification of various sorts.

Buddhists define desire or craving very broadly, but ascetic discourse is especially concerned with eradicating sexual desire. Given the centrality of sexual desire to Butler's theories of identity formation, it is important to underscore that the formation of a Buddha or liberated being entails the repudiation of sexual desire rather than the production of a particular kind of sexual desire.[43] The principal issue here is the distinction between sexuality and celibacy rather than between heterosexuality and homosexuality.[44] One way that Buddhist ascetics attempted to eradicate desire is by cultivating an abject body image. In this context abjection is not feared or shunned as it is in the context of a conventional discourse on bodies; to the contrary, *abjection is valorized as a soteriological tool to produce virtuous/liberated bodied beings.* Further, identification with an abject body image is made without being disavowed. Normative heterosexuality is produced, according to Butler's analysis, by repudiating the identification with an abject homosexuality. In the Buddhist context a virtuous/liberated bodied being is produced by affirming the identification with an abject body image. In both instances, however, abjection is key to the formation of determinate types of bodied beings.

Buddhist monastic practitioners developed a variety of techniques to cultivate an abject body image. Such techniques included systematic meditation on the thirty-two repulsive features of the body such as urine and excrement, meditations on decaying corpses (traditionally such meditations were undertaken in cremation grounds, but today these are sometimes performed in autopsy rooms),[45] and a range of meditations on the body's impermanence and lack of enduring essence or worth.[46] Buddhists characterize the experience of identifying with an abject body image as one of extreme shock (saṃvega).[47] This is the moment when one finally realizes that all Buddhist teachings about the body's inherent foulness, impermanence, and lack of enduring essence actually apply to oneself. It is an experiential realization of the truth of these teachings. For instance, practitioners contemplating decaying corpses learn to identify their own bodies with the rotting corpses, saying, "this [my own] body is of the same nature as that, will become like that, cannot avoid [becoming like] that."[48] Identification with an abject body image—an identification that is affirmed and not disavowed—eradicates desire and thereby materializes a virtuous/liberated bodied being.

Although ascetic discourse cultivates detachment from the conventionally valued body, its aim is the eradication of desire and not a repudiation of the body in itself. To the contrary, ascetic discourse that codes all bodies as abject produces bodies conventionally defined as virtuous, for instance the well-disciplined bodies of monks or the beautiful body of a Buddha.[49] In other words, a discourse that negates all bodily distinctions is in the service of producing bodies with distinct bodily features. This is nowhere more apparent than in traditional representations of the Buddha's body, conventionally regarded as exquisitely beautiful. The Buddha's body is marked with very specific physical features, codified in lists of thirty-two major and eighty minor characteristics.[50] Among the thirty-two major characteristics are a golden complexion, a skin texture so smooth no dust can stick to the body, the imprint of auspicious symbols on the soles of his feet, sparkling white teeth, an unusually long tongue, arms that reach down to his knees, long and shapely eyelashes, body hairs that curl to the right, and a sheathed penis—the latter apparently marking the Buddha as male (a point I shall return to below).

Like ascetic practitioners, Beautiful Woman identifies with an abject body image in order to materialize a virtuous and eventually liberated bodied being. Narratives about bodily mutilation and sacrifice evoke an ascetic discourse on bodies that marks all bodies as abject.[51] "The Story of Beautiful Woman" opens with a description of Beautiful Woman's good looks—that is, conventionally speaking, Beautiful Woman has a virtuous body. But immediately Beautiful Woman offers a different image of herself, a mutilated image of herself. Recall, Beautiful Woman reflects that her hands, feet, ears, noses, and various other body parts have been cut off again and again in countless past lifetimes. The effect of such reflection is similar to the effect of ascetic discourse which defines all bodies, no matter how virtuous, as abject. Further, just as ascetic discourse reminds a practitioner that no amount of care can protect one's body from an inevitable—and apparently often gruesome—death, so too this narrative reminds its audience of the same point.

Beautiful Woman's vision of herself as repeatedly mutilated constitutes an identification with an abject body image. However, she goes a step beyond the ordinary ascetic practitioner and affirms that identification by mutilating herself, in effect, performing her own abjection.[52] This act of self-mutilation differs from all of the previous mutilations she has experienced in past lives because it is intentional. Beautiful Woman chooses to abject herself. She is not a victim, but an agent. Beautiful Woman's experience of abjection is very different from that of abject beings such as the starving mother in the story who has not chosen abjection; she has simply attained a conventionally defined abject rebirth. Whereas the starving mother experiences abjection as suffering, Beautiful Woman does not appear to suffer. To the contrary, she feels no regret, even while cutting off her breasts. Further, she gains great benefit by abjecting herself. She makes progress on the Bodhisattva path and eventually becomes a Buddha. Ascetic discourse evaluates abjection differently from conventional discourse. Whereas conventional discourse shuns and fears abject bodies, ascetic discourse affirms identification with an abject body image because such identification is liberative.

What are the material effects of mutilating or sacrificing one's body—that is, performing one's own abjection? All acts of bodily mutilation and sacrifice in this story produce ever more virtuous Bodhisattva bodies, culminating in the most virtuous body of all—that of a Buddha. These virtuous bodies appear to conform to conventional representations of body ideals in that they are male, of high-caste or family status, and beautiful. Yet I argue that choosing abjection produces virtuous bodies in tension with normative representations of body ideals, specifically with respect to sex. To that end I now consider whether Beautiful Woman's bodily mutilation really materializes male sex and whether it materializes only one kind of sex.

Sexing Beautiful Woman

The question of Beautiful Woman's sex(es) is particularly pressing because of an intriguing narrative detail. Before cutting off her breasts Beautiful Woman generates in her body (*ātman*)[53] three qualities—strength (*sthāma*), power (*bala*), and virility (*vīrya*).[54] I shall suggest different ways of interpreting these qualities, beginning with the suggestion that they—and especially virility—are masculine qualities. *Vīrya* can mean anything from "valor," "courage," or "vigor," to "manliness," "virility," and "semen." The breadth of *vīrya's* semantic field offers no definitive interpretation of the term, whether to a premodern South Asian reader or to this modern North American reader. In a story about the transition of a female Bodhisattva to a male Bodhisattva, I find most suggestive a masculine reading of *vīrya* as virility. According to such a reading, Beautiful Woman generates masculine qualities in her body prior to becoming male. Remember, she does not become male until the god, Śakra, prompts her to make a declaration of truth at which point her female sex faculty is replaced by a male sex faculty. Before Śakra's visit Beautiful Woman has both a female sex faculty and male qualities in her body. Beautiful Woman blurs the distinctions between male and female sex and is thus indeterminately sexed.

Support for reading Beautiful Woman's sex as indeterminate at this stage of the narrative also comes from the instability of Beautiful Woman's bodily form. Beautiful Woman cuts off her breasts, her husband restores them, and Beautiful Woman presumably loses them again when Beautiful Woman gains a male sex faculty and becomes Beautiful Man. This is hardly a straightforward shift from female to male sex. Beautiful Woman's very name calls attention to her bodily form and hence also the instability of that form. "Beautiful Woman" is a translation of "Rūpāvatī" which means "possessing a bodily form" and, by extension, a beautiful bodily form. Her name could also be translated as "Shapely Woman." The shifting shape of this Shapely Woman underscores the indeterminacy of Beautiful Woman's sex.

The indeterminacy of Beautiful Woman's sex is also suggested by the unusual exchange Beautiful Woman has with the husband when Beautiful Woman arrives home dripping with blood. Beautiful Woman asks the husband to prepare food for the starving mother. The husband immediately refuses and makes his declaration of truth, which restores Beautiful Woman's breasts. At precisely the moment in the narrative when Beautiful Woman's sex is in question, Beautiful Woman attempts a subversion of normative gender roles.

Beautiful Woman temporarily materializes an indeterminately sexed body that blurs the distinctions between male and female sex. Conventionally speaking, such a body is an abject body. Significantly, Beautiful Woman is never called *paṇḍaka* or any of the other terms that refer to abject sex. Further, Beautiful Woman's indeterminately sexed body is the result of merit (an act of generosity), not sin. Beautiful Woman's indeterminately sexed body represents a counterhegemonic materialization of virtue, that is, a virtuous body in tension with normative body ideals. Beautiful Woman demonstrates that indeterminate sex can be virtuous.

Both Beautiful Woman's husband and the god, Śakra, compel Beautiful Woman to assume normative female or male sex. The husband makes a declaration of truth that restores Beautiful Woman's female appearance and conduct. Śakra prompts Beautiful Woman to make her own declaration of truth, which replaces her female sex faculty with a male sex faculty. Beautiful Woman makes her declaration of truth specifically because Śakra tells her that no one will believe that she gave away her breasts without regret. Beautiful Woman makes her declaration of truth in order to prove she is not lying. If we read the qualities of strength, power, and virility as masculine qualities, the generation of a male sex faculty removes any sexual indeterminacy. Beautiful Man is just that—a beautiful man. Beautiful Woman's bodily mutilation produces a temporary counterhegemonic materialization of virtue and subsequently a normatively virtuous male body.

The qualities of strength, power, and virility, however, need not be interpreted as explicitly masculine qualities. The narrative also supports an interpretation of these qualities as *Bodhisattva*, rather than *masculine*, qualities (although the two interpretations are not necessarily mutually exclusive). *Vīrya* (virility) could be translated in a less gender-specific manner as "vigor" or "energy." Significantly, strength, power, and vigor are not generic masculine qualities in this story; ordinary men do not manifest these qualities. Only the Bodhisattva, Beautiful Woman, manifests these qualities. In the context of the anthology as a whole, these are qualities a Bodhisattva generates right before sacrificing her or his body.[55] If these are Bodhisattva qualities rather than masculine qualities, they are alterior to both men and women. Rather than produce indeterminate sex, Beautiful Woman may have produced alterior sex. That is, Beautiful Woman's sex does not blur the distinctions between male and female sex (indeterminate sex), but is instead a sex that is radically other (alterior sex). Alterior sex challenges the very validity of male and female sex as exclusive markers of sexual identity. Beautiful Woman's shape-shifting and attempted subversion of a female gender role may indicate alterior sex as much as indeterminate sex. Reading strength, power, and vigor as alterior Bodhisattva qualities also calls into question Beautiful Man's sex. Beautiful Man may have a male sex faculty but he also manifests alterior Bodhisattva qualities.

In a story ostensibly about the shift from female to male sex, we find a surprising proliferation of sexes. Beautiful Woman's bodily mutilation does not produce (only) a conventionally virtuous male sex. Rather, Beautiful Woman's performance of abjection produces indeterminate and/or alterior sex. Her identification with an abject body image produces counterhegemonic materializations of virtue, that is, non-normatively sexed but virtuous bodied beings. Beautiful Woman illustrates the instabilities of all normative performances (for Butler, gender performances; for this story, Bodhisattva performances) because Beautiful Woman's affirmation of an abject identity produces bodies that challenge normative representations of virtuous bodied beings.

Beautiful Woman and Beautiful Man both possess female and male sex faculties, respectively, suggesting that radical sexual alterity has not yet been attained, since their identities (i.e., their names) still depend on a distinction between female and male sex faculties. Beautiful Woman and Beautiful Man are Bodhisattvas and not yet Buddhas. Only the Buddha is portrayed as a fully alterior being. What signifies his alterity? The Buddha's alterity is signi-fied by his representation as a mother, adding another level of complexity to the narrative's exploration of sex.

Buddha-mother

In what sense is the Buddha a mother? One scholar of Buddhist ethics remarks that "the ideal moral attitude to other beings . . . is the 'love a mother shows towards her one and only son.'"[56] Mothers are commonly regarded as exemplars of love, compassion, generosity, and self-sacrifice.[57] Because the Buddha too exhibits such virtues, he is sometimes likened to a mother. Yet the Buddha differs from mothers in the scope of his love. He loves every liv-ing being with the same intensity a mother feels for her only son.[58] The Bud-dha is thus both *like* other mothers and also *better than* other mothers.[59] In "The Story of Beautiful Woman" the Buddha-mother represents the epitome of care for others. In his past lives he feeds starving beings with her/his own flesh and blood. Beautiful Woman's gift of her breasts is "an obvious evoca-tion of the idea of breastfeeding."[60] The Bodhisattva's performances of abjec-tion (i.e., bodily mutilations and sacrifices) are represented as acts of mater-nal care that culminate in the formation of a Buddha-mother.[61]

The Bodhisattva and Buddha stand in sharp contrast to the murderous mothers that populate this narrative. On more than one occasion the Bod-hisattva rescues children—human and animal—from their starving mothers. In Buddhist traditions motherhood has negative as well as positive connota-tions. Starving mothers about to eat their children are a common metaphor for desire or craving that, as we have seen, is the cause of all suffering.[62] Unrestrained desires cause harm to oneself and others. Had the starving mothers actually eaten their children, they would have suffered severe kar-mic consequences, namely further abject rebirths. The contrast between Buddha-mother, in particular, and starving mothers is especially apt because the Buddha teaches us how to gain some control over our desires and ensure virtuous rebirths. In the case of religious ascetics, he teaches the means of eradicating desire altogether and attaining liberation that brings an end to all suffering. The Buddha is by far the best mother of all; indeed he some-times appears to be the only viable mother in this story.[63] Not only does the Buddha lavish maternal care on beings in her/his past and present lifetimes, but, as a Buddha in his present lifetime, he also teaches living beings how to control or eradicate desire. The Buddha is the only mother who can promise his children permanent protection from all suffering.

Motherhood signifies the Buddha's alterity, that is, "a form of otherness irreducible to and unable to be modelled on any form of projection of or identification with the subject . . . an independent and autonomous other with its own qualities and attributes."[64] Buddhists say this succinctly when they call the Buddha "unthinkable" (*acintya*). The Buddha is a unique class of being, radically different from everyone else. Contrary to modernist representations of the Buddha (beginning around the nineteenth century) that emphasize the Buddha's humanity, premodern Buddhists represented the Buddha as an extraordinary being with vast miraculous powers who could barely take a step without the earth quaking, gods raining down flowers from the heavens, and divine music sounding in the air.[65] The Buddha's alterity is salvific. His difference guarantees his ability to save others.[66]

The Buddha's alterity is also with respect to sex. Although the Buddha is maternal, he is not feminine in this story. For instance, the Buddha does not suckle his children at his breasts like Christ in medieval European Christian visions.[67] In fact, the Buddha (in his incarnation as Beautiful Woman) is a mother who feeds with her/his breasts by cutting them off. The Buddha is also not androgynous. There is no attempt to define the Buddha as a composite of specifically masculine and feminine qualities. Nor is there a trace of Buddhist tantric physiology, which assumes that all humans have both male and female elements within them. Like Beautiful Woman (and perhaps Beautiful Man), the Buddha defies normative expectations of male and female sex. Yet normative sex is not demanded of the Buddha as it is of Beautiful Woman. No spouse or god intervenes to compel female or male sex. In fact, the Buddha's body is the telos of all the acts of bodily mutilation, the materialization of repeated identifications with an abject body, the end point of all the narrative's shape-shifting. In a story seemingly about the acquisition of male sex, the culmination of all Bodhisattva performances is an alterior bodied being whose sex is radically other to male or female sex. The link between virtue and male sex has become rather tenuous in this narrative.

But what about the Buddha's sheathed penis? Traditionally Buddhists and scholars of Buddhism regard this as evidence of the Buddha's masculinity. Yet the sheathed penis marks the Buddha as *different* from other men.[68] Reading against tradition, I suggest we have the option of interpreting the sheathed penis as a marker of alterity rather than as a marker of normative masculinity. Even if male sex is a required condition for attaining Buddhahood (as much of Buddhist tradition claims), male sex is not necessarily a defining feature of Buddhahood, just as a career as a graduate student is a condition for becoming a professor, but a professor is not defined as a graduate student. Rather than attribute male or even female sex to the Buddha, I suggest we simply speak of "Buddha sex" and allow that sex its difference.

What effect does the maternal care of Bodhisattva and Buddha have on other beings in the narrative? Typically, the Buddha is said to regard every living being as if that being were his one and only son. But in this story the Bodhisattva's and Buddha's maternal love is reserved primarily for the Buddha's male monastic community. With one exception all the mothers and children the Bodhisattva rescues are reborn as men who become monks during the Buddha's lifetime. The fact that some of these future monks are also blood relations of the Buddha, including the Buddha's own son, further underscores the familial imagery of the story.[69] (The Buddha conceived a son before abandoning his family to pursue meditation.) The Buddha is depicted as the mother of a monastic community, and that community is depicted as an alternative family.[70] This family represents a better alternative to the normative one because it is the context in which one can learn how to eradicate desire and thus attain liberation.

Significantly, the formation of particular subjects—Bodhisattva and Buddha—form in turn *other subjects*. The repeated gift of the Bodhisattva's body—a body ascetic discourse codes as abject—is a gift in two senses: first, the gifted body satisfies an immediate need for food, and second, it enables the radical transformation of other subjects both in the present and in the future. For instance, in the present the murderous mothers are given food so that they can care properly for their own children; the Bodhisattva's maternal care enables these mothers to become better mothers. Consequently, both mothers and children develop the ethical capacity to care for other beings. In the future they therefore attain better rebirths and are eventually reborn as men who are ordained in the Buddha's order. By intentionally abjecting her/himself, the Bodhisattva transforms abject beings—who themselves have not chosen their abjection—into virtuous beings. By choosing abjection, the Bodhisattva materializes not only an individual virtuous/liberated body but also an entire monastic community, suggesting that abjection can be both individually and communally liberative. Yet the Bodhisattva is also dependent on the abject starving mothers for her/his progress toward Buddhahood. Without these mothers the Bodhisattva would have had no opportunity to cultivate generosity and develop the extraordinary degree of maternal love manifest by the radically and salvifically alterior figure of the Buddha-mother. In effect, these abject mothers also teach the Bodhisattva how to become a better mother. Varieties of abject beings, both those who choose abjection, namely, the Bodhisattva, and those who do not choose abjection, namely, the starving mothers, are vital to the ethical and religious development of a wider community of beings.

Although the Buddha is known to have founded an order of nuns in India, these are not the focus of his maternal love in this story.[71] The narrative attempts once again to code virtue as male by defining the monastic community as exclusively male in spite of, *or perhaps because of*, the fact that there were nuns' communities of considerable influence at various points in South Asian history.[72] On the most obvious level this story is sexist. Beautiful

Woman becomes Beautiful Man, Beautiful Woman feeds with her breasts by cutting them off, and the maternal love of Bodhisattva and Buddha are directed at creating and sustaining a male monastic community. But the story continuously displays the instabilities of its sexist discourse. One such destabilizing moment occurs in the coding of virtue as a male monastic community. There is one being rescued by the Bodhisattva who is not reborn as a man in the Buddha's lifetime and is not ordained in the Buddha's monastic order. That being is the starving human mother saved by Beautiful Woman's breasts. The starving human mother is reborn as a high-caste woman named Moonlight. Moonlight is also the name of one of the Bodhisattvas in this story (he is the one who offers his body to a flock of starving birds). Sometimes in Buddhist literature a person takes the name of a Buddha they wish to emulate.[73] The female Moonlight is about to embark on her own Bodhisattva career and produce materializations of virtue—individual and communal—that cannot be predicted in advance. The effects of the narrative, to paraphrase Butler, continue to signify in spite of and sometimes against its authors "most precious intentions" (BTM, p. 241).

Fluid Bodies

At the close of the narrative the reader is offered one final vision of the tale as a whole, which, I argue, renders impossible the association of virtue with one particular material form or limited range of material forms. There are two temporal perspectives present in "The Story of Beautiful Woman," as in all stories about the Buddha's past lives. These are diachronic and synchronic perspectives. The former is a linear perspective in which all Bodhisattva performances culminate in the attainment of Buddhahood. Reading diachronically, each Bodhisattva body is abjected in the service of materializing the next body. Virtue has a variety of material forms, but at any given moment it has *one particular form*—be it Beautiful Woman, Beautiful Man, Moonlight, Brahmalight, or Buddha-mother.

The synchronic perspective is a vision of the totality of Bodhisattva and Buddha bodies grasped in one moment. The synchronic perspective dominates at the end of the tale, although to some extent it is operative throughout as well. At the end of the story the Buddha identifies himself with all the Bodhisattvas of the story, saying, "at that time I was Beautiful Woman," and so forth. Such announcements come as no surprise to this story's audience, who knows the pattern of such narratives. The audience knows all along that Beautiful Woman is both Beautiful Woman and Buddha; Moonlight is both Moonlight and Buddha, etc. From a synchronic perspective the Buddha is all these bodies rather than the culmination of a discrete series of bodies. The synchronic perspective offers the reader a vision of the Buddha as omnibodied, omnisexed, and omnigendered. From this perspective it is impossible to associate virtue with any one particular material form; rather, multiple hegemonic and counterhegemonic materializations of virtue appear simultaneously.

Traditionally, Buddhists and scholars of Buddhism have argued that liberation is an experience that transcends material distinctions such as sex. Just as an ascetic discourse on bodies negates all bodily distinctions, so too Buddhist discourse on liberation, for different reasons, defines liberation as an experience that transcends all bodily distinctions—indeed, all forms of conceptualization. Both the ascetic discourse on bodies and the discourse on liberation represent "ultimate" perspectives on reality, which Buddhists intentionally contrast to "conventional" perspectives that value material distinctions such as sex. When Buddhists speak of an "ultimate" perspective they do not deny the conventional existence of bodily differences (or, for that matter, the entire material world), but they deny that these differences have ultimate or permanent validity. Many Buddhists and scholars of Buddhism have found an "ultimate" perspective on reality that relativizes bodily distinctions useful for combating injustices such as sexism. Without denying the efficacy of such an approach in political struggles, I nevertheless have some reservations about the usefulness of exclusively invoking such an ultimate perspective. I propose an alternative representation of liberation and the liberated being in order to revision what virtue looks like—in other words, to contribute to a radical resignification of "what counts as a valued and valuable body in the world" (BTM, p. 22).

I am not the first to note that statements in Buddhist literature about the "ultimate" irrelevance of distinctions such as sex and gender sometimes appear in narratives about female Bodhisattvas who become male in order to prove that they have attained liberation. While Buddhists and scholars of Buddhism, past and present, have frequently interpreted such stories as evidence of women's *capacity to attain liberation*, the fact that male sex is demanded of these female Bodhisattvas demonstrates the persistence of the association of virtue with male sex.[74] Scholars have been less attentive to more subtle ways in which statements about the ultimate irrelevance of sex and gender are undermined in Buddhist literature. For instance, such statements may coincide with praise of Śākyamuni Buddha's physical beauty, thus suggesting that virtue has a particular material form.[75] There is a tension between the rhetoric of liberation, which transcends all difference, and the embodied nature of this religious ideal, which reinscribes difference in the particularity of the body of the Buddha—a body generally presumed to be male.

How do we explain this tension? One scholar rightly suggests that there are conflicting attitudes toward women in Buddhist literature. He contrasts a "soteriological inclusiveness" with "institutional androcentrism" and "ascetic misogyny."[76] Yet, my analysis of "The Story of Beautiful Woman" provides another explanation. We have seen that an ascetic discourse on bodies produces virtuous/liberated bodied beings. In this instance an "ultimate" discourse on bodies that negates bodily differences because it codes all bodies as abject is in the service of a "conventional" discourse on bodies that values bodily differences.[77] I am concerned that the emphasis among Buddhists and scholars of Buddhism on the transcendence of distinctions—that is, an ultimate perspective—overlooks the fact that such a perspective often is in the service of producing determinate types of beings with distinct bodily features. But I do not regard this as an evil. Buddhist tradition values difference as much as it values the transcendence of difference. After all, the Buddha's radical alterity is salvific. Finally, on a more practical note, I am apprehensive that defining liberation primarily as the transcendence of all distinctions may shut down conversations about sex/gender equality as often as it initiates such conversations.[78]

In place of a definition of the liberated being as one who transcends all distinctions, I propose a Buddha such as we find in "The Story of Beautiful Woman," one who is omnibodied, omnisexed, and omnigendered. Instead of speaking about transcending distinctions, let us focus our attention on revisioning what the ideals of a tradition look like. What forms can virtue take? "The Story of Beautiful Woman" demonstrates that virtue may take forms that challenge normative conceptions of virtuous bodies. For instance, the paradigmatic virtuous bodied beings—Bodhisattva and Buddha—need not be male. Indeed, they materialize sexed bodies that defy our limited and limiting definitions of male and female. The challenge for Buddhists today is to materialize—that is, render culturally legible—diverse virtuous bodied beings heretofore abjected in Buddhist literature and/or communities:[79] to materialize, for instance, queer Buddha, differently abled Buddha, low-caste or Dalit Buddha, blue-collar Buddha, black Buddha,[80] Latino/a Buddha. The question is not whether such Buddhas exist; the question is whether and how such Buddhas (or Bodhisattvas) attain "symbolic legitimacy and intelligibility" (BTM, p. 3). In representing the Buddha as omnibodied, omnisexed, and omnigendered, "The Story of Beautiful Woman" provides an occasion for rethinking what virtue looks like—in Butler's terms, rethinking what kinds of bodies "matter." Although my reading of "The Story of Beautiful Woman" focuses on the issue of sex, conceiving of the Buddha as omnibodied suggests the possibility of a much broader reconceptualization of virtuous bodied beings.

Imagining Śākyamuni Buddha as omnibodied, omnisexed, and omnigendered means that we need to conceive of embodiment as fluid rather than static. Although my reading of "The Story of Beautiful Woman" challenges traditional interpretations of Buddhahood, my emphasis on the fluidity of embodiment is actually grounded within normative Buddhist doctrine. Buddhists believe that reality is inherently fluid. Nothing and no one remains the same from one moment to the next—whether in the course of one lifetime or over many lifetimes. A nun and contemporary of the Buddha put it best when she said, "I have been mother, son, father, brother, grandmother."[81] Comprehension and acceptance of the inherent fluidity or impermanence of reality is central to liberation. A vision of the Buddha as omnibodied, omnisexed, and omnigendered is soteriologically efficacious. Further, the synchronic perspective is not just a vision of the Buddha as omnibodied, omnisexed, and omnigendered but of all beings as such. At the end of the story the Buddha identifies the other characters in his past lives so that he reveals to his audience the inherent fluidity of all forms of embodiment. Just as the liberated nun, we have all been "mother, son, father, brother, grandmother."[81]

The Buddhist emphasis on the fluidity of embodied existence offers another vantage on the inherent incoherence of identity (BTM, p. 113). Butler argues that all identities—even lesbian, gay, or queer identities—depend upon the exclusion of disavowed identities (BTM, pp. 111–19, especially p. 115). While identities such as "women," "queer," "gay," and "lesbian" are necessary for political mobilization, Butler insists that all identities be subject to a critique that exposes the constitutive outside of any given identity (BTM, pp. 226–30). Butler calls into question the very notion of a fixed subject position and maintains that a "subject produces its coherence at the cost of its own complexity" (BTM, p. 115). The synchronic perspective is a vision of that complexity—a vision of oneself as a fluid, bodied being whose efforts to hold on to a particular identity or experience inevitably generate suffering. The synchronic perspective is one of radical incoherence, which suggests the possibility of multiple and constantly shifting materializations of virtue.

"The Story of Beautiful Woman" is a "complicated, conflicted, and ambiguous"[82] narrative that may be read in different ways for different purposes. I have read the story to denaturalize the link between virtue and male sex and, more broadly, to challenge normative representations of body ideals displayed in premodern South Asian Buddhist literature. In doing so I have intentionally read against the sexist discourse of the narrative because I believe this discourse is not consistently or persuasively maintained. I have found Butler good to think with because she illuminates a process of subject formation useful for an analysis of the formation of subjects central to Buddhist traditions, namely, Bodhisattva and Buddha. Formation of Bodhisattva and Buddha depends upon identification with an abject body image. From the perspective of an ascetic discourse, abjection is valorized as a soteriological tool to produce a virtuous/liberated bodied being. In spite of significant differences in Butler's analysis of the formation of normative heterosexual subjects and my analysis of the formation of Bodhisattva and Buddha, we agree that choosing abjection, that is, affirming rather than disavowing identification with an abject body image, can be liberative, politically and/or soteriologically. But "The Story of Beautiful Woman" also nuances the liberative potential of Butler's concept of abjection. The story underscores that choosing abjection is not just individually but also communally transformative. A Bodhisattva's performance of her/his abjection materializes *other* virtuous/liberated bodied beings. A Bodhisattva's affirmation of an abject body image has powerful consequences for others—so much so that the story defines such affirmation as the epitome of maternal care.

Butler uses the concept of abjection to illumine the inherent instabilities of heterosexist norms. I have demonstrated that the material effects of a Bodhisattva's identification with an abject body image similarly challenge normative representations of body ideals in premodern South Asian Buddhist literature. Bodily mutilations and sacrifices on the part of the Bodhisattva produce counterhegemonic virtuous bodied beings, specifically, non-normatively sexed bodies. Beautiful Woman materializes bodies of indeterminate and/or alterior sex. The virtuous body of the Buddha is far from male in this story. Rather, the image of Buddha-mother signifies the Buddha's radical and salvific alterity. I do not mean to suggest that every representation of the Buddha is of an alterior rather than a normatively male being. "The Story of Beautiful Woman," however, indicates that Buddhist traditions offer alternatives to traditional male representations of the Buddha.

The story's most significant contribution to revisioning what virtue looks like—i.e., what kinds of bodies "matter"—is that in the end it refuses to associate virtue with any particular body, be it a normatively or non-normatively sexed body. The Buddha is represented as omnibodied, omnisexed, and omnigendered. Embodiment is fluid and so are the materializations of virtue. In a Buddhist typology of generosity the greatest gift of all is the gift of the Buddhist teachings. At the end of the story the Buddha gives that gift in teaching that all reality is inherently fluid. The Buddha makes available to his/her/its audience a potentially liberative vision of all beings as omnibodied, omnisexed, and omnigendered.

Although reality is inherently fluid, most Buddhists cannot materialize a radically different body from one moment to the next any more than Butler's subjects can decide, on any given morning, which gender to perform (BTM, p. x). Buddhists recognize they have only limited agency because of the constraints of karma. "The Story of Beautiful Woman" reminds its audience that the bodied beings and communities present today are the effects of deeds, individual and collective, committed in the past. Similarly, the kinds of bodied beings and communities in the future will be the effects of deeds, individual and collective, committed today. "The Story of Beautiful Woman," with its emphasis on indeterminate, alterior, and fluid bodies, presumes the possibility of future individual and communal materializations of virtue we may not, at present, even be able to imagine. "The Story of Beautiful Woman" thus suggests that choosing abjection is liberative in both soteriological and political senses.

NOTES

For insightful comments on various drafts of this essay I thank Denise Kimber Buell, Karen Derris, Natalie Gummer, Charles Hallisey, Heather Masri, Kesaya Noda, and Suzanne Seger. I thank Ellen Armour and Elizabeth A. Castelli for their perceptive remarks on the oral version of this paper, which was presented at the annual meeting of the American Academy of Religion in 1997. I am indebted to Masatoshi Nagatomi for introducing me to "The Story of Beautiful Woman" in 1990.

1. Butler, *Bodies That Matter: On the Discursive Limits of "Sex"* (BTM), pp. 4–12, especially pp. 9–10.

2. I do not mean to imply that a close relationship between morality and bodies is foreign to Western cultures. See, for instance, Elaine Scarry, *On Beauty and Being Just* (Princeton University Press, 1999), p. 91. My point is that Butler has rightly identified sexual identity as a critical factor in determining which bodies matter in contemporary Western cultures. Therefore the normative ideals in her sources differ from those in my own.

3. There are other religious ideals in Buddhist traditions. For instance, the saint, or *arhat*, has also attained liberation, but his or her capacities do not equal that of a Buddha, especially with regard to his or her ability to teach and transform others. Other religious ideals include those of monk, nun, layman, and laywoman. Each of these ideal categories of Buddhist agents has distinct responsibilities and capacities.

4. Pheng Cheah, "Mattering," *Diacritics* 26, no. 1 (Spring 1996): 118; review of Judith Butler's *Bodies That Matter* and Elizabeth Grosz's *Volatile Bodies*.

5. Whether the materialization of normative heterosexual subjects in South Asian cultures is also the effect of an identification with and disavowal of an abject homosexuality is beyond the scope of this study. My paper examines representations of the Bodhisattva and Buddha in narrative literature.

6. The anthology is called the *Divyāvadāna*. Andy Rotman is currently preparing a translation of the *Divyāvadāna* and has written a dissertation on this anthology (Andy Rotman, "Monks, Merchants, and a Moral Economy: Visual Culture and the Practice of Faith in the *Divyāvadāna*" [Ph.D. diss., University of Chicago, 2003]). I thank him for his generosity in sharing with me his translation of the

anthology. The original composition of the anthology has been dated to the early centuries of the common era in North India (see Reiko Ohnuma, "*Dehadāna*: The 'Gift of the Body' in Indian Buddhist Narrative Literature" [Ph.D. diss., University of Michigan, 1997], p. 34; and John Strong, *The Legend of King Aśoka: A Study and Translation of the Aśokāvadāna* [Princeton: Princeton University Press, 1983], pp. 26–31). The manuscripts that form the basis of the critical edition of the *Divyāvadāna*, however, are considerably more recent, as is the case with most Sanskrit Buddhist literature. The original editors of the text, E. B. Cowell and R. A. Neil, based their critical edition of the *Divyāvadāna* on manuscripts which are modern copies of a single Nepalese Sanskrit manuscript, a manuscript dated to the 17th century by Cecil Bendall (*The Divyāvadāna: A Collection of Early Buddhist Legends*, eds. E. B. Cowell and R. A. Neil [Cambridge: The University Press, 1886]; pp. vi-vii).

Different versions of "The Story of Beautiful Woman" occur in other Sanskrit anthologies. Kṣemendra's eleventh century *Avadānakalpalatā* contains one such version entitled the *Rukmatī avadāna* (*Avadāna-Kalpalatā of Kṣemendra*, ed. P. L. Vaidya, vol. 2, Buddhist Sanskrit Texts no. 23 [Darbhanga, Bihar: Mithila Institute, 1959]). Haribhaṭṭa's, *Jātakamālā* contains another version entitled the *Rūpyāvatī jātaka* (Michael Hahn, *Haribhaṭṭa and Gopadatta: Two Authors in the Succession of Āryaśūra: On the Rediscovery of Parts of Their Jātakamālās*, 2d ed., Studia Philologica Buddhica Occasional Paper Series I [Tokyo: International Institute for Buddhist Studies, 1992]). This paper is based on "The Story of Beautiful Woman" (*Rūpāvatī avadāna*) in the Cowell and Neil edition of the *Divyāvadāna*.

7. Feminine imagery is valorized in tantric Buddhism, but the extent to which this imagery benefited female tantric practitioners is a matter of scholarly debate. For a range of views, see Janet Gyatso, *Apparitions of the Self: The Secret Autobiographies of a Tibetan Visionary* (Princeton: Princeton University Press, 1998), pp. 243–64; Anne C. Klein, "Primordial Purity and Everday Life: Exalted Female Symbols and the Women of Tibet," in *Immaculate and Powerful*, ed. C. W. Atkinson, C. H. Buchanan, and M. R. Miles (Boston: Beacon, 1985), pp. 111–38; and Miranda Shaw, *Passionate Enlightenment: Women in Tantric Buddhism* (Princeton: Princeton University Press, 1994).

8. William R. LaFleur, *Buddhism: A Cultural Perspective* (Englewood Cliffs, N.J.: Prentice Hall, 1988) pp. 11–12.

9. For the most recent discussion of narratives of bodily mutilation and sacrifice, see Ohnuma, "*Dehadāna*" and her "The Gift of the Body and the Gift of Dharma," *History of Religions* 37, no. 4 (May 1998): 323–59. Ohnuma gives an alternative reading of "The Story of Beautiful Woman" in "*Dehadāna*," pp. 226–74, and in "The Story of Rūpāvatī: A Female Past Birth of the Buddha," *Journal of the International Association of Buddhist Studies* 23, no. 1 (2000): 103–41.

10. For instance, one scholastic example of a practical or logical impossibility is a female Buddha (Paul J. Griffiths, *On Being Buddha: The Classical Doctrine of Buddhahood* [Albany: SUNY Press, 1994], p. 118).

11. Toshichi Endo discusses the significance of male sex to a Bodhisattva's progress

in his *Buddha in Theravāda Buddhism: A Study of the Concept of Buddha in the Pali Commentaries* (Nedimala, Dehiwala, Sri Lanka: Buddhist Cultural Centre, 1997), pp. 252–54, and pp. 260–64.

12. I thank Natalie Gummer for the felicitous expression *omnigendered.*

13. I thank Karen Derris for this insight.

14. *Divyāvadāna*, p. 472.12–13.

15. Maria Ruth Hibbets, "The Ethics of the Gift: A Study of Medieval South Asian Discourses on *Dāna,"* Ph.D. diss., Harvard University, 1999, pp. 91–92.

16. *Divyāvadāna*, p. 473.27–28.

17. Michael J. Sweet and Leonard Zwilling, "The First Medicalization: The Taxonomy and Etiology of Queerness in Classical Indian Medicine," *Journal of the History of Sexuality* 3, no. 4 (1993): 604.

18. For additional information on the sex *indriya*, see Y. Karunadasa, *Buddhist Analysis of Matter*, 2d ed. (Singapore: Buddhist Research Society, 1989), pp. 55–58; Diana Y. Paul, *Women in Buddhism: Images of the Feminine in the Mahāyāna Tradition*, 2d ed. (1979; Berkeley: University of California Press, 1985), pp. 166–216, especially pp. 171–72; and L. P. N. Perera, "Faculties of Sex and Related Phenomena in Buddhist Sexual Theory," in *Buddhist Philosophy and Culture: Essays in Honour of N. A. Jayawickrema* (Kelaniya, Sri Lanka: Vidyalankara, 1987), pp. 179–88. Buddhist scholastics debated the definition and function of the sex faculty. "The Story of Beautiful Woman" uses the term *indriya* without defining it.

19. With the exception of Beautiful Man, I follow Andy Rotman in the translation of the Bodhisattvas' names. I have also adopted his translation of the story's title.

20. Other features of a favorable rebirth include the nature of one's physical environment and community as well as access to Buddhist teachings.

21. Caste (*varṇa, jāti*) and family or clan (*kula*) are defined as biological and social categories. See McKim Marriott and Ronald B. Inden, "Caste Systems," *Encyclopedia Britannica*, 15th ed., 3:982–91; and Ronald B. Inden and Ralph W. Nicholas, *Kinship in Bengali Culture* (Chicago: University of Chicago Press, 1977).

22. Scholarly studies of the relationship between body and morality in Hindu traditions include Joseph S. Alter, *The Wrestler's Body: Identity and Ideology in North India* (Berkeley: University of California Press, 1992); E. Valentine Daniel, *Fluid Signs: Being a Person the Tamil Way* (Berkeley: University of California Press, 1984); Ronald B. Inden and Ralph W. Nicholas, *Kinship in Bengali Culture*; Sarah Lamb, *White Saris and Sweet Mangoes: Aging, Gender, and Body in North India* (Berkeley: University of California Press, 2000); McKim Marriott and Ronald B. Inden, "Toward an Ethnosociology of South Asian Caste Systems" in *The New Wind: Changing Identities in South Asia*, ed. K. David (The Hague: Mouton, 1977), pp. 227–38; and Ralph W. Nicholas, "The Effectiveness of the Hindu Sacrament (*Saṃskāra*): Caste, Marriage, and Divorce in Bengali Culture," in *From the Margins of Hindu Marriage: Essays of Gender, Religion, and Culture*, ed. Lindsey Harlan and Paul B. Courtright (New York: Oxford University Press, 1995), pp. 137–59.

23. Steven Kemper, "Wealth and Reformation in Sinhalese Buddhist Monasticism," in *Ethics, Wealth, and Salvation: A Study of Buddhist Social Ethics*, ed. Russell F.

Sizemore and Donald K. Swearer (Columbia: University of South Carolina Press, 1990), p. 167. For an instructive comparative example see a discussion of Greek physiognomy; Maud W. Gleason, *Making Men: Sophists and Self-Presentation in Ancient Rome* (Princeton: Princeton University Press, 1995).

24. Susanne Mrozik, "The Value of Human Differences: South Asian Buddhist Contributions Toward an Embodied Virtue Theory," *Journal of Buddhist Ethics* 9 (2002): 1–33; and Mrozik, "The Relationship Between Morality and the Body in Monastic Training According to the *Śikṣāsamuccaya,*" Ph.D. diss., Harvard University, 1998, especially pp. 36–62.

25. *Śikshāsamuccaya: A Compendium of Buddhistic Teaching Compiled by Śāntideva Chiefly from Earlier Mahāyāna-Sūtras,* ed. Cecil Bendall, Bibliotheca Buddhica 1 (1897–1902; Osnabrück: Biblio Verlag, 1970), p. 80.1–3, 7–8. *Śikṣā Samuccaya: A Compendium of Buddhist Doctrine Compiled by Śāntideva Chiefly from Earlier Mahāyāna Sūtras,* trans. Cecil Bendall and W. H. D. Rouse (1922; New Delhi: Motilal Banarsidass, 1971; rpt. 1990), p. 84. Since the English translation is unreliable, references will be given to both Sanskrit and English editions.

26. *Śikṣāsamuccaya,* Sanskrit ed., p. 69.5–7; English ed., pp. 73–74.

27. Janet Gyatso has written the most comprehensive study to date on *paṇḍakas* in Buddhist monastic and medical literature (Janet Gyatso, "One Plus One Makes Three: Buddhist Gender, Monasticism, and the Law of the Non-Excluded Middle," *History of Religions* 43, no. 2 (November 2003): 89–115.

28. Sweet and Zwilling, "The First Medicalization," p. 592.

29. Leonard Zwilling (speaking specifically about non-normative males), "Homosexuality as Seen in Indian Buddhist Texts," in *Buddhism, Sexuality, and Gender,* ed. José Ignacio Cabezón (Albany: SUNY Press, 1992), p. 205; Sweet and Zwilling, "The First Medicalization," p. 594. Sweet and Zwilling also add that non-normative sex may include "some deficiency of procreative interest or ability" (p. 594).

30. Bernard Faure, *The Red Thread: Buddhist Approaches to Sexuality* (Princeton: Princeton University Press, 1998), pp. 77, 277, 280.

31. Sweet and Zwilling, "The First Medicalization," pp. 603–4.

32. See Gyatso, "One Plus One Makes Three" and José Ignacio Cabezón, "Homosexuality and Buddhism," in *Homosexuality and World Religions,* ed. Arlene Swidler (Valley Forge, PA: Trinity, 1993), p. 86. For an instructive comparative example from the early Christian period see Bernadette J. Brooten *Between Women: Early Christian Responses to Female Homoeroticism* (Chicago: University of Chicago Press, 1996).

33. Sweet and Zwilling, "The First Medicalization," p. 598; see also Leonard Zwilling, "Homosexuality as Seen in Indian Buddhist Texts," in Cabezón, *Buddhism, Sexuality, and Gender,* p. 204.

34. Gyatso, "One Plus One Makes Three," p. 93. See also Bernard Faure, *The Red Thread: Buddhist Approaches to Sexuality* (Princeton: Princeton University Press, 1998), p. 73.

35. Leo M. Pruden, trans., *Abhidharmakośabhāṣyam* (1988–1990; Berkeley: Asian Humanities, 1991), vol. 2, p. 690. This is an English translation of Louis de La Vallée Poussin's French translation (La Vallée Poussin, trans., *L'Abhidharmakośa*

de Vasubandhu: Traduction et Annotations (Paris: Paul Geuthner, 1924). For the Sanskrit, see *Abhidharmakośa & Bhāṣya of Acharya Vasubandhu with Sphutārthā Commentary of Ācārya Yaśomitra,* part 2, vols. 3 and 4, ed. Swami Dwarikadas Shastri (Varanasi: Bauddha Bharati, 1971), p. 651 (4.43).

36. Pruden, *Abhidharmakośabhāṣyam,* vol. 2, p. 620. Shastri, ed., *Abhidharmakośa & Bhāṣya of Acharya Vasubandhu with Sphutārthā Commentary of Ācārya Yaśomitra,* part 2, vols. 3 and 4, p. 651 (4.43).

37. I say "virtuous/liberated" because while all liberated bodied beings are virtuous bodied beings, not all virtuous bodied beings have attained liberation.

38. There are a number of technical terms to express the notion of enduring essence. These are *sāra* (essence or worth), *ātman* (self or soul), or *svabhāva* (intrinsic nature)—the subjects of much scholastic discussion. For our purposes we need only note that Buddhists reject the belief in an eternal self or soul. The fact that there is no eternal self or soul naturally gives rise to the question of what transmigrates from birth to birth. Buddhist traditions have answered this question in different ways. One normative view is that personal identity consists of an unbroken continuity of experiences and their karmic consequences, which, in turn, give rise to new experiences, and so on from life to life. However, since living beings are changing, physically and mentally, from moment to moment, there is no essence that endures unchanged.

39. For instance, *Śikṣāsamuccaya,* Sanskrit ed., p. 229.1–3; English ed., p. 216.

40. For instance, *Śikṣāsamuccaya,* Sanskrit ed., pp. 80.14–82.13; English ed., pp. 85–86. Given the male perspective of much Buddhist literature, women's bodies in particular often were coded as abject (Liz Wilson, *Charming Cadavers: Horrific Figurations of the Feminine in Indian Buddhist Hagiographic Literature* [Chicago: University of Chicago Press, 1996]). The passage cited from the *Śikṣāsamuccaya* refers specifically to women's bodies.

41. Buddhists also acknowledge that some people may have a desire for self-annihilation (see Phra Payudh Payutto, *Buddhadhamma: Natural Laws and Values for Life,* trans. Grant A. Olson [Albany: SUNY Press, 1995], p. 122).

42. Payutto, *Buddhadhamma,* p. 61.

43. Not all Buddhist traditions insist that a liberated person must be celibate. While Hīnayāna traditions do, Mahāyāna traditions do not. However even in Mahāyāna traditions, monasticism is still a highly prized ideal—especially in premodern South Asia. Some tantric traditions believe that sexual practice is essential to the attainment of liberation (Miranda Shaw, *Passionate Enlightenment*). "The Story of Beautiful Woman" draws on Hīnayāna and Mahāyāna, but not tantric Buddhist traditions. Celibacy is valued in this text. For instance, the Bodhisattva Brahmalight rejects marriage in favor of practicing religious austerities. He is the third in the series of Bodhisattvas and has made the most progress towards Buddhahood.

44. Cabezón, "Homosexuality and Buddhism," p. 82. This produces some interesting inversions of normative sexual ideals. Since Buddhist literature defines normative sexual desire as heterosexual desire, sexual encounters between monastics and members of the opposite sex result in expulsion from the monastery, but sexual

encounters between members of the same sex or non-normatively sexed persons do not. With regard to monks, Leonard Zwilling argues that sexual offenses incur decreasing levels of punishment if committed with a woman, a *paṇḍaka*, or a socially normative man, respectively; Zwilling, "Homosexuality as Seen in Indian Buddhist Texts," p. 207. This suggests that the hegemony of heterosexual norms actually codes heterosexual behavior as the most transgressive form of sexual behavior in a monastic context.

45. Mathieu Boisvert, "Death as Meditation Subject in the Theravāda Tradition," *Buddhist Studies Review* 13, no. 1 (1996): 37–54.

46. For an overview of meditations on the body see Steven Collins, "The Body in Theravāda Buddhist Monasticism," in *Religion and the Body*, ed. Sarah Coakley (Cambridge: Cambridge University Press, 1997), pp. 185–204. For an incisive gender analysis of such meditations, see Wilson, *Charming Cadavers*, especially chapter 2.

47. On *saṃvega* see Wilson, *Charming Cadavers*, pp. 15–17.

48. Collins, "The Body in Theravāda Buddhist Monasticism," p. 194.

49. The practitioners of a set of ascetic practicies (*dhutaṅgas*), which include wearing rags and living out of doors, form an exception to this point. Although such severe forms of asceticism receive some praise in Buddhist traditions, more commonly these monks are regarded as little better than social derelicts; Steven Collins, "The Body in Theravāda Buddhist Monasticism," pp. 197–98.

50. For an overview of the thirty-two major and eighty minor characteristics, see Bellanwilla Wimalaratana, *Concept of Great Man (Mahāpurisa) in Buddhist Literature and Iconography* (Singapore: Buddhist Research Society, n.d.), especially chapter 4 and appendixes 1 and 2; Toshichi Endo, *Buddha in Theravāda Buddhism: A Study of the Concept of Buddha in the Pali Commentaries* (Nedimala, Dehiwala, Sri Lanka: Buddhist Cultural Centre, 1997), pp. 135–65; and Griffiths, *On Being Buddha*, pp. 97–101.

51. See Ohnuma, *"Dehadāna,"* p. 177; and Wilson, *Charming Cadavers*, p. 17.

52. The Sanskrit verbs used to describe the Bodhisattva's acts of bodily mutilation or sacrifice are *pari-tyaj* (*Divyāvadāna*, p. 473.15, 16, 17, 18, 20, 21, 23; p. 478.7, 12, 14, 24) and *ut-srj* (p. 476.9) These verbs mean both to give and to discard, abandon, renounce, and cast forth or away. Butler derives her concept of abjection from the Latin, *ab-jicere*, meaning "to cast off, away, or out" (BTM, p. 243, n. 2). Although *pari-tyaj* and *ut-srj* are by no means direct equivalents to Butler's concept of abjection, they share the sense of casting off or repudiating. There is one instance when the verb *dā* (p. 476.6) is used which does not convey the same sense of discarding or repudiating. This verb occurs right before an act of bodily sacrifice in the context of discussing a Bodhisattva's six perfections, one of which is generosity. The standard term for generosity is *dāna*, a derivative of the verb *dā*, accounting for this anomalous choice of verb.

It is unknown to what extent Buddhist practitioners engaged in bodily mutilation or sacrifice in South Asia (see Jean Filliozat, "Self-Immolation by Fire and the Indian Buddhist Tradition" [1963], and "The Giving up of Life by the Sage: The Suicides of the Criminal and the Hero in Indian Tradition" [1967], in

Religion Philosophy Yoga: A Selection of Articles by Jean Filliozat, trans. Maurice Shukla [New Delhi: Motilal Banarsidass, 1991], pp. 91–125, 135–59). Practices such as cutting off or burning fingers and committing religious suicide through self-immolation or other means occurred in East Asia. On such practices in China, see James A. Benn, "Where Text Meets Flesh: Burning the Body as an Apocryphal Practice in Chinese Buddhism," *History of Religions* 37, no. 4 (1998): 295–322; and Jacques Gernet, *Les aspects économiques du bouddhisme dans la société chinoise du Ve au Xe siècle* (Saigon: École Française d'Extrême-Orient, 1956); trans. Franciscus Verellen under the title *Buddhism in Chinese Society: An Economic History From the Fifth To the Tenth Centuries* (New York: Columbia University Press, 1995), pp. 231–47. A more recent example is the self-immolation of Vietnamese monastics beginning in 1963; see Chân Không (Cao Ngoc Phuong), *Learning True Love: How I Learned and Practiced Social Change in Vietnam* (Berkeley: Parallax, 1993), especially pp. 33–48, 96–108; and LaFleur, *Buddhism*, pp. 137–43. Examples closer to home can also be found, for instance, the self-immolation of a Vietnamese Buddhist immigrant in Connecticut in 1993; Irene Sege, "Suicide or Sacrifice?" *Boston Globe*, July 15, 1993. The propriety of bodily mutilation and sacrifice is and has been a controversial issue for Buddhists; see J. Takakusu, trans., *A Record of the Buddhist Religion as Practised in India and the Malay Archipelago (AD 671–695) by I-Tsing* (New Delhi: Munshiram Manoharlal, 1966 [1896]; 2d Indian ed. 1982), pp. 197–98; Sallie B. King, "They Who Burned Themselves for Peace: Quaker and Buddhist Self-Immolators During the Vietnam War," *Buddhist-Christian Studies* 20 (2000): 127–50; Ohnuma, *"Dehadāna,"* p.131; and Wilson, *Charming Cadavers*, pp. 41–43). There are a range of motives for Buddhist performances of bodily mutilation or sacrifice, including expressing devotion to a Buddha, earning merit for oneself or others, ritually affirming one's commitment to the Bodhisattva ideal of helping all living beings even at the expense of one's own safety, political protest, or, as in the case of Beautiful Woman, saving the life of another living being.

53.   *Ātman* literally means soul or self, but can also be translated as body: e.g., Patrick Olivelle, trans., *Upaniṣads* (Oxford: Oxford University Press, 1996; rpt. as Oxford World's Classics, 1998), xlix. The *Divyāvadāna* contains another story about bodily sacrifice that is closely related to "The Story of Beautiful Woman." In this story ("The Story of Moonlight") a Bodhisattva named Moonlight cuts off his head at the request of another human being. Right before making this sacrifice, he generates strength and power in his body. The word for body in this instance is *kāya* (p. 327.2), a word that is generally translated as body. Since the two passages are almost identical in language, I suggest that *ātman* is a synonym for *kāya* in the passage from "The Story of Beautiful Woman."

54.   *Divyāvadāna*, p. 472.6–8.

55.   See "The Story of Moonlight" (*Divyāvadāna* p. 327.2–3). Moonlight generates strength (*sthāma*) and power (*bala*), but not virility/vigor (*vīrya*) in his body.

56.   Gunapala Dharmasiri, *Fundamentals of Buddhist Ethics* (Singapore: Buddhist Research Society, 1986) p. 19, cf. 24; cited in Charles Hallisey, "Recent Work on Buddhist Ethics," *Religious Studies Review* 18:4 (October 1992): 283.

57. See I. B. Horner, *Women Under Primitive Buddhism* (1930; Delhi: Motilal Banarsidass, 1975; rpt. 1990), pp. 11–12; Paul, *Women in Buddhism*, p. 62; Paula Richman, "Gender and Persuasion: The Portrayal of Beauty, Anguish, and Nurturance in an Account of a Tamil Nun," in Cabezón, *Buddhism, Sexuality, and Gender*, p. 112. Horner and Paul both note that mother's love frequently is represented as superior to father's love (ibid.). On this point see also Robert P. Goldman, "Transsexualism, Gender, and Anxiety in Traditional India," *Journal of the American Oriental Society* 113, no. 3 (July-September 1993): 383.

58. See Dharmasiri, *Fundamentals of Buddhist Ethics*, p. 24. On the concept of "Buddha-mother" in Theravāda Buddhism, see R. Gombrich, "Feminine Elements in Sinhalese Buddhism," *Wiener Zeitschrift für die Kunde Südasiens* 16 (1972): 67–93; Jonathan S. Walters, "Gotamī's Story," in *Buddhism in Practice*, ed. Donald S. Lopez Jr. (Princeton: Princeton University Press, 1995), pp. 113–38; and Wilson, *Charming Cadavers*, pp. 29–32. For an example of the use of maternal imagery in meditations on compassion in Mahāyāna traditions, particularly in their Tibetan forms, see Alex Wayman, trans., *Ethics of Tibet: Bodhisattva Section of Tsong-Kha-Pa's Lam Rim Chen Mo* (Albany: SUNY Press, 1991), pp. 38–57; and Donald S. Lopez Jr., "Sanctification on the Bodhisattva Path," in *Sainthood: Its Manifestations in World Religions*, ed. Richard Kieckhefer and George D. Bond (Berkeley: University of California Press, 1988), pp. 189–90.

59. Cf. Paul, *Women in Buddhism*, p. 66.

60. Ohnuma, "*Dehadāna*," p. 233.

61. Further examples of maternal imagery in the *Divyāvadāna* occur at p. 96.7–13. Familial imagery, not specifically maternal, occurs at *Divyāvadāna*, p. 319.21, 27; p. 321.4–5; p. 322.20–21; p. 323.26.

62. See Ohnuma, "*Dehadāna*," p. 237.

63. Cf. Ohnuma, "*Dehadāna*," p. 234: " . . . Rūpāvatī [Beautiful Woman] constitutes the boy's 'true mother' . . . "

64. Elizabeth Grosz, *Sexual Subversions: Three French Feminists* (St. Leonards, Australia: Allen and Unwin, 1989), p. xiv.

65. On modernist conceptions of the Buddha, see Gananath Obeyesekere, "Taking the Myth Seriously: The Buddha and the Enlightenment," in *Bauddhavidyāsudhākarah: Studies in Honour of Heinz Bechert on the Occasion of His Sixty-fifth Birthday*, ed. Petra Kieffer-Pülz and Jens-Uwe Hartmann (Swisttal-Odendorf: Indica et Tibetica Verlag, 1997), pp. 473–82; and Obeyesekere, "Buddhism and Conscience: An Exploratory Essay," in *Daedalus* 120 (1991): 219–39.

66. I use the masculine pronoun because of the lack of a viable alternative for an alterior being.

67. On such medieval visions see Caroline Walker Bynum, *Holy Feast and Holy Fast: The Religious Significance of Food to Medieval Women* (Berkeley: University of California Press, 1987).

68. Buddhist tradition attributes the sheathed penis to a few other beings. The most important of these is the Cakravartin, or Universal Monarch. The Universal Monarch possesses the same thirty-two physical features as a Buddha, but does not possess a Buddha's eighty secondary features. Bellanwilla Wimalaratana suggests

that the sheathed penis signifies strength and kingship (*Concept of Great Man*, p. 97). The sheathed penis appears to produce different effects for different classes of beings. The sheathed penis guarantees the Universal Monarch many children. The sheathed penis signifies a Buddha's sexual restraint and guarantees the Buddha many disciples (Wimalaratana, *Concept of Great Man*, p. 190).

69. Beautiful Woman rescues a human boy who is reborn as Rāhula (the Buddha's son). Moonlight rescues a bird who is reborn as Kauṇḍinya (the Buddha's first disciple), and Brahmalight rescues a tigress mother and two cubs who are reborn again as Kauṇḍinya, Nanda (the Buddha's nephew), and Rāhula. Each are ordained as monks. I discuss the one exception who is not a monk, namely the starving human mother, below.

70. Cf. Bernard Faure, *The Red Thread*, and Wilson, *Charming Cadavers*, p. 30.

71. Nuns only appear at the opening and close of the narrative as members of the larger Buddhist cosmos, consisting of monks, nuns, laymen, laywomen, various classes of human beings, and a host of divine beings who make offerings to the Buddha and his community of 12,500 monks.

72. Gregory Schopen documents historical tensions and even occasions of violence between male and female monastic communities (Gregory Schopen, "The Suppression of Nuns and the Ritual Murder of Their Special Dead in Two Buddhist Monastic Texts," *Journal of Indian Philosophy* 24 [1996]: 563–92). One narrative in the *Divyāvadāna* suggests the presence of tensions between male and female orders. See story number 35 (Cūḍāpakṣa) in which a group of nuns express their conviction that their own knowledge of the Buddha's teachings surpasses that of the monk assigned to them for lessons (*Divyāvadāna*, p. 493ff.).

73. Karen Anne Derris, "Virtue and Relationships in a Theravādin Biography of the Bodhisatta: A Study of the *Sotaṭṭhakīmahānidāna*, Ph.D. diss., Harvard University, 2000, pp. 117–23.

74. Scholarship on narratives of female sex change and/or women's appropriations of such narratives include: Bernard Faure, *The Power of Denial: Buddhism, Purity, and Gender* (Princeton: Princeton University Press, 2003), especially chapters 3 and 4; Ding-hwa E. Hsieh, "Images of Women in Ch'an Buddhist Literature of the Sung Period" in *Buddhism in the Sung*, ed. Peter N. Gregory and Daniel A. Getz, Jr. (Honolulu: University of Hawai'i Press with the Kuroda Institute, 1999), pp. 148–87; Miriam L. Levering, "The Dragon Girl and the Abbess of Mo-Shan: Gender and Status in the Ch'an Buddhist Tradition," *Journal of the International Association of Buddhist Studies* 5, no. 1 (1982): 19–35; Ohnuma, "*Dehadāna*," pp. 244–53; Paul, *Women in Buddhism*, pp. 166–243; Lucinda Joy Peach, "Social Responsibility, Sex Change, and Salvation: Gender Justice in the *Lotus Sūtra*," *Philosophy East and West* 52, no. 1 (Jan. 2002): 50–74; Nancy Schuster, "Changing the Female Body: Wise Women and the Bodhisattva Career in Some *Mahāratnakūṭasūtras*," *Journal of the International Association of Buddhist Studies* 4, no. 1 (1981): 24–69; Hae-ju Sunim (Ho-Ryeon Jeon), "Can Women Achieve Enlightenment? A Critique of Sexual Transformation for Enlightenment," in *Buddhist Women Across Cultures: Realizations*, ed. Karma Lekshe Tsomo (Albany: SUNY Press, 1999), pp. 123–41.

75. For instance the "Devadatta" chapter of the *Lotus Sūtra; The Lotus Sutra*, trans. Burton Watson (New York: Columbia University Press, 1993), pp. 182–89, especially 187.

76. Alan Sponberg, "Attitudes Toward Women and the Feminine in Early Buddhism," in Cabezón, *Buddhism, Sexuality, and Gender*, pp. 3–36.

77. Further examples can be provided to prove my point that an "ultimate" perspective may be in the service of a "conventional" perspective. For instance, a medieval Indian compendium claims that comprehension of an "ultimate" perspective on reality will materialize a body adorned with the major and minor marks characteristic of a Buddha's body. Such comprehension also has the added benefit that one will never fall into the power of women again. The "ultimate" perspective in this case is the quiescence of all dharmas, or phenomena—another way of indicating the sameness of all reality (*Śikṣāsamuccaya*, Sanskrit ed., pp. 242.12–243.2; p. 243.11–12; English ed., p. 225).

 Even those Buddhist traditions which define Buddhahood as a nondual, non-conceptual awareness of the ultimate nature of the universe—in other words, as an experience that transcends all conceptualization including that of sex and gender—assume that experience of liberation is coincident with conceptual expressions of Buddhahood, i.e. the appearance of various types of Buddha bodies. See Malcolm David Eckel, *To See the Buddha: A Philosopher's Quest for the Meaning of Emptiness* (New York: Harper Collins, 1992), p. 75.

78. Bernard Faure, Rita M. Gross, and Sara McClintock have expressed similar concerns; Bernard Faure, *The Power of Denial: Buddhism, Purity, and Gender* (Princeton: Princeton University Press, 2003), pp. 119–42; Rita M. Gross, "The *Dharma* of Gender," *Contemporary Buddhism* 5, no. 1 (2004): 11; Sara McClintock, "Gendered Bodies of Illusion: Finding a Somatic Method in the Ontic Madness of Emptiness," in *Buddhist Theology: Critical Reflections by Contemporary Buddhist Scholars*, ed. Roger R. Jackson and John J. Makransky (London: RoutledgeCurzon, 2003), p. 261.

79. I am heartened to see other scholars beginning to think along similar lines. McClintock writes that Buddhists need to "take a greater interest in re-imagining the shape of our future buddhahood" so that "we may aspire to create a world in which diversity of embodiment is a cause for celebration and not a source of suffering and oppression; McClintock, "Gendered Bodies of Illusion," pp. 269–70.

80. Cf. bell hooks, "Waking Up to Racism," *Tricycle* (Fall 1994): 42–45.

81. Susan Murcott, *The First Buddhist Women: Translations and Commentaries on the Therigatha* (Berkeley: Parallax, 1991), pp. 18–19.

82. See Gerald Graff, "Determinacy/Indeterminacy," in *Critical Terms for Literary Study*, ed. Frank Lentricchia and Thomas McLaughlin, 2d ed. (Chicago: University of Chicago Press, 1995), p. 169.

2. THE GARDEN OF EDEN AND
THE HETEROSEXUAL CONTRACT

KEN STONE

[1]

In her lectures on Antigone, Judith Butler demonstrates the potential value of rereading ancient texts as part of the project of interrogating structures of kinship and gender.[1] For a reader such as myself—a self-identified "gay man" engaged professionally in biblical interpretation—such a project can hardly fail to stimulate one's own interpretive practice. For among the ancient myths implicated today in public debates over kinship and gender, surely none are more often cited than those found in the Bible.

When gay men, lesbians, and bisexuals do turn to the Bible, however, they all too often focus on a handful of passages that refer to, or can be interpreted as referring to, same-sex sexual contact. Because these passages are frequently used as proof texts to condemn homosexuality, careful attention to them is both easily understood and justifiable.[2] Yet such a focus also carries with it certain risks. For example, the continuing debate over texts that are thought to refer to homosexuality can deflect adequate attention from other texts that simply assume sexual relations between women and men are socially normative and divinely ordained.

Consider, in this context, the frequency with which one hears such statements as "God created Adam and Eve, not Adam and Steve." Although it is tempting to dismiss this sort of statement with scorn, the appeal to such an "argument" underscores the need for reflection on the ways in which biblical texts that do not refer to same-sex sexual activity at all are nevertheless characterized by what we might call, borrowing a phrase from Teresa de Lauretis, "heterosexual presumption."[3] I use this term, *heterosexual,* with some hesitation here since the term (like *homosexual*) often carries with it certain assumptions about identity that should not be imposed anachronistically upon the ancient world.[4] Nevertheless, rhetorical appeals to God's creation of "Adam and Eve, not Adam and Steve" do rest upon recognition that the book of Genesis presupposes throughout, and often seems to emphasize, the sexual relation between women and men, especially in terms of its reproductive potential.

In a series of provocative essays that have had some influence on Butler's work, Monique Wittig argues that this valorization of heterosexual relations and sexual reproduction is in fact already implicit in the binary sexual differentiation of humankind. According to Wittig, the division of the human species into male and female is a historical and social phenomenon accomplished through language rather than a self-evident biological fact, but it is often mistaken for the latter. "And although it has been accepted in recent years," Wittig adds, "that there is no such thing as nature, that everything is culture, there remains within that culture a core of nature which resists examination, a relationship excluded from the social in the analysis . . . which is the heterosexual relationship. I will call it the obligatory social relationship between 'man' and 'woman.'"[5] Wittig insists that "the categories 'man' and 'woman' . . . are political categories and not natural givens" (*Straight Mind,* p. 14). As her use of the adjective "political" indicates, such categories are, in Wittig's estimation, never innocent. Among other things, they lead us to grant social and ontological significance—to "mark" (pp. 11–12) bodies in terms of—to exactly those parts of the body that are most useful to sexual reproduction. Thus the binary categories of sex are defended with such vehemence precisely because they constitute the foundation upon which the heterosexualization of society and the imperative of sexual reproduction rest. In Wittig's words, "the category of sex is the political category that founds society as heterosexual" (ibid).

Wittig's discussion suggests that binary sexual differentiation works to the disadvantage of those whose lives do not conform to conventional expectations about sex, gender, and sexual practice—for example, lesbians, gay men, bisexuals, and transgendered persons. Indeed, careful reflection in particular on the experiences and bodies variously thrown together under such labels as "transgender," "intersex," "transsexual," and so forth reveals in a startling fashion the inadequacies of the rigid binary system of sexual categorizing that Wittig attacks.[6] But Wittig also argues that the category of "sex" is detrimental to all women inasmuch as it "conceals the political fact of the subjugation of one sex by the other" while grounding heterosexual relations in the order of nature itself (*Straight Mind,* p. 5). Building upon Jean-Jacques Rousseau's notion of the "social contract," Wittig goes on to refer to the system of assumptions and institutions that rests upon binary sexual division as "the heterosexual contract" (p. 32; cf. pp. 33–34).

In the wake of Wittig's argument the implicit appeal of such statements as "God created Adam and Eve, not Adam and Steve" becomes more apparent. Once the binary sexual division of humanity is attributed to God and located at the moment of the creation of humankind, endless arguments over the explicit biblical attitude toward homoeroticism can appear to be somewhat beside the point. The emphasis can now fall not so much upon the occasional biblical condemnation of same-sex sexual activity but rather upon the divine imperative to have sexual relations with the opposite sex. And since the binary sexual differentiation upon which this imperative rests does appear to be presupposed throughout much of the Bible, the fact that the Bible has so few explicit references to same-sex sexual contact becomes less problematic for religious proponents of the heterosexual contract. What is important is that the Bible does so often promote, naturalize, and sanctify a particular "obligatory social relationship between 'man' and 'woman.'"

In the remainder of this essay, I would like to consider certain aspects of this problem in relation to the two creation accounts that appear at the beginning of the book of Genesis. Although these two accounts, which were written at different times by different authors, are in many respects quite distinct from one another, the structure and contents of both accounts seem to make them especially attractive to readers who are looking to the Bible for rhetorical support for the heterosexual contract. After a brief discussion of the first biblical creation account (Gen. 1:1–2:4a) and its reception, a discussion that underscores the usefulness of the text for those who wish to stress binary sexual difference, I will turn to the second biblical creation account (Gen. 2:4b–3:24)—that is, the story of "Adam and Eve." Although this text, too, is often read as a foundation for compulsory heterosexuality, I wish to reflect upon the possibilities for a reading that, inspired in part by certain of Butler's arguments, focuses upon the instability and incoherence of this textual foundation. While such a rereading can never turn Genesis into a queer manifesto, it may reveal potential openings for queer contestation of the heterosexual contract or, in any case, of biblical justifications given for that contract. In the final section of the essay, then, I turn briefly to reflection on possible directions for and effects of such contestation, articulated specifically in relation to gay male readers of the Bible and in dialogue with Butler and Foucault.

[2]

The creation account in Genesis 1:1–2:4a (generally referred to as the "priestly" creation account) moves, as has often been noted, in an orderly and progressive fashion. From its beginning in a time of watery chaos to its conclusion on the day of God's rest, the narrative constructs a picture of the process whereby God creates the ordered structures of the cosmos. Although it incorporates mythological themes that appeared throughout the ancient Near East, the story was probably written to foster confidence in Israel's God in the wake of the Babylonian exile.[7] By representing Israel's God as the creator of an orderly cosmos, the priestly writers hoped to encourage trust in the power and might of that God at a time when such power and might seemed to have been called into question by the events of history.

At a crucial point in this story, God creates humankind. The priestly creation account notes at the first appearance of humanity its twofold sexual division: "So God created the human [ha-'adam] in his image, in the image of God he created it, male and female he created them" (Gen. 1:27).[8] The binary sexual differentiation of humankind seems, therefore, to be part of God's orderly cosmos from the beginning. While this initial statement says nothing about sexual relations, such relations are implied in the verse that follows. There we find God's first commandment to the new human beings: "Bear fruit, and increase in number, and fill the earth" (Gen. 1:28). The commandment is concerned with procreation and not with sexual ethics, but sexual intercourse between males and females is obviously presupposed.

Now historical and comparative evidence indicates that readers should proceed with caution when interpreting this commandment. Sexual relations with members of the opposite sex were not always understood to be exclusive of same-sex sexual contact in the ancient world, as studies of Greek and Roman attitudes and practices clearly demonstrate.[9] Thus, we cannot simply assume that an imperative to produce offspring—and, hence, to participate in opposite-sex sexual intercourse—would automatically be understood by ancient readers to imply a prohibition on all forms of same-sex sexual contact.

On the other hand, neither should we underestimate the effects of this representation of the creation of humanity or ignore the possible relations between that representation and a hostility toward homoeroticism. Because the linguistic structure of Genesis 1:27 does underscore a binary division of humankind ("male and female he created them") and moves immediately to an emphasis upon reproduction, the text easily lends itself to interpretations that valorize the relation between woman and man and make that relation key to the understanding of human ontology and vocation. Indeed, it is not difficult to find such interpretations. The theologian Karl Barth, for example, makes the following comments in his discussion of creation in the influential *Church Dogmatics*:

> Men [*sic*] are simply male and female. Whatever else they may be, it is only in this differentiation and relationship. This is the particular dignity ascribed to the sex relationship. . . . As the only real principle of differentiation and relationship, as the original form not only of man's confrontation of God but also of all intercourse between man and man, it is the true *humanum* and therefore the true creaturely image of God. Man can and will always be man before God and among his fellows only as he is man in relationship to woman and woman in relationship to man. . . . The fact that he was created man and woman will be the great paradigm of everything that is to take place between him and God, and also of everything that is to take place between him and his fellows. . . . In all His future utterances and actions God will acknowledge that He has created man male and female, and in this way in His own image and likeness.[10]

Notice the rhetorical drift of this passage. Barth seizes upon the fact that human binary sexual division is juxtaposed, in Genesis 1:27, with an affirmation that human beings are created in the image of God. Thus, within the course of a few sentences, Barth can imply a direct link between these two, arguably distinct, phenomena: sexual dimorphism and the image of God. The "image and likeness" of God in humankind seems in fact to consist, in Barth's discussion, at least in part in humanity's having been created male and female. And, as if to illustrate in advance Wittig's argument that an emphasis upon binary sexual difference underwrites the heterosexual contract, Barth returns to this theological interpretation of humanity in a later volume of the *Church Dogmatics*. Raising the specter of "the malady called homosexuality . . . the physical, psychological and social sickness, the phenomenon of perversion, decadence and decay," Barth calls his reader's attention once again to the fact that "humanity . . . is to be understood in its root as the togetherness of man and woman."[11]

I shall leave it for others to debate whether any of the theological points that Barth wished to make with such statements can be redeemed today for a nonheterosexist theological project.[12] In the present context I am more interested in noting how the structure of Genesis 1:27—with its juxtaposition of a reference to binary sexual division, on the one hand, and a reference to the "image of God" in humankind, on the other—encouraged such a reading. Indeed, this juxtaposition has led other sorts of readers, working on very different types of projects, to make remarkably similar arguments.

Consider, for example, a widely read feminist study by Phyllis Trible. Trible also suggests, on the basis of a close literary analysis, that "'male and female' correspond structurally to 'the image of God'" in Genesis 1:27.[13] Humankind,

Trible argues, "is the original unity that is at the same time the original differentiation." The differentiation to which Trible refers is, of course, binary
sexual differentiation: "From the beginning, the word 'humankind' is synonymous with the phrase 'male and female'" (*Rhetoric,* p. 18). And, by taking
her reader through a consideration of parallelism, tenor and metaphor, Trible
can conclude from Genesis 1:27 that "'male and female' is the finger pointing to the 'image of God'" (p. 20). The binary division of humankind into two
sexes, male and female, thus becomes for Trible as for Barth an indicator
of what it means to be created in "the image of God." Trible, of course, in
distinction from Barth, deploys this argument strategically toward the goal of
fostering religious communities structured by gender equality—a goal that I
share—and she nowhere includes negative statements about homosexuality
such as those we find in Barth. Yet it has to be recognized that her argument
veers perilously close to the rhetoric of "gender complementarity" so often
used in support of heterosexist positions. A recent religious diatribe against
homosexuality by the Presbyterian writer Robert Gagnon, for example, which
makes numerous appeals to sexual and gender "complementarity," relies
in part on an interpretation of Genesis 1:27 that is quite similar to the one
adopted by Trible.[14]

It may be worth pointing out here that the reading of Genesis 1:27 put forward by Trible and Barth, which tries to interpret the phrase "image of God"
in light of the reference to sexual difference, has not always been accepted
in biblical scholarship. On the contrary, a number of biblical scholars have
argued that the phrase *image of God* in Genesis 1:27 probably does not refer
at all to binary sexual division (which is apparently shared by humans with
the animals, which are also commanded to "be fruitful and multiply" [Gen.
1:22]).[15] The primary point I wish to make, however, is that whatever the
original authorial intentions behind Genesis 1:27 might have been, the structure and content of the text as it stands do seem to encourage interpretations
that grant a foundational status to binary sexual division as a crucial defining
feature of humankind. And, when we compare the interpretations of Barth,
Trible, and Gagnon with one another and with Wittig's argument, we become
aware of the extent to which Genesis 1:27 lends itself to readings that buttress the heterosexual contract.

[3]

Wittig's response to the problems presented by the heterosexual contract seems to involve some sort of movement beyond such categories as sex
and gender altogether. As she puts it, "the refusal to become (or to remain)
heterosexual always meant to refuse to become a man or a woman, consciously or not" (*Straight Mind,* p. 13). Since compulsory heterosexuality and

male domination establish themselves through the continued inscription, by way of language and ideology, of binary sexual difference, it is important in Wittig's opinion to refuse the categories "woman" and "man" through which the heterosexual contract is constructed.

Butler, however, though obviously indebted to Wittig's analysis, nevertheless carves out some distance between that analysis and her own. Butler agrees with Wittig that the naturalization of sex and gender categories needs to be exposed as a means of grounding the heterosexual contract, but in Butler's view it is not sufficient to reject the categories of sex and gender altogether in hopes of moving beyond them to some utopian space. If Wittig seems at times entranced by what Butler calls "the Marcusean dream of a sexuality without power," Butler positions herself closer to the Foucault of *The History of Sexuality,* volume 1, which, while also arguing against naturalized categories of "sex," nevertheless seeks not the transcendence of culture and power relations but rather the proliferation of possibilities within them.[16] Even when categories of sex and gender are deployed, in Butler's view they seldom succeed in reaffirming what Butler calls the "heterosexual matrix" of society in quite so total a fashion as Wittig sometimes seems to imply. Butler, therefore, emphasizes instead the instabilities and multiple effects of the norms and categories of sex and gender. These instabilities and multiple effects allow us to contest sex and gender in a fashion "that robs compulsory heterosexuality of its claims to naturalness and originality."[17] We contest the sex and gender norms associated with the heterosexual contract not by seeking to get outside of them or beyond them but rather by proliferating their possible forms. The "critical promise" of such proliferation for Butler seems to lie not in the essentially subversive nature of the forms themselves, but rather in the consequent "exposure of the failure of heterosexual regimes ever fully to legislate or contain their own ideals."[18]

It is partly as a way of thinking such contestation that Butler develops her influential "performative" theory of gender, which surely has potential consequences for religious debates over sex and sexuality.[19] But is it possible to transpose this philosophical discussion into the context of biblical interpretation? Could we suggest, for example, that if Wittig's work encourages us to look with suspicion at biblical texts that undergird the heterosexual contract, Butler's work encourages us to focus upon instabilities and ambiguities in those texts, instabilities and ambiguities that might represent weak spots in the supposed biblical foundations for the heterosexual contract and, hence, openings for queer contestation?

In order to explore this possibility, let us turn to the second biblical creation account. This story, generally considered older than the priestly account that precedes it and often referred to as the "Yahwist" account (in part because its writer, in distinction from the writer of the priestly account, uses the name *Yahweh* to refer to God), can also be seen as serving the interests of hegemonic heterosexuality. It is here, after all, and not in the priestly account, that we find Adam and Eve rather than Adam and Steve. The text is often read as a sort of explanation for the origins of opposite-sex "marriage," an attempt to explain and perhaps justify that institution by narrating the way in which it came into existence. For after recounting an operation on the original human being that results in two humans, one male and one female, the narrator is careful to note that "therefore a man leaves his father and his mother and clings to his woman [often translated here as "wife"], and they become one flesh" (Gen. 2:24). At a later point in the story, Yahweh God's response to the transgressions of the human pair in the Garden of Eden includes decrees that—particularly in the case of the woman—consolidate the reproductive imperative. From now on, Yahweh insists, the woman will desire her man (often translated here as "husband") in spite of the fact that the pain associated with childbirth has been increased. Thus, the story as a whole seems not only to insist upon binary sexual difference but also to underscore the inevitability of sexual reproduction (with particular consequences for the woman), to affirm the subordination of women to men (Gen. 3:16), and to highlight the importance of desire (at least in the case of the woman) for the opposite-sex partner. In all these respects the Yahwist creation account appears at first to serve as a paradigmatic example of Wittig's heterosexual contract.

Yet there are certain features of this text that make its support for the heterosexual contract somewhat problematic. It is interesting to note, for example, that the text finds it necessary to specify in 3:16b that the woman's "desire" or "longing" will be directed toward her man, and that this specification of heterosexual desire occurs in a list of those features of human existence that result from the pair's transgressions. What are we to make of this surprising and often ignored statement? A reader might very well conclude from it that heterosexual desire on the part of the woman is itself a consequence of—or even a punishment for—the woman's misdeeds rather than an original component of her created nature.[20] Perhaps it is true, as some scholars have suggested, that the writer of the story simply assumed that Adam and Eve had sexual relations with one another already, before this decree.[21] The text never states this, however, which is one of the reasons why Christian readers concluded in antiquity that Adam and Eve were "virgins" in the garden.[22] And it is striking that the text as worded seems to display a certain amount of insecurity about the woman's desire for the man, having to insist upon that desire as something that God ordains while also allowing a reader to reach the conclusion that such desire is a consequence of the woman's rebellion, a consequence that might not have been any more certain than other such consequences as, for example, the woman's increased pain in childbirth, the man's having to toil and labor as he works a recalcitrant earth, or the snake's having to crawl upon its belly. Moreover, this statement about the woman's desire is followed immediately by the infamous recognition that, from now on, her man will "rule" over her. The conjunction of these two statements almost makes it sound as if the text recognizes, with Wittig, that women might have good reasons for refusing to submit to the terms of the heterosexual contract, so that the text has to insist upon the installation of heterosexual desire in the woman as a guarantee of such submission.[23]

Moreover, the Yahwist creation account, in distinction from the priestly text that precedes it, makes no reference to sexual division at the initial creation of humankind. Rather, the text simply states that "Yahweh God formed ha-'adam [with definite article, literally, "the 'adam"] from the dust of the ground ['adamah] and breathed into its nostrils the breath of life" (Gen. 2:7). A single creature is produced here rather than a pair, a creature referred to as the 'adam. To be sure, Genesis 2:7 has often been read as a reference to the creation of a specifically male creature named Adam. It is therefore frequently said that God created man before woman; and this interpretation has sometimes been given, already as early as the time of the New Testament (e.g., in 1 Tim. 2:13), as a justification for the subordination of women to men. In recent years, however, the obviousness of this interpretation of Genesis 2:7 has been called into question, especially by feminist literary analyses of the Bible.[24] Such readings point out that the word 'adam functions within the Hebrew Bible not only as a proper name but also as a generic term for humanity. The word is in fact used in precisely this sense in the previous priestly creation account (Gen. 1:27). The sexually differentiated terms 'ish ("man") and 'ishah ("woman"), on the other hand, do not appear in the Yahwist story until Genesis 2:23, after the creation of the second creature. Is it legitimate, then, to read binary sexual difference into the text prior to this moment?

There are, in fact, some logical difficulties raised by any interpretation that would argue that the 'adam is male prior to the appearance of the woman. Just what exactly does it mean to have a single "male" creature prior to the creation of a female one? Is he "male" by virtue of his genitalia? If so, what functions might we imagine to have been served by these genitalia at a time when sexual reproduction or sexual contact with any other human creature was impossible? And if we close off this uncomfortable question (to which, however, I return below) by arguing (though without textual support) that specific biological and anatomical features associated with sexual reproduction were not yet present, then we have to ask ourselves whether there is any sense in which it remains meaningful to speak of the first creature as male.

Such feminist readers as Trible and Mieke Bal suggest, therefore, that it is preferable to think not of God's having created Eve out of Adam but rather of God's having created Adam *and* Eve by dividing a single androgy-nous being, the *'adam*, into two creatures, *'ish* ("man") and *'ishah* ("woman"). Since the word *'adam* is clearly used in Genesis 2 in the context of a wordplay with *'adamah*, "ground" or "earth," from which *'adam* is taken, Trible offers the translation "earth creature" for *'adam* and notes that this creature is not yet sexually differentiated.[25] This understanding coheres in certain respects with the interpretations of early Jewish readers who, by reading the Yahwist creation account in light of the reference to "male" and "female" that appears alongside a reference to *'adam* in the first account (Gen. 1:27), also concluded that the *'adam* was an androgynous creature, containing within itself *both* male and female.[26]

Now there are obviously some attractive features of this reading of *'adam* as an androgynous "earth creature" rather than a man. From a feminist point of view it gives the reader a biblical text with which to question religious attempts to ground male supremacy in the secondary creation of the first woman. In the context of the present article it also presents us with a coun-tertext to the priestly creation narrative, a countertext in which it is not self-evident that binary sexual division is assumed from the beginning of human existence.

On the other hand this interpretation, too, runs into problems that make it difficult to accept without qualification. For example, the term *'adam* con-tinues to be used with reference to the male character even after the cre-ation of the woman. This continuity between *'adam* and the man implies per-haps that *'adam* was understood to have been male already before that time. Indeed, the speech given by *'adam* in 2:23 seems to assume a continuity of identity between *'adam* and the "man" when it notes that "woman" was taken "from man" just after verse 21 has specified that God caused the *'adam* to fall asleep and then took "one from its ribs" in order to create the second human. Furthermore, the male who is punished in 3:17–19 is assigned agricultural tasks, just as *'adam* was assigned agricultural tasks by God in 2:15, prior to the creation of the second creature.

So in spite of the literary and linguistic features that lead some readers to argue that the first creature is androgynous or sexually undifferentiated, there are other features of the text that lead other readers—including other feminist readers—to reject this interpretation and argue that the text must presuppose that the first creature, *'adam*, is already a male creature.[27] Hence, as several perceptive commentators have noted, the Yahwist creation account as it now stands is riven with tensions and contradictions, problems of logic that can never be completely resolved but that the story attempts to paper over in an attempt to account for human existence as experienced and under-stood by the story's male authors. Such a conclusion underlies the argument of David Jobling, for example, who—reflecting upon the implications of his structuralist reading for feminist analyses—resists the conclusion that "'positive' features" of the story's female character result from a nonpatriarchal consciousness underlying the text:

> Rather, they are the effects of the patriarchal mind-set tying itself in knots trying to account for woman and femaleness in a way which both makes sense and supports patriarchal assumptions. Given that there must be two sexes, why cannot they be *really* one. . . . In the face of the irreducible twoness, the text strives for a false unity by making maleness the norm, and accounting for human experience by making "humanity as male" its protagonist; but it fails in this, for "humanity as male and female" inevitably reasserts itself as the true protagonist .[28]

Now I agree with Jobling that the text as it stands is characterized by tensions and contradictions related to sex and gender and that these tensions and contradictions result from the social ideology that generated the text. I would like to suggest, however, that the situation is even more complex than Jobling's analysis indicates and that what we find "tying itself in knots" in this text is not simply "the patriarchal mind-set" but also the version of the heterosexual contract upon which biblical patriarchy logically relies. Instead of suggesting that "humanity as male and female inevitably reasserts itself" here, I propose that it is precisely one goal of this text—as it is also one goal of the priestly creation account—to *buttress* the heterosexual contract by sketching the etiology of "humanity as male and female." In order to accomplish this goal, the Yahwist text—in distinction from the priestly account—attempts to speak about a moment prior to the establishment of binary sexual difference, but it does so from an ideological position (inhabited also by most of the subsequent readers of this text) that both presupposes and promotes compulsory heterosexuality and male domination. It is this difficult project, of trying to imagine a moment before the establishment of an institution—the heterosexual contract, which is nevertheless everywhere presupposed—that leads the Yahwist to formulate a text with interpretive problems that continue to vex readers to the present day.

Let us think further about the paradox that results. Given the fact that the Yahwist text was clearly written (as Jobling recognizes) in a thoroughly, if not uniformly, patriarchal society, it is certainly plausible to imagine that the text inscribes a wish to assert the temporal priority of male over female and perhaps also hint at the closer (because prior) relationship between the male creature and the male god who creates him. This wish, however, results in the potentially disconcerting scenario according to which the male creature is, by virtue of being male, presumably sexed but without an appropriate human partner, prior to the creation of the woman. God has created neither Adam and Eve, nor Adam and Steve, but simply Adam, who stands alone in the garden with no one but God. For whom, then, are this male creature's sexual components intended? Yahweh God is only subsequently represented as noticing the lack of a partner or "helper" and as searching for one, first of all by assuming naively that the animals will serve this role and only then by creating a second creature out of the first one.

However, God's search can be read as implying recognition that Yahweh alone is not a sufficient companion for Adam.[29] And in that light it may be productive to read this text in dialogue with the work of Howard Eilberg-Schwartz. For, in a provocative study indebted to Freud, Eilberg-Schwartz argues that the discourse of the Hebrew Bible is overdetermined at numerous points by an attempt to deny the implications of an unconscious homoerotic relation between Israel's male deity and that deity's male worshiper.[30] Is it possible, then, that the representation of Yahweh's search for an appropriate partner for Adam is the reflex of a felt need, on the part of the text's writer, to preclude the possibility of this sort of homoerotic relationship? After all, the fact that divine-human sexual relations were in principle imaginable in ancient Israel is clear enough from one of the other stories in Genesis associated with the Yahwist tradition, a story in which sexual relations between divine males and human females are both acknowledged and condemned (Gen. 6:1-4). While in that case there are no homoerotic connotations, we know that other ancient gods—Zeus, for example—are represented as pursuing not only female but also male objects of desire, such as Ganymede. And, partly in that light, at least some biblical texts have been construed by recent readers as representations of a homoerotic relationship between Israel's god, Yahweh, and certain of his male favorites such as David.[31]

It is fairly clear, I think, that the story of Yahweh and 'adam is in various ways different from those I just mentioned. But in the light of the existence of those stories, one might very well wonder whether *discomfort* with the potential for homoerotic relations between male Israelites and their male deity, which Eilberg-Schwartz emphasizes, in fact motivates the *ambiguity* of 'adam's gender assignment in the Yahwist creation account. If this account, while hinting that 'adam is "male," nevertheless refuses to specify as much until the moment of the creation of the "woman," is it not possible to imagine that this refusal functions partly to prevent unwanted interpretive speculations about Yahweh and 'adam? Yet such a refusal also ironically enables, perhaps against the author's intentions, the interpretation of 'adam as a sexually undifferentiated "earth creature," an interpretation that—however contested—opens a textual space from which feminist readers have challenged the patriarchal assumptions that have also shaped both the story and its reception.

In the light of Butler's work one might well suggest that an appropriate "queer" response to this text is not to resolve the tensions and contradictions that I have just highlighted but rather to emphasize them. For such tensions and contradictions underscore the fact that biblical contributions to the heterosexual contract, though clearly present and certainly visible in the Genesis creation accounts, are less secure or stable than many readers wish to admit. The exposure of this instability, in Genesis and elsewhere, will never in itself be a sufficient condition for the elimination of religious heterosexism, but it may prove to be a productive contribution to such elimination. For if we are able to contest what Butler calls "the regulatory fiction of heterosexual coherence" by showing that the rhetorical foundations of this fiction—including the supposed biblical foundations—are never quite so coherent as we have been led to believe, we may open up spaces for the production of alternative, queer subjects of religious or theological discourse and practice.[32]

[4]

But can we say more than this about such queer subjects, or the ways in which they are produced in part through interaction with biblical texts? To explore this question further we may have to think about the relation between ancient texts and contemporary readers in ways other than, or in addition to, that provided by Butler in her reading of Antigone. Butler's attempt, there, to bring the reading of an ancient text to bear on contemporary matters of sex, gender, and kinship takes the form, in part, of critical engagement with Lacanian rereadings of Freud. Although some of Butler's own readers are not entirely convinced that her ongoing dialogue with psychoanalysis is compatible with other elements of her critical toolbox,[33] it does have a certain logical relation to her reading of Antigone; for Antigone can be offered as something like an alternative, within Greek literary traditions, to Oedipus, whose significance for psychoanalytic notions of kinship and desire is obvious. Indeed because she is Oedipus's daughter and something of a mythical figure in Western thought in her own right, to reread Antigone is potentially to reroute the Oedipal narrative and the traditions that have grown up around it subsequently. But more seems necessary, given the role biblical narratives play in contemporary debates. It may therefore be helpful to find some additional way of imagining the relevance of reading biblical literature if one is going to argue with any specificity that such a reading of ancient texts can contribute to the creation of interpretive effects—and subject effects—that will challenge religiously grounded heteronormativity.

Butler may point us in the direction of one such alternative in her unexpectedly moving meditation on Foucault's notion of critique as virtue.[34] For in that essay she begins to engage Foucault's later work, which gives more and more attention to the "arts of existence," that is, those techniques by which individuals "seek to transform themselves, to change themselves in their singular being, and to make their life into an *oeuvre* that carries certain aesthetic values and meets certain stylistic critera."[35] We appear to have, in this emphasis, something of a new development in comparison with the Foucault of *Discipline and Punish* and *The History of Sexuality,* volume 1 that has been more important for most of Butler's work. Such a transformation in perspective is consistent, however, with the emphasis of the new perspective itself. For if Foucault begins in the later work to underscore the techniques by which certain ancient figures labored to create and recreate themselves through a range of practices that included (significantly for my purposes here) reading and writing,[36] so also he began to claim that his own writing resulted in part from his own ongoing attempts at self-stylization. The processes of reading certain texts and writing texts of his own were undertaken in part, as Foucault put it, "to prevent me from always being the same."[37] He also hoped that his readers, in turn, would be changed through the reading process, as he made clear when asked at one point about the historical research he carried out on psychiatric institutions and madness:

> But the problem isn't that of humoring the professional historians. Rather, I aim at having an experience myself—by passing through a determinate historical content—an experience of what we are today, of what is not only our past but also our present. And I invite others to share the experience. That is, an experience of our modernity that might permit us to emerge from it transformed. Which means that *at the conclusion of the book we can establish new relationships with what was at issue.*[38]

Here transformation is linked to reading, which appears to have as one of its aims the practice of forming new relationships with matters handled by or "at issue" in the texts one reads. Foucault is recommending for himself and for us an approach to reading that is very much like the approach he claims to have found among those ancient figures who worked at the cultivation of the self, not along the lines of modern individualism but rather as part of "a true social practice" that aimed, among other things, and always in specific contexts, at forming political subjects.[39] Since Foucault at one point also speculates on the possibility that these self-forming and transforming projects offer us a notion of "spirituality" with some potential usefulness in the present, it seems plausible to ask whether the reading of religious texts, in particular, could be helpfully rethought as a practice of the self.[40] Indeed, Foucault's essay on critique as virtue seems to suggest that the practice of "finding another function for the Scriptures" was one of the ways in which enlightenment thinkers in their time raised the question, "What, therefore, am I?"[41] And inasmuch as Foucault, when giving interviews in the gay press, also recommends this practice of stylizing and working on the self explicitly to his assumed gay male audience (as when he argues, for example, using a vocabulary of asceticism often associated with religion, that "it's up to us to advance into a homosexual ascesis that would make us work on ourselves and invent—I do not say discover—a manner of being that is still improbable"),[42] a gay audience in particular might find it useful to reconceptualize biblical interpretation, not in a neotraditional way but rather as one of those practices by which subjects create and transform themselves, especially in relation to matters of sex, gender, and kinship that are "at issue" in particular biblical texts.[43]

Let us imagine, then, one among many specific situations of reading. Let us say that a reader identifies himself, under current discursive conditions, as a "gay man"—and so as a reader for whom matters of sex, gender, and kinship are, within a world structured by heteronormativity and partly under the influence of biblical interpretation, very much "at issue." What kinds of reading effects, and subject effects, become possible when this reader encounters the tensions and contradictions that fracture the story of the Garden of Eden, tensions and contradictions that I have attempted to highlight here and that complicate the story's presumed contribution to the coherence of the heterosexual contract? How might this gay reader bring his labor on the text to bear on his ascetic labor on himself and on the "improbable" modes of individual and social existence that he is trying to bring about?

Among the possible directions, let me point toward two.

In the first place, such a reader might discover that interaction with this text does offer an opportunity for critical reflection on—and transformation of—the relationship between contemporary gay men and binary notions of sexual and gender difference. For the gay male reader may well catch a glimpse, in some of the tensions and contradictions that shape the story, of a subject position that refracts a certain complicated relation to gender with which he has some familiarity. After all, here in the story of the Garden of Eden we have a creature that is and is not recognizably "male." We find a creature that appears to be "male" at certain moments but not at others. And if this creature does eventually identify itself as a "man," at the moment of acknowledging explicitly the existence of "woman" (Gen. 2:23), it is nevertheless striking that it apparently has no need to speak in such a way as to relegate "woman" to some space of radical alterity such as we find valorized in much contemporary thought. What we find instead is that the character recognizes—and says out loud—that the "woman" who now stands over against him was also already within him, as bone of bone and flesh of flesh. If, in the second half of 2:23, the creature does give voice to the binary differentiation between "man" and "woman" that undergirds the heterosexual contract, it does so only while noting as well that here in front of him stands the other who is also, always, in some way himself.

Now there may be some danger, at just this point, of reintroducing notions of gender complementarity. Religious proponents of such complementarity sometimes argue, after all, that the apparent presence in the first human of both "man" and "woman" corresponds to a wholeness that can only ever be achieved again through heterosexual union.[44] However, Butler's work reminds us that heteronormativity generally rules out the "intelligibility" of individual bodies and experiences that are not easily categorized as either "male" or "female." What Butler at one point calls "the gender norm that establishes coherent personhood" is premised on the assumption that a single lived bodily experience is only "conceivable" as human so long as it conforms unambiguously—or can be made to conform—to one sex and one sex only.[45] Persons whose bodily experiences do not so conform may therefore find it useful to recognize that, in the story of the Garden of Eden, the first human creature is initially formed by Yahweh God instead as what Butler might call an "inconceivable" creature. Yahweh's initial created human may incorporate both "man" and "woman," but for exactly that reason it corresponds neatly to neither "male" nor "female" as defined by the binary norms of sex and gender. Such a character may thus come to serve as a useful rallying point, against the wishes of proponents of "gender complementarity," for readers who today also embody or wish to embody "inconceivable" gendered and/or sexed human lives—that is, lives that fall outside or at the limits of the social norms of sex and gender that shape our notions of intelligible human existence.

Now these readers will no doubt be potentially quite diverse and could include for example the intersexed, transsexuals, individuals labeled with the pathologizing term "gender identity disorder," and so forth. However, it is not difficult to imagine how the strangely gendered human character initially created by God might catch the attention also of gay male readers who, confronted with recurring cultural and religious imperatives to be (in the terms used by a gay male character created by the gay novelist Michael Cunningham) "ladylike" or "manly," frequently conclude instead that "I was something else altogether."[46] Such readers might discover in this story a text that enacts complications of gender often associated with gay men themselves. It will, of course, be tempting to avoid that discovery out of phobic reaction to the accusation of gay male "effeminacy," particularly since one can always point out (correctly) that individual gay men exist in many different—and complex—actual relations to a so-called "feminine" identification and habitus. The point, however, is not only that numerous gay men do, by their own testimony, experience lived complications of gender but also that, rather than avoiding engagement with this topic by claiming anxiously that it "merely" reflects a stereotype, it will be more productive to use gender to rethink the possible contributions of gay men to the transformation of religious communities and discourse. God does not first create Adam and Eve but rather a creature who is in some strange way neither "man" nor "woman," in any strict binary sense: a creature who is instead, to borrow Cunningham's phrase again, "something else altogether." Armed with the insight that the story of the Garden of Eden represents humans as having first been created by God in a form that does not cohere with binary gender distinctions, a gay reader might be encouraged to notice just how often the actual deployment of religious symbols and practices disrupts binary gender codes, even in what appear to be relatively orthodox religious texts and contexts.[47] Indeed, if one goal of reading is (as Foucault's account suggests) the creation or fostering of "improbable" modes of being in the present, it is even possible to imagine that the cultivation of forms of gender subversion could come to be understood as an indispensable component of gay male religious vocation, "authorized," as it were, by the gender instability that exists in the Garden of Eden.

Of perhaps greater potential significance, however, is the way in which tensions and contradictions in the Genesis text might lead a gay male reader to position himself differently in relation to another set of matters currently very much "at issue": specifically, matters of marriage. It is, after all, often assumed and asserted that the story of the Garden of Eden provides a religious foundation for the institution of heterosexual marriage. And, as we have seen, there is a sense in which the story does offer a narrative of origins for that institution.

This narrative is, however, hardly a stable one; and it is not difficult to imagine (to stick with our reading scenario) how gay men might find some of the textual instabilities useful for repositioning themselves relative to contemporary debates—though perhaps in unexpected ways. For if Yahweh does, in fact, wind up creating something like "marriage," he does not set out to do so initially. Marriage is not the vocation for which the human creature is initially created in this story. That vocation is clearly focused on tending Yahweh's garden (Gen. 2:15). This horticultural vocation allows us to understand the fact that Yahweh, having first decided that the human needs a "helper," initially creates not another human but rather the animals (Gen. 2:18–19), for some of these animals do, in fact, "help" the human in agricultural tasks.[48] But after the animals have been brought to the human it becomes apparent that a "helper like himself" has still not been found for him; only at this point does Yahweh, finally, create a "woman" (Gen. 2:22). Moreover, while the first human does acknowledge the existence of "woman," the still later reference to something like marriage (in 2:24) is not voiced by either of the human creatures as something to be desired. We find only an observation from the narrator indicating continuity between the sexual division of the two creatures and the fact that men do, in the *narrator's* own present (by which point the "fathers" and "mothers" mentioned by the narrator exist), leave their parents and "cling" to their women. Indeed, it is too infrequently noted that the first human nowhere actually asks for another human companion at all. The decision to create a second human out of the first one is in fact made by Yahweh, as part of a chain of events that could almost be described as clumsy, trial-and-error efforts on Yahweh's part to figure out what ought to be done

with his creation. To the extent that the human creature is initially created
in relationship, then, the relationship in question is much closer to a homoerotic than a heterosexual one. That is to say, an ambiguously male human
character and a(n ambiguously) male divine character are the only beings yet
in existence. And while the human's words in 2:22 indicate happiness about
human companionship, nothing like marriage or even sexual intercourse is
ever requested. As we have seen, it is only when their punishments are being
announced in chapter 3 that the humans are first told explicitly about opposite-sex desire, childbirth, and the dominion of man over woman. Even quite
orthodox Christian readers, we should remind ourselves, often understand
these announcements to contain the consequences of a "fall" rather than an
order ordained from creation; and although the language of "fall" comes from
later Christian doctrine rather than the text, certainly the divine speech in
chapter 3 describing the workings of the heterosexual reproductive household appear at a negative moment in the trajectory of the plot.

Might a reader not conclude, then, that the story of the Garden of Eden,
far from being an obviously celebratory account of an institution (heterosexual marriage) toward which everyone should aspire, can be read differently?
Does it not begin to look like a complicated tale of the human creatures'
gradual but forced submission to the constraints of the heterosexual contract? And if even religious readers of the text routinely understand today that
life legitimately takes the shape of attempts to get out from under the weight
of some of the punishments imposed on the humans—when, for example,
we routinely arrange for food to be produced in ways that do not involve
the sweat of the brow (Gen. 3:19) or for childbirth to take place in ways that
allow a mother's birth pangs to be less severe (Gen. 3:16)—why should opposite sex desire, announced at the very same moment, not be understood also
as a constraint that some of us might wish to undo or alleviate?

I am not saying, of course, that the implied answers to these questions
lead us to a single, clear "meaning" for this text but only that the text's instabilities allow it to be interpreted—or, perhaps I should say in the context
of a dialogue with Butler's work, "cited," "iterated"—in such a fashion. And
should gay male readers (to remain with my imagined reading situation)
come to understand the text in anything close to this manner, perhaps they
will find themselves establishing new relationships with the various matters—kinship, companionship, sexual desire and practice, reproduction and
childbirth, household organization, gender roles, and so forth—that are "at
issue," in the text and in the interpretive situations where the text is so often
referenced today. These new relationships might take the form of advocacy
for something like "gay marriage." But, then again, they might take very different forms. The continuity between biblical organizations of household and
family and modern notions of "marriage" that many readers of the Bible seem
to presuppose is actually not at all clear; but, to the extent that anything like

"marriage" is established in the story of Adam and Eve, that establishment takes place at a late moment in the chain of events constituting the story. As we have seen, it is associated more with punishment than with creation and paradise. It functions in the plot more as tragic consequence than as desirable goal. Perhaps gay readers of this story will therefore find in it reasons to be more cautious about the valorization of marriage and so more inclined to look carefully at the arguments of those thinkers—including Butler—who, while countering homophobic arguments made against gay unions, have also raised serious questions about the limits or even deleterious effects of a focus on "gay marriage." Perhaps such readers will then be encouraged instead to participate in—or to recognize ways in which they are already participating in—what Butler calls the performative "reiteration of sexuality beyond the dominant terms" of state-sanctioned marriage. Perhaps they will work to fashion and cultivate—or to become aware of ways in which they have already created and are already cultivating—multiple "forms of intimate alliance" that show marriage itself to be only "one practice among many that organize human sexual life."[49] If it turns out that engagement with biblical literature actually contributes to the recognition and fostering of such multiple practices, and not simply to the defensive war waged against them, the assumed normative correspondence between the Garden of Eden and the heterosexual contract may be in great "trouble" indeed.

NOTES

Portions of this essay appeared in an earlier form in Robert E. Goss and Mona West, eds., *Take Back the Word: A Queer Reading of the Bible* (Cleveland: Pilgrim, 2000), pp. 57–70. I wish to thank Pilgrim Press for permission to reuse that material and Ellen Armour for helpful conversations that contributed to the expansions found here.

1. Butler, *Antigone's Claim: Kinship Between Life and Death* (AC).
2. Helpful studies of such passages include Saul M. Olyan, "'And with a Male You Shall Not Lie the Lying Down of a Woman': On the Meaning and Significance of Leviticus 18:22 and 20:13," *Journal of the History of Sexuality* 5, no. 2 (1994): 179–206; Dale M. Martin, "Heterosexism and the Interpretation of Romans 1:18–32," *Biblical Interpretation* 3, no. 3 (1995): 332–55; Daniel Boyarin, "Are There Any Jews in 'The History of Sexuality'?" *Journal of the History of Sexuality* 5, no. 3 (1995): 333–55; Bernadette J. Brooten, *Love Between Women: Early Christian Responses to Female Homoeroticism* (Chicago: University of Chicago Press, 1996); Martti Nissinen, *Homoeroticism in the Biblical World: A Historical Perspective*, trans. Kirsi Stjerna (Minneapolis: Fortress, 1998). For my own comments on some of the issues, see Ken Stone, "Gender and Homosexuality in Judges 19:

Subject-Honor, Object-Shame?" *Journal for the Study of the Old Testament* 67 (1995): 87–107.

3. Teresa de Lauretis, "The Female Body and Heterosexual Presumption," *Semiotica* 67, nos. 3–4 (1987): 259–79.

4. Cf. Jonathan Ned Katz, *The Invention of Heterosexuality* (New York: Dutton, 1995); David M. Halperin, *One Hundred Years of Homosexuality and Other Essays on Greek Love* (New York: Routledge, 1990), especially pp. 15–40; Daniel Boyarin, *Unheroic Conduct: The Rise of Heterosexuality and the Invention of the Jewish Man* (Berkeley: University of California Press, 1997), esp. pp. 13–23.

5. Monique Wittig, *The Straight Mind and Other Essays* (Boston: Beacon, 1992), p. 27. Subsequent references to Wittig's volume in this section of my paper are included parenthetically in the body of the text.

6. Cf. Michel Foucault, *Herculine Barbin: Being the Recently Discovered Memoirs of a Nineteenth-Century French Hermaphrodite*, trans. Richard McDougall (New York: Pantheon, 1980); Pat Califia, *Sex Changes: The Politics of Transgenderism* (San Francisco: Cleis, 1997); Anne Fausto-Sterling, *Sexing the Body: Gender Politics and the Construction of Sexuality* (New York: Basic, 2000); Butler, *Undoing Gender* (UG).

7. Cf. Bernard E. Batto, *Slaying the Dragon: Mythmaking in the Biblical Tradition* (Louisville: Westminster/John Knox, 1992), esp. pp. 73–101; Jon D. Levenson, *Creation and the Persistence of Evil: The Jewish Drama of Divine Omnipotence* (San Francisco: Harper and Row, 1988); Robert B. Coote and David Robert Ord, *In The Beginning: Creation and the Priestly History* (Minneapolis: Fortress, 1991).

8. Except where noted, translations are my own. The reader will no doubt notice the use of masculine pronouns for the deity in my translation of this verse and elsewhere in the essay. Such usage does not reflect a resistance to "inclusive language" for purposes of religious ritual or theological construction but rather recognizes the analytical importance of uncovering androcentric assumptions when they appear in the language of the text. For a helpful discussion of the issues, see Phyllis A. Bird, "Translating Sexist Language as a Theological and Cultural Problem," in her *Missing Persons and Mistaken Identities: Women and Gender in Ancient Israel* (Minneapolis: Fortress, 1997), pp. 239–47.

9. See, e.g., Kenneth Dover, *Greek Homosexuality*, 2d ed. (Cambridge: Harvard University Press, 1989); Halperin, *One Hundred Years of Homosexuality*; John J. Winkler, *The Constraints of Desire: The Anthropology of Sex and Gender in Ancient Greece* (New York: Routledge, 1990); Michel Foucault, *The Use of Pleasure*, trans. Robert Hurley (New York: Random House, 1985); Craig A. Williams, *Roman Homosexuality: Ideologies of Masculinity in Classical Antiquity* (New York: Oxford University Press, 1999).

10. Karl Barth, *Church Dogmatics III/1, The Doctrine of Creation*, ed. G. W. Bromiley and T. E. Torrance, trans. J. W. Edwards, O. Bussey, and Harold Knight (Edinburgh: Clark, 1958), pp. 186–87.

11. Karl Barth, *Church Dogmatics III/4, The Doctrine of Creation*, ed. G. W. Bromiley and T. E. Torrance, trans. A. T. Mackey, T. H. L. Parker, H. Knight, H. A. Kennedy, and J. Marks (Edinburgh: Clark, 1961), p. 166.

12.   Cf. Graham Ward, "The Erotics of Redemption—After Karl Barth," *Theology and Sexuality* 8 (1998): 52–72; Eugene F. Rogers Jr., *Sexuality and the Christian Body: Their Way Into the Triune God* (Oxford: Blackwell, 1999), pp. 180–91 passim; Geoffrey Rees, "'In the Sight of God': Gender Complementarity and the Male Homosocial Signification of Male-Female Marriage," *Theology and Sexuality* 9, no. 1 (2002): 19–47.

13.   Phyllis Trible, *God and the Rhetoric of Sexuality* (Philadelphia: Fortress, 1978), p. 17. Subsequent references to this volume are included in the body of the text.

14.   Robert A. J. Gagnon, *The Bible and Homosexual Practice: Texts and Hermeneutics* (Nashville: Abingdon, 2001), p. 58 passim.

15.   See, e.g., Phyllis Bird, "'Male and Female He Created Them': Genesis 1:27b in the Context of the Priestly Creation Account," in her *Missing Persons and Mistaken Identities*, pp. 123–54; James Barr, *Biblical Faith and Natural Theology* (Oxford: Clarendon, 1993), pp. 159–73; Levenson, *Creation and the Persistence of Evil*, pp. 111–17.

16.   Judith Butler, "Variations on Sex and Gender: Beauvoir, Wittig, and Foucault," in Seyla Benhabib and Drucilla Cornell, eds., *Feminism as Critique: On the Politics of Gender* (Minneapolis: University of Minnesota Press, 1987), p. 137 passim. Cf. Michel Foucault, *The History of Sexuality,* vol. 1: *An Introduction*, trans. Robert Hurley (New York: Random House, 1978).

17.   Butler, *Gender Trouble: Feminism and the Subversion of Identity* (GT), p. 124.

18.   Butler, *Bodies That Matter: On the Discursive Limits of "Sex"* (BTM), p. 237.

19.   Cf. Mary McClintock Fulkerson, "Gender—Being It or Doing It? The Church, Homosexuality, and the Politics of Identity," in Gary David Comstock and Susan E. Henking, eds., *Que(e)rying Religion: A Critical Anthology* (New York: Continuum, 1997), pp. 188–201.

20.   See, e.g., Brooten, *Love Between Women*, p. 275; cf. Rebecca Alpert, *Like Bread on the Seder Plate: Jewish Lesbians and the Transformation of Tradition* (New York: Columbia University Press, 1997), p. 25.

21.   James Barr, *The Garden of Eden and the Hope of Immortality* (Minneapolis: Fortress, 1992), pp. 66–69.

22.   See chapter 1 of my *Practicing Safer Texts: Food, Sex and Bible in Queer Perspective* (London: Clark, 2005) and the various sources cited there.

23.   Thus even Carol Meyers, an archaeologically inclined biblical scholar who tries to read the text in such a way as to avoid the implication that the woman's desire is a product of God's oracle of punishment, notes that the text acknowledges the potential negative consequences of sexual reproduction for women living in the harsh environment of ancient Israel and therefore tries to explain women's participation in activities they might, because of those consequences, otherwise wish to avoid. See Meyers, *Discovering Eve: Ancient Israelite Women in Context* (New York: Oxford University Press, 1988), pp. 110–13.

24.   See, e.g., the otherwise quite different feminist interpretations of Trible, *God and the Rhetoric of Sexuality*, pp. 72–143; and Mieke Bal, *Lethal Love: Feminist Literary Readings of Biblical Love Stories* (Bloomington: Indiana University Press, 1987), pp. 104–30.

25. Trible, *God and the Rhetoric of Sexuality*, p. 80; cf. Bal, *Lethal Love*, pp. 113–14.

26. See Daniel Boyarin, *Carnal Israel: Reading Sex in Talmudic Culture* (Berkeley: University of California Press, 1993), esp. pp. 35–46.

27. See, e.g., Susan S. Lanser, "(Feminist) Criticism in the Garden: Inferring Genesis 2–3," *Semeia* 41 (1988): 67–84; Beverly J. Stratton, *Out of Eden: Reading, Rhetoric, and Ideology in Genesis 2–3* (Sheffield: Sheffield Academic, 1995), esp. pp. 102–4.

28. David Jobling, *The Sense of Biblical Narrative: Structural Analyses in the Hebrew Bible II* (Sheffield: Sheffield Academic, 1987), p. 43. For similar conclusions about the text's tensions and contradictions see Danna Nolan Fewell and David M. Gunn, *Gender, Power, and Promise: The Subject of the Bible's First Story* (Nashville: Abingdon, 1993), pp. 22–38; Pamela Milne, "The Patriarchal Stamp of Scripture: The Implications of Structural Analysis for Feminist Hermeneutics," reprinted with a new afterword in Athalya Brenner, ed., *A Feminist Companion to Genesis* (Sheffield: Sheffield Academic, 1993). The original version of Milne's article appeared in *Journal of Feminist Studies in Religion* 5, no. 1 (1989): 17–34.

29. See Fewell and Gunn, *Gender, Power, and Promise*, p. 27.

30. Howard Eilberg-Schwartz, *God's Phallus: And Other Problems for Men and Monotheism* (Boston: Beacon, 1994).

31. See Theodore W. Jennings Jr., "YHWH as Erastes," in Ken Stone, ed., *Queer Commentary and the Hebrew Bible* (Sheffield/Cleveland: Sheffield Academic/Pilgrim, 2001).

32. Butler, GT, p. 136.

33. See, e.g., William B. Turner, *A Genealogy of Queer Theory* (Philadelphia: Temple University Press, 2000), pp. 113–23; cf. John Hood-Williams and Wendy Cealey Harrison, "Trouble With Gender," *Sociological Review* 46, no. 1 (1998): 73–94, especially p. 90.

34. See Judith Butler, "What Is Critique? An Essay on Foucault's Virtue," in David Ingram, ed., *The Political* (Oxford: Blackwell, 2002), pp. 212–18.

35. Michel Foucault, *The History of Sexuality*, vol. 2: *The Use of Pleasure*, trans. Robert Hurley (New York: Random House, 1985), pp. 10–11.

36. See, e.g., Michel Foucault, *Ethics, Subjectivity, and Truth: The Essential Works of Foucault 1954–1984*, ed. Paul Rabinow (New York: Free, 1997), 1:207–22, 232–33, 272–77; Foucault, *The History of Sexuality*, vol. 3: *The Care of the Self*, trans. Robert Hurley (New York: Random House, 1986), pp. 50–51.

37. Michel Foucault, "How An 'Experience Book' Is Born," in Foucault, *Remarks on Marx: Conversations with Duccio Trombadori*, trans. R. James Goldstein and James Cascaito (New York: Semiotexte, 1991), p. 32; cf. Foucault, *Ethics*, pp. 130–31.

38. Foucault, "How An 'Experience Book' Is Born," pp. 33–34, emphasis mine.

39. Foucault, *The Care of the Self*, p. 51; cf. pp. 52–54, 71–95 passim.

40. Foucault, *Ethics*, pp. 294–95.

41. Michel Foucault, *The Politics of Truth*, ed. Sylvère Lotringer and Lysa Hochroth (New York: Semiotexte, 1997), pp. 29–31, 46.

42. Foucault, *Ethics*, p. 137.

43. See, further, Ken Stone, "Biblical Interpretation as a Technology of the Self: Gay Men and the Ethics of Reading," in Danna Nolan Fewell and Gary A. Phillips, eds., *Bible and Ethics of Reading*, *Semeia* 77 (Atlanta: Scholars, 1997).

44. See, e.g., Gagnon, *The Bible and Homosexual Practice*, pp. 60–61.

45. Butler, "Doing Justice to Someone: Sex Reassignment and Allegories of Transsexuality," in UG, p. 67 passim.

46. Michael Cunningham, *A Home at the End of the World* (New York: Picador, 1990), p. 10.

47. For examples specifically from Christianity see, e.g., Stephen D. Moore, *God's Beauty Parlor: And Other Queer Spaces in and Around the Bible* (Stanford: Stanford University Press, 2001); Mark D. Jordan, *The Silence of Sodom: Homosexuality in Modern Catholicism* (Chicago: University of Chicago Press, 2000).

48. Theodore Hiebert, *The Yahwist's Landscape: Nature and Religion in Early Israel* (New York: Oxford University Press, 1996), p. 61; cf. pp. 32–38, 59–61 passim.

49. Judith Butler, "Competing Universalities," in Butler, Laclau, and Žižek, *Contingency, Hegemony, Universality: Contemporary Dialogues on the Left* (CHU), p. 177. See also Butler's important essay "Is Kinship Always Already Heterosexual," in UG.

3. THE ANNOYING WOMAN: Biblical Scholarship After Judith Butler

TERESA J. HORNSBY

J UDITH BUTLER RULES. Her assertions about gender, complex and clear, are born out in daily (as well as nightly) observations of human relationships. Just as Copernicus's interpretations of stellar relationships prompted dread, fear, and imagination, so Butler's insights into the gendered nature of power. Her readers are awed by her intellect yet dread her exposure of a big and ugly truth: regardless of (and because of) subversion, an androcentric dominant culture, or patriarchy, is sustained, reified, and empowered. Butler tells us that protests, queerness, or anything deemed "countercultural" may do nothing toward weakening a dominant culture but, just like the B-movie monster who consumes the power from weapons bent on its destruction, the blob that we call patriarchy gains definition and strength as it moves toward the village and swallows everyone and everything in its path. In such schema feminism is not only an impotent assault on the villain but also a source of its power. No wonder the villagers are up in arms! From Butler's claim that every reference to a pure body is a further formation of that body,[1] combined with her observation that one is "implicated in that which one opposes,"[2] emerges a realization that has launched a major offensive against her by some feminists.[3]

As I have charted the evolution of biblical interpretations, particularly of feminist scholarship on Luke 7:36–50,[4] an anointing of Jesus's feet by an unnamed woman, I am convinced that Butler's observations of feminism and its unintentional complicity in women's own oppressions are accurate. In that work I demonstrate that feminist biblical scholarship participates in the definition and perpetuation of ideologies that sustain gendered, hierarchical systems. More, gendered, categorical, and hierarchical systems create and define feminisms as well.

To turn a feminist lens toward the Bible was an endeavor mandated by centuries of its misuse. The Bible has long been used against women and a whole host of "others" as an authoritative bedrock beneath the idea that men should rule over women, that white should rule over nonwhite, that some are masters, some are slaves. In my thinking, within the foundational texts of Western culture are all the issues that have spawned the necessity of feminism—women as chattel, the control of reproduction, women's poverty, violence against women, for example. While it is impossible to extricate these texts from our culture, it is possible and necessary to deconstruct each text and expose its foundation as flimsy, just as Butler has done with many of these classic Western works. To do feminist biblical criticism is not only to recognize the damage that biblical interpretations have done in this culture; it is an attempt to undo some of that damage. Yet Butler has troubled those waters as well.

In *Bodies That Matter* Butler asks a question that, for me, was like that bit of gravel that a huge dump truck shot against my car windshield a few years ago. It formed a tiny, almost invisible crack—but a year later the whole window shattered and had to be replaced. Here is the question: "How will we know the difference between the power we promote and the power we oppose?"[5] In other words, in my own works as a feminist biblical scholar is it possible to distinguish what I produce *with the intention* of alleviating gender constructions that oppress from works that contribute to and reinforce oppressive constructions of gender? The feminist scholars whom I identify below as perpetuating divisive and hierarchical understandings of "women" in the Christian scriptures, such as Luise Schottroff, Elizabeth Schüssler Fiorenza, and Kathleen Corley, initially understood their own work to be liberating; they worked in earnest toward "correcting" biblical exegeses that justified power structures subordinating women. And the works—such as the writings of Ben Witherington III, Leonard Swidler, H. Howard Marshall, Joachim Jeremias—those feminists sought to dismantle perceived themselves to be liberating in their own right. Yikes. The frightening thought then settled in my mind: no doubt, as I write to dismantle, to deconstruct, to liberate, I also write to edify, to construct, and to oppress. Next year someone will be writing an article naming all the ways that this present project reinforces dominant destructive ideologies. Thank you, Judith Butler. Yet I say "thank you, Judith Butler" with sincerity and with sarcasm. I sincerely thank her because she has defrocked the perception that "I" as feminist biblical scholar stand in a place that is objective and unwavering in its knowing of what is "right" and "good" for "women." I say an almost bitter thank you because, now that I know I cannot escape the complicity with which I have charged my predecessors and colleagues, do I continue to make the critiques, throwing rock after rock from within my glass house? The fact that I am inevitably forging the weapons of my own demise inspires me to consider whether or not silence is indeed golden.

Once it becomes clear that feminist biblical studies is a performative genre, one that not only reiterates a gendered subjectivity but also punishes "those who fail to do their gender right,"[6] then the feminist biblical scholar must ask the enormous question, is it possible to do biblical interpretation without doing further harm to women or to those who become "decentered" as a result of biblical exegeses? One should be prepared to hear "no" as an answer to this question. More, if it is impossible to talk about biblical formations and understandings of gender without a further formation of gender and its subsequent subsumption into a dominant ideology, should feminists do biblical scholarship at all? In other words, if one understands that she or he is contributing to the oppression of women, for example, in the very act of biblical scholarship, wouldn't biblical exegesis then become a specifically "unfeminist" enterprise? This short article will address Butler's "genre troubling" of feminist biblical studies. I show that it is a "performative genre" in that feminist biblical studies reproduces gender roles as "norms which precede, constrain, and exceed the performer." More, feminist biblical scholarship produces and perpetuates categories of gender that it claims to be opposing. Yet I usher in through a Butlerian reading of Luke's Anointing a hope—even an ethical obligation—to do *helpful* feminist biblical interpretation. Because of the position of authority that the Bible has held and continues to hold in formative public debate it is a moral imperative to do no less.

Since Butler implies that feminism is not the warrior against oppression that it claims to be, she has had to explain and defend her feminist identity as well as answer charges that her theories suggest hopelessness against hierarchy. She has been compelled to think, write, and speak about the relationship of feminism to political activism. Though Butler's implications are clear—i.e., just the process of doing feminist critiques, particularly those that concern women's bodies, contributes to *harmful* social constructions of those bodies—she claims that feminism can be rescued. The problems with "traditional" feminism are complex. One problem, according to Butler, is that classic foundations of feminist theory are anchored in dialectical and hierarchical dualism. De Beauvoir, for example, preserves a dualistic distinction between mind/body. In "Subjects of Sex/Gender/Desire," Butler writes that

> the preservation of that very distinction can be read as symptomatic of the very phallogocentrism that begins with Plato and continues through Descartes, Husserl, and Sartre, the ontological distinction between soul (consciousness, mind) and body and hierarchy. . . . As a result, any uncritical reproduction of the mind/body distinction ought to be rethought for the implicit gender hierarchy that the distinction has conventionally produced, maintained, and rationalized.[7]

Another infestation within feminism's roots is a preimposed limit on the category of "woman." A definition is, as Butler observes, limiting. Something is defined, sharpened, honed in on by saying what it is not; thus, a category "woman" forces exclusion upon those who do not conform to a preconceived notion of what "woman" is. Butler writes:

> The domains of political and linguistic "representation" set out in advance the criterion by which subjects themselves are formed, with the result that representation is extended only to what can be acknowledged as a subject. . . . Juridical formation of language and politics that represents women as "the subject" of feminism is itself a discursive formation and effect of a given version of representational politics. The feminist subject turns out to be discursively constituted by the very political system that is supposed to facilitate its emancipation.
>
> ("Subjects," p. 274)

Butler's criticisms of feminism are not defeatist—she proposes options, thoughts, suggestions. One is simply this: do not expect unity within feminism. A predetermined goal of a unification of disparate voices will always silence some and render others invisible:

> Without the compulsory expectation that feminist actions must be instituted from some stable, unified, and agreed-upon identity, those actions might well get a quicker start and seem more congenial to a number of "women" for whom the meaning of the category is permanently moot. . . . When agreed-upon identities or agreed-upon dialogic structures, through which already established identities are communicated, no longer constitute the theme or subject of politics, then identities can come into being and dissolve depending on the concrete practices that constitute them.
>
> ("Subjects," p. 288)

Butler, in recent works, refines feminist theory in the dimensions she describes above. For example, in *Antigone's Claim*, a work in which she deconstructs classic interpretations of Sophocles' character, Butler suggests that in spite of, or because of, each interpretation of Antigone, there are readings that offer subversion rather than reiteration.[8] The reading strategies Butler offers in *Antigone's Claim* hold much promise for reading the Bible— particularly for reading the text of Luke 7:36–50. Each woman, fictional, is perceived as out of place, is assumed to be in resistance of social (and legal) mores. Each has been endlessly appropriated throughout history; both are tragically associated with death and transgression (sin).

Feminist Biblical Scholarship as a Performative Genre

"Performativity," according to Butler, "describes this relation of being implicated in that which one opposes, this turning of power against itself to produce alternative modalities of power, to establish a kind of political contestation that is not a 'pure' opposition, a 'transcendence' of contemporary relations of power, but a difficult labor of forging a future from resources inevitably impure" (BTM, p. 241). In exactly the same way, feminist biblical scholarship is implicated in that which it opposes, which is, at least, the use of Scripture as justification for oppressing and subjugating women and others who are perceived to be marginal. It certainly seeks to forge a future from impure resources.

In Luke 7:36–50 an unnamed woman approaches Jesus as he is dining with a pharisee, Simon, in his home. She anoints Jesus's feet with oil, weeps, uses her hair to wipe his feet, and repeatedly kisses his feet. While she is engaged with Jesus's body, Simon thinks to himself, "If this man is really a prophet, he would know what kind of woman this is, a sinner" (v. 39). Then, Jesus tells Simon a story about being in debt, having those debts forgiven, and love. Jesus tells him that the woman has fulfilled all the obligations that Simon, as host, has failed to do. Then Jesus turns to the woman and tells her, "Your sins are forgiven" (v. 48).[9]

Luke's narrative of the woman who anoints Jesus is an example of Scripture that has been interpreted relentlessly (even after feminism) to the detriment of women. I first read Luke's story of the anointing when I was beginning my doctoral program. From that initial reading I found the account of a woman wiping Jesus's feet with her hair as she weeps on them to be most provocative. Indeed, I found the image of the woman with her hair and hands full of ointment, and the image of her rubbing this mess on Jesus's feet with her hair somewhat erotic. I was conscious of a physicality that went beyond (I assumed) what was acceptable in "proper society." I was captivated by the messiness of what the woman was doing as she poured and wiped ointment on Jesus' feet and by what I perceived to be an act of intimacy forced into public space. But, above all, I remember thinking that this woman in Luke 7 was one of the most powerful and memorable characters in the New Testament.

The mere depiction of a woman's physicality, with no apparent fear of reprisal and without any type of shame associated with her act, made me glad. I was glad, I think, because I found that I could finally identify with a character in the biblical text, a character who—at least in my initial reading—was not only a woman acting independently but also one who blended together the movements of her whole body with the expression of raw emotion. And I was even more pleased to read that Jesus responded positively to the lavish gestures of wiping hair, wiping tears, wiping feet. Further, I was glad to see a woman unabashedly using her body without the stipulation of procreation. Of course, these musings about who the woman is, what she is doing, and why were my own inventions, but they were reflections that, to my mind, esteemed her and her acts rather than disparaged them.

But when I looked at the interpretations of Luke's passage, I could not find the woman whom I encountered. I was disappointed to discover that the anointing woman has been used, since interpretations of this pericope have been recorded, as a symbol of every woman's lewdness, as a symbol of a woman's sexuality that stands over and against what is "good" and "proper." With few exceptions, especially in any work prior to the mid-1980s, scholars either call her a whore or claim that the label *sinner* surely indicates that the anointing woman is a sexual sinner; her effusive weeping, they write, must be indicative of sexual shame-inspired remorse and repentance.[10] Yet, for Luke's male sinners, such as Peter in 5:8 or Zacchaeus in 19:1–10, the taint of shame is never the central detail of their interpretations. Peter refers to himself as a sinner and Jesus invites him to follow him. No one ever assumes that Peter's sins were sexual. Even though Jesus affirms the anointing woman, commentators typically fail to absolve the woman of the shame they associate with her "sexual" sins.

The label *prostitute* is consistently evoked from the time of the Church Fathers, through the Byzantine era, the Middle Ages, the Reformation, and into the modern age. Across the diversity of interpretive cultures, the responses to the anointing woman are quite similar. Interpreters first sexualize her and her sins, then they either exclude her from the dominant culture by declaring her too immoral to exist within proper society or her physicality (which has been sexualized) gets shifted into nonphysical categories, spiritual, linguistic, or economic, after which the anointing woman is allowed to enter normal society or the dominant discourse. A typical reading in the Middle Ages identifies the anointing woman with the "great harlot" Mary of Magdala, only then to turn her into "the great penitent." According to the legends told about her, her sins are so great and her shame so complete that she exiles herself to the wilderness for thirty years.[11] Even during the Reformation, when Protestant Christian rhetorical malice was aimed primarily at Catholics and Jews, Luther spiritualizes the physicality of the anointing woman and Jean Calvin's exegesis of the passage justifies the anointing in economic terms.

Yet the most extensive explorations into the labeling of the anointing woman stem from the feminist scholarship of the pericope of the last two decades. In the latter half of the twentieth century a debate has raged over whether or not the gospel of Luke is "good" or "bad" for women. Some scholars, such as Leonard Swidler and Ben Witherington III, argue that Luke has such a positive portrayal of women, the evangelist may have very well been a woman.[12] Feminist scholars like Turid Seim, Jane Schaberg, and Mary Rose D'Angelo have argued that, though Luke may include more stories about women and give women what may appear to be central roles, Luke undermines the subjectivity of many of those women by leaving them nameless and relegating them to the domestic sphere where they perform menial tasks.[13] For example, D'Angelo notes that Luke de-emphasizes women's roles of spiritual leadership in the early Church. She argues that Luke seeks to present an apologetic that depicts Christian women as conforming to the gender norms of Greco-Roman society, just as Philo and Josephus sought to "demonstrate that Judaism is not less circumspect in its control of women and sexuality."[14] Schaberg even calls the gospel of Luke "dangerous" for women. She writes that

> even as this gospel highlights women as included among the followers of Jesus . . . it deftly portrays them as models of subordinate service, excluded from the power center of the movement and from significant responsibilities. . . . The danger lies in the subtle artistic power of the story to seduce the reader into uncritical acceptance of it as simple history, and into acceptance of the depicted gender roles as divinely ordained.[15]

Likewise, Seim perceives that Luke contains a "double message" for women: they can be active in the Christian church but their activity should be confined to the domestic sphere and to acts of service. Additionally, all three scholars, Seim, Schaberg, and D'Angelo, note that the women who receive praise and support from Jesus in Luke are those women who are silent, nameless, or passive.

D'Angelo, Seim, and Schaberg assert that Luke takes an active and central character, such as the anointing woman in Luke 7, and positions her in established gender roles. Luke's presentation of the anointing, they claim, reestablishes the subordination of the woman in the following ways: he labels her a sinner, which sets up the potential for readers to see her as immoral or unclean; he diverts focus from the anointing itself to the woman's "excessive" display of emotion and physicality; through Jesus's praise Luke characterizes her gestures as acts of servitude. An underlying assumption is that the woman "is," independent from the text, an active, autonomous individual. It is also assumed that Luke corrupts "her" in his representation by portraying the anointing woman as passive, silent, submissive. More, the labels *passive, silent, submissive* are presumed to be negative, powerless, and above all, *feminine* qualities.

Feminist biblical scholarship tends to construct a woman (or a community of women) to which it attaches certain attributes—attributes that in turn are ascribed positive value. By naming these traits as "historical" and, therefore, "real," and as "good" counters to the "bad" values assigned to certain activities deemed to be feminine, the scholarship perpetuates gendered dualities of vocal/silent; active/passive; dominant/submissive; named/unnamed, and, above all, masculine/feminine. These dualities figure prominently as primary targets of feminist scholarship. When feminists critique and oppose the portrayals of women as passive and silent, as submissive, and as "unclean," they create and vilify the thing they name.

Surprisingly, acceptance of the premise that Luke's sinner is a prostitute goes without question, for the most part. I say "surprisingly" because I expected a feminist defense of the woman's labeling instead of an attack on how Luke constructs her. But a recent and dominant strand in Lukan scholarship has been to focus on how negatively the third evangelist depicts women—a response to scholarship in the 1970s that claimed Luke not only as an excellent gospel for women but one that may even have been written by a woman.[16] A current feminist response to Luke 7:36–50 has been to assume that the woman is a prostitute and then to reconsider the value placed on that label.[17]

Kathleen Corley, Luise Schottroff, and others perceive that the pejorative labeling of the anointing woman and her actions is injurious to the social status of women. To remedy the negative portrayal of Luke's sinner, they seek to reconstruct or revalue the term *prostitute* as one that is not harmful to women. In order to do this they unconsciously shift *prostitute* from being a physical label to an economic one. The shift, according to the implications of their work, makes the prostitute an acceptable category because it is no longer only attached to women's bodies but has found a place within the social structure. If a woman is a prostitute and if prostitution can be considered a viable economic venture—i.e., as an alternative to a woman who is sexual without "proper" justification—then the "economic prostitute" becomes a relatively acceptable label.[18] Nevertheless, it only becomes so in relation to the prostitute as a physical label. There appears to be something about the physicality of the anointing woman that threatens the social space of the dinner, and the move to dephysicalize that body reduces whatever threat it introduces.[19]

What goes unsaid in the former feminist redemption of "prostitute" is that the woman who is perceived to be sexual, whether for pleasure or for no apparent reason at all, and who does not "belong" to a man remains socially condemned. Nothing really changes as far as the status of a woman's physicality goes in Corley or Schottroff's reassessment of prostitute: a woman who succumbs to economic pressures is justified, and is "in her place," but a sexual woman who uses her body outside economic justification and without clear association with one man remains deviant.

Another feminist hermeneutical move (in both modern feminist theory and modern feminist biblical studies) is to critique the depiction of women as submissive and subservient.[20] The image of the anointing woman cowering at Jesus's feet or groveling under the table while he towers above her is not common in text-based interpretations, but it is pervasive in paintings and films. Again, critiquing Luke's text for presenting such images produces the same two complicated issues that arise when we declare the anointing woman a prostitute: some feminists assume, first, that Luke is producing the images of the anointing woman as submissive and, second, that being submissive is a "bad" thing for women.

In the artistic depictions the woman is most often illustrated as crawling under the table to get to Jesus's feet as he sits upright at a table; he is surrounded by men who look shocked by her display.[21] Luke clearly writes, however, that Jesus reclines at the table (v. 36) and the anointing woman is standing behind Jesus's feet, above them so that her tears fall on them.[22] The facial expressions of the observers in the paintings and the murmuring in the movies by those around the table register shock and disgust. Yet, Luke's text gives no indication that the woman's presence at the meal is abnormal; Simon, Jesus's Pharisaic host, merely questions Jesus's prophetic abilities: "If this man were a prophet, he would know who and what sort of woman is touching him." Further, there is no verb of entering for the woman. From Jesus's comment in verse 45, "from the time I came in she has not stopped kissing my feet," we could even assume that the anointing woman was already in the room when Jesus arrived; her presence there may not have been out of the ordinary at all. Still, the woman is always portrayed as a stranger and an unwelcome intruder into Simon's house.

Further, when feminist biblical critics assail Luke or any interpreter for depicting the woman as submissive, they place an underlying negative value judgment on the submissive woman.[23] In part, the anointing woman's label as submissive comes from her devotion to Jesus's feet and the fact that Jesus praises her for performing acts of hospitality that Simon (or Simon's slave) has neglected to do. There is an assumption by some feminists (not all) that being submissive is a "bad" thing for a woman, and that submissiveness and service are traits only connected to women. But an additional move by interpreters transforms an image of submission to Jesus—an image that is certainly encouraged for Christians, male or female—into an image of humiliation and of shame. In other words, the anointing woman's submission to Jesus and her willingness to serve him get interpreted as masochism; the critics do not, then, see her as a model Christian.

The complexities of either the presences or absences of speech in a narrative cannot be simplified into the valued categories of "good" or "bad." For example, Jesus's silence at his trial (Mt. 26:63) has never, as far as I can determine, signified Jesus's weakness; we could even consider the absence of speech in that context a sign of power. On the other hand, silence in Luke tends to indicate an acceptance of a subordinate position to Jesus (e.g., 4:35, 9:36, 14:4, 20:26). Jesus's remarks tend to silence the voices of his adversaries. Male subordination and submission and silence and passivity toward Jesus are accepted as "good" things.

Even though the anointing woman could be observed as actively and independently involved in *something*, her critics (or, rather, Luke's critics) draw attention to the fact that she is nameless and silent (and therefore, they insist, powerless and passive). Schüssler Fiorenza points out how ironic it is that Jesus tells all who hear that Mark's anointing woman will always be remembered for what she has done. And, as Schüssler Fiorenza observes, we do not even know her name.[24] Yet in fact, she *is* still remembered for what she did, just as the nameless and silent centurion in Luke is remembered for his faith in Jesus (7:1–10).[25] I wonder: are we (as feminist Lukan scholars) weaving the rope with which we hang ourselves? In other words (Butler's), are we "being implicated in that which we oppose"? Are we "turning power against itself to produce alternative modalities of power" and "forging a future from resources inevitably impure?" (BTM, p. 241)

Either Luke's depiction of the anointing woman is extremely potent, because the perceptions of her as they are reflected through centuries of interpretation are virtually unified in their negative assessment of her character or all of us are so habitually familiar with vilifying women's physicality that the mere flicker of the word *sinner* pointed at a woman instinctively and reflexively evokes from us only condemnation. Even if Luke has nuanced the narrative with sexual codes, e.g., the allusions to "feet" (which is a sexual euphemism in both Greek and Hebrew texts) or the detail of her loose hair, so that we read the anointing woman as a sexual character, I doubt that her ascription as prostitute by interpreters is based on much more than the label *sinner*. The tendency to judge an actively physical woman negatively, especially a woman not connected to one particular man, is the sludge that remains when all else is washed away.

Rather than reading the anointing in Luke 7 as an act of adoration in which a woman sinner uses her body—perhaps in a sexual way but certainly in an effort that involves her whole body—interpreters of this passage have chosen to fill in the gap between "sinner" and "woman" with sex. To assume that the woman is sexual is not necessarily damaging to the woman, but the sex that is assumed of her is not sex that can be affirming or celebrated but a sex that is rendered deviant, i.e., counter to everything proper or normal—a sex that is defiling and necessitates her redemption. Just assigning the woman a physical label should not (necessarily) be a negative valuation, but the next hermeneutical step is that sexuality attached to an independent woman becomes "sinful" or bad. Thus not only does the anointing woman take on a negative labeling of "sexual sinner" but, in the interpretive corpus, that ascription is most often articulated as prostitute as well. The label *prostitute* functions to categorize all women whose physicality does not conform to what is "normal" or socially acceptable. Feminist scholarship on the Gospel of Luke provides an excellent example of Butler's laws of motion.

Rereading the Anointing: Is She Really So Bad?

There are alternatives to how one can read the anointing in Luke: First, we could question the assumption that "silence" and "namelessness" are "bad." As I have shown above, it is not essential that women's silence and namelessness are signs of passivity or powerlessness. In most feminist criticisms the silent and nameless woman has been assigned a negative value. There is an assumption that nameless women or women who listen without responding through speech are rendered weak or helpless by the author. For example, Schaberg and others assert that Luke praises the silent (and passive) Mary and scolds the active and vocal Martha (10:38–42).[26] And Evelyn Thibeaux assumes that the silence of the anointing woman creates a gulf in the text that invites readers to make negative assumptions about her.[27] But, with this critique, scholars are privileging speech and language over silence; they are assuming that silence and namelessness are passive traits and that passivity is of a lesser domain and a debasement of women. Adele Reinhartz, however, argues that anonymity can open a gap in the text into which the reader is invited. The absence of a name, she asserts, provides a narratival flexibility.[28] While scholars critique Luke's manipulations of women, they are in fact constructing the roles and the values of those roles to which they assign each woman. In other words (again those of Butler), we are attempting to fix "the identity" of the anointing woman. With a stabilization or definition of her identity also comes her "limitation, prohibition, regulation, and control" ("Subjects," p. 274). The text gives us a mystery woman. Her character, as Butler might suggest of all "women," should remain without definition, without limits, discursive.

Another reading strategy for Luke 7:36–50 parallels Butler's reading of Antigone in *Antigone's Claim*. In such a reading one might discover a route toward challenging normative systems and a way to resist reading the anointing woman as "bad": "It is her very impurity—her imbrication in systems that simultaneously oppress and empower her—that makes her such a resource."[29] This strategy makes positive use of precisely those aspects that so trouble readers of this pericope: the silence, the mystery, and the eroticism.

Antigone, like the anointing woman, is an ancient, mythic figure whose interpreters concern themselves with significations of propriety and transgression, eroticism and desire, defiance and submission. The play opens with Antigone, a daughter of Oedipus, telling her sister that she plans to perform funereal rites for her brother Polyneices, even though Creon, the ruler, has forbidden it. Antigone transgresses Creon's edict and is caught by soldiers who have set a trap for her. Creon, against all advice, condemns her to be sealed up in a tomb—a living being among the dead. After the seer Tiresias warns Creon that he will bring doom upon everything and everybody, Creon changes his mind—too late! We hear through a messenger that Hamon, Creon's son and Antigone's betrothed, has gone to Antigone. When he finds that she has hanged herself, he tries to kill Creon (who has just arrived at the tomb), fails, and kills himself instead.

In *Antigone's Claim* Butler makes the case that previous definitive readings of *Antigone* have a performative function; like the interpreters of the anointing woman, readers create exactly who they *need* Antigone to be.

> But who is this "Antigone" that I sought to use as an example of a certain feminist impulse? There is, of course, the "Antigone" of Sophocles' play by that name, and that Antigone is, after all, a fiction, one that does not easily allow itself to be made into an example one might follow without running the risk of slipping into irreality oneself. Not that this has stopped many people from making her into a representative of sorts.
>
> (AC, pp. 1–2)

Hegel, for example, uses the play in both the *Phenomenology* and in *Philosophy of Right*. He sees in "Antigone" the personifications of the familial in conflict with the polis and human law in conflict with divine law. Perhaps most significant for Hegel is the relationship between Antigone and Polyneices. According to Hegel, the relationship between a brother and sister is the most perfect relationship between a man and a woman because it is without erotic desire. When Antigone loses Polyneices, she has forever lost the possibility of having a perfect and egalitarian relationship with another man.

The postmodern French philosopher Luce Irigaray, according to Butler, also insists upon the "representative function" (AC, p. 2) of Antigone. Irigaray, quoted in Butler, writes that, "Her example is always worth reflecting upon as a historical figure and as an identity and identification for many girls and women living today. For this reflection, we must abstract Antigone from the seductive, reductive discourses and listen to what she has to say about government of the polis, its order and its laws."[30] Irigaray sees Antigone as one who expresses a "pre-political" condition, a representation of kinship as "the sphere that conditions the possibility of politics without ever entering into it" (Butler, AC, p. 2). Butler's critique is that Irigaray's and Hegel's readings set up Antigone as representative of something that opposes the polis. That even as Irigaray, for example, seeks to portray Antigone as symbolic of kinship, linked to "blood" and an irreducible foundation of the polis, Butler poses that Irigaray's notions of kinship are still laden with binary oppositions.

Butler goes on to argue that Hegel's and Irigaray's readings of Antigone are unstable. Even Irigaray's insistence that Antigone be "defended and championed as a principle of feminine defiance of statism and an example of anti-authoritarianism" (AC, p.1) is unstable:

> But can Antigone herself be made into a representative for a certain kind of feminist politics, if Antigone's own representative function is itself in crisis? As I hope to show in what follows, she hardly represents the normative principles of kinship, steeped as she is in incestuous legacies that confound her position within kinship. And she hardly represents a feminism that might in any way be unimplicated in the very power that it opposes.
>
> (AC, p. 2)

What Butler does, then, is to read Antigone as one who stands in a liminal position between family and state, public and private, life and death; her birth, her family, all her relationships are non-normative. Whatever it is that a woman is said to "be," the character Antigone defies, or, rather, slips in and out of all of them. Most important, it seems, to Butler, the text never brings Antigone into "compulsive heterosexuality: it "fails to produce heterosexual closure for that drama" (ibid.)

The anointing woman, like Butler's Antigone, can be recognized for her destabilizing potential. The anointing woman is a [fictional] woman who is perceived by some feminists to be in opposition to the powers that be. As Antigone defies the edict of Creon, the anointing woman, perhaps, defies an unwritten law of gender activity. She appears in what is generally perceived as male space[31] just as Antigone "enters" into the affairs of the polis. The anointer is actively physical toward a passive male body, just as Antigone is doubly active—over Creon and over Polyneices. The anointing woman becomes the focus of everyone's attention and, like Antigone, is the subject of all subsequent discourse (within and without the initial text). Like Antigone, who becomes a living body in the realm of the dead, the anointing woman stands at an intersection of life and death as she performs a fragrant anointing, a rite of the dead onto a living body. Both characters stand at an interstice of power; the acts they perform challenge traditional power centers. Finally, both evoke images of displaced desire as each attend to forbidden erotic subjects. The anointing woman rubs the feet of the divine Son of God[32] and Antigone defiantly attends to the needs of her brother.

Though the anointing woman's critics say that she is somewhere she shouldn't be, doing things she shouldn't be doing, the destabilizing blow of this text, I suspect, is that the object of her physicality (erotic desire?) is Jesus. Is she a daughter of God who caresses and desires the Son of God? Might one read her acts as evidence of a forbidden desire, like Antigone's desire for Polyneices?[33] The specter of "perverse" desire has silently haunted this passage throughout the centuries. When "sex" does appear, it is a deviant sexuality heaped upon a woman portrayed as a whore, in opposition to a perfect, sexless, sinless, Son of God. Often, a reader ignores the tensions and traces of erotic physicality in this narrative. For example, that "feet" was a euphemism for male genitals in the Septuagint as well as Hellenistic and Greco-Roman literature has already been convincingly argued.[34] As I think about this, I recall several occasions in which I quickly deflected inquiries about the anointing of Jesus' euphemistic "feet" with a glib, "sometimes a cigar is just a cigar." I find it odd now that I did not even consider an explicitly genital reading of this passage that would have explored the contingent meanings of the question "what if the woman is anointing Jesus's genitals?"

The Church fathers, such as Ambrose, also desexualize the passage and read Luke 7 allegorically. The primary metaphor is that the relationship between the anointing woman and Jesus is a relationship between the Church and God. The delayed presence of God is manifested in the sexual tension of the narrative: the Church has rejected "indulgence and fleshly delights and pleasures" in anticipation of the union with her lover, Jesus. Thus, when the woman Church is finally joined with Jesus, a single kiss is not enough to "fulfill her desire . . . for as a lover, she is not satisfied with the meager offering of a single kiss, but demands many, claims many as her right."[35] The excessive kissing in Luke 7, as Ambrose describes it, is a symbol of the fulfillment of the Church's desire, or, in other words, a sexual consummation. Origen, the first interpreter to call the anointing woman a harlot, also sees the relationship between Jesus and the anointing woman as erotic; he presents them as the lovers in Song of Songs.[36]

Origen also—accidentally—evokes an incestuous desire into this text. He confuses Luke's version of the story with the account of an anointing in the Gospel of John and calls the anointer Mary of Bethany, the sister of the resurrected Lazarus (Jn. 12:1–8). In the misnaming of Luke's anointer, the identities of the anointing woman and Jesus become entangled with the identities of Mary of Bethany and her brother Lazarus. As one who is raised from the dead, is a target of "the Jews," is interred in a cave for three days, and is the brother/companion of Mary and Martha, Lazarus is a strong literary parallel for Jesus. More, in the story of Lazarus' resurrection, the ambiguity of Jesus's/Lazarus's identity is heightened when Jesus says to Mary, "Your brother shall rise again" and, then, "I am the risen one" (Jn. 11:23, 25).

According to John 12:7, the anointing is specifically meant for a corpse, yet which corpse is not clear. The story of the anointing immediately follows the raising of Lazarus, and John tells us that Lazarus is present at the house. Maybe the resurrected one still stinks (see Jn. 11:39) and needs to be anointed. Who is the resurrected corpse? Who is in need of anointing? And, who is the anointer's brother? John's text is ambiguous, and Origen imports the ambiguity and potential of perverse desire into Luke's narrative of the anointing.

It is intriguing to consider a latent desire in this text, a prohibited eroticism either between a woman and God or a woman and her brother. It is a reading that blurs boundaries between the forbidden desire and the norm. It is an interrelationship wherein each requires the other, both are fluid, both are temporal. It is a reading in which perverse desire is not perceived as the "negative feature of the norm" (AC, p. 76). Butler asks,

> Can such a rule, understood as a prohibition, actually operate, however effectively, without producing and maintaining the specter of its transgression? Do such rules produce conformity, or do they also produce a set of social configurations that exceed and defy the rules by which they are occasioned? . . . How interesting, then, that so many of the readings of Sophocles' play insist that there is no incestuous love here, and one wonders whether the reading of the play does not in those instances become the very occasion for the insistence of the rule to take place: there is no incest here, and cannot be.
>
> (AC, p. 17)

Thus, we could read the physicality of this passage—passionate weeping, caressing feet with expensive oil, rubbing the oil between the toes, around the feet, and with long, thick hair—as a forbidden desire between Jesus and the anointing woman; it is a desire that requires some readers to respond with vehement prohibition. Through repudiations and denials it is made clear that "the norm has a temporality that opens it to a subversion from within and to a future that cannot be fully anticipated" (AC, p. 21). To paraphrase Butler a bit, "the point, then, is not to unleash [forbidden desire] from its constraints but to ask what forms of [normativity] are understood to proceed as structural necessities from that taboo" (AC, p. 30). Just as Antigone "becomes the occasion for a reading of a structurally constrained notion of kinship in terms of its social iterability" (AC, p. 29), Jesus's anointing by the woman sinner becomes an occasion for reading structurally constrained notions of gender and eroticism in terms of their own social iterability. Like Antigone, the anointing woman escapes compulsive heterosexuality: she does not marry, have children, or become further attached to Jesus. Her actions that have been read as harmful to the construction of "woman" can also be read as subverting that same term. Because she never speaks, never explains her presence or her actions, is without a name, the anointing woman's character can defy assimilation into "a symbolic order that requires the communicability of the sign" (AC, p. 52). She can be read as maintaining a certain autonomy while she is proclaimed sinless. More, any prohibition of erotic desire between the woman and Jesus could problematize, to some extent, all configurations of heterosexual desire. In other words, if readers ignore, deny, or prohibit an interpretation of an erotic instance between Jesus and the anointing woman, all heteronormative relationships come under suspicion. Thus the erasure of heterosexual desire from this text leaves an invitation to insert into the gap alternative, non-normative desire.

A Butlerian reading of this text presents some alternatives to previous readings that tend to perpetuate more negative claims about women. I am sure this reading does its own damage in some ways, but in identifying a perverse desire and seeing the performance as a validation of women's activity, this reading challenges some assumptions of heteronormative structure and disrupts some constructions of the term *woman*. While this reading may not topple dynasties or rewrite laws, it whittles away at a bedrock that holds these kingdoms in place.

NOTES

1. Butler, *Bodies That Matter: On the Discursive Limits of "Sex"* (BTM), p. 10.
2. Ibid., p. 241.
3. See, for example, Martha Nussbaum, "The Professor of Parody: The Hip Defeatist Feminism of Judith Butler," *New Republic* 220, no. 4 (1999): 38–45; Teresa Ebert, "Ludic Feminism, the Body, Performance, and Labor: Bringing Materialism Back Into Feminist Cultural Studies," *Cultural Critique* 23 (1992–1993): 5–50.
4. Teresa Hornsby, *The Gendered Sinner* (Ann Arbor: UMI, 2000).
5. Ibid.

6. Judith Butler, "Performative Acts and Gender Constitution: An Essay in Phenomenology and Feminist Theory," in *Performing Feminisms: Feminist Critical Theory and Theatre*, ed. Sue-Ellen Case (Baltimore: Johns Hopkins University Press, 1990), p. 273.

7. Judith Butler, "Subjects of Sex/Gender/Desire," in *Feminism and Politics*, ed. Anne Phillips (New York: Oxford University Press, 1998), p. 285.

8. Judith Butler, *Antigone's Claim: Kinship Between Life and Death* (AC).

9. This same story occurs in the three other gospels, but in Mark and Matthew a woman anoints Jesus's head. In John, Jesus seems to understand the gesture as symbolic of the anointing of his corpse.

10. E.g., Origen, *Origenes Werke: Origenes Matthäuserklärung* (Leipzig: Hinrichssche Buchhandlung, 1935), book 12, section 4, lines 10–14,10:75; J. Duncan Derrett, *Law in the New Testament* (London: Darton, Longman and Todd, 1970), p. 277.

11. For a brief history of the legends of Mary Magdalene and her conflation with the anointing woman in Luke and with Mary of Bethany, see Susan Haskins, *Mary Magdalen: Myth and Metaphor* (New York: Harper Collins, 1993), pp. 113–33.

12. Ben Witherington III, *Women in the Ministry of Jesus: A Study of Jesus' Attitudes to Women and Their Roles as Reflected in His Earthly Life* (New York: Cambridge University Press, 1984); Leonard Swidler, *Biblical Affirmations of Women* (Philadelphia: Westminster, 1979).

13. Turid Seim, *The Double Message: Patterns of Gender in Luke and Acts* (Nashville: Abingdon, 1994); Jane Schaberg, "Luke," in *The Women's Bible Commentary*, ed. Carol Newsom and Sharon Ringe (Louisville: Westminster/John Knox, 1992), pp. 275–92; Mary Rose D'Angelo, "Women in Luke/Acts: A Redactional View," *Journal of Biblical Literature* 109, no. 3 (1990): 441–61.

14. D'Angelo, "Women in Luke/Acts," p. 460.

15. Schaberg, "Luke," p. 275.

16. See, for example, Swidler, *Biblical Affirmations of Women,* and Constance Parvey, "The Theology and Leadership of Women in the New Testament," in *Religion and Sexism*, ed. Rosemary R. Ruether (New York: Simon and Schuster, 1974), pp. 139–46. Even as early as 1887, one male scholar writes, "Luke delighted in pointing out that … [Jesus] had sympathy with weaker suffering womanhood and that everywhere departed from the common Oriental habit of degrading womanhood, and how the gospel was to elevate womanhood all over the world"; Thomas M. Lindsay, *Handbooks for Bible Classes* (Edinburgh: Clark, 1887), p. 117.

17. Kathleen Corley argues that the mere presence of the anointing woman at a Greco-Roman dinner setting is enough to suggest that she is a prostitute, according to custom. But Corley insists that the woman does not have to be read as a common streetwalker; she could be a type of prostitute that is known to be aristocratic and philosophically educated; Corley, "Were the Women Around Jesus Really Prostitutes?" *SBL Seminar Papers* (Atlanta: Scholars, 1989), p. 490; and Corley, *Private Women, Public Meals: Social Conflict in the Synoptic Tradition* (Peabody, MA: Hendrickson, 1993). Schottroff also accepts that the anointing woman is a prostitute but calls for scholars to read that designation as a position

of power rather than powerlessness; Luise Schottroff, *Let the Oppressed Go Free: Feminist Perspectives on the New Testament*, trans. Annemarie S. Kidder (Louisville: Westminster/John Knox, 1991), pp. 150, 154–55. For contemporary feminist theory on revaluing the prostitute, see Shannon Bell, *Reading Writing and Re-Writing the Prostitute Body* (Bloomington: Indiana University Press, 1994). Some biblical scholars have followed this line of thinking in their reassessment of women in the Christian world.

18. Jacques Roussiaud asserts that by 1300 the prostitute as "the impoverished foreigner selling her body in order to survive" became distinguished from "the lustful woman searching for pleasure"; *Medieval Prostitution* (New York: Blackwell, 1988), p. 160. The former, an economic category, was deemed as socially necessary and protected under the law. The distinction and saving grace of the prostitute as opposed to the promiscuous woman becomes a circumstance of economics. According to Roussiaud, if a woman can convince authorities she is selling her body in order to live, her body is a valid economic resource and therefore legitimate. Thus it seems that a prostitute that has been brought into the economy is no longer valued negatively or as socially deviant.

19. This hermeneutical transformation is consistent with what Paul De Man describes as a displacement that occurs to circumvent something in a literary text that is perceived to be dangerous or at least disruptive to social standards. Paul De Man, *Allegories of Reading: Figural Language in Rousseau, Nietzsche, Rilke, and Proust* (New Haven: Yale University Press, 1979), p. 300.

20. Robin Linden, Darlene Pagano, Diana Russell, Susan Leigh Star, *Against Sadomasochism: A Radical Feminist Analysis* (East Palo Alto, CA: Frog in the Well, 1982), p. 2; specifically regarding Luke's anointing woman, see Evelyn Thibeaux, "Known to Be a Sinner," *Biblical Theology Bulletin* 23 (1991): 151–60; T. K. Seim, *The Double Message: Patterns of Gender in Luke and Acts* (Nashville: Abingdon, 1994), p. 92; Barbara Reid, *Choosing the Better Part? Women in the Gospel of Luke* (Collegeville: Liturgical, 1996), p. 205.

21. See, for example, paintings of the anointing in Haskins, *Mary Magdalen*, pp. 15, 22, 45, 107, 195, 223, and 352.

22. Fred Craddock notes that since "dining occurred in a reclining position, anointing Jesus' feet should not conjure up the image of a woman crawling around under a table." Fred Craddock, *Interpretation: A Bible Commentary for Teaching and Preaching—Luke* (Louisville: Knox, 1990), p. 105. John's version (12:1–8), the only other rendering in which the woman uses her hair to wipe Jesus's feet, does not use the verb "to recline" but does place Jesus at a meal.

23. See, for example, Jane Schaberg, "Fast Forwarding to the Magdalene," in *Semeia* 74 (1996): 33–45; Reid, *Choosing the Better Part?* p. 205.

24. Elisabeth Schüssler Fiorenza, *In Memory of Her: A Feminist Theological Reconstruction of Christian Origins* (New York: Crossroad, 1992), p. xiii.

25. The centurion never speaks directly—in fact, he does not even appear in the text. His words are spoken first through a contingency of Jewish elders and then through slaves. The centurion is never named, nor is he given direct speech. Like the anointing woman, he is praised by Jesus for his faith.

26. Schaberg, "Luke," p. 377; Judith Applegate, "And she wet his feet with her tears: A Feminist Interpretation of Luke 7:36–50," in Harold Washington, Susan Lochrie Grahm, and Pamela Thimmes, eds., *Escaping Eden: New Feminist Perspectives on the Bible* (Atlanta: Sheffield Academic, 1998–1999), p. 89; Elisabeth Schüssler Fiorenza, "A Feminist Interpretation for Liberation—Martha and Mary: Lk. 10:38–42," *Religion and Intellectual Life* 3 (1986): 21–36; Corley, *Private Women,* p. 142. See Reid's critique of this model, *Choosing the Better Part?* pp. 144–62; and Adele Reinhartz's critique, "From Narrative to History: The Resurrection of Mary and Martha," in *Women Like This,* ed. Amy-Jill Levine (Atlanta: Scholars, 1991), pp. 161–84.

27. Evelyn Thibeaux, "The Narrative Rhetoric of Luke 7:36–50: A Study of Context, Text, and Interpretation," Ph.D. diss., Graduate Theological Union, p. 475.

28. Adele Reinhartz, *Why Ask My Name? Anonymity and Identity in the Biblical Narrative* (New York: Oxford University Press, 1998), p. 186.

29. Ellen Armour, comments in an e-mail to me, June 15, 2001.

30. Luce Irigaray, *Speculum of the Other Woman,* trans. Gillian Gill (Ithaca: Cornell University Press, 1985), p. 70; quoted by Butler, *AC,* p. 2.

31. I do not think she enters; elsewhere I have argued that the woman is there all along. See Hornsby, *The Gendered Sinner.*

32. The Church Father Clement wrote: "A luxury without a useful purpose gives grounds for the charge of being sensual in character, and is a drug to excite the passions. But it is entirely different to rub oneself with oil out of necessity [as opposed to being anointed for pleasure]. The one makes a man womanish but to anoint out of necessity is the better." *Le Pédagogue,* book 2, section 68,4b, trans. Marrou and Harl, quoted in *Christ the Educator,* trans. Simon P. Wood (New York: Fathers of the Church, 1954), p. 152.

33. I do not mean to say that the anointing woman's desire for Jesus is incestuous. Rather, eroticism in this passage has been understood to be as much a taboo as the incestuous desire of Antigone.

34. See Marvin Pope, "Euphemism and Dysphemism in the Bible," *The Anchor Bible Dictionary,* 6 vols. (New York: Doubleday, 1992), 1:720–25, and Amy-Jill Levine, "Ruth," *The Women's Bible Commentary,* pp. 78–84. The locus classicus is the Delphic oracle in Euripides' *Medea* 679–81: Aegeus must not loosen the "foot" (πους)—i.e., spout—of the wineskin until he returns home; this comment comes within a passage that addresses the begetting of children. The critical notes for *Medea* say that πους indicates the phallus. See Denys L. Page, *The Plays of Euripides: Medea* (Oxford: Oxford University Press, 1955), p. 121. Liddell-Scott notes that the singular of πους can mean "the neck of the bladder" or "the neck of the penis"; H. G. Liddell and Robert Scott, *Greek-English Lexicon* (Oxford: Oxford University Press, 1940), pp. 1456–57.

35. Ambrose, *Seven Exegetical Works,* trans. Michael P. McHugh (Washington, DC: Catholic University of America Press, 1974), pp. 15–16.

36. Origen, *The Song of Songs: Commentary and Homilies,* trans. and annotated R. P. Lawson, no. 26, in *Ancient Christian Writers: The Works of the Fathers in Translation,* ed. Johannes Quasten (Westminster, MD: Newman, 1957), p. 23.

EMBODYING IDENTITIES

The incarnation of the Word took place according to the male sex: this is indeed a question of fact, and . . . while not implying an alleged natural superiority of man over woman, cannot be disassociated from the economy of salvation. . . . That is why we can never ignore the fact that Christ is a man.

—Sacred Congregation for the Doctrine of the Faith

Men are only sometimes men, but a woman is always a woman; everything reminds her of her sex.

—Jean Jacques Rousseau

I don't think one can pretend to imitate adequately that to which one is bound.

—Gayatri Chakravorty Spivak

In the end, in the beginning, now as then, there is only the performance.

—John Dominic Crossan

4. DISTURBINGLY CATHOLIC: Thinking the Inordinate Body

KAREN TRIMBLE ALLIAUME

FOR CATHOLIC WOMEN gender matters theologically. It matters most peculiarly when it comes to the question of ordination to the priesthood, which, for Catholics obedient to the Church's official teaching, has been "definitively" answered: "Women are not to be admitted to ordination."[1] The silence enjoined by the Church on this matter is constituted less by the absence of speech than by the inarticulability of bodies: to understand why Catholic women may not, according to Church teaching, be ordained, we must understand how and why gender comes to matter in the theology promulgated by the Catholic magisterium[2] and in dissenting theologies by those theologians, feminist and otherwise, who question its conclusions. "Theologies are never sexually neutral. The Roman Catholic Church's theology is a heavily sexual theology, obsessed with the regulation and control of sexual performances, roles and behavioural patterns of people. . . . Gender roles are not an extra element but a constitutive one of an understanding of being church."[3] For a Catholic woman gender identity and Catholic identity are not separable. Both the magisterium and those who contest its teachings with regard to ordination rely on certain understandings of women's identities as members of the "Body of Christ." Both also rely on certain construals of Jesus's corporeal identity in arguing for what the identity of "his" corporate body, the Church, is and should be. Links between bodies, seen by the Catholic magisterium as naturally and primordially sexed, and the Body of Christ, the communal identity of the Church—in turn based on the physical and sexed body of the historical Jesus of Nazareth as well as on the "spiritual" body of the risen Jesus Christ—form a complex web of symbolism determinative of women's inclusion and exclusion in the Catholic Church.

If you are not Catholic, why does this matter to you? Because the gender construction—and abjection—of women in official Catholic pronouncements on ordination may be helpfully analyzed as a case study illuminating both exclusion of and resistance by women in other institutions and communities. The body of Jesus is a potent trope, and tracing its shifting contours through a Butlerian lens illuminates not only the effects of the Church's judgment of women as illegitimate subjects of ordination, and the constructive possibilities of feminist resistance to that judgment, but other exclusive cultural constructions of women that rely, overtly or covertly, on Christian underpinnings.

For instance, the ambiguities of Catholic women's Church membership can be seen as analogous to the tensions attending women's rights as citizens in the modern nation-state. Feminist political scientist Jan Jindy Pettman argues that, while in theory they are full citizens, in practice women are often denied full citizenship rights on various grounds of unsuitability (as not male, not reasonable; as emotional; as sexual and therefore disruptive or dangerous; or as having family attachments precluding the disinterested work of citizenship). Asymmetry between women's claims to and full enjoyment of citizenship rights tends to rest on the grounds of motherhood: the maternal is located in the family, which is "private," yet (certain) women are also claimed by the state to perform civic duties such as giving birth to, bringing up, and offering to the state future citizens, soldiers, and workers.[4] Church defenses of the "dignity and vocation of women" with regard to their role in the Church strike a remarkably similar note:

> By defending the dignity of women and their vocation, the Church has shown honor and gratitude for those women who—faithful to the Gospel—have shared in every age in the apostolic mission of the whole People of God. They are the holy martyrs, virgins and mothers of families, who bravely bore witness to their faith and passed on the Church's faith and tradition by bringing up their children in the spirit of the Gospel."[5]

The "Letter to the Bishops of the Catholic Church on the Collaboration of Men and Women in the Church and in the World," issued by the Sacred Congregation for the Doctrine of the Faith on May 31, 2004, reaffirms this explicitly complementary view of sex and gender, finding "woman's" dignity firmly rooted in her capacity for nurturing and existing "for the other."[6] It explains that men's and women's equal dignity as persons "is realized as physical, psychological and ontological complementarity" that only sin renders conflictual.[7] The letter attempts to defend this understanding from charges of biological determinism by invoking virginity as a historical option for women, explaining that "although motherhood is a key element of women's identity, this does not mean that women should be considered from the sole perspective of physical procreation," and argues that "the existence of the Christian vocation of virginity . . . refutes any attempt to enclose women in mere biological destiny."[8] However, it is noteworthy that women's options and status are still defined here as based on *sexual* status. And motherhood, far from disappearing as a defining characteristic of womanhood, is confirmed as an ontological quality of all women: The letter defends the role of women in the workplace by invoking their inherent "mothering" qualities, seen as the capacity to give life, to be attuned to the concrete rather than the abstract, and to value human life. While these are seen as "above all human values . . . it is only because women are more immediately attuned to these values that they are the reminder and the privileged sign of such values."[9]

There is admittedly a disjunction between this language of rights and democratic citizenship and the language of faithfulness and discipleship used to characterize membership in the Catholic Church. The "Declaration on the Question of the Admission of Women to the Ministerial Priesthood" asserts that "priesthood does not form part of the rights of the individual, but stems from the economy of the mystery of Christ and the Church."[10] The writers distinguish the Church's organizing and governing principles from modern democracy:

> One must note the extent to which the Church is a society different from other societies, original in her nature and in her structures. The pastoral charge in the Church is normally linked to the sacrament of Order; it is not a simple government, comparable to the modes of authority found in the States. It is not granted by people's spontaneous choice: even when it involves designation through election, it is the laying on of hands and the prayer of the successors of the Apostles which guarantee God's choice; and it is the Holy Spirit, given by ordination, who grants participation in the ruling power of the Supreme Pastor, Christ (Acts 20:28). It is a charge of service and love: "If you love me, feed my sheep" (Jn. 21:15–17).
>
> For this reason one cannot see how it is possible to propose the admission of women to the priesthood in virtue of the equality of rights of the human person.[11]

Yet the analogy to women's rights as citizens remains salient, in view of Church capitulation to other "democratic values" of modernity. Mark Chaves argues that "sacramental" Christian denominations such as the Roman Catholic Church, as well as Protestant fundamentalist traditions, identify resisting women's ordination with resisting modernity.[12] Gene Burns demonstrates that the Catholic Church, having capitulated to other modern values such as church-state relations, capitalism, and freedom of conscience outside the Church, resists modernity most strenuously in the area of "faith and morals" read as (particularly women's) sexuality.[13] Marian Ronan argues that the Church has settled on issues surrounding women's sexuality, including ordination, as the primary symbol of this resistance because "women as a class have less power to fight back than liberal states or the market do."[14]

As in the case of citizenship, Catholic women's (non)ordination demonstrates in ways pertinent to other arenas that identities are embodied and not abstract and that bodies are inscribed in ways that are read not only to grant or deny rights but also to create the subjectivity of the bodies to which they seem merely to refer. Women are constructed as separate but equal in their roles and responsibilities in the Church by the Church's complementary understanding of gender, displayed in the theological "economy of salvation." The declaration explains this economy, in which the priest must be male because Jesus Christ was male, as follows:

> The unity which [Christ] re-established after sin is such that there are no more distinctions between Jew and Greek, slave and free, male and female, but all are one in Christ Jesus (Gal. 3:28). Nevertheless, *the incarnation of the Word took place according to the male sex:* this is indeed a question of fact, and this fact, while not implying an alleged natural superiority of man over woman, *cannot be disassociated from the economy of salvation:* it is indeed in harmony with the entirety of God's plan as God himself has revealed it. . . . *That is why we can never ignore the fact that Christ is a man. And therefore, unless one is to disregard the importance of this symbolism for the economy of Revelation, it must be admitted that, in actions which demand the character of ordination and in which Christ himself . . . is represented, exercising his ministry of salvation—which is in the highest degree the case of the Eucharist—his role (this is the original sense of the word "persona") must be taken by a man.* This does not stem from any personal superiority of the latter in the order of values, but only from a *difference of fact* on the level of functions and service.[15]

The problem inherent in this strong linkage between divinity and maleness has been most classically expressed by feminist theologian Rosemary Radford Ruether: "Women's inability to represent Christ is sealed by . . . the male disclosure of a male God whose normative representation can only be male."[16] The language of "reminder and privileged sign" used of women's putative and preeminent "nurturing" qualities, in the Church's letter "On the Collaboration of Men and Women" discussed earlier, echoes the logic of that used in the declaration to uphold the male-only priesthood, in which men are seen as the reminder and privileged sign of *divinity*. The theological and theoretical "equality" posited by a complementary understanding of gender cannot and does not translate into practical equality. Women who do not wish to be restricted to the Church-sanctioned and gender-complementary roles of mother, virgin, and/or martyr, and who may not "represent" Jesus Christ as priests, need alternatives. Exploring those alternatives may prove to apply not only to the particular case of women's ordination within Catholicism but to other situations where women's access to certain rights or roles is controlled based on similar logical "economies of imitation."

An Economy of Imitation

The problematic linkage of maleness and salvation may be traced back to the Council of Chalcedon's affirmation of Christ's humanity and divinity in 451, as expressed in Gregory of Nazianzus's assertion that "what has not been assumed [by Christ] cannot be restored; it is what is united with God that is saved."[17] In other words, Jesus Christ can be understood as saving humanity from sin and death only if he "takes on" all it means to be human and unites it with the divine. In particular, the council wished to affirm Christ's humanity through an emphasis on his corporeality: if Christ was *really* human, then he had a physical body that was truly capable of suffering and death.[18] This Chalcedonian affirmation of Christ's humanity and divinity was not meant to be an exhaustive account of Christ's meaning and identity, but a rule determining what kinds of faithful accounts of Christ could be given in the future.[19] In other words, orthodox Christian theology confirmed that belief in Jesus' full humanity and full divinity had a crucial role in salvation. This "rule" is still operative, it seems to me, both in the problematic links between Christ's maleness and salvation that feminists criticize as well as in feminists' own remedial reconstructions. If Christ had to be physically like us in order to save us, logic suggests, then in order to be saved we must in turn have to be like *him*.

To the extent that feminist theologians continue to assert that women must resemble Christ (or that Christ must resemble them) in order to be saved, we remain indebted, I argue, to the same Christological economy of imitation espoused by official Church teaching, in which Jesus Christ is seen as the norm that individuals must resemble for the salvific economy to work and from which resemblance women are ultimately (in full or in part) precluded. Dissolving the intransigence of both poles of this imitative economy by employing theorist Judith Butler's deconstruction of the sexed body, I argue for a shift in Christological discourse to a "performative" economy in which the meanings of both "Jesus Christ" and "women" are understood to be performed in community. I develop Butler's understanding of performativity as citational to demonstrate that Christ's body is discursively reproduced through a process that creates the continuity and stability of those bodies to which it seems only to refer. Butler uses the term *citationality* to name the process through which material reality takes shape and has meaning for us, focusing in particular on the production of the sexed body as one such material reality. She asserts that "sex," rather than being the raw physical material upon which "gender" writes, is one of the norms through which subjectivity becomes possible at all.[20] In other words, one's sex must be made intelligible, made easily determinable, for one to qualify as human in the first place. "Sex" precedes "body" and thus "humanity." Citationality, I argue, allows us to see how Jesus's body and women's bodies are *mutually* constructed both in the traditional Christological discourses that feminists criticize as well as in the alternative formulations feminists offer as more redemptive to women.

In recommending that we would do better to understand Christians as "citing" rather than "resembling" Jesus, I suggest a different configuration of the relationship between his body and women's bodies. Jesus's body is a textual body, made up of stories and sayings and their reiterations.[21] But Christians also understand him as Body, the members of the Church; his is a corporate body. The relationship between these two is what is at stake in feminist contestation for women's representation of divinity. Feminists ask whether or not women, as subjugated members of the latter Body, may represent or be represented by the former. How does lack of resemblance to the male body of Jesus work to exclude women from the Body of Christ? In other words, what makes some bodies "inordinate?"

I refer to dominant patterns of Christological discourse (such as that found in the Catholic magisterium's statements on ordination) as an *economy of imitation* that begins with the theological presupposition that Christians are to be like Christ. The term *economy* designates at least two poles that mean what they mean only in relation to one another. Christological discourse displays an economy of meaning that takes *Jesus Christ* and *humans* as its terms, linked by a relationship of resemblance. On an everyday level this holds true for all Christians: Jesus is a model of ethical behavior, or perfect "humanity," and thus both men and women are enjoined to "imitate" him. But when Jesus can be represented only by men in those functions that pertain directly to salvation (as experienced through the sacraments, which can only be administered by priests) the economy excludes women. They may represent "humanity," but not the divine.

Feminist theologians affirm the former meaning of the principle, emphasizing that our definition of humanity must explicitly include women. If Jesus Christ is understood to have assumed all aspects of what we understand humanity to be, then these aspects must include sex and gender for women truly to be able to experience redemption. If women cannot "see themselves" in Jesus, then their salvation is in jeopardy. Womanist theologian Jacquelyn Grant expresses this contemporary understanding of the power of the Christological economy of imitation in her statement "There is a direct relationship between our perception of Jesus Christ and our perception of ourselves."[22] Both traditional and feminist Christologies take this relationship as given but define the nature of the relationship quite differently. I will further explore the traditional Christological economy of imitation that feminists critique, as represented by the issue of women's ordination in the Roman Catholic Church, and then look at some of the ways feminist attempts to redress this problem reinstate the original terms of the imitative economy. Finally, I will read one feminist proposal through the lens of citationality in order to discern its liberating effects.

As we have already begun to see, debate over women's ordination in the Roman Catholic Church helpfully demonstrates the logic of the economy of imitation that feminists resist. This logic is primarily, although not completely, one of "natural bodily resemblance" between the man Jesus and male priests. Christine Gudorf helpfully recapitulates the main points of the argument of the Sacred Congregation for the Doctrine of the Faith in the "Declaration on the Question of the Admission of Women to the Ministerial Priesthood": women may not be ordained as priests because 1. Jesus was male, 2. the apostles were male, 3. the Church has a two-thousand-year-old tradition of ordaining only males; 4. since signs must resemble what they signify, women are not to be ordained because they cannot resemble Jesus, and 5. the symbolism of the Church as feminine bride to the male Christ would result in symbolic homosexuality if women were ordained.[23]

Numerous feminist and other religious scholars have pointed out the theological and logical distortions and inconsistencies of these arguments.[24] Counterarguments usually deemphasize Jesus's maleness as theologically meaningless while highlighting other aspects of his life and message as the more salient characteristics of his identity. But in distinguishing between the "historical" and the "redemptive" aspects of Jesus's identity these counterarguments often fail to take into account the constitutive relationships between them. Feminist refutations of the ultimate theological significance of Jesus's maleness often, and ironically, reinscribe that "historical maleness" as necessary to their own liberating conclusions. For instance, Elizabeth Johnson interprets Jesus's maleness as essential to the contemporary reception of his saving message during his lifetime, asserting that "if a woman had preached compassionate love and enacted a style of authority that serves, she would have been greeted with a colossal shrug."[25] Johnson's attempt to disprove the ultimate theological import of Jesus's maleness vacillates between assurance of its theological *insignificance* (it is no more or less important than his Jewishness, his age, his profession, etc.) and its *significance* as necessary to her positive evaluation of Jesus's effect on his hearers.

Similarly, Rosemary Radford Ruether suggests that in order to rediscover what is redeeming about Jesus for women, it is necessary to return to the historical Jesus. "Stripping" Jesus of accumulated doctrine, she redresses him as "representative of liberated humanity."[26] Jesus's redemptive power is seen by Ruether to lie ultimately in this ideal humanity, not in his maleness. His maleness is significant, rather, only insofar as he renounces the privileges that accompany it. Ruether interprets Jesus's redeeming power as extending to the whole community, members of which continue his identity through history by their imitation and replication of his ideal humanity and the kinds of acts that display it. We can now encounter Christ, Ruether asserts, "even in the form of our sister."[27]

Jesus is interpreted by Ruether not only as an ideal human being but as the initiator and spirit of a new kind of community. She resituates the power of this renounced masculine privilege in the community, a relocation that is meant to have—and, to some extent, does have—liberating effects for women. If it is the *community* who is to give up patriarchy, to give up unjust ways of relating to one another, then it is the community qua community that is seen to imitate Christ, rather than specific individuals. If "sisterhood" is now that which resembles Jesus most, then it would seem that the logic of the economy of imitation that reads maleness as inherent to redemption has lost all force. Yet I argue that maleness continues to signify here, to do work in the economy of imitation, in two important ways.

First, Ruether reaffirms Jesus's masculinity in the very act of portraying him as a renouncer of patriarchy. In her feminist reconstrual of the (in)significance of Jesus's maleness, he must "have" maleness in order to give it up, along with the privileges that accompany it. Jesus's sacrifice is seen by Ruether not as willing conformity to his Father's will but as an achievement of his own will: his choice to forego the pleasures of male privilege. If Jesus were not first (re)construed as "historically male," his significance would not be able to be read in this way. Ruether's argument reaffirms Jesus's maleness as theologically important, as does Johnson's, precisely in the task of trying to prove its theological irrelevance.

Second, Ruether's continued reliance on the category of humanity as that aspect of Jesus women resemble also belies the conclusion that maleness is insignificant to redemption. The economy in which women imitate (are included in) "humanity" tends to backfire on women. The category of humanity has always been constructed in a patriarchal vein. Many feminist theorists have demonstrated that the prototypical human is male, while the female has always been seen as lesser than or other to full male humanity. Uncritical use of this category is in danger of reinscribing (at best) women's occasional and circumstantial status as "honorary" humans. For instance, Denise Riley argues that before the Enlightenment women and men enjoyed a "democracy of the soul."[28] Women were seen as the spiritual, if not the political, equals of men. Once women's spirituality and character began to be defined as distinctly "feminine," man and woman became complementary (and thus even more unequal—there is no longer even a question of the woman imitating the man, as she is considered fundamentally different in her very substance).[29] Riley's arguments trace some of the ways in which women have historically been included and excluded from "humanity." Jean-Jacques Rousseau's comment that "men are only sometimes men, but a woman is always a woman; everything reminds her of her sex," is reworked by Riley to claim that, in fact, women are only *sometimes* women, that they "sway" in and out of gender depending on the context. Her examination of when women have or have not counted as human suggests that the degree to which they have so counted has depended upon the degree to which they were considered to be women "all the way through."[30] In other words, to the extent to which women are seen as "saturated" with gender they recede from full humanity.

Humanity, then, is a category to which women are not easily restored without a fundamental critique of this history. In becoming a prime exemplar of "humanity," redefined as right relation, Ruether's Jesus is feminized. The theological significance of his maleness is meant to be canceled out by his nonmale behavior, yet the category of women remains unchanged. The economy of imitation works here in Ruether's argument to essentialize women as "relaters" and as thus better able (even than men) to "resemble" Jesus. His disavowal of male privilege makes Ruether's Jesus what "women" already (stereotypically) are: relaters, connectors, those who live for others rather than for themselves. If the intention behind this reinterpretation of Jesus's maleness is to redress the historic imbalance of power between men and women, this cannot be done, I argue, by claiming that Jesus *really* represents the kind of humanity displayed more frequently by women than by men. The argument does not work, because Jesus is the only term of the economy of imitation that (seems to have) changed. The economy of imitation that Ruether critiques is simply reversed in her rebuilt Christology: it is now Jesus who resembles women, by engaging in the female-identified ability to model right relationship.

Reinterpreting what it is about Jesus that women can imitate in order to be saved merely redefines the ways in which Jesus can be understood to be like us, or we like him. Attempts to solve the problem of Jesus's maleness by focusing on Jesus's exemplary humanity, as a standard of imitation inclusive of women, rather than on his maleness, a standard that excludes women, nevertheless remain within the same economy of imitation assumed by the posing of the problem. It seems, then, that Jesus's male body (re)materializes in Christology at points where women want most to deconstruct it. Feminist appeals to Jesus's disavowal of his male privilege and his consequent exemplary humanity or relationality as the redemptive aspect of Jesus women need to imitate simply reinstantiate women's bodies as oppositional to Jesus's (male) body. According to the logic of the magisterial statements already dis-cussed, women "naturally" embody and signify the "human" qualities of nur-turing and right relationship, while only men can signify Jesus in his saving aspects. Feminist claims that women, "too," represent the kind of humanity displayed by Jesus recapitulate the terms of the magisterial imitative econ-omy in which women may still not "represent" the divine.

Although these feminist reconstructions of Jesus fail to solve the problem of Jesus's maleness and its symbolic link to redemptive power, they do gesture toward a better understanding of redemptive power as existing only in and through our relations with one another as these emerge from our *citations* of Jesus. A performative and citational reading is better able to account for the ways in which women already *do* "re(as)semble" Jesus. *Re(as)sembly* connotes an alternative to resemblance, since the latter is understood as imitation of or representation of Jesus, a representation from which women are liable to disqualification. Re(as)sembly of Christ denotes communal performances of Jesus rather than individual women's representations. In further specify-ing how Jesus Christ is the norm that is cited to (re)produce the communal Body of Christ, I demonstrate that both poles of the feminist Christological economy of imitation, "Jesus" and "women," form one another in more com-plex ways than can be accounted for by "resemblance."

From Imitation to Performativity: Re-citing Feminist Christology

To *imitate* is "to follow as a pattern, model or example; to be or appear like: resemble; to produce a copy of: reproduce, mimic, counterfeit."[31] The synonyms here imply complete congruence between imitator and original—all but the last, *counterfeit,* which implies falseness, inauthenticity, even dishonesty. According to this definition of imitation, women trying to imi-tate a male figure are doomed to failure. To *perform,* on the other hand, is to "adhere to the terms of: fulfill, carry out, do; to do in a formal manner or according to prescribed ritual; to give a rendition of, present; to carry out an action or pattern of behavior, act, function." If imitation needs an original, performance needs only a script, a text, a ritual, something that is not to be reproduced but to be *cited.* I therefore read feminist Christologies as *perfor-mances* of Jesus, as citational practices, rather than as attempts to replicate a standard. Performances cannot help but recall previous performances, but they need not, and cannot, duplicate them perfectly or entirely.

Butler's notion of performativity as citational, as the power of discourse to produce that to which it "refers," is the lever I use to dislodge both poles, "women" and "Jesus," from the Christological economy of imitation. Butler demonstrates that the body, as "matter," is not best understood as a preexisting site or surface, as the "stuff" upon which gender socialization imprints masculinity or femininity. Rather, the body "materializes," or comes to be understood as preexisting its attribution of sex, only through a repetitive process in which the norms of sex, cited and re-cited, produce that to which they seem to refer. The always already sexed body is an effect of citationality.

For instance, when a newborn (or even preborn) child is pronounced a "girl," this performative statement—"it's a girl"—at once establishes the child's sex, posits that sex as preexisting this performative statement, and compels further citations of the statement (remember, "everything reminds her of her sex"). The girl will continue to be "girled" as the girl herself compulsorily enacts girlhood in accordance with cultural norms of gender by wearing dresses, playing with dolls, or otherwise conducting herself "like a girl." These citations of norms are not merely a matter of the girl's own choice of feminine clothing or of stereotypically feminine pursuits but will also include her unconscious bodily gestures and habits such as her manner of walking. In this way sex is prior to humanity, because one must be understood as a "he" or a "she" before one is understood to have any of the other capacities attributable to "humanity."

It is the repetitive nature of citations of gender, of the acts appropriate to one's "sex," that produce the appearance of sex as natural.[32] But, precisely because citation of gender norms *must* be constantly repeated in order to maintain this appearance of stability or naturalness, citations are subject to slippage and inaccuracy. Our citations of the laws regulating gender are never exact, but are instead more like parody.

Butler describes parody in relation to practices of cross-dressing. Dressing in drag mocks, by foregrounding, the heterosexual norms it is citing. It is subversive in its implicit question, why may only "women" wear dresses or high heels? Why may only *this* gender desire this "opposite" one? The transvestite, Butler argues, invites recognition that it is impossible to completely embody the norms of heterosexuality, or to completely embody any other kind of norm. Parody, for Butler, specifies the relationship between the citation and the "original" as one of radical contingency.[33] In provoking laughter, cognitive dissonance, or even unease, a parody such as a drag performance provokes inquiry into how the standards it mocks came into being.

But the interpretive value of parody is not restricted to the kinds of "intentional" performances represented by drag. Butler extends parody to refer to the citational practices that are necessary in order to be understood as "being" one sex or another. These practices are parodic, even though they are not (always) intentional, because they, too, can never completely live up to the norms they attempt to approximate. For example, sometimes I wear lipstick and sometimes I don't. Am I closer to being a "real woman" on those days that I do wear it? The answer has little to do with my own intention to look feminine or not and much more to do with how others "read" my lipstick or its absence. One may "fail to matter" to others, to be defined as human, or woman, no matter what one's conscious "choice" of identification may be. Identities are fundamentally relational; this is why protesting that I am *really* human does not work unless others agree with me.[34] How others "identify" us is as crucial to our "mattering" as how we see ourselves. "Failing to matter" in one community can be redeemed only in an alternative community.

The feminist impulse to fix "women" as indisputably human, then, fails because the fixing of women as human, just like the fixing of women *as women*, is an arduous and repetitive process. We can never "be" women (just as we can never be "human") completely, can never fully inhabit the norms we cite. Identity, then, is not a pregiven asset or substance but an ongoing *practice* of the citation of certain rules. A sexual identity or a Christian identity is performative, then, in that it materializes through the invocation or citation of certain norms.

How does citationality work in terms of Christian identity, an identity that is not generally understood as "visible" in the way that race or sex generally is and that, moreover, is understood as voluntary in a way that sex or race generally are not? Citationality shifts our gaze away from the fallacy of a preexisting "body" and allows us to scrutinize instead how it is that bodies come to be in *communal* citational processes. Just as being a "woman" is a continued citation of certain culturally intelligible norms of "womanhood," so being a Christian is a citation of certain culturally intelligible norms of "Christianity." Both citations are *corporate*, are manifested bodily, because the norms that are cited are communally constructed and upheld.

Butler's notion of citationality suggests that the inclusion or exclusion of women from humanity and/or from "resembling" Christ is not performed by comparing their "female" bodies with Jesus's "male" body and discovering resemblance or explaining away its lack. This is because Jesus's body and women's bodies do not preexist the moments of their citation but are mutually constructed and reformed in those moments. Because Jesus's body is a canonical text for Christians, citation of Jesus is constitutive of Christian identity. Jesus's "body" provides the material both for patriarchal reification of the maleness of divinity and for feminist resistance to this reification. Jesus is the norm Christians must cite in order to perform Christian identity.

Performance of one's gender and one's Christianity are not "choices" whose intentions are transparent to their observers. Rather, our citations of these identities are out of our conscious control, not only because we can never fully express our intentions in practice but because the effects of our practices escape and exceed us, involving others in ways we cannot predict. This is why it is so hard to counter the logic of the Christological economy of imitation promulgated by the Catholic magisterium that says only men can resemble Jesus as priests. The practice of an identity materializes only in community, in a context in which a particular performance is able to be read as such an identity. The discursive practices that make identity "mean," that materialize certain kinds of bodies, also produce (or fail to produce) some bodies as recognizable.[35] Bodies and identities that do not successfully approximate communal norms are not recognized. The "failing to matter" of bodies, or their abjection, is what feminists protest in the exclusion of women as candidates for ordination.

Inordinate Bodies: the Violence of Constitutive Exclusion

As we have seen, the official Catholic Christological economy of imitation functions in ways that feminists read as harmful to women. This harm is not easily smoothed over or done away with through arguments that reinstate women into the Christological economy of imitation, because this harm takes the form, not only of the exclusion of some bodies, but of the inability of certain bodies to "matter," to be recognized as existing, at all. If agency arises, as Butler argues, only in and through the constraints that compel us into subjectivity, then these constraints may also operate to *prevent* subjectivity, by defining a realm of unintelligible bodies.[36] Butler's deconstruction of the body looks also at the way bodies *fail* to matter, by failing to achieve cultural intelligibility. In bringing to our attention those bodies that cannot fully materialize under the regulatory schemas of normative heterosexuality, Butler indicates the deeper level at which violence and harm to bodies, including women's bodies, needs to be resisted.

Butler argues that identification as a "woman" or a "man" re-cites a normative heterosexist economy in which a "real man" or a "real woman" can be understood only in distinction from its "outside" of homosexuality. In other words, identities materialize partly through the repudiation and refusal of alternative identities; they are defined by what they are not. Heterosexuality and homosexuality come into being together, the one requiring the repudiation of the other. The grids of cultural intelligibility (male/female, hetero-/homosexual) that make it possible for us to identify as men and women also necessarily reinforce standards of unintelligibility that work to keep certain bodies from materializing.

This exclusionary logic applies as well to the economies of Christian identity criticized by feminists. Butler's explanation of the workings of the exclusionary logic constructing sexed bodies is better able to account for the everyday kinds of harm that feminists claim result from practices such as the refusal to ordain women or gender-exclusive language for God. The cognitive dissonance that leads feminists to protest women's exclusion from Church leadership, to criticize male pronouns for God, or to refuse to recommend suffering to women in Christ's name, stems from the different ways these practices prevent women from materializing as subjects. Women cannot materialize in the economy of salvation as other than recipients, while men may be recipients and/or conduits of that salvation. Every man is potentially a priest; no woman can be.

In pushing our analysis to this level, Butler's deconstruction of the body gets at the embeddedness of violence in ways that the feminist reinstantiation of a Christological economy of imitation cannot. It demonstrates that what feminists are really protesting are the ways in which a Christian identity seems to them to call for the suppression or repression of other identities, when "Christian" and "women" begin to seem incompatible or even oxymoronic. When bodies fail to matter in Christian community, I argue, this failure cannot be attributed to pernicious texts or doctrines that need only to be corrected in order to function more benignly, nor to misunderstanding of the "tradition" whose essentially liberating message has merely been distorted or disguised. Rather, this failure is due to any given community's ability to re(as)semble the conventional terms of recognition in ways that allow Christ's Body to matter.

Let us return to the example of women's ordination to demonstrate that the inclusion or exclusion of women as putative representatives of Christ is not decided once and for all on the basis of the preexistence of "sex." The Roman Catholic Church's practice of ordaining only men as a citational practice at once affects women's bodies and Jesus's body. In other words, if Jesus is the standard or norm cited by Church leadership, to which women do not conform, then they fail to "matter" in relation to this standard.

Pope John Paul II addressed a group of American bishops visiting Rome in the spring of 1998, admonishing them to explain to their congregations why the Church does not have the authority to ordain women. In doing so, he did not, this time, refer to the necessity for the priest to resemble Christ *physically*. Rather, he told them,

> As Bishops, you must explain to the faithful why the Church does not have authority to ordain women to the ministerial priesthood. . . . Ordination . . . can never be claimed by anyone as a right; no one is "due" Holy Orders within the economy of salvation. That discernment belongs, finally, to the Church through the Bishop. And the Church ordains only on the basis of that ecclesial and episcopal discernment.
>
> The Church's teaching that only men may be ordained to the ministerial priesthood is an expression to the witness of the New Testament and the constant tradition of the Church of East and West. . . . Jesus himself chose and commissioned men for certain specific tasks.[37]

The pope concludes that "the church's practice of ordaining only men is not a matter of discrimination, but of fidelity to Christ. . . . By reserving ordination to men, the church acts in fidelity to Christ's own example and to the constant tradition of the church."[38] Here, the refusal to ordain women does not rest on the positive attribution of "sex" to women and thus their purported physical or biological disqualification from representing Jesus. The economy of imitation in which the pope's statement operates is not one in which women are precluded from ordination on the grounds of physical dissimilarity. In fact, "women" are altogether absent from the economy. The only "resemblance," the only congruity to be found here, is that between the absence of women and the absence of Jesus's practice in ordaining them. Based on something Jesus did not do, the Church—as Christ's Body—grounds its inability to act in the example of Jesus's inaction.

The refusal to ordain women here rests on the statement's disavowal of authority, a disavowal whose effect is that of occluding women, making them unrecognizable. Jesus's apparent lack of instruction on the ordination of women is employed by the pope as a failure to *subject* women, to make subjects of them, to find a place for them in this Christological economy. Women are not "called" to ordination by this reading, are not *interpellated* in the Church's economy of imitation, because Jesus's textual body does not, on the pope's reading, address women. *Interpellation* is the term used by Louis Althusser to refer to the moment of recognition that inserts us into an economy of intelligibility as recognizable subjects.[39] For instance, when a policeman hails you on the street, "Hey, you," and you turn around in answer to this call, you have been interpellated as a citizen of that jurisdiction: you have recognized that the call applied to you, and you have answered it. Butler explains interpellation as the process by which "the address constitutes a being within the possible circuit of recognition and, accordingly, outside of it, in abjection."[40] To say that women are not "called" to ordination according to the pope's statements is to say that women are constituted outside the Church's "circuit of recognition" as subjects in relation to Jesus and thus abjected. The Church's very identity, the pope seems to be saying, depends on this disavowal of women; they are now the "outside" that must be repudiated in order to maintain the Church's fidelity to Christ.

When women, "as women," then, assert that we are just as able as men to represent Jesus and thus deserve equal consideration for leadership roles in the Church, we find ourselves entirely outside the economy in which this prohibition takes place. It is our position in the grid of (un)intelligibility used by the magisterium that determines our occlusion. An early example of the magisterial position that ordination simply will not "take" on a woman is evidenced by medieval theologian St. Thomas Aquinas, who wrote that

> certain things are required in the recipient of a sacrament as being requisite for the
> validity of the sacrament, and if such things be lacking, one can receive neither the

sacrament nor the reality of the sacrament. Other things, however, are required, not for the validity of the sacrament, but for its lawfulness, as being congruous to the sacrament; and with these one receives the sacrament, but not the reality of the sacrament. Accordingly we must say that the male sex is required for receiving Orders not only in the second, but also in the first way. Wherefore even though a woman were made the object of all that is done in conferring Orders, she would not receive Orders, for since a sacrament is a sign, not only the thing, but the signification of the thing, is required in all sacramental action. . . . Accordingly, since it is not possible in the female sex to signify eminence of degree, for a woman in the state of subjection, it follows that she cannot receive the sacrament of Order.[41]

The Sacred Congregation for the Doctrine of the Faith updates this understanding without essentially altering it: "It is sometimes said and written in books and periodicals that some women feel that they have a vocation to the priesthood. Such an attraction however noble and understandable, still does not suffice for a genuine vocation. . . . Since the priesthood is a particular ministry of which the Church has received the charge and the control, authentication by the Church is indispensable here and is a constitutive part of the vocation: Christ chose 'those he wanted' (Mk.3:13)."[42]

But failing to materialize in this economy does not mean that women thus fail to materialize completely. If it did, this would mean that women belonged only to one economy, one grid of intelligibility. If ordination of women were truly "unthinkable," then Roman Catholic women active in the pro-ordination movement would not be thinking it.[43]

To "cite" Jesus with one's own body, then, as do the seven Roman Catholic women recently "illegitimately" ordained near Passau, Germany, by bishops not officially recognized as being in communion with Rome, is to refer to what appears to be a nonexistent relationship of congruity between Jesus and women, a relationship that takes place only in citation.[44] Women's citations of Jesus are correctives to the (lack of) interpellation performed by the Church's citation of Jesus: they "seek to introduce a reality rather than report on an existing one . . . through a citation of existing conventions."[45] For a woman to take the place of a priest, whether or not she is officially ordained, is to cite the conventions governing who may be a priest. The woman priest's citation recontextualizes the body (and the Body) of Jesus, by putting into question the very conventions she is citing. She is able to do this by occupying more than one economy at a time.

The Church's refusal or inability to ordain women needs to be read, I argue, not as the failure of women to matter but of the failure of the Church to matter. The conventions belonging to the grid of intelligibility that refuse ordination to women do not result in the utter disavowal of women because there are alternative conventions, an alternative Christian "grid," to which women can appeal. Ordination becomes thinkable to Roman Catholic women because Christ is the "other" upon whose address they are fundamentally dependent for their identity as children of God, and Christ does not materialize only in the confines of the institutional Church.

According to this understanding of bodies and identities as citational (rather than imitative), the feminist Christological proposals read above misconstrue "agency" as issuing from only one pole of an imitative economy. If agency and authority are located in the Church's hierarchy, understood unilaterally to mandate certain "imitations" of Christ that demand that women (and men) match up to a preexisting model, then it is understandable that feminists portray resistance to this authority as arising from an individual, autonomous subject who is portrayed as "choosing" her own imitation: of Christ's humanity, or of his right relationality, rather than of his maleness. This understanding of agency and authority transforms power into a possession, and the exercise of power becomes a zero-sum game in which, if one side "has" it, the other side has none.

Understanding identity as citational complicates feminist attributions of "choice" to individual performances of Jesus. Power, in my view, "invests" bodies with meaning. Therefore power cannot be understood as something one chooses to exercise either against or on behalf of another. Rather, one's own bodily investment with power (one's "identity," one's very existence) provides the conditions of possibility for any exercise of agency. Agency and authority are not found either in Church hierarchy or in resisting feminist subjects but instead are created in the interaction between them, in the moment when the very constraints of the "norms" we cannot help but cite (like Jesus's maleness) allow the possibility of our citing them differently and thus reshaping them. "A church involved at the margins of society, a church in dialogue and involved in democratic models, will be a church in which we will look like Christ."[46] In order to explore further the liberating possibilities of citationality, I turn to another feminist proposal for rereading Jesus in relationship to women to see if it can help to dismantle Jesus's male body in ways conducive to furthering the Body that performs him.

Performing the Body of Jesus

Eleanor McLaughlin's essay "Feminist Christologies: Re-Dressing the Tradition" displays in many ways a typical understanding of the "maleness-of-Jesus" problem as an economy of imitation.[47] Yet it offers creative suggestions for how to understand Jesus Christ in a way that would mitigate this problem. Her proposals serve as a thought-provoking test case for how "citationality" furthers the economy of performativity in shifting Christological discourse to a different understanding of relationality.

McLaughlin argues that the most pressing Christological problem for us today is that of gender, of how to understand Jesus as "representing" not only men but women. While liberal theologians dismiss Jesus's gender as theologically insignificant, McLaughlin notes, more conservative churches "understand the maleness of Jesus as a necessary symbol," as relating in a particularly material way to the necessary maleness of the priest as resembling Christ.[48] McLaughlin agrees that theological emphasis on Jesus's *humanity* in preference to his maleness does not work to solve this problem because it ignores the skewing of the category "humanity" to individualistic, male-identified norms. Noting that for first-century Christians it was Jesus's *bodiliness* that provided the stumbling block to understanding Jesus as redemptive, McLaughlin argues that understanding Jesus as embodied *today* means understanding Jesus in terms of female embodiment. If "humanity" is a male-default category in our culture, McLaughlin argues, then "bodiliness" can be represented only by the feminine.[49]

McLaughlin is well aware of the dangers of essentialism in adopting such a position. She appreciates, for example, Caroline Walker Bynum's interpretation of medieval women's devotion to the eucharist as stemming from their (bodily) ability to signify humanity, and thus Jesus, in a way that men, signifying divinity, could not.[50] Yet she also understands that such imagery will not necessarily function in the same relatively liberating way for contemporary women. How can McLaughlin reinterpret Jesus as representative of women without reinscribing the problems of the very gender complementarity she is attempting to critique?

I believe that the risks of this reinscription are high, but that it is worth paying close attention to McLaughlin's constructive argument, because her proposal for how we can understand Jesus as either man or woman offers novel promise for finding a way beyond the "maleness-of-Jesus" problem. McLaughlin's updating of our sense of productive Christological crisis, from the pre-Chalcedonian problem of Jesus's humanity and divinity to the problem of "his" gender, displays the rich theological possibilities of the latter crisis. But her argument must still invoke that humanity and divinity, must "cite" the Chalcedonian "rule," to express the theological force of symbolizing Jesus's gender differently. Her argument thus serves as a good example of citationality, understood as our constraint by the norms that have already formed us, even in forging something "new."

McLaughlin figuratively "re-dresses" the problem of Jesus's maleness by likening him to a transvestite, understood as someone who shatters the opposed duality of male and female. McLaughlin finds that the most salient characteristic of our experience of the transvestite, of a man dressed as a woman, is the suspension of the moment of recognition and definition. The transvestite is neither "he" nor "she," but a "third thing."[51] The transvestite tricks our senses and makes us question what it means to be a "man" or a "woman." McLaughlin, like Butler, characterizes the liberating potential of cross-dressing as parodic. Cross-dressing puts into question the naturalized status of the norms that constitute us as sexed and gendered, norms that map two and only two "genders" onto two and only two "sexes."

Jesus's behavior functions in a directly analogous way to the parodic performance of the transvestite, McLaughlin argues. "He" behaves in a manner inconsistent with our expectations of him as a man, provoking surprise, anxiety, or confusion among his disciples and others. This surprising behavior (eating with the poor and unclean, refusing the traditional boundaries of family, even rising from the dead) shakes up conventional understanding not only of proper gender roles but of the proper relationship between different classes and ethnicities. For McLaughlin, Jesus confounds and multiplies all dualities: male/female, rich/poor, life/death. His practices challenge our attempts to categorize him; he always slips away. Like the cross-dresser, who cannot be plainly designated male or female, Jesus does not fit an either/or definition.[52]

This reading of Jesus allows McLaughlin to play most exuberantly with gender dualities and their reversal. "Christians believe in a Jesus 'dressed' in flesh," she writes, "that most female of symbols, and they believe in a God in man-flesh who behaves like a woman."[53] The transvestite Jesus's "womanly" practices of love, forgiveness, and sacrifice allow us to read him, like Ruether's Jesus, as divesting male privilege. Yet McLaughlin deliberately distinguishes her reading from a "feminized" reconceptualization of Jesus, arguing that the analogy of the transvestite complicates binary gender categories by multiplying the available options. McLaughlin wants to highlight the theological significance of Jesus's transformation of conventional categories. As transvestite, she argues, Jesus is a trickster whose maleness is no longer available for theological reification.[54]

How does the interpretation of Jesus as transvestite open up the possibilities of representation? Does it serve to multiply the terms of the imitative economy, even if, as I shall argue, it does not quite abandon this economy? McLaughlin proffers examples of women who can now participate in a Christological economy of imitation. She sees St. Joan of Arc, along with other female saints who display "male" qualities, and women priests as peculiarly apt embodiments of Jesus' transgressive, cross-dressing figure. These women "represent" Christ because they, too, are tricksters, dressed in cultural (and sometimes literal) garb that codes them as male.

McLaughlin sees particular promise in the figure of the woman priest or deacon, the "woman (dressed as a man, dressed as a woman)" who startles and confounds the gaze of a congregation.[55] Her proposal that we see Jesus as a transvestite is an attempt to startle us into the recognition that women can indeed "represent" Jesus, that their occupation, however "illegitimate," of the conventions of Christ's office changes the contours of that office in surprising and ultimately liberating ways.[56] Her work troubles the very assumptions underlying the Christological dictum that "what is not assumed is not redeemed." Her reading of Jesus as cross-dresser has the effect of displacing our convictions about the "historical maleness" of Jesus. It does this by bracketing more conventional prefaces to feminist discussions of the maleness-of-Jesus problem that hasten to assure us that Jesus *really was* a man, that "the fact that Jesus of Nazareth was a male human being is not in question."[57] The subversive fun of McLaughlin's transvestite Jesus is that, for the moment at least, Jesus's maleness is precisely what is in question. But does the subversion last, and what effects does it have?

I emphasize that what we "recognize" in McLaughlin's momentary subversion of the norm of Jesus is not women's inherent formation according to the divine image, "our" essential resemblance to Jesus that has been obscured by patriarchal misinterpretation. Instead, I read this "recognition" as a claim made by women, such as McLaughlin's priests, who *cite* Jesus. McLaughlin's metaphor of cross-dressing draws our attention to the body as that which is hidden or disguised but, when unearthed, displays the "truth" of the transvestite's identity. The productive disorientation brought about by our confusion, by our being fooled, is only effective when we are able to juxtapose the "real" body against its disguise. If the man dressed as a woman is able to pass for a woman, then the binary norms of the sex-gender system are not subverted but reinforced, "sex" becoming again the raw material for "gender." Does the metaphor of cross-dressing really work as liberating, then, in dismantling patriarchal citations of Jesus's body? That will depend on the economy in which it is invoked.

Read within an economy of imitation, inserting women into Christic roles formerly (or formally) reserved for men may serve only to interpellate them as honorary men. This seems to be one of the reasons why some Roman Catholic feminists, for instance, oppose the ordination of women: simply inserting women into a male-dominated structure, they argue, will not change the contours of that structure. (We might term this understanding, "clothes *do* make the man.") But read within an economy of performativity, as citational, the woman priests' inhabitation of Jesus's position provokes dissonance because it incites simultaneous recognition of two supposedly incompatible things, priesthood and womanhood. She looks right (she is wearing the right things, performing the right movements, saying the right words), but her body belies our reading of her.

What does it mean to say that the truth of the priest's body or of the transvestite's body differs from her imitation? The slippage from imitation, from an "exact copy," to performance, has already begun. McLaughlin's rereading of Jesus as transvestite and trickster begins to pry Jesus loose from "his" fixed position in the imitative Christological economy. Read as a *performance* of Jesus—that is, as the citation of a "male" norm—rather than as an imitation of Jesus, the woman priest/transvestite serves as an example of how both terms in the economy create one another. The woman priest complicates the reproduction of the male-only priesthood as a function of bodily resemblance. Women priests are interpellated in a performative economy that mimes the economy of imitation in which only men can resemble Jesus, thus calling into question the terms of that economy.

The constructive potential of McLaughlin's transvestite Jesus can be elaborated further, then, by revisiting the parodic potential of "citationality." Where McLaughlin sees liberating potential for women in Jesus's confusion of gender boundaries (his behavior is like donning feminine garments), Butler sees liberating potential for gay men and lesbians in the process by which, for instance, homosexual behavior "mimes" conventional heterosexual behavior or gay men in drag "cite" femininity. Citation of gender is parodic in that no one—heterosexual or homosexual, male or female—can ever adequately represent or reproduce the "real" gender relations they are citing. "Citing" one's sexual orientation is performative rather than imitative because "gay is to straight *not* as copy is to original, but as copy is to copy."[58] In other words, gay miming of "straight" norms, or female miming of "male" norms, throws into relief the constructed and unoriginal character of those norms, parodying the very idea of an "original."

But there are no *automatically* liberating consequences to drag. It is not parody in and of itself, as imitation leading to excess, that opens up space for resistance to oppressive norms but the *repetition* inherent to parodic citational practice that does so. Jacques Derrida describes the repetitive property of citationality, explaining that every sign can be placed in quotation marks, can be *cited*, and in being cited can break with every previous context and generate an unlimited number of new contexts. "This does not imply that the [sign] is valid outside of a context," he assures us, "but on the contrary that *there are only contexts without any center or absolute anchoring*."[59] Because a sign, as an identifying mark or norm, can be so detached from its original context and re-cited, women's performances of Jesus can be read as citational practices that recontextualize the Church as the Body of Christ.

I apply these insights about citationality to McLaughlin's construction of Jesus as cross-dresser in order to conclude that "women" are to Jesus not as copy is to original but as copy is to copy. Women's citations of Jesus (as priests or ministers, for instance) call attention not only to the heretofore illegitimate congruities of women's bodies and practice with Jesus's body and practice but to men's likewise illegitimate "representation" of Christ.

Because we cannot ultimately compare ourselves with the "original," we cannot know whether men or women "really" resemble the historical Jesus. The excessive quality of theological emphasis on Jesus's maleness is emphasized when Jesus is "represented" by a woman in "male" drag, or when Jesus is seen as a transvestite. McLaughlin's Jesus suggests that, for women, "representing" Jesus means both "putting on" and subverting the norm that places men closer to Jesus Christ on a divine-human continuum.

Gayatri Spivak's distinction between types of representation is helpful in explaining the nature of this subversion.[60] Spivak notes the inevitability of an "essentialist" moment in any discourse. That is, we cannot escape the moment of positing ourselves as part of a group and thus reinforcing that group as a naturalized entity or essence. In this sense we cannot avoid the identity politics of representation. As an aid to our critical assessment of the others created in such moments, Spivak differentiates between two moments or types of representation. She translates the first as "stepping in someone's place" or "walking in their shoes."[61] This is the kind of representation we think of as political. Our congressperson is our proxy in this sense, for instance; he or she "stands for" us. The second type of representation refers to the portrait of that which is represented. This portrait is always *catachrestic*, argues Spivak, meaning that it has no literal referent. The congressperson cannot encompass her entire constituency in herself. She is not a literal reflection or copy of all of "us."

The first kind of representation, Spivak argues, always includes the second; proxy always includes portrait. This insight needs to be applied to women's relationship of Jesus. Our representation of Jesus, in these terms, is at once a practice of imitation and the citation of a catachrestic norm, one we can never fully live up to. Understanding citation of Jesus as catachrestic underlines the radically situated nature of our claims about Jesus without mourning an unreachable perfection before which women (or men, for that matter) always fall short.

In citing Jesus, then, we are all always copies of copies. The search for an original Jesus is itself a construction of that Jesus. The term *citation* points, as *redressing* does not, to the fluidity and built-in vulnerability of our "representations" of Christ. Citation highlights the artificiality, the constructed character, of norms we inhabit either as "natural," or, equally problematically, as "chosen": norms of gender, of sexuality, of race, of religious identity. Citation destabilizes both ends of the continuum between natural and chosen in ways redressing cannot. It does so by more adequately explaining how the "given" character of that which we experience as given is constructed. Citationality also exposes the fallacy that we can, in resisting harmful consequences of the identities in which we are implicated, choose our own alternative identities in an uncomplicated way. The norms that shape us are not the ones we choose but the ones that have already chosen us.[62]

My preference for a theoretical lens of performativity/citationality, for an economy of performativity rather than of imitation, should not be construed as imparting conscious choice to the process of citation; this is the problem, ultimately, with the cross-dressing analogy. I asked whether or not cross-dressing is able to "dismantle" pernicious citations of Jesus, but performativity/citationality implies that the solidity of the norm of Jesus Christ does not preexist our citations. Redressing works as a metaphor for feminist resistance and theological reconstruction only if we don't think of it as following stripping, which does not reveal an original, just more layers. In other words, it is only in the constant repetition of the norms that constrain us that bodies materialize and that "subjectivity," "agency," or "choice" appear. The citation of the norms that materialize us is always already a condition of our resistance but provides the possibility of their citation to other effects. Because we cannot cite these norms in such a way as to make them wholly present or known, the norms are in fact "known" only in and through their citations. As Spivak observes, "we cannot imitate adequately that to which we are bound," and in performing that to which we are bound we are bound to change it.

Merely recognizing that norms such as "sex" or Jesus's body are performatively stabilized, rather than permanent and unchanging essences, does not lessen their power. We live by these norms, we become recognizable to one another through them. A man "citing" femininity, a woman "citing" priesthood, can be read as undermining the originary and factual status of that norm *or* as reinstating the value of "femininity," of "priesthood." Similarly, not every recitation of Jesus is good news for women. McLaughlin's provocative suggestion that Jesus can be read analogously to a transvestite, and that women who stand at the altar *in persona Christi* reshape this norm through the apparent contrast between their position and their "womanliness," may be profoundly unsettling and liberating to some and for others may serve only to recite women as (sole) bearers of embodiment. This is surely not McLaughlin's intent, but then it is not good intentions that *matter*, in the sense of signifying, materializing, or becoming real. Even subversive citations of Jesus reinvoke the authority of Jesus, of his textual body, to shape our lives. It matters *which* citations we find ourselves inhabiting and which citations these citations themselves compel.[63]

The historical Jesus is the body that haunts feminist Christological reconstructions as pervasively as it does hegemonic ones. I conclude that the inability of women to represent Christ, as understood by feminist critique, is fundamentally a body problem. I also conclude, contrary to feminist fears of poststructural dissolution of women's agency, that deconstruction of the body, including Jesus's body, provides a lot more maneuverability for women in relation to Jesus than do more traditional feminist retrievals of the body. Feminism, and thus feminist theology, grapples with the slipperiness of terms like *body, subject, sex, gender, women,* terms that refuse to be pinned down to serve a feminist politics. This refusal *can* be seen as their weakness, their vulnerability, but when I read the poststructural erosion of these foundations through a Christian lens I find it coded rather—as weakness is so often coded in Christianity—as paradoxical strength.

NOTES

Some material in this essay appeared in earlier form in "The Risks of Repeating Ourselves: Reading Feminist/Womanist Figures of Jesus," *CrossCurrents* 48, no. 2 (Summer 1998), http://www.crosscurrents.org/alliaume. html.

1. "Although the teaching that priestly ordination is to be reserved to men alone has been preserved by the constant and universal Tradition of the Church and firmly taught by the Magisterium in its more recent documents, at the present time in some places it is nonetheless considered still open to debate, or the Church's judgment that women are not to be admitted to ordination is considered to have a merely disciplinary force.

   "Wherefore, in order that all doubt may be removed regarding a matter of great importance, a matter which pertains to the Church's divine constitution itself, in virtue of my ministry of confirming the brethren (cf. Lk 22:32) I declare that the Church has no authority whatsoever to confer priestly ordination on women and that *this judgment is to be definitively held by all the Church's faithful*" (my emphasis). Pope John Paul II, *Ordinatio Sacerdotalis,* May 22, 1994, an apostolic letter to the bishops of the Catholic Church, http://www.usccb.org/pope/letters/52294. htm. See also Sacred Congregation for the Doctrine of the Faith, "Declaration on the Question of the Admission of Women to the Ministerial Priesthood," written and published at the behest of Pope Paul VI, October 15, 1976, http://www. newadvent.org/library/docs_df76ii.htm.

2. The magisterium is the official teaching authority of the Roman Catholic Church, comprised of the bishops in concert with the pope. When speaking as a body on matters of faith and morals, its teachings are held to be infallible.

3. Marcella Althaus-Reid, "On Not Looking Like Christ . . . " *Catholic Women's Ordination,* no. 18 (July-August 2000), pp. 2–7.

4. Jan Jindy Pettman, *Worlding Women: A Feminist International Politics* (New York: Routledge, 1996), pp. 17–21.

5. Pope John Paul II, Apostolic Letter *Mulieris Dignitatem,* no. 27: AAS 80 (1988), 1719, http://www.vatican.va/holy_father/john_paul_ii/apost_letters/documents/ hf_jp-ii_apl_15081988_mulieris-dignitatem_en.html.

6. Sacred Congregation for the Doctrine of the Faith, "On the Collaboration of Men and Women," May 31, 2004, http://www.vatican.va/roman_curia/congregations/cfaith/documents/rc_con_cfaith_doc_20040731_collaboration_en.html.

7. Ibid.

8. Ibid.

9. Ibid.

10. Sacred Congregation for the Doctrine of the Faith, "Declaration on the Question."

11. Ibid.

12. Mark Chaves, *Ordaining Women: Culture and Conflict in Religious Organizations.* (Cambridge: Harvard University Press, 1997), p. 91.

13. Gene Burns, *The Frontiers of Catholicism* (Berkeley: University of California Press, 1992).

14. E-mail communication, May 26, 1998. Thanks also to Ronan for pointing out the links between Chaves's and Burns's arguments.

15. Sacred Congregation for the Doctrine of the Faith, "Declaration on the Question"; my emphases.

16. Rosemary Radford Ruether, *Sexism and God-Talk: Toward a Feminist Theology* (Boston: Beacon, 1983), p. 125.

17. Gregory of Nazianzus, *Epistle* 101, quoted in Walter Lowe, "Christ and Salvation," in *Christian Theology: An Introduction to its Traditions and Tasks*, ed. Peter C. Hodgson and Robert H. King, rev. ed. (Philadelphia: Fortress, 1985), p. 228.

18. The denial that Jesus was fully human is known in Christian theology as *docetism* and is seen as heretical to orthodox Christianity.

19. Lowe, "Christ and Salvation," pp. 228–29.

20. Butler, *Bodies That Matter: On the Discursive Limits of "Sex"* (BTM), pp. 12–16.

21. The notion of a "textual body" is adapted from Jan William Tarling, "'I Went in Bitterness in the Fury of My Spirit': Materializing a Prophetic Body in Ezekiel 1–4," paper presented at the annual meeting of the American Academy of Religion, San Francisco, November 1997.

22. Jacquelyn Grant, *White Women's Christ and Black Women's Jesus: Feminist Christology and Womanist Response* (Atlanta: Scholars, 1989), p. 63.

23. Christine E. Gudorf, "Encountering the Other: The Modern Papacy on Women," *Social Compass* 36:3 (1989), p. 305.

24. See, for instance, Gudorf, "Encountering the Other;" Leonardo Boff, "Quaestio Disputata III: Women's Priesthood and Its Possibilities," in *Ecclesiogenesis: The Base Communities Reinvent the Church*, trans. Robert R. Barr (Maryknoll, NY: Orbis, 1986), pp. 76–97; Eleanor McLaughlin, "Feminist Christologies: Re-Dressing the Tradition," in *Reconstructing the Christ Symbol: Essays in Feminist Christology*, ed. Maryanne Stevens (New York: Paulist, 1993), pp. 119–21; Elisabeth Schüssler Fiorenza, *Jesus, Miriam's Child, Sophia's Prophet: Critical Issues in Feminist Christology* (New York: Continuum, 1994), p. 39.

25. Elizabeth A. Johnson, "The Maleness of Christ," in *Concilium* 6, "The Special Nature of Women?" ed. Anne Carr and Elisabeth Schüssler Fiorenza (Philadelphia: Trinity Press International, 1991), p. 112.

26. Ruether, *Sexism and God-Talk*, p. 135.

27. Ibid., p. 138.

28. Denise Riley, *Am I That Name? Feminism and the Category of "Women" in History* (Minneapolis: University of Minnesota Press, 1988), pp. 18–43.

29. As discussed above, while the hierarchy of the Catholic Church defends the dignity and equality of women, both in statements on ordination and on other matters, it generally adopts a complementary view of gender in which women are separate (in role and vocation) but equal. "It therefore remains for us to meditate more deeply on the nature of the real equality of the baptized which is one of the great affirmations of Christianity; equality is in no way identity, for the Church is a differentiated body, in which each individual has his or her role. The roles are distinct, and must not be confused" (Sacred Congregation on the Doctrine of the Faith, "Declaration on the Question"). See Gudorf, "Encountering the Other" for further analysis.

30. Riley, *Am I That Name?* p. 37, quoting Jean-Jacques Rousseau, *Émile, ou de l'Education* (Amsterdam, 1962; London: Everyman, 1905, p. 321). This oscillation of women's identification as women and as human is not to be construed as women's own choice but as a comment about the different ways oppression "as women" intersects with other forms of oppression such as race, class, ethnicity, sexual orientation, physical disability, etc.

31. *Merriam Webster's Collegiate Dictionary*, tenth edition (1994). All further definitions are from the same source.

32. Butler, *Gender Trouble: Feminism and the Subversion of Identity* (GT), p. 33.

33. Butler, GT, pp. 137–38.

34. Here Christian feminist theologians have a resource with which to counter official theological tradition on its own terms: we may argue that God is the "other" who agrees that we are human. See below.

35. Butler, BTM, pp. 15–16.

36. Ibid., p. 3.

37. Pope John Paul II, "Priest's Ministry and Spiritual Life Are Intimately Connected" (*Ad Limina Apostolorum*-6), *L'Osservatore Romano,* weekly edition in English, May 27, 1998, p. 5; online database, Eternal Word Television Network, http://www.ewtn.com.

38. Cindy Wooden, "John Paul II to Bishops: You Must Explain That Women Cannot Be Ordained!" *Catholic News Service,* May 22, 1998.

39. Louis Althusser, "Ideology and Ideological State Apparatuses (Notes Toward an Investigation)," in *Lenin and Philosophy and Other Essays,* trans. Ben Brewster (New York: Monthly Review Press, 1971), pp. 170–77.

40. Butler, *Excitable Speech: A Politics of the Performative* (ES), p. 5.

41. St. Thomas Aquinas, *Summa Theologica*, part 3 supplement, question 39, article 1 (Benziger Bros. edition, 1947), trans. Fathers of the English Dominican Province, http://www.ccel.org/a/aquinas/summa/XP/XP039.html#XPQ39A1THEP1.

42. Sacred Congregation for the Doctrine of the Faith, "Declaration on the Question."

43. For instance, the Women's Ordination Conference has been working for women's

ordination and related issues in the Catholic church for twenty-seven years. See website at http://www.womensordination.org.

44. John L. Allen Jr., "Seven Women 'Ordained' Priests June 29," National Catholic Reporter Online, July 1, 2002. http://www.natcath.com/NCR_Online/archives/071902/ordinations.htm.

45. Butler, ES, p. 33.

46. Althaus-Reid, "On Not Looking Like Christ."

47. McLaughlin, "Feminist Christologies," pp. 118–49.

48. Ibid., p. 119.

49. Ibid., pp. 127–28.

50. See Caroline Walker Bynum, *Holy Feast and Holy Fast: The Religious Significance of Food to Medieval Women* (Berkeley: University of California Press, 1987).

51. McLaughlin, "Feminist Christologies," p. 139. McLaughlin borrows the term *third thing* from Marjorie Garber. See Garber, *Vested Interests: Cross-Dressing and Cultural Anxiety* (New York: Routledge, Chapman and Hall, 1992).

52. McLaughlin, "Feminist Christologies," pp. 141–42.

53. Ibid., p. 144.

54. Ibid., pp. 141–42.

55. Ibid., p. 139.

56. For a more detailed study of the signifying effects of women's bodies as ministers, see Elaine J. Lawless, "Writing the Body in the Pulpit: Female-Sexed Texts," *Journal of American Folklore* 107, no. 423 (1994): 55–81.

57. Johnson, "Maleness of Christ," p. 108.

58. Butler, GT, p. 31.

59. Ibid., p. 12; my emphasis.

60. Gayatri Chakravorty Spivak, "Practical Politics of the Open End," in *The Post-Colonial Critic: Interviews, Strategies, Dialogues*, ed. Sarah Harasym (New York: Routledge, 1990), pp. 108–9.

61. Ibid., p. 108.

62. Butler, GT, p. 127. Postmodernism has not so surprising affinities with theology in its interventions: both claim that our lives and bodies are not "our own" in the way that modern construals, including feminist versions, would have us think.

63. See Butler, BTM, p. 13.

In all the futures I have walked toward
I have seen a future I can hardly name.
      —Muriel Rukeyser, *Body of Waking*

Vital then, that we widen the "I" that we are as much as we can.
      —Jeanette Winterson, *Art Objects*

5. UNCONFORMING BECOMINGS: The Significance of Whitehead's Novelty and Butler's Subversion for the Repetitions of Lesbian Identity and the Expansion of the Future

CHRISTINA K. HUTCHINS

Inclusivity, Categorization, and the Discourse on Gays and Lesbians in Churches and Society

At the turn of the millennium in the United States many Christian churches are theologically positioning themselves in relation to, or reaction against, various considerations of lesbian and gay lives in social and religious institutions. The wrenching emotional and ecclesial turmoil characterizing the debates suggests that far more than academic abstractions are at stake in the shiftings of cultural concepts of identity and the relational construction of the subject. Drawing on theoretical interactions of process and deconstructive postmodernisms, this chapter points to the importance of understanding identities as processes of becoming that can open novel possibilities for the future of Christianity and of humanity itself.

In the past decade rifts have widened between those who believe that lesbians and gay men should be fully included in religious, social, and political life and those who oppose the full humanity and participation of "practicing" homosexuals.[1] An extreme of the latter position, the Religious Right, attempt simultaneously to regulate the heterosexual nuclear family *and* access to God and political power by fixing the "naturalness" of heterosexuality onto a Christian identity defined in binary opposition to "homosexual" identity.[2] Yet even those who risk a great deal to work for the full inclusion of gays and lesbians, including many queer[3] people, often attempt to regulate terms of the debate in ways that can be understood as heteronormative (displayed, e.g., by the increasing focus on "gay marriage"); that is, they often "fix" the identity of lesbians and gay men in binary opposition to heterosexuality, citing the genetic, biological origin of same-sex orientation, with the unwitting effect of reifying dominant cultural categories. By utilizing essentialist arguments in the debate surrounding lesbian and gay lives in religious and social insti- tutions, do even progressive positions threaten to narrow social and sacred possibilities for our shared and open-ended future?

As a member of the United Church of Christ, a liberal denomination marked by a prominent and public stance of affiliation of gay and lesbian persons and relationships, I am both grateful for and troubled by the terms of discourse surrounding the inclusion of gay, lesbian, bisexual, and trans- gendered persons in church and society. I am grateful, because as an "out" lesbian and an ordained minister, I can inhabit a still-too-rare space of voice, visibility, and community. I am troubled, however, because positions of inclu- sivity increasingly rely on essentialist arguments and heteronormative con- structions of social and religious acceptability.[4]

Essentialist arguments depend upon and reify an ontology based on the metaphysics of substance as the hermeneutical lens for interpreting human identity. Therefore they reinforce the Cartesian subject/object split and the subsequent binary oppositions of "self" and "other," exemplified by the sen- tence, "I am _____ because I am not _____." Such binary oppositions inevi- tably fund culturally oppressive dualisms, since even nonhegemonic identi- ties are implicated in, enforced, and created by the same repressive regimes they may be seeking to resist. In other words, when the second blank space in this sentence is occupied by a hegemonic identifier such as "white, man, straight, wealthy, physically able, or Christian," the first blank space becomes dependent upon its opposition to the second for its own self-definition. In such a way nonhegemonic identities may be understood not as essential dif- ferences but as cultural constructions, which even when used as resistance, may continue to reify hegemonic powers of definition and binary categoriza- tion, reinforcing the universalizing tendencies of dominant positions. Thus essentialist positions, utilized by those arguing for greater inclusion of lesbi- ans and gay men in churches, however progressive in comparison with the overt exclusion of the Religious Right, do not escape the heteronormatively privileged straight/gay binarism. Such binary oppositions limit the possibili- ties of the future and replace the concrete reality of the complexities and dynamisms of human relationships with abstracted categories constructed as dualistic opposites. The naturalization of cultural categories, the plac- ing of man/woman and gay/straight as *opposites* becomes one characteristic of what Judith Butler calls the "fiction of compulsory heterosexuality." For Alfred North Whitehead such a substitution or act of mistaking of abstract categories of thought and social construction for the relational dynamisms of actuality commits the gravest of philosophical errors, the "fallacy of misplaced concreteness."[5] The immensity of the error cannot be underestimated, because when we believe that the categories have more concrete reality than the creative motion of actuality we narrow the possibilities of and for the future. To mistake constructed categories, such as the heteronormatively privileged straight/gay binarism in church conversations on lesbian and gay inclusion, for actuality or "nature," limits the freedom and power of love that Christianity claims as its raison d'être and narrows the possibilities for future human relationships in general.

This chapter explores identity understood as ongoing, creative process(es) in which "the subject" always exists only in relation to, and as a result or effect of, the event of her own becoming, an event that is at once *both* freely shaped by the becoming subject *and* limited, formed, and deformed by its context. In order to personalize and concretize an otherwise abstract exploration, I offer an example of a recent denominational gathering in which, as a participant, I found myself wondering what it means to "be" a lesbian, a question that problematizes issues of representation, identity, and categorization that are often obscured in the debate surrounding lesbian and gay lives in religious and social institutions. After a brief extension of categorization and identity politics into the more philosophical questions of essence and ontology, the essay proceeds by way of an active juxtaposition of ideas from the process metaphysics of Whitehead with insights of Butler on performativity and the fluid, always-in-process, iterating subject.[6] I analyze the relationships between repetition and novelty (Whitehead) and repetition and subversive resignification (Butler) and conclude by addressing the political effectiveness and religious significance of the dynamic insights generated by the interplay of Butler's and Whitehead's thought. My thesis is that an emphasis on the "unconformity" (nonconformity + unconventionality) by which the repetitions of lesbian identity are performed destabilizes the very institutions and cultural categories in and by which that identity is shaped. Such destabilizations open and broaden the public space for future becomings, expansions that carry religious significance, as does the manner in which such destabilizations act as lures for increasing the experiential richness, dynamism, and intensity of human existence.

Some Discursive Problems with Representation, Identity, and Categorization

One sunny Saturday morning in May of 1997 members of the United Church of Christ (UCC) in northern California entered into deliberate conversation about multiculturalism and identity in the UCC and in our wider society, Each participant had been carefully selected to represent a particular identity group.[7] I was asked to "be" the "lesbian."

I had agreed to be present, but nonetheless remained uncomfortable at being asked to *represent* "lesbians" as an identity group and at how that act necessarily would exclude from view or voice those who may not live out or understand that identity as I do. Any attempt to speak *for* lesbians carries in it an assumption that there is some essential character that we commonly share. I was aware of my own privilege in being a part of the conversation and of a heavy and impossible responsibility to those not present.[8] I was also disturbed at the idea of fixing *my own identity* in a primary way to the category of "lesbian." Not only has my own sexuality been fluidly expressed in a variety of ways over my lifetime, but by naming myself within the category of "lesbian," I was defining myself *as a fixed identity* (and perhaps a rather reductively sexualized identity) rather than as a subject *in ongoing, multiple processes of becoming*. In addition, the fixed identity of "lesbian" is a category that has been named and projected with attributes and values by the hegemonic position of compulsory heterosexuality in the discourse of our culture and religious traditions. While the planners of the multicultural discussions had some sensitivity to issues of race, sexual orientation, and other "isms," the fact was that there were a designated "gay" and "lesbian" but no "heterosexual" representative. All other participants of various ethnic and social categories were presumed to be heterosexual, an unexamined operation of heteronormativity in which gay men and lesbians were being defined as "Other."[9] By using the category "lesbian," how would I be allowing that category, and thus the dominant view or hegemonic norm, to define me? By doing so would I be actively reinforcing the binary terms of the dominant discourse? How would I be affecting and perhaps foreclosing relational possibilities in, for, and of the future?

Each participant was asked to state in a single sentence the most important gift that our "identity group" brings to the wider gathering of the United Church of Christ. When my turn came, I said, "My name is Christina Hutchins, and I was asked to participate as a lesbian." As soon as the word *lesbian* was pronounced, I noticed an instant hush in the room, a kind of snapping into a deeper listening. That word certainly claims people's attention. Feeling that tiny and vast pause, I tried to discern what might be the most politically effective and religiously significant response to the question that we'd been asked. I actually ended up voicing *two* gifts that I think lesbians particularly bring to the larger church: 1. an insistence on an embodied faith and 2. a sense that identities are culturally constructed rather than natural, fluid rather than fixed or given, and that the categories themselves and acts of categorization, while often helpful, are also restrictive.[10] The remainder of this chapter is an expansion of the second statement: that the *destabilization* of identity categories is a gift that lesbians bring to the wider church.[11]

Essentialism and Ontology

Questions and concerns about identity, inclusion, exclusion, subjectivity, representation, and categorization are relevant to dilemmas surrounding what it means to be a representative subject. When we make "I am" statements, such as "I am a woman," "I am a lesbian," "I am a feminist," or "I am a Euro-American" (an identifier that, by the way, is usually used as an adjective rather than as a substantive noun like "lesbian"), we are usually making particular claims not only about what categories we "belong to" but also about what it means to *essentially be* who we are. To begin to question one's identity categories also initiates a critique of one's *essentialism* and one's *ontology*. Essentialism is the notion that one has or can be primarily defined by a central characteristic or "core" shared with all others "within" a category, such that I might have a shared "essence" as a woman, a white person, a lesbian, or even as a human being.[12] *Ontology* involves the underlying way(s) in which culture defines what it means "to be" or to exist as a human being.

While drawing on a supposed common "essence" has often been useful for feminists and for gay men and lesbians in particular political contexts, including many church contexts, it is important to ask what (and *who*) such essentialism obscures, invisibilizes, and excludes. When a person is asked to define herself by a single, defined category, such as "lesbian," in the situation above, she is being asked to choose *between* parts of herself, to claim that one identifying characteristic or behavior, such as sexual orientation, is more *essential* to her being than another, such as race, age, class, income, or educational level.[13]

The feminist theorist Jane Flax points out a different problematic face of essentialism: "Man and woman are posited as exclusionary categories. One can be only one gender, never the other or both." Likewise, categories of sexuality are oppositionally defined, creating a problem not only for bisexuals but in and for the freedom of expression of sexual desire in general. Flax continues: "gender relations have been (more) defined and (imperfectly) controlled by one of their interrelated aspects—the man."[14] Not only is "woman" set in essential opposition to "man," and "homosexual" defined only in mutual oppositional relation to "heterosexual," but the exact nature of the oppositions and the various facets of the "essential nature" of "woman" or "homosexual" have been constructed in service of more or less conscious purposes of domination.[15]

Often either "God" or "nature" (or both, as is the case with some religious conservatives) are named as authorities in the definitive act of essentialist claims. In secular and political arenas many thinkers, as well as our mass media, draw upon "nature" in the form of biological and/or psychological theories of origin/archetypes to justify definitions of essentialism. The historian

Thomas Laqueur well describes our current two-sex model undergirded by a widespread biological essentialism of "hormones and other chemicals that are meant to serve as a sort of ontological granite for observable sexual differences."[16] In broad-based political discussions of gay/lesbian identities, whenever questions of "the cause" of homosexual behaviors come up (questions that are themselves hegemonically generated), it is amazing how much more "accepting" many people *seem* if they can be assured that such behaviors result from genetically determined, biological essentialism rather than from an indeterminate number of factors, including free choice and cultural construction. While often politically useful, the reliance on biology in justifying homosexual behaviors omits so much of what it is to be queer: layers of history carried in/on the body, freedoms to relate sexually and otherwise in noncoercive ways as one *chooses* and finds joy and satisfaction in a relationship.[17] Is it possible that we are constraining ourselves *politically* and *religiously*, as well as personally, by allowing acceptance to revolve around biological essentialism rather than a more creative way of being human? Is it possible that by utilizing essentialist arguments we are narrowing social and sacred possibilities, doing irreparable damage to our shared and open-ended future?

Teresa de Lauretis offers several helpful definitions of "essence": "1. Absolute being, substance in the metaphysical sense; the reality underlying phenomena. 2. That which constitutes the being of a thing, that 'by which it is what it is' . . . Objective character, intrinsic nature as a 'thing-in-itself.'"[18] She reminds us that questions of essentialism are related to those of ontology and the metaphysically fixed subject. In fact, it is through philosophical questions and critiques of ontology that the problematic limitations of essentialism may be most profoundly and clearly addressed. Most modern philosophies, ethical theories, and theologies have assumed an ontologically fixed subject as a starting point for philosophical thought, human agency, and divine relation: a "doer" precedes her (actually, it's usually *his*) deeds and processes of relation. Certainly the UCC leadership who set up the categories at the denominational multicultural event I attended assumed that the "selves" who *fit* into a particular *identity group* would do so from basically fixed subject positions. However, with deconstruction, the "fixed or "foundational" nature of the choosing subject loses its authority as an automatic assumption or starting place for thought or action. In fact, the "subject" falls to pieces; the "subject" becomes *subjectivity*, a shifting, fully contextualized, nonunified perspective inseparably related to its world. Chris Weedon expresses this shift quite clearly:

> Subjectivity is produced in a whole range of discursive practices—economic, social and political—the meanings of which are a constant site of struggle over power. . . . Moreover for poststructuralism, subjectivity is neither unified nor fixed. Unlike

humanism, which implies a conscious, knowing, unified, rational subject, poststructuralism theorizes subjectivity as a site of disunity and conflict, central to the process of political change and to preserving the status quo.[19]

In other words, "being" a subject no longer exists; rather, one is always in the act of "becoming" a subject: subjectivity is a process. "Against [the] irreducible humanist essence of subjectivity, poststructuralism proposes a subjectivity which is precarious, contradictory and in process, constantly being reconstituted in discourse each time we think or speak."[20] Whitehead and Butler each offer philosophical insights that reach toward a nonessentialist subjectivity. In the sections that follow, their approaches are analyzed in terms of politically and religiously significant insights for reconstituting discourse and opening a relational future less constricted by the fixing grip of normative categories defined and regulated by the status quo.

Metaphysics and Deconstruction: Universals and Antifoundational Thought

Bringing Butler and Whitehead together itself suggests a fairly unconventional academic practice. Butler is widely recognized as representing the contemporary deconstructive "edge," her work informed in primary ways by Friedrich Nietzsche, Jacques Derrida, Michel Foucault, and the poststructuralist unfastenings of the rational, universalizing foundations of modernist discourse.

Whitehead, on the other hand, the author of the 1928 *Process and Reality*, is often understood primarily as having created a "metaphysics," a massive construction that attempts rationally and universally to account for experience through systematic claims. However, this difference between the two may not mark as wide a gap between them as an oversimplification of each of their positions might make it appear. In addition to enhancing the reach of both thinkers in relation to the social and religious significance of fluid subjectivities, I hope to demonstrate some general affinities between poststructuralist claims and process thought. While I propose neither to *apply* the entire metatheory of process metaphysics to Butler's thought nor to comprehensively *critique* process thought using the work of Butler, I do want to utilize places of overlap or affinity between the two. Therefore, the tensions or contrasts between Whitehead's metaphysics and Butler's deconstructive antifoundationalism warrant a brief examination.

Whitehead's development of process thought (or "philosophy of organism," as he called it) in many ways qualifies as a metaphysics, based as it is in part on observations of post-Newtonian physics: the basic notion that what *seems to be* substantive matter can be understood as dynamic interplays of energy. Though Whitehead's philosophy does attempt to explain the total-ity of the universe through the notion of creative acts of becoming, it also understands itself as historically generated and conditioned. For Whitehead and other process philosophers, the cosmos is composed of open-ended, plu-ral processes, as is, necessarily, the *ongoing* philosophical task. Whitehead writes, "In philosophical discourse, the merest hint of dogmatic certainty as to finality of statement is an exhibition of folly" (PR, p. xiv). This whimsical admission of uncertainty, along with Whitehead's methodological commit-ment to begin and end each philosophical thinking-act in the particularities of experience, loosens up much of what might otherwise now be read as an oppressive metatheory. Not only is there nothing absolute in his claims,[21] but "hermeneutical scheme" might be a better phrase than "metaphysics" for characterizing Whitehead's attempt to provide "generic notions that add lucidity to our apprehension of the facts of experience" and a frame of "gen-eral ideas in terms of which every element of our experience can be inter-preted" (PR, pp. 10, 3).[22] In fact, what Whitehead calls "metaphysics" "is nothing but the description of the generalities which apply to the details of practice" (PR, p. 13).

In addition, the concern and content of Whitehead's endeavor is a delib-erate departure from the metaphysics that so much postmodern thought also attempts to abandon. Poststructuralist and process critiques of metaphysics share the distinction of aiming their reformulations primarily at the meta-physics of *substance*. Butler, for instance, describes her task in *Gender Trouble* as "the challenge for rethinking gender categories outside of the metaphys-ics of substance" (*GT*, p. 25). Likewise, when Foucault, whose genealogical method Butler takes up and expands, distances himself from "metaphysics," he attacks the same metaphysical system that Whitehead is concerned with unhinging: the metaphysics of substance, which limits itself to singular ori-gins and linear relations of cause and effect: "If interpretation were the slow exposure of the meaning hidden in *an* origin, then only metaphysics could interpret the development of humanity. . . . The development of humanity is [instead] a series of interpretations. . . . They must be made to appear as events on the stage of historical process."[23] In outlining the role of genealogy, Foucault describes a method and worldview that resonate in many ways with a process-oriented metaphysics. In fact, Whitehead's project can be under-stood as a motion from a substance-oriented metaphysics, with its Carte-sian subject/object split and singular cause and effect relations, to a more postmodern worldview, an interrogation of *how* "interpretations . . . appear as events on the stage of . . . process."

Butler's clear developments and extensions of poststructuralist figuring of identities as constellations of multiple and unstable positions create poten-tial tensions with Whitehead's stretch toward metaphysical universalization. However, while Butler explicitly distances herself from any task "which would articulate a comprehensive universality," she does not undo the category of "the universal" altogether. Perhaps because realities are shaped and constrained by foundationalist claims, which attempt to totalize and thus "shut down rather than authorize . . . unanticipated claims," she understands "the universal" as a category that must be left "permanently open, permanently contested, permanently contingent, in order not to foreclose in advance future claims for inclusion."[24] Because the primary universal in Whitehead's metaphysics is "creativity," which by definition is open-ended, plural, and unfixed, as well as always contingent and conditioned, it is interesting to place Whitehead's "universal," the "principle of *novelty*" (PR, p. 21) in direct conversation with Butler's urgent stance that the very category of the "universal" must be "a site of insistent contest and resignification" ("Contingent Foundations," p. 7).[25] While Butler hopes that her work has "no normative ground," she does admit to a "normative direction," a motion of expanding and complexifying the views of what categorical identities might be, "without filling in the content of what that's going to be."[26]

In terms of "the universal," she writes, "I am not trying to do away with the category, but trying to relieve the category of its foundationalist weight in order to render it as a site of permanent political contest" ("Contingent Foundations," p. 8).[27] In order to do so she suggests that we "pursue the moments of degrounding, when we're standing in two different places at once; or we don't know exactly where we're standing; or when we've produced an aesthetic practice that shakes the ground. That's when resistance to recuperation happens" ("Gender as Performance, p. 122). Thus, Butler's antifoundationalism occurs in her unwillingness to fix, purify, or totalize the meaning or content of a particular category in comprehensive ways, which would foreclose future possibilities. She is not saying, however, as her detractors often claim, that *there are no* foundations; rather, she claims "that wherever there is one, there will also be a foundering, a contestation" ("Contingent Foundations," p. 16). For those parts of each of us and of our social relations existing "outside" of hegemonic norms, such founderings and contestations are a way of life, a survival mechanism. I suggest that such contestations also expand future human relational possibilities, in general, and that such dynamic expansions are motions of the holy.

In exploring lesbian identity as (an) ongoing process(es) of becoming in the sections that follow, I hope to convey a sense of motion that Butler and Whitehead each reach toward but have difficulty expressing in a grammar still based on a metaphysics of substance. The notion of becoming is an apt point of linkage between the two thinkers. Not only does it refer back to Nietzsche's metaphor of becoming, which both thinkers invoke, but *becoming* carries an inarticulable sense of motion, of the possibilities of an unknown future.[28]

Whitehead: Process Thought

Whitehead's philosophy of organism is perhaps most succinctly expressed by Whitehead in the statement, "Process is the becoming of experience" (PR, p. 166). Whitehead, along with certain other American philosophers, for example, Charles S. Peirce, William James, John Dewey, and Charles Hartshorne, attempted to develop a philosophy, cosmology, or hermeneutical system that would begin not with transcendental reason but with the dynamism of experience and a view of reality as social process.[29] Process thought reconceives of matter as process, act, or event. "Actual entities," which are also called "actual occasions," "are the final real things of which the world is made up. There is no going behind actual entities to find anything more real" (PR, p. 18). Actual entities are events or moments of "concrescence," of the *becoming* of a "subject." They are atomistic becomings, blips, noncontinuous moments, drops of existence, and they "perish" as soon as they have fully "prehended" their universe. Prehension involves an occasion's taking into its "becoming," by the act of valuing either positively or negatively, the contents of its context, the past occasions, and then integrating the felt content of that context (those occasions) into the shape of its own becoming. A "prehension . . . involves emotion, and purpose, and valuation, and causation" (PR, p. 19) so that the "becoming" of a moment of subjectivity is a moment of *feeling* every other entity in its universe. Process thought can be understood as a metaphysic of feeling, of felt valuation, a hermeneutic both aesthetic and ethical, because acts of prehension are decisions, never neutral, always involving value judgments of inclusion and exclusion. In this way all events or actual occasions are self-creative, though our language is problematic, since that "self" is only apparent in the event itself.[30] "*How* an actual entity becomes determines *what* that actual entity *is*. . . . Its 'being' is constituted by its 'becoming.' This is the 'principle of process'" (PR, p. 23).

This process is always "atomistic": the act of becoming is also an act of perishing. Since "'becoming' is the transformation of incoherence into coherence, and in each particular instance ceases with this attainment" (PR, p.25), existence is discontinuous. The observed world has a more or less seeming continuity or coherence only because there is a constant unfolding of infinite acts of self-determination. This self-creative process is shared, in Whitehead's view, by the tiniest atoms and subatomic energy particles, stars, galaxies, trees, God, rocks, and humans. In the case of humans and rocks (and, for Whitehead, God) there are "real individual facts of the togetherness of actual entities, which are real, individual and particular. . . . Any such particular fact of togetherness among actual entities is called a 'nexus'" (PR, p. 20). When such a nexus is related temporally, that is, "forms a single line of inheritance of its defining characteristic," it is called an "enduring object."

It "enjoys a personal order" and is a "society" (PR, p. 34).[31] Every human embodies or conjoins a complex "society" or "nexus" composed of countless, multiple becomings related both temporally and spatially. As humans we can say that we *are* or *have* consciousness, corporate feelings, a body. We *become* bodily, both unconsciously and consciously: "It is by reason of the body, with its miracle of order, that the treasures of the past environment are poured into the living occasion. . . . It receives from the past; it lives in the present" (PR, p. 339).

Repetition plays a crucial role in process thought. Enduring objects result from multiple repetitions of occasions that occur with more or less exactness or variety. For a rock or a table fewer and smaller variations happen in and between repeated acts of becoming than for a living tree or a human woman. Repetition acts as a means by which feelings are intensified to the point of physical sensations and consciousness. The body concentrates the past, moving related past occasions toward consciousness. "Intensity," which Whitehead believes characterizes the direction into which the universe (*multiverse* might be a more accurate term) is increasing and moving, arises "from the force of repetition" (PR, p. 253). When repetitions occur with a sense of what Whitehead calls "width," which is both an aesthetic and ethical term for positively prehending with greater depth, breadth, and clarity the possible contrasts in any particular act of becoming, greater complexity and intensity are expressed in the acts of becoming. The responsibility of *how* we become, of determining *who* we become, moment by moment, is ethically and aesthetically informed by how deeply and clearly we feel the complexities, the contrasts of the contexts or universe that surround and enter into those becomings. "The savouring of the complexity of the universe can enter into satisfaction only through the dimension of width . . . the function of width is to deepen the ocean of feeling" (PR, p. 166).[32] Increases in complexity and intensity of acts of becoming open more possibilities for future becomings.

And yet, though concrescence, or becoming, is a self-creative act, in that it carries the responsibility for how and therefore what/who it becomes, "the character of an actual entity is governed by its datum" (PR, p. 110). We are limited, constrained in the repetitions of our becoming by what Whitehead calls "stubborn fact." Thus, process thought simultaneously develops *both* a kind of artistic freedom for the creative play of self-shaping of the becoming subject *and* a kind of determinism, a sense of limitation—inscribed upon and into the act of becoming—by the reality of that which already exists.

In terms of the problems raised by categorically defined identities, Whitehead effectively addressed some of the issues of essentialism and fixed ontology by positing, like poststructuralist views half a century later, a subjectivity in process. Whitehead writes, "The philosophies of substance presuppose a subject which then encounters a datum, and then reacts to the datum. The philosophy of organism presupposes a datum which is met with feelings, and progressively attains the unity of a subject. But with this doctrine, 'super-ject' would be a better term than subject" (PR, p. 155). "Subject," because it implies stasis, or something fixed, is problematic for Whitehead. By using "superject" he conveys the motion of efficient causation: the completed and perished "becoming" of one "subject" affects subsequent "becomings." The "subject" is always a subject arising out of the process of prehending its past, its context, *and*, having perished, affecting other, future processes of becoming by being prehended by those concrescing others.

Performativity and the Deconstruction of Fixed Identity

Butler begins her article "Imitation and Gender Insubordination" with a complaint that "being" is too fixed of a category for her comfort. She writes, "the prospect of *being* anything, even for pay [she has a great sense of humor], has always produced in me a certain anxiety, for 'to be' gay, 'to be' lesbian seems to be more than a simple injunction to become who or what I already am" ("Imitation," p. 13). Part of the discomfort comes in the realization that "identity categories tend to be instruments of regulatory regimes," such that Butler says she is "permanently troubled by identity categories, consider[s] them to be invariable stumbling-blocks, and understand[s] them, even promote[s] them as sites of necessary trouble" ("Imitation," pp. 13, 14). She would like it to remain "permanently unclear" precisely what is being signified by a sign that says "Lesbian" under which she is willing to stand at a political occasion. In addition, she claims that "pleasure" is produced for her by the instability of the category.

For Butler, what we experience are performative moments of identity, which share some affinities with Whitehead's actual occasions. She writes playfully about being invited to a public speaking event *as* a lesbian:

> When and where does my being a lesbian come into play, when and where does this playing a lesbian constitute something like what I am? To say that I "play" at being one is not to say that I am not one "really"; rather, how and where I play at being one is the way in which that "being" gets established, instituted, circulated, confirmed. This is not a performance from which I can take radical distance, for this is deep-seated play, psychically entrenched play, *and this "I" does not play its lesbianism as a role.* Rather it is through the repeated play of this sexuality that the "I" is insistently reconstituted as a lesbian "I."
>
> ("Imitation," p. 18)

There are several key ideas packed into this description. First of all, identity is *performative*, which for Butler means "constituting the identity it is purported to be. In this sense, gender [and sexual orientation] is always a doing, though not a doing by a subject who might be said to preexist the deed" (GT, p. 25). Thus, when Butler "plays at being lesbian," this play constitutes the *reality* of her being lesbian. She is always becoming. This is serious play, because it determines not only *who* she is and will become, but affects the future possibilities of the cultural discourse in which it takes place. She plays "with" and "in" the mechanisms or motions by which categorical identity is established, instituted, and circumscribed. Cultural discourse takes place not only—or even primarily—*within* her, but by her act of playing with/out the ways in which she is externally, culturally inscripted. Butler continues by exploring this "play" as a process of repetition:

> paradoxically, it is precisely the *repetition* of that play that establishes so well the *instability* of the very category that it constitutes. For if the "I" is a site of repetition, that is, if the "I" only achieves the semblance of identity through a certain repetition of itself, then the "I" is always displaced by the very repetition that sustains it. In other words, does or can the "I" ever repeat itself, cite itself, faithfully, or is there always a displacement from its former moment that establishes the permanently non-self-identical status of that "I" or its "being lesbian"?
>
> ("Imitation," p. 18)

Any sense of a "stable" identity results from, is an effect of repetition, as is the "instability" of the category itself. *Becoming* involves *repetition* because each performative instance is both discrete, displacing the "former moment," and delimited, shaped by, and inseparably related to that former moment and to the constraints that preceded and shaped its relation with its context. *Citation* is the act of this repetition within the relational dynamism of the process, and, because of the dynamism, repetitions never happen with exact uniformity or sameness. In *Bodies That Matter* Butler writes, "let us remember that reiterations are never simply replicas of the same" (BTM, p. 226). The sense that an identity, such as that of lesbian or woman, is fixed, stable, *like* an essence, comes about through the "sedimentation" of these repetitions over time within particular power dynamics. "The process of that sedimentation or what we might call *materialization* will be a kind of citationality, the acquisition of being through the citing of power, a citing that establishes an originary complicity with power in the formation of the 'I'" (BTM, p. 15). This means that while Butler retains and amplifies deconstruction's critique of essentialism, she also opens a way of understanding and still being able to speak from subject positions: We can say "I am a woman" or "I am a lesbian." The idea of sedimentation allows for the feelings and intimations we experience *as* essences, norms, and continuities within hegemonic culture. Without sacrificing the iterated dynamism of performativity, sedimentation allows us to talk about and form experienced categorical identities without drawing on a metaphysics of substance that philosophically naturalizes those identities as essences. Identity can be understood as provisional, as culturally constituted and constrained, and an identity category can be viewed as a repeated site of relational dynamism:

> The repetition of one's subjectivity is not a choice. Nor can it be stopped: The subject is not *determined* by the rules through which it is generated because signification is *not a founding act, but rather a regulatory process of repetition* that both conceals itself and enforces its rules precisely through the production of substantializing effects. In a sense, all signification takes place within the orbit of the compulsion to repeat: "agency," then, is to be located within the possibility of a variation on that repetition.
>
> (GT, p. 145)

Not unlike process thought, both the inevitability of the repetition and the limitations of the datum, "stubborn fact" for Whitehead or "rules of signification" for Butler, confine the possibilities of becoming. However, there is still the notion that *how* one becomes affects *what* and *who* one becomes and the wider future of discourse itself. To be constituted by discourse is not necessarily to be determined by discourse. Though inscription is relational and societal, and though iteration happens under and through the force of prohibitions, there is nonetheless a self-creativity or agency possible *in the activity of varying the repetitions.*

Butler focuses this creativity of variation in and through the example of "drag." In the inevitable process of repetition, compulsory heterosexuality has set itself up as an "original way of being" or "the essence of identity," a regulatory norm that is to be copied moment by moment and generation by generation. Butler calls it "the regulatory fiction of heterosexual coherence" because it is a "fabrication manufactured and sustained through corporeal signs [like clothing and bodily gestures] and other discursive means" ("Gender Trouble, Feminist Theory," p. 336) and is widely believed to be the only "coherent" way to put a life together. By performing "drag" a lesbian, gay, or transgendered person not only replicates the culturally constructed heterosexual compulsory repetition in a way that parodies those constructs but she or he also *resignifies* those constructs, becoming a *deinstituting* repetition. By bringing "into relief the utterly constructed status of the so-called original," the resignification of drag shows that "heterosexuality only constitutes itself as the original through a convincing act of repetition. The more 'act' is expropriated, the more the heterosexual claim to originality is exposed as illusory" (GT, p. 31). Parody becomes a strategy of resistance; drag—playing between or with "mismatches" of gender—becomes a practice that in imitating gender implicitly reveals the imitative structure of gender itself and draws attention to those processes that consolidate identities.[33] In other words,

> drag enacts the very structure of impersonation by which any gender is assumed. Drag is not the putting on of a gender that belongs properly to some other group. . . . Drag constitutes the mundane way in which genders are appropriated, theatricalized, worn, and done; it implies that all gendering is a kind of impersonation and approximation. If this is true, there is no original or primary gender that drag imitates, but *gender is a kind of imitation for which there is no original.*[34]
>
> ("Imitation," p. 21)

For Butler subjectivity *is* performative. Identity and identity categories are neither essential nor fixed, nor the outcome of some inner substance of who we are, waiting for fulfillment. Rather, identity is formed *in moment by moment activity*, an activity that requires and creates/constructs a body and is sedimented through time.[35] In the introduction to *Bodies That Matter* Butler claims that a part of her project is

> a rethinking of the process by which a bodily norm is assumed, appropriated, taken on as not, strictly speaking, undergone *by a subject*, but rather that the subject, the speaking "I," is formed by virtue of having gone through such a process of assuming a sex; and a linking of this process of "assuming" a sex with the question of *identification*, and with the discursive means by which the heterosexual imperative enables certain sexed identifications and forecloses and/or disavows other identifications.
>
> (BTM, p. 3)

To the extent that she has found a way to understand the "subject" as constituted or occasioned by the performative process, and the subject's particular cultural "identity" as an effect or occasion of that process, Butler offers a wonderful tool for deconstructing identities as belonging to fixed categories. The object is not to do away with categories or coalitions altogether, but to understand them as *permanently unfixed, open sites of becoming and cultural valuation,* where individuals and culture itself are constantly reified, redefined, and redefining. In Butler's words,

> The antifoundationalist approach to coalitional politics assumes neither that "identity" is a premise nor that the shape or meaning of a coalitional assemblage can be known prior to its achievement. Because the articulation of an identity within available cultural terms instates a definition that forecloses in advance the emergence of new identity concepts in and through politically engaged actions, the foundational-

ist tactic cannot take the transformation or expansion of existing identity concepts as a normative goal.[36]

(GT, p. 15)

In addition, Butler hints that lesbians, in particular, inhabit a unique site within cultural discourse. Because lesbians experience oppression partly through being considered "a domain of unviable (un)subjects—*abjects,* we might call them—who are neither named nor prohibited within the economy of the law," who inhabit a "domain of unthinkability and unnameability," we perhaps embody or perform unique possibilities for rendering ourselves "visible" beyond "existing regulatory regimes. . . . Lesbianism is not explicitly prohibited in part because it has not even fully made its way into the thinkable, the imaginable, that grid of cultural intelligibility that regulates the real and the nameable. How, then, to 'be' a lesbian in a political context in which the lesbian does not exist?"("Imitation," p. 20).[37] Though Butler's 1988 suggestion that the lesbian does not exist may not now be quite so uncontested (after "Ellen" has come out on prime-time TV and all), I think it is still relevant. Her further question, "Can the exclusion from ontology itself become a rallying point for resistance?"("Imitation," p. 20), remains with me as a very hopeful possibility.[38] Butler's question suggests that an exclusion from cultural intelligibility may also involve an exclusion from the tyranny of the fixed subject and thus from the metaphysics of substance. Each day people throughout the world are killed and kill each other in the name of identity politics. How might our visions, parameters, and worldviews shape human relations if we based those visions and worldviews not on fixed subject positions and identities but on the creative and fluid acts of multiple becomings? How do we imagine, discover, and perform such politics, ethics, and theologies into existence? How might insights drawn from nonfixed identity subjectivities move into our existing, identity-based habits of relating, thinking, and believing in ways that heal and liberate human relations in academic institutions, in the broad social institutions of media and government, and in the various religious organizations we rely upon to emancipate and vivify our lives?

The Importance of Repetition and of "Resignification" or "Novelty"

Though the two projects differ in purpose, method, and proposed scope, I believe that Judith Butler's well-nuanced development of social identities as effects of hegemonic discourse displays several shared affinities with Alfred North Whitehead's process thought. Both share a sense of a fluid, creative subjectivity that shapes and is shaped by the activity of becoming a "subject" in relation with the confines of the repetitions of the "subject's" context or past reality. These dynamic models abandon the metaphysics of substance in order to understand matter itself as a process and to characterize the "subject" as an *effect* of performativity (Butler) or as a concrescent *event* (Whitehead).[39]

Each mode of thought also develops both complex, nondualistic relations between the reality of being conditioned and constrained by the world (discourse or datum) that is inescapably inscribed into/onto our becoming and the agency of the self- and future-creating activity of performance or concrescence. In Whitehead's philosophy, which involves not only cultural inscription but the inscription of the entire universe, every actual occasion is both determined ("the datum both limits and supplies" [PR, p. 110]) and free ("each concrescence is to be referred to a definite free initiation and a definite free conclusion" [PR, p. 47]). Butler, too, unhinges the oppositional "either/or" between agency and cultural constructedness and constraint. Near the end of *Gender Trouble*, she writes, "the feminist discourse on cultural construction remains trapped within the unnecessary binarism of free will and determinism. Construction is not opposed to agency; it is the necessary scene of agency, the very terms in which agency is articulated and becomes culturally intelligible" (GT, p. 147).[40] For Butler the fluidity of subjectivity means that we are simultaneously and inseparably *interpolated into* systems that preexist us (a notion she uses from Foucault) *and* we have to actively *become* moment by moment, reminiscent of Simone de Beauvoir's notion of becoming a woman: "One is not born a woman, but rather becomes one."[41]

The necessary, inescapable repetition of becoming, for both Whitehead and Butler, carries in itself hope of and for the future, because repetition is the way in which *novelty* (Whitehead) or *subversive resignification* (Butler) can enter into the ongoing processes of discourse in the world. Butler writes,

> for if the performance is "repeated," there is always the question of what differentiates from each other the moments of identity that are repeated. And if the "I" is the effect of a certain repetition, one which produces the semblance of a continuity or coherence, then there is no "I" that precedes the gender that it is said to perform; the repetition, and the failure to repeat, produce a string of performances that constitute and contest the coherence of that "I."[42]
>
> ("Imitation," p. 18)

For Butler it is the "string of performances" that both "constitute and contest the coherence" of the subject that creates a space for the creative activity of subversively resignifying the self and the categories of discourse themselves. This is perhaps the clearest and most vivid and crucial of the affinities between Butler and Whitehead. Whitehead writes,

Thus an enduring object gains the enhanced intensity of feeling arising from contrast between inheritance and novel effect, and also gains the enhanced intensity arising from the combined inheritance of its stable rhythmic character through-out its life-history. It has the weight of repetition, the intensity of contrast, and the balance between the two factors of the contrast.[43]

(PR, p. 279)

For Whitehead the experience of the contrast between inheritance and novelty or, using Butler's words, between constituting and contesting the coherence of the enduring "I," is "an intense experience of aesthetic fact" (PR, p. 279). The experienced contrasts increase the intensity of experience and are thus *aesthetically and ethically* valuable: "All aesthetic experience is feeling arising out of the realization of contrast under identity" (PR, p. 280). I find this insight of Whitehead's returning me to Butler's sense of the trouble and the pleasure of working with and from identity categories. "In fact if the category [of lesbian] were to offer no trouble, it would cease to be interesting: it is precisely the *pleasure* produced by the instability of those categories which sustains the various erotic practices that make me a candidate for the category [of lesbian] to begin with" ("Imitation," p. 14). Identity categories, then, can be sites in which to experience the *intensity* of feeling and the aesthetic *pleasure* of creating ways of subverting those very categories. Finally, in the dance between the two, Butler's Foucauldian invocation of the *pleasure* of troubling categories turns toward the esteemed place *enjoyment* holds in Whitehead's endeavor. Becoming itself is enjoyment.[44] And particular enjoyment floods from the prospect of broadening future relational possibilities through the realization of increased contrasts in one's present becoming. "The function of being a means is not disjoined from the function of being an end. The sense of worth beyond itself is immediately enjoyed as an overpowering element in the individual self-attainment" (PR, p. 350).[45]

For both Whitehead and Butler, the deep-seated play of contrasts is both aesthetically pleasurable, a felt enjoyment of efficient causation (Whitehead), and an ethical responsibility. The future opens outward: its possibilities and its limitations open out from the playful juxtaposition of contrasts and affinities in the becoming of the present moment. In a sense, for both thinkers, we live both for and into ourselves and, at the same time, for and into an undetermined future where the activity of our becoming will deeply and irrevocably affect the possibilities of future becomings. The actions of our performativity *matter*. They have no purely private meaning or value but extensively effect and affect one another's futures.

The past flows into the present through the becoming occasion from which particular future possibilities will be rendered. Whitehead calls this effective motion "creativity." It is *the* "universal" in his metaphysics. "'Creativity' is the principle of *novelty*. . . . The 'creative advance' is the application of this ultimate principle of creativity to each novel situation which it originates" (PR, p. 21). For Whitehead creativity means not only that the universe and the possible increase of intensity, complexity, and plurality expand endlessly, but that the ongoing, multiple unfoldings of reality are uncontrolled, uncontrollable, and the future is unknowable and fully open. He writes, "Thus, if there is to be progress beyond limited ideals, the course of history by way of escape must venture along the borders of chaos" (PR, p. 111). Butler shares with Whitehead this sense of excitement and trepidation at the realization of the dynamism of the processes in which we participate. If there is no closure on the category (and there can never be complete closure), a category can and will be a site spawning unexpected and uncontrollable permutations. While Butler writes not of "novelty" but of "resignification," strong affinities surface between Whitehead and her far more developed notion of power relations:

> The effects of performatives, understood as discursive productions, do not conclude at the terminus of a given statement or utterance, the passing of legislation, the announcement of a birth. *The reach of their significance cannot be controlled by the one who utters or writes, since such productions are not owned by the one who utters them.*[46]
>
> (BTM, p. 241; my emphasis)

In other words, "the incalculable effects of action are as much a part of their subversive promise as those that we plan in advance" (BTM, p. 241).[47] We live with both the risks and the promise as well as the relief of not being able to control the unknowable reaches of our resignifying activities that creatively subvert the hegemonic norms, the novelty of our own becomings that enter the world.

Toward Some Conclusions: Unconfoming Becomings

So, then *what*, in the midst of these provocative connections that remain speculative and abstract, unless connected to particular, embodied, contextual events, might carry *political effectiveness and religious significance* in the world in which we come into being? How might we utilize categories of identity in ways that subvert their hegemony and open novel possibilities for human relationship? What *matters* here and how? For instance, what, in the debates over inclusion of gay men and lesbians, do churches *miss* when conversations are focused and limited by heteronormative essentialism and a metaphysics of substance? How might such debates obscure particular and ongoing creative revelations that queer relationships embody and engender within communities of faith? And, if we do not deliberately question our ontological assumptions, how might the vivifying pulse or motion of the holy, which the Christian faith claims as its raison d'être, be obscured or even diminished by notions such as the binary opposition of genders, of hetero/homosexualities, and of the divine and the human with assumptions of the fixed essence of the human person and declarations of Christian identity claiming an essential unity of all who are "one" in Christ?

I return to the denominational gathering where, as the representative "lesbian," I said that identity is more fluid than the stated categories and that, however useful or helpful those categories, they also confine and restrict us. As soon as I voiced that thought aloud most of the people in the room, including the planners of the event, who were four straight, white clergy males in their sixties (an interesting group to be planning multicultural discussions and creating a list of categories with which nonhegemonic others are to "self-identify," though, the fact is, it was through their commitment that the event occurred at all), said, "yes, yes, yes, you're right." One of the members of the planning team added, "Yes, these categories are, after all, just categories. We are, after all, all human together. We are all *one* in Christ." Inwardly, I immediately asked, "*Whose* definition of 'we,' of 'after all,' of 'all,' of 'human,' of 'together,' of 'one,' of 'Christ' . . . *yours*?" Why did those who, though not necessarily less progressive ideologically, nonetheless benefit most from hegemonic norms so quickly agree that categorical identities are transcendable and perhaps disposable? Why the hurry to move to a sense of *unity*, of being *one* together? Why can't we just remain *many* together: many people, many Christianities, many ways, without foreclosing the conversations that might, over time, reveal the effects of our power relations on the very real differences between us?[48] And what are the possibilities of *using* our differences to effect change on those power relations? Is it possible that the categories are necessary sites for undoing the very binary oppositions that define and reify them?

In that situation I immediately regretted having spoken of the fluidity of identity from a site that people who comfortably live the hegemonic norm of compulsory heterosexuality would rather not have to acknowledge after all. If hegemonic society functions by co-opting the energies, creative insights, and discourses of nonhegemonic positions, why should it be any different with ideas of a fluid, becoming subject, which arrive on the scene just when the category of lesbian (as with categories of race and gender) is becoming a problematic, disruptive voice and thus a *reality* in the dominant discourse?[49] But, if having only my single sentence or two, it was not expedient to bring up the fluidity of identity and the problem of categorization, without being able to more fully explain how radical antifoundational thought undercuts the essentialist, ontological assumptions of the dominant discourse, what might I have said instead?

If we are, as humans, fluidly and necessarily repeating (performing) whatever cultural categories we live and are defined by, it is in the *unconformity* (nonconformity + unconventionality) *within the forcefield of expectations of compulsive and compulsory repetition* that the creative power of novelty (Whitehead) and subversive activity of resignification (Butler) reside. And it is in *emphasizing* that aspect of our fluid identities, by publicly articulating the *nonconforming, unconventional* character of our repetitions, that we have the most effectiveness in destabilizing the hegemonic assumptions that underlie the categories of identity politics. The subtlety of emphasis in Butler's work is on the subversiveness, and in Whitehead's aesthetically informed metaphysic the ethical impulse finds expression in the "width" produced by including increased contrast within and by performative iterations. At this time and place it does not seem expedient (or possible) to do away with the category "lesbian" itself and to collapse into the cultural invisibility and lack of voice of a hegemonic "one." Neither is that the intent of Butler's antifoundationalist approach. She *does* seek to undermine and complexify the understanding of "lesbian" as stable, unified, or fully defined within and by available cultural terms. She writes, "The assumption of its essential incompleteness permits [the] category to serve as a permanently available site of contested meanings. The definitional incompleteness of the category might then serve as a normative ideal relieved of coercive force" (GT, p. 15).[50] If categorical identities remain in a sense inescapable, never merely descriptive but always normative and therefore exclusive, the work of becoming focuses on making those categories sites of permanent openness and instability. Increased agency only becomes possible in the midst of the dynamic unfixing and expansion of the categories that constrain.[51] For a lesbian involved in the ongoing processes of becoming in, by, and in resistance to the effects of compulsory heterosexuality, what matters are *how* the iterations carry and reveal contrasts and thus can begin to differ from that which is expected. Rather than citing iterations that seek unobtrusively to increase cultural coherence or to slip into adapted cultural universals, it is the active, playful, parodic citations, those that refuse to unproblematically conform to conventional binarisms of sexuality and gender, that reveal the confines of the norms that seek to prohibit human difference and relational complexification. The intense, powerful, beautiful play of embodied, seemingly unresolved contrasts opens new ethical and aesthetic dimensions. The novel conjunctions and disjunctions of such iterations dissolve the hegemonic binary oppositions that numb and limit social relationality, and they trouble the categories of woman and man, feminine and masculine, gay and straight, human and divine. In other words, effecting structural change politically and religiously requires that the *differ-*

ences by which we are differently inscribed make ourselves differently than the expected norms *be made visible, audible*.

I wish I had said at the denominational gathering that lesbians bring not only a willingness to break silence and step into visibility, but that we do so in ways that by their *unconforming becomings* constantly stretch and redefine the very institutions and categories in which we reside, thus revealing their permanent incompleteness. This is a gift that those persons and relationships "outside" of hegemonic norms bring to the wider churches and to the wider culture. When novelty and subversion enter and (re)form the experiential processes of identity formation, the creative space or freedom (future possibilities) for all human becoming expands. The *public articulation of unconformity* enables its disruptive and creative power to enter into the conscious discourse of social change, reminding us that public space for social change lives always already right in our midst.[52] The space of becoming resides in the instability and incompleteness of the categories we live by, always shrinking or expanding according to the ways in which we iterate and articulate our becomings. The expansion of public space for the discourse of becoming carries significance for and beyond the political. In the language of religious intuition, such expansion embodies the motion of the holy.

To articulate those becomings that *unconform* hegemonic or dominant norms *expands* the future space of and for becoming. More possibilities become available for prehension by future occasions, and those possibilities carry within them a greater degree of contrast or width and thus a capacity for more—and more intense—internal relations with other possibilities in future becomings. Butler characterizes this as the work of "assisting a radical resignification of the symbolic domain, deviating the citational chain toward a more possible future to expand the very meaning of what counts as a valued and valuable body in the world" (BTM, p. 22).[53] For Whitehead the expansion involves an extension of and into future potentialities, of and for dynamic interconnections in the world.[54] To contribute to an expansion of future relational possibilities is an act of hope, of resistance to the tyranny of compulsory heterosexuality, in particular, and to the metaphysics of substance, in general, and the reliance of that metaphysics on binary oppositions that function culturally as hierarchical dualisms. Because hegemonic forms remain dominant by actively seeking to narrow down possibilities available for the becomings of the future, the sense of expansion, of breaking open space for the future is particularly important for gay/lesbian/queer persons and for others who live at the "margins" or "beyond the borders" of dominant cultural paradigms.[55]

To enter into the expansive motion of creativity, by subversive resignification or by becoming *differently*, with a greater degree of width, and thus more novelty, even (and especially) among and within and limited by the repetitions of the dominant society, is to participate in and with a *holy motion*. The interplay between Butler's and Whitehead's dynamic insights is extremely useful in the articulation of this experiential process, an articulation that allows the process and its invaluable, subversive, and creative power to enter into the conscious discourse, the speech acts, and actual world of social change.

The Expansion of the Future: Divinity and Excess, Responsibility and Hope

Whitehead's concept of divinity offers one way of connecting the motion of expanding relational possibilities with that which is holy. Whitehead's God can be understood as the motion of creativity characterized into its primordial and consequent trajectories, lure and memory. "Viewed as primordial," God "is the unlimited conceptual realization of the absolute wealth of potentiality . . . the lure for feeling, the eternal urge of desire" (PR, pp. 343–44). The primordial nature is not *before* act(s) of creation but is *with* creation; likewise, the consequent nature is not *after* "but in unison of becoming with every other creative act" (PR, p. 345). The consequent character reflects a reaction of the world on God, on/into the reservoir of future possibility: "This final phase of passage in God's nature is ever enlarging itself" (PR, p. 349), a motion that expands the "wealth of potentiality" for the primordial trajectories. I understand this motion of the expansion of future relational possibilities as holy, as the freedom and power of love, a revelation that Christianity claims and embodies yet too often has obscured by the "fallacy of misplaced concreteness," by categorical imperialisms that reify a metaphysics of substance, and by the violence of attempting to contain and control the always plural dynamism of creative love breaking open new possibilities.

In addition to opening future relational possibilities, unconforming repetitions can be viewed as politically powerful and religiously significant, *holy*, partly because, by their *intensity*, they act as lures for further felt experiences. In a society and in religious institutions where uncritical, automatic repetitions within hegemonic norms predominate, conforming becomings (assuming dominant cultural habits of prehension or signification) may be experienced as confining, as dreary and "unfulfilling," however thoroughly those losses are concealed. Whitehead writes of the "tedium arising from the unrelieved dominance of fashion in [European] art" (PR, p. 339). A kind of cultural fatigue and listlessness result from repetitions that lack "width," variety, subversion, critical novelty, from repetitions that gradually shrink public spaces of becoming. The limitations iterated into human becomings by the unrelieved dominance of binary gender norms and compulsory heterosexuality, and by the assumption that categories and institutions are definitionally complete, are experienced as such "tedium." In the midst of that "tedium" often unacknowledged needs and yearnings pulse, barely discernible: long-ings for new and creative ways to experience deepened aesthetic pleasure and conscious ethical commitments, desire for active participation in the critical reshaping of relational possibilities for society and our own lives. Voiced dif-ferences of unconforming becomings reveal themselves as politically power-ful and religiously vital *tools* as well as experiences, because the creation of novel conjunctions not only embodies the motion that expands our universe but also acts as a *lure for further engagement*. By presenting novel possibili-ties for creativity's further conditioning, unconforming becomings respond to the pulse of a world yearning for intensity. While novelty in itself is neither life-giving nor destructive, it opens future possibilities that are necessarily disruptive, uncontrollable, and multiple, and therefore intensely terrifying, interesting, and exciting. The possibilities presented by novelty draw forth, elicit in human becoming, both the aesthetic pleasures and the ethical com-mitments of further creative, subversive, constructive activity.

Finally, in addition to utilizing Butler and Whitehead to demonstrate some general affinities between poststructuralist claims and process thought, I claim that the intensities created by novel categorical constructions, which arise through iterated contrasts between genders, sexual desires, and behav-iors of lesbians, not only act as lures for further felt experience of contrasts but open a broader future. When novelty and subversion (re)form the expe-riential processes of identity formation, the creative space or freedom for all human becoming expands. In this expansion we might recognize a motion of the holy. In particular, for Christians, the motion of perpetual categori-cal remaking, opening, dissolving, breaking, and expansion characterizes the discipleship that Jesus of Nazareth taught and lived. Such ongoing expansion of the relational future is a call that institutional churches, in fixing creeds and scripture, in regulating marriage, ordination, conditions of membership, and, perhaps most of all, Christian identity as primarily gendered and het-erosexual—thus establishing both human and divine identities as essentially separate, culturally independent, and complete—have sadly, hugely failed. The attempt to fix, confine, control, or entomb the creative motion of love that expands the relational future characterizes the concept of idolatry. To seek to free the ever expanding relational performativities of love character-izes a holy motion that forms, informs, and reforms human and divine lives.

In conclusion, the juxtaposition of Butler and Whitehead offers two con-nected directives: responsibility and hope. Both remind us of *the responsi-bility involved in our own activities of becoming*. Whitehead writes of "the insistent craving that zest for existence be refreshed by the ever-present, unfading importance of our immediate actions, which perish and yet live for ever more" (PR, p. 351). And Butler asks, "if repetition is bound to per-sist as the mechanism of the cultural reproduction of identities, then the crucial question emerges, What kind of subversive repetition might call into question the regulatory practice of identity itself?" (GT, p. 32). How might we turn each of the categorical sites in which we repeat our lives into a perpetual site of dynamic complexification? How might we ask ourselves, "What kind of subversive repetition might call into question the present and future constraints set into this moment of becoming?" Agency happens in pursuing and naming the moments of unconforming becoming, moments that exceed and thereby shift the categorical limitations we live in and by. Responsibility involves a constant carrying along with us—in the ongoing activities of our becomings—something like Whitehead's awareness of the "unfading importance of our immediate actions" and Butler's continual question, "What kind of subversive repetition might call into question" the very regulatory practices we live by?

Hope resides in the process(es), in the multiplicities and excesses of becoming. This contextualized, process-oriented critique of culturally imposed dominance contains and offers a possibility of trusting in the process itself. In addition to underlining the responsibility involved in ongoing creation, Whitehead suggests relaxing into what he calls "the multiple freedom of actuality" (PR, p. 349). He writes,

> The social history of mankind exhibits great organizations in their alternating functions of conditions for progress, and of contrivances for stunting humanity. The history of the Mediterranean lands, and of western Europe, is the history of the blessing and the curse of political organizations, of religious organizations, of schemes of thought, of social agencies for large purposes. The moment of dominance, prayed for, worked for, sacrificed for, by generations of the noblest spirits, marks the turning point where the blessing passes into the curse. Some new principle of refreshment is required. . . . Life refuses to be embalmed alive. The more prolonged the halt in some unrelieved system of order, the greater the crash of the dead society.
>
> (PR, p. 339)

Life's refusing "to be embalmed alive" resonates with Butler's notion of the "excess that necessarily accompanies any effort to posit identity once and for all" (GT, p. 143). Butler, too, in addition to pointing to the necessity of the play, work, and responsibility involved as our identities are continually reiterated, relates a trust in the process itself. "Excess" is characterized by that which exceeds, disrupts, or cannot be contained or expressed within, by, or through categorical "sites" of identity such as gender, race, or sexual orientation. Excess describes that which cannot be expressed in or by any single performative category, binary opposition, or act of identity yet, despite all regulatory regimes and institutional powers, persists. If Whitehead's language about God offers one way of characterizing and valuing the motions of expanding relational possibilities into and for the future, I believe that Butler's invocation of excess is another way of naming those motions as sacred or holy, though Butler does not do so. For Butler, excess is that which is systematically denied by the traditional philosophical notion of a fixed, volitional subject and by the habitual processes of categorization that characterize our thought, language, and ways of relating with one another. Excess orients itself toward and into the open and unknowable future: "the effects of an action always supersede the stated intention or purpose of the act" ("Contingent Foundations," p. 10).[56] I characterize excess as that which no site can fully contain, as a holy motion that broadens public space, a catalyst on which future freedoms depend. The "gaps and fissures" that bear the promise of the future are opened by "that which exceeds the norm . . . that which cannot be wholly defined or fixed by the repetitive labor of that norm" (BTM, p. 10).[57] In this spilling toward the future, Butler implies a guarded hope:

> How then to expose the causal lines as retrospectively and performatively produced fabrications? . . . Perhaps this will be a matter of working sexuality against identity, even against gender, and of *letting that which cannot fully appear in any performance persist in its disruptive promise*.
>
> ("Imitation," p. 29; my emphasis)

And what exactly *is* "that which cannot fully appear" but "persists" in its "disruptive promise?" Is it power, the invisible, the holy? Perhaps "that which cannot fully appear" both obscures and points not toward "it"—not to a metaphysical substance—but to the motion(s) of a *how*. If so, that which "refuses to be embalmed alive" and "cannot be fully known" is no *noun*, but a *verb*, the creative process itself, the bursting open, the novel connecting, the queering, dissolving, fracturing, and excessive blooming, the expansion of social and sacred possibilities for our shared and open-ended future. If we participate in the blooming and queering, the fracturing and novel connecting, if we unconform our own becomings, we will participate in the relational expansion of an undreamable future. Perhaps, in the midst of the pleasure of that conjoined responsibility and hope, we might name the motion, that verb which cannot fully appear: love . . . or might it be play?

NOTES

1. I use *gay, lesbian,* and *homosexual* deliberately here, aware that I am excluding bisexual, transgendered persons, and other sexual minorities from the "debate." But I do so not because I want to simplify the terms or contestability of the conversations. On the contrary, I hope to demonstrate that it is precisely the degree to which a straight/gay binarism operates as definitional—thereby reifying a metaphysics of substance—that reiterates and conserves the "simplifying" norms of compulsory heterosexuality, constraining broader relational possibilities.

2. See Kathy Rudy's helpful exposition, *Sex and the Church: Gender, Homosexuality, and the Transformation of Christian Ethics* (Boston: Beacon, 1997). Rudy analyzes the Christian Right's commitment to re-create the gendered theology of the nineteenth century's Cult of Domesticity, in which access to God depended on the binary opposition of gender. Rudy also explores not whether gay people should be allowed to "fit" into churches but which historically gay practices, including gay male promiscuity as a model for Christian community, might renew and invigorate contemporary churches.

3. I occasionally use the word *queer* in this chapter, a term that seeks to play off of the energy of reversal from its common derogatory usage. Queer, according to Annamarie Jagose, "describes those gestures or analytical models which dramatize incoherences in the allegedly stable relations between chromosomal sex, gender and sexual desire. . . . Queer locates and exploits the incoherences in those three terms which stabilize heterosexuality"; Jagose, *Queer Theory: An Introduction* (New York: New York University Press, 1996), p. 3.

4. For example, essentialist views often come into play when tolerance is based on assertions of biological or genetic determinism, being "born that way." Tolerance or acceptance based on essentialist views tends to be inclusion "into" heteronormativity. That "acceptable" lesbian and gay lives must be heteronormatively constituted is exemplified by the UCC's 1997 General Synod statement on "fidelity in covenant." While not using the phrase "heterosexual marriage" (in deference to the 1985 statement of affirmation of gay and lesbian persons), the 1997 statement affirms only covenanted, monogamous, partnered relationships. Thus the "otherness" of the binarism is not undone but simply shifts to "other" nonhegemonic relations or identities, such as nonmonogamy, promiscuity, and excessive gender blurring. "Inclusion" then becomes not about the free motion of love but about being heteronormative.

5. Whitehead calls "the fallacy of misplaced concreteness" an "overstatement" of generalization: "This fallacy consists in neglecting the degree of abstraction involved when an actual entity is considered merely so far as it exemplifies certain categories of thought"; Alfred North Whitehead, *Process and Reality: An Essay in Cosmology*, ed. David Ray Griffin and Donald W. Sherburne, corrected ed. (New York: Free, 1978), pp. 7–8.

6. Process insights are drawn primarily from Whitehead's *Process and Reality*, hereafter cited as PR. In this chapter I draw primarily from Butler's article "Imitation and Gender Insubordination," in *inside/outside: Lesbian Theories, Gay Theories*, ed. Diana Fuss (New York: Routledge, 1991). I also use insights drawn more broadly from "Gender Trouble, Feminist Theory, and Psychoanalytic Discourse," in *Feminism/Postmodernism*, ed. Linda J. Nicholson (New York: Routledge, 1990) and other major works by Butler concerning the deconstruction of fixed gender identity.

7. Identities included in the conversation were Samoan, Filipino/American, African American, commonwealth countries, Native American Hawaiian, congregational Christian, seniors, youth, gay, lesbian, Urban, multiracial, rural, other Protestant, Catholic, Asian American, metropolitan (between suburban and urban), small town, suburban, and Euro-American.

8.   An interview between Gayatri Chakravorty Spivak and Sneja Gunew in *The Cultural Studies Reader*, ed. Simon During (New York: Routledge, 1993) contains an interesting discussion of, among other things, representation. Spivak says, "this question of representation, self-representation, representing other, is a problem. . . . And there has to be a persistent critique of what one is up to, so that it doesn't get all bogged down in this homogenization; constructing the Other simply as an object of knowledge, leaving out the real Others because of the others who are getting access into public places due to these waves of benevolence and so on. I think as long as one remains aware that it is a very problematic field, there is some hope" (p. 198).

9.   Being able to "choose" or be representative of only *one* identity group is particularly difficult for people who "fit" more than one nonhegemonic category. A forced choice of "which identity is primary" often ensues, and usually the primary identity is that category that is experienced as most oppressed by, or oppositional to, hegemonic norms. The person with many nonhegemonic traits or characteristics is split into various facets and forced choices between identity-based alliances, while the person with many hegemonic traits is able to be "whole" and does not feel tension or conflict between categorical identifiers such as race, ethnicity, class, gender, sexuality, ablebodiedness, education level, or income level. In such a way hegemonic norms remain both powerful and obscured.

10. That lesbians may bring a "gift" of a faith or spirituality that cannot ignore the body or its behaviors and desires, reflects an insistence partly enforced through a history of exclusion/invisibility from within the church due to the judgment of lesbian bodies and acts as "deviant." The sense of the sacred as embodied may also partly come from those bodies in the joyful, pleasurable acts of sexual relations.

11. In claiming destabilization as a gift that "lesbians" bring, I do not mean to imply that others can and do not bring that gift, too! Rudy is excellent on this point: "From a Christian perspective, gay and lesbian people are good for the entire church because they can lead us all closer to God. (This is something like an extreme liberationist perspective of God's 'option' for the oppressed.) This line of argument is extremely dangerous. I resist the narrative that gays, lesbians, and other sexual minorities are spiritually oriented in a way that straight or celibate people are not, because such an assertion relies on the very distinctions I am trying here to challenge. That is, the major mistake of homophobic Christianity has been to think that solely because of their sexual preference, lesbian and gay people have nothing to contribute to the church. However, the reverse proposition, that gays, lesbians, bisexuals, and transgendered people—as a result of their natures—inherently have a special connection to God, is equally essentialist and problematic" (*Sex and the Church*, pp. 122–23).

12. For an essentialist thinker, identity is natural, fixed, innate, culturally independent, and intrinsic; identity is an empirical category. For a social constructionist thinker, identity is culturally dependent and relational, an effect of processes of identification.

13. When faced with opportunities to self-select or self-name the cultural category(s) to which we "belong" or have affinities, we often "choose" those categorical assertions in and by which we experience or *feel* the most pain of exclusion, violence,

and oppression. Perhaps we gain awareness of the power of the culture's dominance at those categorical sites where we are at odds with its hegemonic assumptions. In fact, those places where we rub up against culture in our nonhegemonic
traits (rather, where culture rubs up against *us* in those places) may be the *only*
windows we have into the mechanisms and structures of our culture, the only
places we experientially *feel* and are *aware* of the power of discourse in culture
at all. In the UCC multiculturalism/identity conversations I would guess that I
was chosen as a "representative" or "token" lesbian because my other identities,
particularly race and class, "fit" easily into the hegemonic norms of the dominant
discourse. It is easier to abstract "lesbianism" as my essence, because I am not
as "complicated" by other nonhegemonic identities. By so doing, however, the
categorical essence of "lesbian" becomes defined in that discourse in ways that
exclude and obscure the heterogeneity both within and breaking beyond that
category. Butler, discussing the category of "woman," makes a similar comment.
She claims that when we rely on an identity category in a fundamental way, it
"becomes normative in character and, hence, exclusionary in principle," and "the
category effects a political closure on the kinds of experiences articulable as part
of a feminist discourse"; Butler, "Gender Trouble, Feminist Theory," p. 325.

In contemporary feminisms the question of essentialism, the question of
whether there is an "essence of *woman*," of whether you and I speak *primarily* "as
women," is becoming ever more clearly articulated as it becomes more crucial to
the ways in which we understand each other and ourselves. Elizabeth Spelman
describes the problem well: "I try to show that the notion of a generic 'woman'
functions in feminist thought much the way the notion of generic 'man' has functioned in Western philosophy: it obscures the heterogeneity of women and cuts
off examination of the significance of such heterogeneity for feminist theory and
political activity." Spelman, *Inessential Woman: Problems of Exclusion in Feminist
Thought* (Boston: Beacon, 1988), p. ix. Linda Nicholson echoes Spelman's concern: "In so far as the category is given substantive, cross-cultural content, there
arises the possibility that it becomes totalizing and discriminating against the
experiences and realities of some." Nicholson, "Introduction," *Feminism/Post-
modernism*, p. 15.

14.   Jane Flax, "Postmodernism and Gender Relations in Feminist Theory," in *Femi-
nism/Postmodernism*, p. 45.

15.   That "essential woman" has been culturally constructed as a tool of hegemonic
discourse is startlingly apparent in a book that I recently happened to pull (nearly
at random; I was attracted by the age of its cover) from a shelf in the feminism
section of the Graduate Theological Union library. In *The Mirror of True Womanhood: A Book of Instruction for Women in the World*, 18th ed. (New York: P. J.
Kenedy, 1877), the author, the Reverend Bernard O'Reilly, L.D., writes, "it is precisely because women are, by the noble instincts which God has given to their
nature, prone to all that is most heroic, that this book has been written for them."
It is not insignificant that most of the essentially feminine traits that the author
reveres as God-given "nature" are actually husband-benefiting *behaviors*, revealed
by chapter headings such as "Generosity in Forgetting One's Pain, to Please Oth-

ers" (chapter 3, p. 229). In an achingly common move, both God and "nature" are invoked to justify the author's hegemonic definition of essential woman.

16. Thomas Laqueur, *Making Sex: Body and Gender from the Greeks to Freud* (Cambridge: Harvard University Press, 1990), p. 21.

17. In suggesting that acceptance avoid biological essentialism, I have no intention of denigrating gay, lesbian, bisexual, or transgendered persons, nor well-meaning heterosexual allies who have utilized such arguments in their courageous commitments toward opening political rights and religious freedoms. On the contrary, I carry deep gratitude and daily benefit from such commitments. However, I *am* critiquing the habits of thought that fund biological and other essentialism. By utilizing unexamined habits of thought, depending on heterosexually sedimented arguments to buttress g/l/b/t rights, we may end up forfeiting the extraordinary opportunities queer lives open for the dynamic rethinking and shaping of human lives, relations, and patterns of thought.

In addition, I am not suggesting here that sexual identities are necessarily chosen. Rather, I suggest that a tendency on the part of progressives to shun the view that sexual relationality may be at least partially fluid or chosen inadvertently reinforces heteronormative habits of thought. Thus I advocate that g/l/b/t and well-meaning heterosexuals *refrain from* using biological determinism—or any single *cause—as a condition for the acceptability* of queer lives and relations. I share theorist Eve Kosofsky Sedgwick's view that the concept of ontogeny itself, the question of "the cause" of homosexuality, has developed through "gay-genocidal nexuses of thought" and that queer-affirmative work "does well when it aims to minimize its reliance on any particular account of the origin of sexual preference and identity in individuals"; Kosofsky Sedgwick, *Epistemology of the Closet* (Berkeley: University of California Press, 1990), p. 40. For more on the critique of "cause" see Christina Hutchins, "Holy Ferment: Queer Philosophical Destabilizations and the Discourse on Lesbian, Gay, Bisexual and Transgender Lives in Christian Institutions," *Theology and Sexuality* 15 (2001): 9–22. For a study, including extensive interviews, exploring the possibilities of chosen homosexualities, see Vera Whisman, *Queer by Choice: Lesbians, Gay Men, and the Politics of Identity* (New York: Routledge, 1996).

18. Teresa de Lauretis, "Upping the Anti [sic] in Feminist Theory," in *The Cultural Studies Reader*, ed. Simon During (New York: Routledge, 1993), p. 76.

19. Chris Weedon, *Feminist Practice and Poststructuralist Theory* (Cambridge: Blackwell, 1987), p. 21.

20. Ibid., p. 33.

21. "Philosophers can never hope finally to formulate these metaphysical first principles . . . however such elements of language be stabilized as technicalities, they remain metaphors mutely appealing for an imaginative leap" (PR, p. 4). Not only does Whitehead understand the lack of the absolute in philosophy as a problem of language, but he perceives it as one of the philosophical enterprise itself: "There is no totality which is the harmony of all perfections. Whatever is realized in any one occasion of experience necessarily excludes the unbounded welter of contrary possibilities. There are always 'others,' which might have been and are

not. . . . This doctrine is commonplace in the fine arts. It also is—or should be—a commonplace of political philosophy"; Whitehead, *Adventures of Ideas* [1933] (New York: Free, 1967), p. 276.

22.　For Whitehead "the primary method of philosophy is descriptive generalization" (PR, p. 10). I am indebted to Luis G. Pedraja's excellent treatment of the topic for the phrase "hermeneutical scheme." He writes, "although it may not seem evident, Whitehead does not want to establish an absolute metaphysical scheme. What he wants is to develop a comprehensive hermeneutical scheme to serve as an interpretive context in which individual experiences can acquire meaning"; Luis Pedraja, "Whitehead, Deconstruction, and Postmodernism," *Process and Difference: Between Cosmological and Poststructuralist Postmodernisms*, ed. Catherine Keller and Anne Daniell (Albany: SUNY Press, 2002), p. 75. And the possibility of utilizing a relative metaphysics offers novel possibilities for contemporary feminist and critical theory. Catherine Keller writes, "this emerging feminist vision requires something like metaphysical sensibility, because such vision drives beyond the sphere of the interpersonal, seeking a broader context in which all relations may be reassessed"; Keller, *From a Broken Web* (Boston: Beacon, 1986), p. 158.

23.　Michel Foucault, "Nietzsche, Genealogy, History," in *Language, Counter-Memory, Practice*, ed. D. F. Bondchard (Ithaca: Cornell University Press, 1977), pp. 151–52. Butler further supports the view that Foucault's genealogical method of exposing "causes" as "effects" of regulatory regimes overtly critiques the metaphysics of substance: "The strategic displacement of that binary relation and the metaphysics of substance on which it relies presuppose that the categories of female and male, woman and man, are similarly produced within the binary frame . . . Foucault's genealogical inquiry exposes this ostensible 'cause' as 'an effect,' the production of a given regime of sexuality that seeks to regulate sexual experience by instating the discrete categories of sex as foundational and causal functions within any discursive account of sexuality. . . . His analysis implies the interesting belief that sexual heterogeneity . . . implies a critique of the metaphysics of substance as it informs the identitarian categories of sex" (GT, pp. 23–24).

　　Whitehead also shares affinities with Derrida (and through Derrida with Butler) on the ways in which the very grammar of our language constrains and is constrained by a metaphysics of substance, making it difficult to conceptualize, write, or speak in/through an alternative metaphysical hermeneutic. Substance metaphysics is *sedimented* into our language *structures* in which a *subject* is followed by a verb in the *predicate*, indicating a preexisting, fixed subject that subsequently acts or is acted upon. Both Whitehead and Butler struggle with how to use language without further foreclosing the dynamism of reality.

24.　Judith Butler, "Contingent Foundations: Feminism and the Question of 'Postmodernism'" in *Feminists Theorize the Political*, ed. Judith Butler and Joan W. Scott (New York: Routledge, 1992), p. 8. Later in the same essay, Butler addresses a common misconception about deconstruction: "To deconstruct is not to negate or to dismiss, but to call into question and, perhaps most importantly, to open up a term, like the subject, to a reusage or redeployment that previously has not been authorized" (p. 15).

25. For Whitehead each concrescent occasion unifies its universe, such that "the many become one and are increased by one" (PR, p. 21). However, each universalizing moment of concrescence is only a moment, and it ceases with its attainment. In addition, though each occasion concresces as a universalized *one*, the *many* always remain. Because all unification is momentary, the fragmentation and plurality of the universe are neither erased nor diminished, but rather increased. In this way Whitehead unhinges the potential dualism between the one and the many.

26. Butler, "Gender as Performance," in *A Critical Sense: Interviews with Intellectuals* (New York: Routledge, 1996; first published in *Radical Philosophy* 67, Summer 1994), p. 125.

27. Elsewhere Butler suggests that what is needed "is a dynamic and more diffuse conception of power, one which is committed to the difficulty of cultural translation as well as the need to rearticulate 'universality' in non-imperialist directions" ("Gender as Performance," p. 125).

28. Nietzsche wrote, "What does your conscience say? 'You should become him who you are'"; Nietzsche, *The Gay Science,* trans. Walter Kaufmann (New York: Vintage, 1974), p. 155. Butler explicitly invokes Nietzsche: "The challenge for rethinking gender categories outside of the metaphysics of substance will have to consider the relevance of Nietzsche's claim in *On the Genealogy of Morals* that 'there is no "being" behind doing, effecting, becoming; "the doer" is merely a fiction added to the deed—the deed is everything'" (GT, p. 25). In my referring "becoming" to both thinkers it is important to point out that Whitehead never developed a concept of the "self"; rather, "becoming" was always ontological and cosmological. Yet Keller, along with others, has utilized very effectively Whitehead's notion of concrescence, bringing it into conversation with feminist thinkers, in order to interrogate selfhood and subjectivity: "Self is an event, a process, and no fixed substance, no substantive" (*Broken Web,* p. 194). See also "The Selves of Psyche," the fourth chapter of *Broken Web.*

29. In addition, process metaphysics have been used to develop "process theologies" by John B. Cobb Jr., David Ray Griffin, Rita Nakashima Brock, Marjorie Suchocki, and others, as well as used in conjunction with fields such as environmental ethics (Jay McDaniel) and feminist philosophy and ethics (Keller).

30. See note 23. Grammatical structuring of the sentence is based on and further sediments metaphysics of substance.

31. Whitehead continues: "these enduring objects and 'societies,' analyzable into strands of enduring objects, are the [comparatively] permanent entities which enjoy adventures of change through time and space" (PR, p. 34).

32. In addition, "width," or the inclusion of contrasts in the act of concrescence, enhances the permanence of an occasion, the durability of its ability, upon perishing, to affect future becomings (PR, p. 163).

33. I cannot resist bringing a bit of Whitehead into conversation here with Butler's use of parody as a strategy of resistance to the conventions of gender consolidation. Whitehead writes, "The last flicker of originality is exhibited by the survival of satire. Satire does not necessarily imply a decadent society, though it flourishes upon the outworn features in the social system . . . [when] there remains

the show of civilization, without any of its realities" (*Adventures of Ideas,* pp. 277–78).

34. In a conversation Mary Ann Tolbert pointed out an important critique of Butler's use of "drag." When discussing the activity of "drag," Butler does not address the difference between male to female and female to male drag in our society. Due to power imbalances, male to female drag is a more shocking, playful, and subversive act—a giving up or turning over of power—while female to male drag may involve an active complicity with existing power relations. There are also complexities and differences within the activities of female to male drag. For instance, a woman who puts on a "power suit," stylized after men's clothing but tailored specifically for a woman, is performing something different than a lesbian butch who wears "real" men's clothes.

35. An example of how repetitions of becoming actively consolidate, sediment, or *matter*, might be a body builder: a person who lifts weights repetitively over months or years, literally (re)shaping her body under/within cultural norms, and further reifying or resisting hegemonic norms (depending perhaps on whether the body builder is a man or a woman and/or which muscles are worked, emphasized, delineated, etc.).

36. Butler continues, "An open coalition, then, will affirm identities that are alternately instituted and relinquished according to the purposes at hand; it will be an open assemblage that permits of multiple convergences and divergences without obedience to a normative telos of definitional closure" (GT, p. 16).

37. The word *abject* describes a domain that is neither subject nor object, that which cannot be known by its opposition to another. Butler relates the word to "lesbian unthinkability" because if, following de Beauvoir, "man" has named himself Self, subject, active, and so forth, and woman as the Other, object, passive, and so forth, and defined the two in opposition to one another, then the active relation of one woman with another problematizes the opposition, because an "object" cannot actively have or possess another "object," nor is she a "subject," living out a relation with an opposite, an "object," who defines her "subject" status. "Abject," as that which cannot be fully named or thought, implies a lack of the content of either object or subject (or perhaps the presence of the content of both at once). And because the boundaries of a subject or an object are defined and constrained by the act of naming, abjects are not limited by the boundedness, fixity, ontological weight, or "being-ness" of a subject or by the static passivity of an object.

By developing some of the exclusions from the binary opposition of "sex," Monique Wittig, a French anti-essentialist materialist feminist, claims "lesbian" as a concept beyond the categories of sex (woman and man). Because for Wittig "women" only expresses meaning in heterosexual systems of thought (and economic arrangements), lesbians are not women. In fact, for Wittig, lesbians, by breaking out of the binarism of sex, demonstrate that "women" are not a natural group or an essential category. It is interesting to note that Wittig engages in essentialist thinking in the act of trying to discredit it—by homogenizing lesbians into a single harmonious group. See Monique Wittig, *The Straight Mind and Other Essays* (Boston: Beacon, 1992).

38. Lesbian "unthinkability" certainly remains an issue. The *Ellen* show was pulled off the air within a year of April 1997, when both the television character and "real life" Ellens "came out." One reason given by an ABC executive was that the show had "too much" lesbian content. Ellen Degeneres's portrayal of the daily life and relational issues that would be considered mundane on a "heterosexual" show were too much of a challenge to the popular unthinkability of lesbianism. Another, more personal example: When my partner and I hold hands in public or simply do errands, stand in line together, and so forth, we are very often asked, "Are you two sisters?" If one of us replies, "actually, we're lovers," the response is often either silence or, occasionally, an insistent, "No, you're sisters!"—a blatant refusal or inability to *see*, to *hear*, to perceive the "nature" or name of our relation.

39. In *Bodies That Matter* Butler writes, "What I propose in place of these conceptions of construction [in which there is no self-creative power] is a return to the notion of matter, not as site or surface, but as a *process of materialization that stabilizes over time to produce the effect of boundary, fixity, and surface we call matter*" (p. 9). Butler uses the word *matter* to convey not only *whose* bodies are important (all bodies and potential bodies) but that bodies *are mattering*, that is, coming into existence through a discursive, metaphysical process of continual resignification. In several places Butler comes quite close to Whitehead's notion of concrescence in her characterizations of performativity: "It is not simply a matter of construing performativity as a repetition of acts, as if 'acts' remain intact and self-identical as they are repeated in time, and where 'time' is understood as external to the 'acts' themselves. On the contrary, an act is itself a repetition, a sedimentation, and congealment of the past which is precisely foreclosed in its act-like status" (BTM, p. 244, n. 7).

40. In "Contingent Foundations" Butler explicitly notes that it is the contingency of the subject that engenders or preconditions its agency: "We may be tempted to think that to assume the subject in advance is necessary in order to safeguard the *agency* of the subject. But to claim that the subject is constituted is not to claim that it is determined; on the contrary, the constituted character of the subject is the very precondition of its agency" (p. 12).

41. Simone de Beauvoir, *The Second Sex* (New York: Bantam, 1952), p. 249.

42. Note that for Butler the "failure to repeat" refers to the inability to perfectly or exactly repeat an "original" (or "get it right")—an impossibility because there is no original. For Whitehead exact repetition is also impossible (and undesirable), neither are actual occasions "originals" for the becoming of subsequent occasions, though they do shape/effect future occasions. In terms of "societies," "there is disorder in the sense that laws are not perfectly obeyed, and that the reproduction is mingled with instances of failure. There is accordingly a gradual transition to new types of order" (PR, p. 91).

43. What a dance when these words of Whitehead's are placed in conjunction with Butler's double movement of invoking a category and opening it as contested! "To ameliorate and rework [the specific violences that a partial concept enforces], it is necessary to learn a double movement: to invoke the category, and hence provisionally to institute an identity and at the same time to open the category as a site

of permanent political contest" (BTM, p. 222). Agency is that double movement (BTM, p. 220).

44. "The experience enjoyed by an actual entity" is "what the actual entity is in itself, for itself" (PR, p. 81).

45. Whitehead's *enjoyment* may be even closer to the particularity of Butler's *pleasure* in "troubling," disturbing, or destabilizing categories. A few sentences later, after noting the enjoyment of efficient causation ("It is in this way that the immediacy of sorrow and pain is transformed into an element of triumph"), Whitehead specifically relates this enjoyment to the redemptive value of *discord*, of which a "very minor exemplification" is "the aesthetic value of discords in art" (PR, p. 350).

46. This passage is preceded by a clear description of agency: "This *resignification* marks the workings of an agency that is (a) not the same as voluntarism, and that (b) though *implicated* in the very relations of power it seeks to rival, is not, as a consequence, reducible to those dominant forms. Performativity describes this relation of being implicated in that which one opposes, this tuning of power against itself to produce alternative modalities of power, to establish a kind of political contestation that is not a 'pure' opposition, a 'transcendence' of contemporary relations of power, but *a difficult labor of forging a future from resources inevitably impure*" (BTM, p. 241; my emphasis). It is important to note that, since there can never be complete closure on a category or site of a performative event (Butler's notion of excess), any attempts at closure will necessarily produce other subversive constructions. However, categorical subversion or agency may be enhanced by deliberately utilizing the process of resignification against itself.

47. In "Gender as Performance" Butler says, "You can't plan or calculate subversion. In fact, I would say that subversion is precisely an incalculable effect" (p. 121).

48. Here I critique an emphasis on "Christian unity" over/against fragmentation, multiplicity, and ruptures of difference. My argument is against a hegemonic "one" that erases, obscures, or excludes non-normativity, even as such a "one" *produces* the non-normative. My intention is not to belittle or weaken contemporary avowals of the commitment that all persons should enjoy common rights and freedoms. In fact, it is the need for such common freedoms that elicits my own provisional appeal to Whiteheadian creativity as a universal and to a Butlerian view of human capacities and characteristics as relationally constituted (and constrained) processes of becoming.

49. A far more disturbing instance of the use (abuse) of the "fluidity of identity" notion is being propagated by conservative Christian organizations in the "transforming movement" of "ex-gay ministries" in which "homosexuals" learn to be attracted to the "opposite sex" so they can enter into heterosexual marriage. An example of this was a full page advertisement in the *New York Times,* July 13, 1998, that read, "Thousands of ex-gays like these have walked away from their homosexual identities. While the paths each took into homosexuality may vary, their stories of hope and healing [from nonheterosexual identities] through the transforming love of Jesus Christ are the same. Ex-gay ministries throughout the U.S. work daily with homosexuals seeking change, and many provide outreach programs to their families and loved ones." It is important to notice that for the

Radical Right the "transformation" never goes in the other direction: from heterosexuality into and toward homosexuality. The motion is rather always toward the conventional, the status quo, *toward and into* compulsory heterosexuality and hegemonic power relations, which stabilize what for the Radical Right is a fixed, stable, enforced category: *gender*. (For an excellent discussion of this see Rudy, *Sex and the Church*.) In this sense, though there is "motion," and the word *transformative* is being used, there is very little "novelty" or "subversion"; future relational possibilities are not being widened, but further confined.

50.   Note that Butler is speaking in *Gender Trouble* of the category "woman," and I have related the quotation here to the context of "lesbian." It is important to make clear that categorical incompleteness, disruption, and the resulting expansion of relational possibilities are not limited to the category "lesbian"; there is no *one* site from which to resist hegemonic namings and to recreate relational possibilities effectively. Such sites are always multiple and surprising.

51.   Butler writes about this in terms of "women": "to authorize or safeguard the category of women as a site of possible resignifications is to expand the possibilities of what it means to be a woman and in this sense to condition and enable an enhanced sense of agency" ("Contingent Foundations," p. 16).

52.   This is reminiscent of Jesus's teachings about the realm of God, which is "always in the midst." The realm of God, characterized in Jesus's parables of the mustard seed or leaven hidden in measures of dough, is also a metaphor about expanding the future, breaking open the containers that constrain the present through the very power of novel becoming that relationally resides in them (cf. Matthew 13: 31–33.)

53.   In *Gender Trouble* Butler points to subversive citations within established norms of continuity as "critical opportunities to expose the limits and regulatory aims of that domain of intelligibility and, hence, to *open up within the very terms of that matrix of intelligibility rival and subversive matrices* of gender disorder" (p. 17).

54.   "The extensiveness of space is really the spatialization of extension" (PR, p. 289).

55.   While expanding or opening space for the relational future is both a necessity and an act of resistance for queer lives, it is imperative that the *self-creativity* of this event be emphasized. I am not advocating the forcible breaking of another's boundaries as happens in events of sexual violence or in the inappropriate "outing" by others, especially by those who iterate within more dominant categories of a queer person or act.

56.   Here Butler explicitly draws on Foucault. The idea of effects that "supersede" the purpose of the act also carries affinities with Whitehead's notion of the "superject," which is the public trajectory(ies) created by an act of becoming: "An actual entity considered in reference to the publicity of things is a 'superject'; namely, it arises from the publicity which it finds, and it adds itself to the publicity which it transmits. It is a moment of passage from decided public facts to a novel public fact" (PR, p. 289).

57.   I am aware that I am utilizing Butler's insights, particularly in this discussion of excess, not only in ways that she does not herself do, but in ways that move in the hegemonic direction that has been all too familiar in Western history:

supersessionism of the work of Jewish persons by and for Christian constructions. I can only hope that my purpose is sufficiently subversive—opening cultural categories that have become sedimented in violently constraining ways by Christian institutions, habits, and ways of thought and that affect and confine secular as well as religious life.

Queer theory . . . offers us little insight for ethics.

—Kathy Rudy, *Sex and the Church*

If there is a "normative" dimension to this work, it consists precisely in assisting a radical resignification of the symbolic domain, deviating the citational chain toward a more possible future to expand the very meaning of what counts as a valued and valuable body in the world.

—Judith Butler, *Bodies That Matter*

6. TURNING ON/TO ETHICS

CLAUDIA SCHIPPERT

WHEN ENGAGING JUDITH Butler's work from the perspective of feminist ethics in religion, it seems that one cannot avoid the tension illustrated by the two epigraphs that introduce this essay. Christian feminist ethicist Rudy's evaluation of queer theory as offering "little insight for ethics" corresponds with perceptions of Butler's work as paradigmatic of the poststructuralist and queer critique of, and resistance to, identity, materiality, and agency.[1] Indeed, Butler's claim that both the body's materiality and the subject are discursively effected through the ritualized repetition of norms has sparked debates about the reality of the material body, social relations, and the possibility of resistant political agency. Although *Gender Trouble* and subsequent works were positioned within, and concerned with, feminist contexts, Butler has had to defend herself against accusations of political quietism, ethical irrelevance, and even collaboration with evil.[2]

Despite her attempts to clarify arguments about the body's materiality, the political promise of citationality, and resistant agency, Butler's critics, among them a number of feminist ethicists in religion, remain unconvinced. Often Butler is disqualified from any relevance for feminist political or ethical discussions because the strategies of subversion and resignification that are central to her argument seem incompatible with constructive ethics based on the specificity of bodily materiality and the experience of domination. Given this great suspicion toward Butler's work, especially among feminist ethicists in religion, it may be a surprise that she has described part of her critically queer project of resignifying the symbolic domain as having, possibly, a normative dimension, indicated in the epigraph by Butler to this chapter. While this normative dimension need not suggest a constructive ethics, it may point to ethical implications, albeit unexplored in her text. I find the quotation a striking moment in *Bodies That Matter*, perhaps similar to Foucault's invocation of bodies and pleasures at the end of the first volume of *The History of Sexuality* (where "bodies and pleasures" has been read to indicate a promise in terms of agency and bodily practices that may evade normalizing operations of power).[3]

In this essay I first briefly outline the sense of bodily materiality I find in Butler's account. Turning to Katie Cannon's work in the second section, I read Cannon's central methodological moves in *Black Womanist Ethics* as parallel to some of Butler's critical concerns.[4] After exploring in the third section how the language of abjection might be usefully deployed in this conversation, I conclude by drawing on the resource offered by Evelynn Hammonds's work in order to illustrate the different sense of resistant agency and bodily materiality to which my essay gestures throughout.

In Butler's case it seems difficult to suggest (or imagine) a turn to ethics.[5] By exploring her description of a normative dimension as a striking and promising moment, I engage the often perceived tension between Butler's work and religious ethics. Placing her work at the intersection with ethics can demonstrate in one specific cross-disciplinary parallel what a queer normative dimension might look like and what strategies may result from it.

In reading Butler and Cannon together I use each to shape my reading of the other in order to explicate aspects of each that are important to explore at the particular intersection of "queer" with "ethics." Thinking about Butler's work in light of Cannon's ethical project allows me to envision more of the normative dimension at which Butler hints but does not fully develop in *Bodies That Matter*. In this way I demonstrate that Butler's queer theoretical work does not act *against* ethics (as Rudy or Nussbaum would have it) but can rather generate a move toward a queer ethics. Considering the tension I described through the two epigraphs, to trace Butler's gesture toward a normative dimension by reading Cannon allows me to illustrate how queer theoretical work, instead of turning *on* ethics (in the sense of evading, defying, or betraying), can enact a turn *to* ethics.

Conversely, reading Cannon with Butler in mind allows me to foreground the radical dimension of Cannon's project in a way that goes beyond familiar readings of Cannon in a Christian liberationist trajectory. Cannon refuses the operative assumptions in Christian ethics that rely on (and constitute) black women as either amoral or immoral. She then draws on the black literary tradition as complex resource for the formulation of a black womanist ethics. Formulating moral values and normative trajectories that need not rely on the abjection of black women, Cannon—and womanist ethics more generally—have altered "what counts as a valued and valuable body" (BTM, p. 22). By taking Butler as lens for my reading of Cannon, I focus on the radical challenges to the very assumptions of "doing ethics" as they are uncovered in Cannon's womanist approach.

Although Cannon's womanist writing is more familiar to feminist ethicists than Butler's *Gender Trouble* and more often appropriated by religious ethicists than any queer theory, my turn to Cannon nevertheless might seem less than obvious.[6] *Black Womanist Ethics* predates the emergence of queer theory and *Bodies That Matter.* More important, it has usually been read within a constructive liberation ethical trajectory rather than within anything like queer ethics—and rightfully so. Cannon is committed to a model of agency, subjectivity, and bodily materiality unlike Butler's. Cannon would not claim to be resignifying the symbolic domain, nor would she be interested in illustrating Butler's or queer theory's normative dimension. Although I do not suggest that there is an obvious connection, I nevertheless find a useful correlation between these strategies that may open up new questions and connections within and beyond fields of religion or ethics.

By suggesting that Katie Cannon's *Black Womanist Ethics* has already illustrated in helpful ways what a strategy of transforming abjection into political agency might look like in the domain of Christian ethics, I place this womanist text in direct conversation with queer theory. However, this is not to apply feminist or womanist ethical methodology to queer theoretical writings—or to apply Butler's arguments to Cannon's text or the complex discourse of feminist and womanist ethics. Rather, in this essay I consider the unintended effects or excesses of both texts and claim that what Butler describes as the attempt to "assist in a radical resignification of the symbolic domain" (BTM, p. 22) can be a turn toward ethics similar to what Cannon's *Black Womanist Ethics* has already performed in deviating the citational chain within the realm of feminist and womanist ethics. Read together and against the grain, both texts demonstrate how a move "toward a more possible future to expand the very meaning of what counts as valued and valuable body in the world" might be(come) a feasible ethics project (BTM, p. 22).

While these authors' ethical strategies or conceptions of resistant agency differ, my essay seeks to demonstrate that moving simultaneously from within these related but not parallel normative dimensions opens up new realms and new ways of thinking about what something like a queer ethics might turn out to be. Reading together what seems not to fit together and reading from within shifted correlations may usefully intervene in normative constellations of discourse and power. In suggesting a connection that may be unexpected to either author of the two texts that centrally concern me, I indicate one possibility across disciplinary fields to relate subversive strategies and forge new, perhaps unintended directions for resistant ethics.[7]

Real Bodies with Agency

Judith Butler argues that the materiality of the body is produced within regulatory regimes of heterosexuality. "Sex," far from being a natural fact or an existing category prior to the advent of cultural gender-norms, can be shown to "be a performatively enacted signification (and hence not 'to be' at all)" (GT, p. 33). However, this need not be an argument *against* the reality of bodies and their experience or an argument *against* feminist politics. Rather, shifting the use of construction, Butler's approach points toward new or different political possibilities despite or maybe because of a radical critique of identity and materiality.[8] By shifting the discussion to that of power operating as a constitutive constraint, attention is shifted away from the question of who does the constructing to the operations and complex networks through which power operates.[9]

The following simplified example illustrates what such a shift to the discursively effected materiality of gender may entail: a body's materiality is produced performatively, through repeated invocations of norms. Within these citational processes various sets of norms become/are available, yet not all sets of available norms actually match. Indeed, many networks are incoherent. Nevertheless, the heteronormative goal in current gender-regimes is to cite the right norms in the right order and context and to bring into compliance aspects such as sex, gender, and sexuality in order to materialize a body that is culturally intelligible and viable. This is not necessarily done by a self-sufficient, prediscursive subject who, after checking its genital situation, decides to put on a particular gender at birth and every morning subsequently. Nevertheless, it seems obvious that throughout a day we engage in many—more or less conscious—reinvocations or bodily citations of norms aimed (mostly) at compliance with the normal, natural world around us. Through these processes bodies in their very essence become materialized and maintain intelligibility. Most interesting, the success of such processes of materialization is not guaranteed; it often does not work out. Things can go wrong (no matter what the intention of the actor). In the case of a great deal of discrepancy and (too much) disturbance, bodies may become unintelligible, impossible, queer.

In this sketch of discursive bodily materiality, questions of who acts in Butler's conception of performativity cannot be easily resolved by concentrating solely on discourse-analysis. Butler insists that performativity is unlike performance.[10] If readers perceive gender to operate like a closet filled with a variety of options from which the independent actor picks and chooses, i.e., performs according to free will, many of the disciplinary operations of power are left out of consideration. Such a scenario does not accurately describe how gender operates. However, neither is it beneficial to draw too drastic a distinction between gender as performative, on the one hand, and theatrical acts or notions of performance, on the other hand. Indeed, we still do act and enact relations and specific constellations of norms. It need not be the case, however, that there is a linear relation between intention and act—or a relation between intentions and the effects of actions. In this context performativity is a helpful concept to unlearn familiar notions of the voluntary subject. At the same time, it should not be read, I think, to dissolve all notions of responsibility or agency.

Another aspect of Judith Butler's description is significant for the material production of bodies. In addition to a Foucauldian description of normalizing power producing bodily materiality through "regulatory ideals," Butler offers an account of the psychic process that is involved in the formation of the subject and the material body. Within the procedures that performatively produce bodies, a realm is simultaneously produced and repudiated that is distinct from the realm of normal, or culturally intelligible, bodies and subjects. Drawing on the Freudian terminology of *Verwerfung,* Butler refers to this process of casting out as "abjection." For her the abject designates "the constitutive outside to the subject, an outside, which is, after all, "inside" the subject as its own founding repudiation" (BTM, p. 3). In Butler's terms, for a subject (or body) to reach intelligibility identification with the abject(ion) of the regulatory ideal has to be persistently disavowed. At the same time, the abject threatens to expose the resumption of the subject, "grounded as it is in a repudiation whose consequences it cannot control" (BTM, p. 3).

If we are to follow Butler's suggestion and shift conceptions of how bodies are materialized and effected by power, conceptions of agency will shift as well. When power works as a constrained and reiterative production and operates through the foreclosure of effects, the materialization of gender or the subject is not a voluntary or singular act but compelled through highly complex and regulated practices within the constraints of the heterosexual matrix. This account does not include a model of agency that is easily recognizable within a liberation ethics framework (which emphasizes voluntary agency). Yet Butler does not therefore lack descriptions—or *any* conception—of change or agency. Paralleling a Foucauldian account of the operations of power, in which relations of resistance are immanent in power relations, Butler's concept of gender performativity bears within it possibilities of resistance to, or subversion of, the regulatory process of gender production. Despite the multiple complex networks of norms and their various connections that compel and constrain the body, the performative production of sexed bodies does not always take place but might fail to take place. This failure need not be a bad thing, however. Butler suggests "the task [for resistant/political practice] will be to consider such threat and disruption not as a permanent contestation of social norms condemned to the pathos of perpetual failure" (BTM, p. 3). The latter often happens in ethics, though not because ethicists want to comply with social norms per se. Rather, in the attempt to find *better* norms, ethicists often constrict the range of their critical action by insisting on producing constructive ethics. Instead of attempting to avoid appearing as unrelated or not constructive for/within *real* feminist ethics, we might want to consider the failed reiteration "as a critical resource in the struggle to rearticulate the very terms of symbolic legitimacy and intelligibility" (ibid.).

Continuous reiteration of norms is necessary for coherence to be maintained, which can be taken as a sign that materialization is never quite complete. Bodies never *quite* comply with the sets of norms through which their materialization is impelled. Indeed, the instabilities and the possibility for rematerialization opened up by this process mark one domain in which, in Butler's words, "the force of the regulatory law can be turned against itself to spawn rearticulations that call into question the hegemonic force of that very regulatory law" (BTM, p. 2). The necessity of reiteration points to the site where the promise of resistant agency is located. The disavowed abject/ion threatens to expose the presumptions of the sexed subject, i.e., the repudiation whose consequences it cannot fully control. Processes of reiteration can be deviated; the process may shift and produce unintended results. Butler describes the abject as the trace of the constitutive reiterative process; the domain of the abject is "the illegible domain that haunts the [domain of intelligible bodies] as the specter of its own impossibility" (BTM, p. xi). The processes of citation that produce intelligibility could be used, repeated, or deployed for different purposes; the abject might insert itself into the normative framework and disturb, dislodge, and reiterate it differently.

Especially when engaging Butler's conception vis-à-vis Christian feminist ethics, it should be noted that the abject is not a margin or a standpoint on the periphery, in the way in which these concepts have functioned in liberation ethics. The reworking of the process of abjection into political agency assumes not a specific (static) abject *position* but an ongoing *process* that is reiterative and reiterable, i.e., it can be engaged and can be reworked for other purposes.[11] The status of the abject as threatening specter might invite parallels to what liberation ethicists have considered to be the epistemological privilege of the oppressed. However, the abjection to be reworked into political agency does not point to an embodied position in the sense of a personification of the abject, ready to engage in the well-planned disillusion work of debunking the myths of identification. The processes Butler describes as abjection—and the unintelligible abjects it effects—are not to be undone or taken back. What remains promising, however, is that the citational work necessarily has to be repeated and reiterated. Resistant agency and possibility of change are located in this temporal promise that, in ongoing reiteration, a shift can occur, altering the available grid of norms and how they are networked with other norms. This realm of necessarily constant and continuous reiteration may resemble what Butler gestured to with her normative dimension.

Turning to Cannon

By formulating moral values and normative trajectories that need not rely on the abjection of black women, Katie Cannon—and womanist ethics more generally—has altered "what counts as a valued and valuable body" (BTM, p. 22). Cannon's point of departure in *Black Womanist Ethics* is the observation that the "assumptions of the dominant ethical system implied that the doing of Christian ethics in the Black community was either immoral or amoral" (BWE, p. 2). This includes an important distinction. Cannon points to the negative evaluation (immoral) of the moral choices and actions in the black community within dominant "Christian ethics." However, she also points out the assumed amorality, the lack of morality, or nonexistence within the moral or ethical realm. Silences or invisibilities are productive by materially effecting bodies as always already abject, outside any recognizable morality. The dominant ethical system and the operative moral spheres of black life constitute two mutually exclusive or seemingly unrelated realms. Christian dominant ethics is defined and continuously reestablished around specific combinations of norms, networks of norms that reiterate and produce normative conceptions of morality and immorality. For example, moral choices are made from positions of freedom or its corollary: suffering is a choice deriving its value precisely from being chosen by the moral actor (rather than constituting normal or unavoidable existence in a racist and sexist society). Cannon challenges these assumptions by demonstrating how a reliance on freedom as constitutive moral condition is networked with other norms in ways that exclude or negatively affect blackness and black women in various normative pairings of regulatory ideals.

> Dominant ethics . . . assumes that a moral agent is to a considerable degree free and self-directing. Each person possesses self-determining power. For instance, one is free to choose whether or not she/he wants to suffer and make sacrifices as a principle of action or as a voluntary vocational pledge of crossbearing. In

dominant ethics a person is free to make suffering a desirable moral norm. This is not so for Blacks. For the masses of Black people, suffering is the normal state of affairs. Mental anguish, physical abuse and emotional agony are all part of the lived truth of Black people's straitened circumstances. Due to the extraneous forces and the entrenched bulwark of white supremacy and male superiority which pervade this society, Blacks and whites, women and men are forced to live with very different ranges of freedom. As long as the white-male experience continues to be established as the ethical norm, Black women, Black men and others will suffer unequivocal oppression.[12]

(BWE, pp. 2–3)

At the same time, Cannon describes the rich moral wisdom in a different realm and explicates moral operations that are acutely aware of the constitutive constraint through which freedom or choices are produced.

The cherished [dominant] ethical ideas predicated upon the existence of freedom and a wider range of choices proved null and void in situations of oppression. The real-lived texture of Black life requires moral agency that may run contrary to the ethical boundaries of mainline Protestantism. Blacks may use action guides which have never been considered within the scope of traditional codes of faithful living. Racism, gender discrimination and economic exploitation . . . require the Black community to create and cultivate values and virtues in their own terms so that they can prevail against the odds with moral integrity.

(BWE, p. 2)

Cannon's project throughout the book develops an ethics that, rather than justifying particular moral action guides or arguing for their inclusion into the cherished ethical ideas of dominant Christian ethics, is grounded in the "real-lived texture of Black life" (BWE, p. 2). Thus she describes an ethics drawing on values and norms that may sound—and in fact are—contradictory to dominant ethical discourse yet are the foundation for survival in black people's, and specifically black women's, moral agency. She writes of her work's focus in the following way:

To show how Black women live out a moral wisdom in their real-lived context that does not appeal to the fixed rules or absolute principles of the white-oriented, male structured society. Black women's analysis and appraisal of what is right or wrong and good or bad develops out of the various coping mechanisms related to the conditions of their own cultural circumstances. In the face of this, Black women have justly regarded survival against tyrannical systems of triple oppression as a true sphere of moral life.

(BWE, p. 4)

Cannon turns to the life and work of Zora Neale Hurston as example for the kind of moral agency she is investigating—and draws on terms originally formulated by Mary Burgher, who sees in Hurston's life and literature "the Black woman's daring act of remaking her *lost innocence into invisible dignity*, her *never-practiced delicacy into quiet grace*, and her *forced responsibility into unshouted courage*."[13]

These terms, much like examples from Hurston's life and work, correspond to recognizable operative values and norms within black life, yet simultaneously point to tensions or impossibilities within a dominant ethical imagination. In discussing the central importance of suffering and the value of unctuousness in her conception of a black womanist ethics, Cannon continues to draw on Hurston as example:

> Hurston, like Black people generally, understood suffering not as a moral norm nor as a desirable ethical quality, but rather as the typical state of affairs. Virtue is not the experiencing of suffering, nor in the survival techniques for enduring. Rather, the quality of moral good is that which allows Black people to maintain feistiness about life that nobody can wipe out, no matter how hard they try.
>
> (BWE, p. 104)

By not justifying specific normative relations as better or more true, Cannon opens the possibility that new locations and alternative modes of moral reasoning become visible and recognizable as such.

> In the Black community, the aggregate of the qualities which determine desirable ethical values regarding the uprightness of character and soundness of moral conduct must always take into account the circumstances, the paradoxes and the dilemmas that constrict Blacks to the lowest range of self-determination.
>
> (BWE, p. 3)

Cannon claims that thinking about and writing her womanist ethics helped her "to demolish internalized myths about Black inferiority, to criticize whole bodies of literature which imply evaluation of Blacks by standards not relevant to oppressed people, and to locate irrefutable evidence of moral sensibility within Black life and culture" (BWE, p. 4).

In doing ethics from a place in which no ethics can be done, Cannon does not merely seek to validate a position on the margins—or one that affects the "lower" positioned or oppressed half of a binary pair. Rather, her project targets the very process through which moral value is established and perpetuated. It is here that a possible relation to Butler's work emerges: Rather than a fight for inclusion, Cannon fundamentally challenges the dominant way of valuing.

However, *Black Womanist Ethics* is not an "anti-ethics" book. It would be wrong to suggest that its only or primary concern is resistance to normativity, since it is in fact an attempt to reformulate and shift specific constellations *within* normative ethics.

> My goal is not to arrive at my own prescriptive or normative ethic. Rather what I am pursuing is an investigation (a) that will help Black women, and others who care, to understand and to appreciate the richness of their own moral struggle through the life of the common people and the oral tradition; (b) to further understandings of some of the differences between ethics of life under oppression and established moral approaches which take for granted freedom and a wide range of choices. I am being suggestive of one possible ethical approach, not exhaustive.
>
> (BWE, pp. 5–6)

Cannon's argument performs a dual move: she addresses the oppressive aspect of the dominant system that affects black bodies in specific ways by acknowledging its effective operation. At the same time she asserts that there is a realm outside the normative constellation of (white) Christian ethics that, precisely because this realm is not considered as moral or in existence within the normative matrix, challenges the very operation of the dominant ethical system (much like the abject in Butler's account of normativity). Throughout Cannon draws on norms, albeit in different constellations.

Tracing Cannon's double move can help illustrate what Butler describes as reworking abjection into political agency and as "a radical resignification of the symbolic domain"(BTM, p. 22). Nevertheless, resignification, symbolic domains, and deviating citational chains are concepts more closely connected to psychoanalytic theory—and are often seen as far removed from Christian ethics or concrete political agency. Interestingly, however, Judith Butler suggests examples for what a politicization of abjection might produce that seem (uncharacteristically?) concrete:

> surviving with AIDS becomes more possible . . . queer lives become legible, valuable, worthy of support . . . passion, injury, grief, aspiration become recognized without fixing the terms of that recognition in yet another conceptual order of lifeless and rigid exclusion.
>
> (BTM, p. 21)

Changing (some aspects of) the relations within the networks of norms—which are configured as normative while continuously depending on abject realms—opens up real change and different possibilities. The examples in the passage above are real-lived illustrations for what Butler describes as "a more possible future to expand the very meaning of what counts as a valued and valuable body in the world" (BTM, p. 22).

According to Cannon, many ideals and norms that inform moral action in the black community do not appear at all in the realm of dominant white Christian ethics, which effectively places the moral actions and actors linked to them outside the realm of recognizable morality. Cannon's concern is with the placing of black (women's) bodies and their actions on the lower half of a set of hierarchical binaries. At the same time, and maybe more important, Cannon targets the tension filled processes through which choices and actions find themselves excluded from the legitimate options or choices the dominant ethical system makes available.

Norms, regulatory ideals, and the citations available in the symbolic domain are already placed in the normative network that counts as Christian ethics. Cannon demonstrates that specific ideals that are action guides and inform the moral sphere in the black community run counter to, or are outside of, the available options in the dominant configuration. At the same time, Cannon argues and demonstrates, they are *real* and they are the choices and values, the real-lived texture and moral wisdom operative in the black community. "The ethical values that the Black community has construed for itself are not identical with the body of obligations and duties that Anglo-Protestant American society requires of its members. Nor can the ethical assumptions be the same" (BWE, p. 3).

When considering Cannon's illustration of unshouted courage and the examples from Zora Neale Hurston's life and work that display unacknowledged, complicated, yet very real courage and moral dignity, it is useful to remember that reworking of abjection does not have to become a reverse discourse "in which the defiant affirmation of queer dialectically reinstalls the version it seeks to overcome" (BTM, p. 3). Or, in Cannon's case, need not result in an inclusive ethic in which previously excluded black woman's moral choice becomes "accepted" or normal—without necessitating any other changes in the constellations of race, gender, and religion in the dominant ethical system.

Taking on the Abject

Cannon's *Black Womanist Ethics* presents a complicated claim about the reality of black women's moral agency, values, and normative constellations. I read Cannon's double move as an illustration of the strategy Butler describes, albeit within a different academic discourse. Moreover, even Butler's own concrete examples gesture to (something like) recognizable positions that, however fleetingly, are embodied along the shifts of various normative networks. In order to account for the ambiguity of the real yet contested characteristics of some bodies' positions and to describe in another way what resistant agency might be in such a queer ethical context, I find useful the phrase *taking on the abject*. *To take on* can point to both, embodying and defying. Much like Cannon's double move to claim ethics and moral wisdom in a sphere excluded—by definition—from such descriptions, taking on the abject suggests a similar double move as both acknowledge/embody and attack/defy. Embodying the abject might seem impossible or in direct contradiction to the abject's very definition (which is precisely *not* an essence or materiality). However, we might want to think of embodying not as a singular act but as nonlinear series of citational moves that contribute to embodiment.[14] This complex embodiment indeed might effect the abject as *a kind* of position.

A related and simultaneous effect of taking on the abject might be the unmaking of its very status as abject and the normalizing operations that involve and require abjection. Such a double sense of taking on the abject responds well to Butler's caution against "assuming and stating that a 'subject-position' is the consummate moment of politics" (PLP, p. 29). For Butler the abject is not a position per se. Rather, the abject is a realm of unintelligibility that contains (constrains?) that which is cast out in the discursive formation of subjectivity, material and psychic coherence. Interestingly, however, the abject in Butler's text, also designates "precisely those 'unlivable' and 'uninhabitable' zones of social life which are nevertheless densely populated by those who do not enjoy the status of the subject, but whose living under the sign of the 'unlivable' is required to circumscribe the domain of the subject" (BTM, p. 3). This description suggests that the haunting specter of the abject, despite producing no essence per se, nevertheless contains material, and variously positioned, bodies. And indeed, after warning against considering the taking of a subject position as the consummate moments of politics, Butler also warns against an approach which would deny the subject's "existence" and thus underestimate the linguistic necessity to inhabit a subject position (PLP, p. 29).

Understood in this sense, taking on the abject has as one of its goals to "rewrite the history of the term" (BTM, p. 21). This historical and temporal dimension, unlike voluntary agency, recalls Katie Cannon's methodological shift that opened up the realm of black womanist ethics. The absence of the black community's moral choices and actions from the normative relations of (white) Christian ethics performs a specific function. What Cannon describes as the "real-lived texture of Black life" is not merely suppressed or erased, but recruited within the production of normative coherence (BWE, p.2). Black women's a/immorality is necessary as a negative foil—an abject and disavowed realm—on which the normativity of the dominant sphere depends through its variously connected normative pairings. Black women's agency, or ascribed lack thereof, could be described as the constitutive outside that is also inside the (white) subject.

Writing an ethics that actively draws on norms deployed within the black community does not function easily—or at all—within a white dominant Christian ethics.[15] Describing and asserting this moral realm as real ethics is to disrupt the operative assumptions in the dominant normativity. Insisting on the validity of these (specifically different) relations between norms can shift and alter the dominant white Christian ethical normativity as well by repeating, teaching, reiterating the womanist constellation.

Such metaethical shifts are not isolated, singular acts that change a static configuration once and for all. Rather, precisely the repetition and reiteration of this altered constellation of norms might disturb and shift the normative grid. The challenge of ongoing resistant engagement can be seen in the process in which womanist ethics has become an academic subdiscipline. Womanism had to confront challenges of normalizing recuperation into the dominant configurations similar to the earlier feminist entry into academic discourse or the later emergence of queer theory as a marketable field of knowledge.[16] The temporal dimension of the symbolic is helpful in illustrating how abjection can be reworked in this context. Resistant agency or the activity of queering is not a singular act, but continuous and reiterative intervention in the processes that require abjection for the production of subjectivity or bodily materiality.

Conclusion: A Different Geometry

In shifting claims of validity and ethical vocabulary, *Black Womanist Ethics* enacts shifts within a specific normativity. Katie Cannon's book provides an instructive example of how to rethink and reconfigure the ways in which norms, sets of norms, and larger matrices are connected, enable each other, preclude certain possibilities while setting up coherence. It is through this discursive coherence that the materiality of bodies is produced. In my reading starting somewhere other than in that place of coherence is useful and can help in enacting and deploying sets of norms that may be contradictory and simultaneously unmake each other.

I do not suggest celebrating this strategy as an unproblematic endeavor. Butler's project of resignifying the realm of the symbolic, Cannon's approach in *Black Womanist Ethics*, or even what I refer to as taking on the abject all involve the embodying and concrete materializing of precisely that which is unaffirmable, unlivable, nonexistent. This is about real bodies that cannot be—yet are constitutively required for the very formation of being and subjectivity.

To address the problematic dimension of this project, I have found Evelynn Hammonds's more recent illustration of a similar issue useful. In "Black

(W)holes and the Geometry of Black Female Sexuality," Hammonds criti-cally discusses the invisibility of black lesbian sexuality in feminist and queer theories.[17] Rather than pursue strategies to increase visibility, Hammonds argues that it is crucial to address and account for the ways in which black female sexuality is absent or invisible as a constitutively necessary function for the construction of (white/straight) norm/al sexuality.

Analyzing how black lesbian and black female sexuality does (not) sur-face in many texts on sexuality (written from various, including feminist and queer, perspectives), Hammonds is concerned with the contestations of such invisibility in institutional terms, specifically the complicated struggles of black women to gain visibility in the academy. She notes that black women's sexuality is invisible as part of the discourse of normal sexuality. Gaining inclusion in this discourse might grant temporary relief from the disciplin-ary pressure, yet it does not change the requirement of a realm of invisible sexuality. Additionally, Hammonds points out that *invisibility* has at times served black women in the academy better than an attempt to gain entry into the operations of visibility and representation in the institution.[18] Strategies for visibility have not always worked because they do not necessarily alter the network of norms, the coherence and pairings that are configured in a particular normativity.[19]

Accounting for the complexity of black female sexuality within the nor-mative discursive formation relying on its invisibility, Hammonds illustrates the paradox by invoking the phenomena and characteristics of black holes, which are thought to be void empty places yet are in fact complex and full.[20] Observing binary star systems, physicists study how one visible, white, nor-mal star orbits in mutual gravitational attraction around another star that is not itself visible (the black hole). Thus the presence of a black hole is dis-cernible by its effects on the region of space where it is located; black holes exert a distorting (and enabling) influence and have a constitutive function for the existence of normal stars.

Staying within Hammonds's useful metaphor, we need to adjust our tools of detection in order to observe such distorting and enabling influences, i.e., in order to deduce the presence of currently invisible, unobservable realms. However, even if such absent presence were to be discerned, we (and phys-icists) do not see, nor do we know what it is like, inside black holes. In Hammonds's critique of texts on black female and black lesbian sexuality, the (seemingly) inaccessible feature of black holes illustrates well the trou-ble involved in attempts to describe them. To begin to resolve the problem, and by extension to develop theories of embodiment that can address and broaden what is valued and a valuable body in the world, Hammonds sug-gests that "we must think in terms of a different geometry" (Hammonds, "Black (W)holes," p. 139).

For me Hammonds poses a metaethical question: what changes in our ethical and political lenses if we consider some realms to be inaccessible to some, yet formative and indeed constitutive for the existence, integrity, or identity of communities or persons? The title of Hammonds's essay, "Black (W)holes," invokes and maintains the ambivalence and contingency of both aspects of this geometry: on the one hand, the abjected realm of invisibility or void and, on the other hand, the complexity and fullness which exerts influence. At the same time, the ambivalence of "(w)holes" points to what Hammonds describes as necessary strategy, "disavowing the designation of black female sexualities as inherently abnormal, while acknowledging the material and symbolic effects of the appellation" ("Black (W)holes," p. 138).

Although primarily focused on literary theory and cultural criticism, the metaphor of the black (w)hole and Hammonds's strategy work well beyond that realm: Hammonds's metaphor invokes ambivalence, yet also takes seriously the possibility of living and thinking in term of a different geometry. Likewise, Cannon's use of the ambivalent character of black real-lived experience insists on (and embodies) the reality of a different geometry. Cannon simultaneously refuses the immorality attributed to the sphere of black moral actions through the process of abjection while taking on this sphere of moral wisdom as an inhabitable position—and thereby establishes it as something altogether different than a/immorality. In so doing, Cannon opens up a new trajectory to approach normativities and to address and subvert the ways in which norms are deployed in their operations.

Hammonds, like Butler, insists that identities and bodily materialities are characterized by contingency and a certain unpredictability of signification. At the same time, both theorists hold it imperative to address (and attack) precisely the contingent, contradictory characteristics. Although norms and their deployment are not linear processes, but characterized by unpredictability, the normative relations reconfigured through practices can, and have to be, engaged nevertheless. In Hammonds's metaphor it is not clear which of the appellations or their effects becomes effective, or real, holes or wholes. There is a tension-filled legacy and process of material and symbolic effecting of inherent abnormality—yet there is also the possibility of simultaneous disavowal that opens up (or takes account of) the existence of a different real(m) with a different geometry.

Hammonds's metaphor usefully invokes the ambivalence yet also takes seriously the possibility of living and thinking in term of a different geometry, which Cannon's work has more explicitly described in a specific context. In a related sense *Black Womanist Ethics* also provides useful insight into some characteristics of what I have called taking on the abject. Insisting on (and embodying) the reality of a different geometry, while refusing the immorality attributed to it through the process of abjection, womanist ethics describes this sphere of moral wisdom as an inhabitable position—and challenges how norms are deployed.[21] In my appropriation of these shifts into a more explicitly queer ethical realm, the position affirmed and taken would be simultaneously dissolved. However, this paradoxically does not negate its reality.

To think of these strategies as taking on the abject has the advantage that it does not rely on agency that is voluntary, intentional, singular, or predictable. Rather, it points out the necessity to deploy networks of norms and, finally, it suggests the need to think and act from within—or in alliance with—different geometries. Such a different geometry adds to a focus on multiple starting points and alliances of contradictory norms that have been useful interventions in recent critical discussions of social movement, theory, and change.[22] Asserting that things operate in terms of a different geometry posits that it is not obvious what things look like inside. Simultaneously, it is not necessarily the case that only those who have been or are inside can participate in the resistant engagement.[23] Rather, being part of a resistant engagement is a continual process; being an ally is not an a priori position but the result of engaging or being in alliance. To recalibrate our tools of detection in such a context is not a project aimed at getting it right and positively describing the inside of the black hole—or the truth of the various interconnected spheres or realms. Rather, we should not assume that we know how to view life in a different geometry. Practically, this might necessitate the deflating of truth claims and positions of authority or critical evaluation.

What I am suggesting, then, is not an approach to ethics that privileges or draws on experience. (This is something that Cannon would likely criticize about my appropriation). Neither am I suggesting an approach that aims to formulate a constructive ethic.[24] Even if, or precisely because, we may have no clue what living in a specifically different geometry is like, we (and I here mean white feminist ethicists) should refuse to trust that our tools of detection are capable of describing all or any geometry or are the only tools of detection out there. What we can see in specific realms (or alliances) will be produced in those specific sites where norms reinforce, contradict, and undo each other.

In conclusion, Butler's normative dimension may not have been intended as a turn to ethics or as a turn like the one I am suggesting here. However, engaging her work together with texts from feminist and womanist ethics proves to be a useful exercise that points to some previously unexplored connections and might lead us to explore yet unexamined dimensions. At the very least, it is an exercise in refuting Kathy Rudy's claim that queer theory offers us little insight for ethics. Indeed, an engagement with Butler's work might serve those of us well who are invested in exploring precisely the productive connections between queer theory and ethics.

NOTES

1. Kathy Rudy, *Sex and the Church: Gender, Homosexuality, and the Transformation of Christian Ethics* (Boston: Beacon, 1997), p. 123.

2. See especially Butler, *Gender Trouble: Feminism and the Subversion of Identity* (GT) and *Bodies That Matter: On the Discursive Limits of "Sex"* (BTM). Martha Nussbaum's scathing critique of Butler's work is noteworthy in this regard for its blatant misreading of Butler's work; "The Professor of Parody," *New Republic*, February 22, 1999, pp. 37–45. It also provoked some rather strange letters to the editor defending Butler. It is unfortunate that Nussbaum's article is useless as a critique or engagement with Butler's work. On the other hand, it is quite entertaining and possibly useful for observations about cultural and intellectual discourse at a specific time. Nussbaum's essay is merely one example in a long line of—mostly more intelligent—engagements that find political significance lacking in Butler's work.

3. Michel Foucault, *The History of Sexuality*, vol. 1 (New York: Random House, 1978; repr. Vintage, 1990). And, indeed, in Foucault's case, a turn to ethics can be observed. In subsequent investigations into the history of sexuality, he explicitly turned his attention back in time and focused on ancient Greeks and Christians in order to explicate practices that drew on norms without being inscribed in the same relations to normativity on which modern constellations of power rely. Although some in the religion academy have written about Foucault, e.g., Jeremy R. Carrette, *Foucault and Religion* (New York: Routledge, 2000), Judith Butler has generally not been taken up on her hesitant normative claim. In attempts to write (about) a queer ethics (in the 1990s), it has been mostly Foucault's turn to ethics which has been useful, expanded, and explicated. See, for example, David M. Halperin, *Saint Foucault: Towards a Gay Hagiography* (New York: Oxford University Press, 1995); and Janet Jakobsen, "Queer Is? Queer Does?" *GLQ* 4, no. 4, pp. 511–36.

4. Katie G. Cannon, *Black Womanist Ethics*. American Academy of Religion Academy Series, no. 60 (Atlanta: Scholars, 1988). Hereafter cited as BWE.

5. When writing earlier versions of this essay in the mid 1990s, I was mostly thinking of the changes from *Gender Trouble* to *Bodies That Matter*. Since then Butler has written about some of these issues herself. Specifically, in the preface to the 1999 edition of *Gender Trouble* she more explicitly discusses some practical dimensions of her radical theoretical critique. In an essay in a recent anthology about the consequences of a perceived "turn to ethics," she discusses the approach to the question of ethics (or lack thereof) in a new way. See her "Ethical Ambivalence" in *The Turn to Ethics*, ed. Marjorie Garber, Beatrice Hanssen, and Rebecca Walkowitz (New York: Routledge, 2000), pp. 15–46.

6. Considering womanist ethics as part of feminist ethics might require an explanatory note. Katie Cannon's book is, strictly speaking, neither feminist nor queer. The 1988 publication of *Black Womanist Ethics* predates any recognizable queer theoretical vocabulary and itself constituted one of the crucial "events" that we may attribute to the emergence of womanist ethics as a *distinct* trajectory within

the academic study of religion. Nevertheless, I suggest that it is not merely a co-incidence that I return again and again to this book when contemplating ways in which ethics may "take on the abject" (see my discussion of this concept below). I wish to point out that personal biography does play a part in this matter, since I essentially learned feminist ethics from Katie Cannon. Thus I learned feminist ethics from a founding scholar of womanist ethics—and always connected or in relation to womanist ethics. In ways that I can probably never entirely retrace, reading *Black Womanist Ethics* enabled me to begin to think—or to imagine and make connections to—what I now refer to as "queer ethics." What I came to call "taking on the abject" is part of that move, which is also a move away from "Katie's Canon."

7. In trying to be/do both (think from queer and engage a text and strategy in ethics) my conversation here parallels those others have engaged at this intersection. Most promising, Janet Jakobsen in "Queer Is? Queer Does?" has demonstrated that the question for strategies of queer is not whether heteronormativity—or any normativity—can be resisted or not, but how it can be done. Resistant agency in such a perspective is not about resisting the normal in general (or any particular norm) but about engaging and intervening in the complex fields and complicat-ed networks of norms that form the enabling possibilities *and* constraints of the body's materiality, legibility, and value.

8. Butler resists writing a political manifesto, which, in a debate that demands such political texts, of course disqualifies her. Although she has elaborated on the po-litical promise of her work and has explicitly warned against considering taking a subject position to be the ultimate political achievement (see *The Psychic Life of Power: Theories in Subjection* [PLP], p. 29), Butler's strengths are on the descrip-tive level. As with other theoretical work, a description of the transformation to action is not necessarily included. Although I find a number of sites that suggest particular applications or effects of reconfiguring the body and agency according to a model of citationality, more explicit translations remain the domain of those attempting to self-consciously write a queer ethics. See, for example, Michael Warner's recent *The Trouble with Normal: Sex, Politics, and the Ethics of Queer Life* (New York: Free, 1999; repr. Cambridge: Harvard University Press, 2000).

9. See BTM, xi. Initial questions about the construction of the material body might have been: if no subject or body before construction, who does the constructing, how can there be agency, etc.? Describing construction as constitutive constraint shifts the questions and issues to a more narrowly focused description of the processes, techniques of power, operations of discourse, and questions of politi-cal agency and/in the cumulative practices that effect the material body as intel-ligible/gendered.

10. Butler's defense against initial readings of *Gender Trouble* to imply voluntary agency are understandable, although her own methodology in that text may have invited such readings. Her preface to the 1999 edition is a helpful addition and corrective in this context.

11. In PLP Butler more explicitly elaborates how the subject, indebted in its very emergence to a specific subjection/subordination simultaneously turns on this subjection—and thus seeks to undo its enabling production.

12. A related example Cannon discusses concerns the virtue of work and self-reliance: "dominant ethics makes a virtue of qualities that lead to economic success—self-reliance, frugality and industry. These qualities are based on an assumption that success is possible for anyone who tried. Developing confidence in one's own abilities, resources and judgments amidst a careful use of money and goods in order to exhibit assiduity in the pursuit of upward mobility have proven to be positive values for whites. But, when the oligarchic economic powers and the consequent political power they generate, own and control capital and distribute credit as part of a legitimating system to justify the supposed inherent inferiority of Blacks, these same values prove to be ineffectual. . . . Analyses demonstrate that to embrace work as a 'moral essential' means that Black women are still last hired to do the work which white men, white women, and men of color refuse to do, and at a wage which men and white women refuse to accept. Black women, placed in jobs that have proven to be detrimental to their health, are doing the most menial, tedious and by far the most underpaid work, if they manage to get a job at all" (BWE, p. 2). For a more recent extensive womanist ethical analysis of the value of work, see Joan Martin, *More Than Chains and Toil: A Christian Work Ethic of Enslaved Women* (Louisville: Westminster/John Knox, 1999).

13. Mary Burgher, "Images of Self and Race in the Autobiographies of Black Women," in *Sturdy Black Bridges*, ed. Roseann P. Bell, Bettye J. Parker, and Beverly Guy-Sheftall (New York: Anchor, 1979), p. 113; quoted on BWE, p. 17.

14. See Jakobsen "Queer Is? Queer Does?" She approaches the question concerning embodiment by shifting to "complicated embodiment," which results in alliances—and a shift to *queer* as a verb. Queering as a verb is useful, particularly in the way deployed here, because it does not focus on a singular norm but on the deployment of networks of norms that disrupt the normative network—however momentarily.

15. Since networked meanings are different, even claiming that particular actions may constitute responsibility and care might not work for a specific normative frame. Toni Morrison's *Beloved* often has been discussed in this regard and illustrates well the lack of relation between some moral spheres or ethical realms.

16. Within the first decade of womanist ethics in academia its normative yet resistant character provoked debates. Insisting on the compulsory inclusion of antihomophobic work in the definition of womanism is but one example of the continuous work to resist the normalizing recuperation into networks that aim to "domesticate" the threat of the abject. For example, Cheryl J. Sanders, Katie G. Cannon, Emilie M. Townes, M. Shawn Copeland, bell hooks, and Cheryl Townsend Gilkes, "Roundtable Discussion: Christian Ethics and Theology in Womanist Perspective," *Journal of Feminist Studies in Religion* 5, no. 2 (1989): 83–91.

17. Evelynn Hammonds, "Black (W)holes and the Geometry of Black Female Sexuality," *Differences: A Journal of Feminist Cultural Studies* 6, nos. 2–3 (1994): 126–45.

18. Hammonds writes, "while hypervisibility can be used to silence black women academics it can also serve them." She quotes Patricia Hill Collins: "paradoxically, being treated as an invisible Other gives black women a peculiar angle of vision, the outsider-within stance that has served so many African-American

women intellectuals as a source of tremendous strength"; *Black Feminist Thought, Knowledge, Consciousness, and the Politics of Empowerment* (Cambridge: Unwin Hyman, 1990), p. 94; quoted by Hammonds, "Black (W)holes," p. 135.

19.   This is, of course, precisely the critique of identity politics that was instrumental for the forging of *queer* as a term of positionality, as an identity without an essence—although black women's sexuality and black lesbian sexuality have not been a particularly visible concern in most queer theory. Hammonds offers insightful comments on the contributions to the initial queer theory volume of *Differences* that, according to Hammonds, replicate problems in the ways black queer sexuality surfaces in critical texts.

20.   Hammonds here appropriates Michele Wallace's image, which originally appeared in "Variations on Negation," *Invisibility Blues: From Pop to Theory* (Seattle: Bay, 1992), p. 218. See Hammonds, ibid., pp. 138ff.

21.   I don't know what physicists think happens when you fly into a black hole, but I am certain that it is much more problematic than what such things look like on *Star Trek*. In real life living according to a different geometry, and insisting that such lives are real and worthy nevertheless, is a dangerous endeavor. Although normativities may be unstable and shifting, and although there may be ways in which performative contradictions can effect shifts and may alter some of their operations, they nevertheless exert great force. To embody/defy the abject is rarely a voluntary act. There is most certainly *no guarantee* and maybe not more than tentative hope (to invoke an uncharacteristic term in this context) that processes of abjection can/will be subverted. Nevertheless—there is promise that lies in moves to validate and think from within a realm which is considered a void, to insist on speaking in terms of a different geometry, and to theorize the very terms according to which such speaking, embodying, and defiance operates.

22.   Here I find myself in conversation with Jakobsen's "Queer Is? Queer Does?" again and her *Working Alliances and the Politics of Difference* (Bloomington: Indiana University Press, 1997).

23.   Indeed, it is the white star that is influenced, enabled, but also fundamentally distorted by the absent presence of the black hole. In attempting a clumsy parallel, white ethicists need to account for and learn to address their white racial identity in some complexity in order to show appropriate—and morally just—engagements with racism.

24.   My work seeks to reflect on the cultural significance of specific discursive constellations and strategies—to explore how such discourses of gender, race, and sexuality produce the materiality of bodies. See, e.g., Claudia Schippert, "Containing Uncertainty: Sexual Values and Citizenship," forthcoming in special double issue of the *Journal of Homosexuality* on "The Contested Terrain of LGBT Studies and Queer Theory."

7. AGENCY, PERFORMATIVITY, AND THE FEMINIST SUBJECT

SABA MAHMOOD

T HIS ESSAY IS born out of a series of analytical and political questions at the heart of the conversation between postcolonial and
poststructuralist feminist theory that I inherited as a feminist
intellectual and activist who came to political consciousness in the Muslim world during the 1970s. If the postcolonial debate that raged through
the 1980s and 1990s put to test the horizon of nationalist politics and the
presumptive divide between North-South and/or East-West, then poststructuralist feminism made many in my generation face the problematic ways in
which we were tied to the liberal tradition, to its epistemological and political presumptions, our own discomfort with this association notwithstanding. These two intersecting intellectual currents found fecund ground among
those of us who had increasingly come to reckon with the force religious
politics had come to command in the Muslim world, particularly after the
Iranian Revolution, which shook our sense of certitude about the potentials
and possibilities of the secular-progressive imaginary. It was not so much that
either postcolonial theory or poststructuralist feminism challenged its own
presumptive secularity and secular commitments (it seldom has), but that
the kinds of questions, both analytical and political, these two intellectual
currents opened up became crucial to working through the conundrums and
challenges thrown up by developments in the Muslim world.

It should come as no surprise that anyone formed by these two broad intellectual movements should find engaging with the work of Judith Butler of utmost importance. I recall, as I am sure others do as well, reading Judith Butler's work when it first came out and being made extremely uncomfortable not only by her critique of liberalism but also its promissory second life within the progressive feminist imaginary of which I found myself to be a part. The questions her work opened up in the first reading morphed over time into a new set of puzzles and conundrums as I came to work with the Islamist movement in Egypt during the 1990s, particularly as her interventions came into conversation with my own struggles with the force secular liberalism commands when attending to the analysis of Islamic politics. In what follows I want to trace this trajectory—if only briefly—in order to make the reader familiar with the landscape of questions and preoccupations that have animated my engagement with Butler's work. As will become clear, even as I recognize that the analytical and the political are indelibly intertwined, my plea often will be to keep the two in tension. This tension owes in some ways to what I consider to be an important point of departure for both understanding and extending Butler's invaluable interventions in the field of feminist and queer theory to the terrain of postcolonial criticism.

In the last two decades one of the key questions that has occupied many feminist theorists is how issues of historical and cultural specificity should inform both the analytics and politics of any feminist project. While this questioning has resulted in serious attempts at integrating issues of sexual, racial, class, and national difference within feminist theory, questions of religious difference have remained relatively unexplored in this scholarship. The vexed relationship between feminism and religious traditions is perhaps most manifest in discussions on Islam. This is due in part to the historically contentious relationship that Islamic societies have had with what has come to be called "the West" and in part to the challenges contemporary Islamic movements pose to secular liberal politics, of which feminism has been an integral (if critical) part. The suspicion with which many feminists tended to view Islamist movements only intensified in the aftermath of the September 11, 2001, attacks launched against the United States and the immense groundswell of anti-Islamic sentiment that has followed since. If supporters of the Islamist movement were disliked before for their social conservatism and their rejection of liberal values (key among them "women's freedom"), their now almost taken-for-granted association with terrorism has served to further reaffirm their status as agents of a dangerous irrationality.[1]

In this essay I will probe some of the conceptual challenges that women's participation in the Islamist movement poses to feminist theorists and gender analysts through an ethnographic account of an urban women's piety movement that is part of the larger Islamic revival in Cairo, Egypt.[2] *Islamic revival* is a term that refers not only to the activities of state-oriented political groups but also to a religious ethos or sensibility that has developed within Muslim societies more generally, and Egypt in particular, since the 1970s.[3] The piety movement with which I worked is comprised of women from a variety of socioeconomic backgrounds who gather in mosques to provide lessons for each other that focus on the teaching and studying of Islamic scriptures, social practices, and forms of bodily comportment considered germane to the cultivation of the ideal virtuous self.[4] Even though Egyptian Muslim women have always had some measure of informal training in piety, the mosque movement represents an unprecedented engagement with scholarly materials and theological reasoning that had, to date, been the purview of learned men. Movements such as this one, if they do not provoke a yawning boredom among secular intellectuals, certainly conjure up a host of uneasy associations, such as fundamentalism, the subjugation of women, social conservatism, reactionary atavism, cultural backwardness, and the rest. My aim in this essay is not to analyze the reductionism these associations entail of an enormously complex phenomenon; nor am I interested in recovering a redeemable element within the Islamist movement by revealing its latent liberatory potentials. Instead I want to focus quite squarely on the conceptions of self, moral agency, and embodiment that undergird the practices of this nonliberal movement in order to come to an understanding of the historical projects that animate it.

My goal, however, is more than to provide an "ethnographic account" of the Islamic revival; it is also to make this material speak back to normative liberal assumptions about freedom and agency against which such a movement is held accountable—such as: the belief that all human beings have an innate desire for freedom, that we all somehow seek to assert our autonomy when allowed to do so, that human agency primarily consists of acts that challenge social norms, and so on. Thus my ethnographic tracings will sustain a running argument with and against key concepts in feminist studies often applied to movements such as the one that concerns me here. In so doing I hope to continue a conversation that explores the tensions attending the dual character of feminism both as an analytical and a political project.[5]

I want to begin by exploring how a particular notion of human agency in feminist scholarship—one that seeks to locate the political and moral autonomy of the subject in the face of power—is brought to bear upon the study of women involved in patriarchal religious traditions such as Islam. I will argue that, despite the important insights it has enabled, this model of agency sharply limits our ability to understand and interrogate the lives of women whose sense of self, projects, and aspirations have been shaped by nonliberal traditions. To analyze the participation of women in religious movements, such as the Egyptian mosque movement I describe, I want to suggest we think of agency not as a synonym for resistance to relations of domination but as a capacity for action that historically specific relations of subordination enable and create. This relatively open-ended understanding of agency draws upon poststructuralist theories of subject formation and is indebted to Judith Butler's work. However, as will become clear, my analysis of agency departs from Butler's argument in that I want to explore those modalities of agency whose meaning and effect are not captured within the logic of subversion and resignification of hegemonic norms. As I will argue, if we want to parochialize the normative liberatory subject of feminist theory, then we must detach the concept of agency from the trope of resistance so as to be able to explore other structures of desire, political imaginaries, social authority, and personhood.

As the second half of this essay makes clear, my interest in locating different modalities of agency is not simply a hermeneutic exercise but remains engaged with questions of social transformation and political change. Following Butler, I want to suggest that any question of transformation must begin with an analysis of the specific practices of subjectivation that make the subjects of a particular social imaginary possible. In the context of the mosque movement this means closely analyzing the scaffolding of practices—both argumentative and embodied—that secured women's attachment to patriarchal forms of life, which, in turn, provided the necessary conditions for both their subordination and their agency. While this approach is deeply indebted to Butler's arguments, it also raises questions about how practices of the women pietists I worked with make us rethink the conceptual relationship between performativity and subject formation, moral action and embodiment, that are at the center of Bulter's theorization of subject formation.

Topography of the Mosque Movement

The mosque movement itself occupies a somewhat paradoxical place in relationship to feminist politics. It represents the first time in Egyptian history that such a large number of women have mobilized to hold public meetings in mosques to teach each other Islamic doctrine, thereby altering the historically male-centered character of mosques as well as Islamic pedagogy.[6] This trend has, of course, been facilitated by the mobility and sense of entitlement engendered by women's greater access to education and employment outside the home in postcolonial Egypt. In the last forty years women have entered new social domains and acquired new public roles from which they were previously excluded. A paradoxical effect of these developments is the proliferation of forms of piety that seem incongruous with the trajectory of the transformations that enabled them in the first place.[7] Notably, even though this movement has empowered women to enter the field of Islamic pedagogy through the institutional setting of mosques, their participation is critically structured by, and seeks to uphold, the limits of a discursive tradition that regards subordination to a transcendent will (and thus, in many instances, to male authority) as its coveted goal.[8]

According to the organizers, the women's mosque movement emerged in response to the perception that religious knowledge as a means of organizing daily life has become increasingly marginalized under modern structures of secular governance. The participants in this movement often criticize what they consider to be an increasingly prevalent form of religiosity in Egypt that accords Islam the status of an abstract system of beliefs with no direct bearing on the way one lives and structures one's daily life. This trend, usually referred to as the secularization (*'almāniya*) or Westernization (*tagharrub*) of Egyptian society, is understood to have reduced Islamic knowledge (both as a mode of conduct as well as a set of principles) to the status of "custom and folklore" (*'āda wa fukloriya*). The women's mosque movement, therefore, seeks to educate lay Muslims in those virtues, ethical capacities, and forms of reasoning the participants perceive to have become either unavailable or irrelevant to the lives of ordinary Muslims.

In Egypt today Islam has come to be embodied in a variety of practices, movements, and ideas.[9] Thus among Egyptians there are those who view Islam as constitutive of the cultural terrain upon which the Egyptian nation has acquired its unique historical character, those who understand Islam as a doctrinal system with strong political and juridical implications for the organization of state and society, and those, such as the women I worked with, for whom Islam consists, first and foremost, in individual and collective practices of pious living. This does not mean, however, that the women's mosque movement is apolitical, in the wider sense of the term, or that it represents a withdrawal from sociopolitical issues. On the contrary, the form of piety it seeks to realize is predicated upon, and transformative of, many aspects of social life.[10] The women's mosque movement has effected changes in a range of social behaviors among contemporary Egyptians, including how one dresses and speaks, what is deemed proper entertainment for adults and children, where one invests one's money, how one takes care of the poor, and what are the terms by which public debate is conducted.

While at times the mosque movement has been seen as a quietist alternative to the more militant forms of Islamic activism, there are many ways in which this movement sits uncomfortably with certain aspects of the secular liberal project promoted by the state.[11] These tensions owe in part to the specific forms of will, desire, reason, and practice this movement seeks to cultivate and in part to the ways in which it reorganizes public life and debate in line with orthodox standards of Islamic piety. It is, therefore, not surprising that the Egyptian government has recently sought to regularize and sanction this movement, recognizing that the proliferation of this kind of Islamic sociability makes the task of securing a secular liberal society difficult if not impossible.[12]

Agency, Resistance, Freedom

The pious subjects of the women's mosque movement occupy an uncomfortable place in feminist scholarship: they pursue practices and ideals embedded within a tradition that has historically accorded women a subordinate status, seeking to cultivate virtues that are associated with feminine passivity and submissiveness (such as shyness, modesty, perseverance, and humility—some of which I discuss below). In other words, the very idioms that women use to assert their presence in previously male-defined spheres are also those that secure their subordination. While it would not have been unusual in the 1960s to account for women's participation in such movements in terms of false consciousness, or the internalization of patriarchal norms through socialization, there has been an increasing discomfort with explanations of this kind. Drawing on work in the humanities and the social sciences since the 1970s that has focused on the operation of human agency within structures of subordination, feminists have sought to understand the ways in which women resist the dominant male order by subverting the hegemonic meanings of cultural practices and redeploying them in their own interests and with their own agendas. A central question explored within this scholarship has been: how do women contribute to reproducing their own domination, and how do they resist or subvert it? Scholars working in this vein have thus tended to explore religious traditions in terms of the conceptual and practical resources they offer, which women may usefully redirect and recode to secure their own interests and agendas, a recoding that stands as the site of women's agency.[13]

It should be acknowledged that the focus on locating women's agency, when it first emerged, played a critical role in complicating and expanding debates about gender in non-Western societies beyond the simplistic registers of submission and patriarchy. In particular, the focus on women's agency provided a crucial corrective to scholarship on the Middle East that had portrayed Arab and Muslim women for decades as passive and submissive beings, shackled by structures of male authority.[14] This scholarship performed the worthy task of restoring the absent voice of women to analyses of Middle Eastern societies, showing women as active agents who live a richer and more complex existence than past narratives had suggested.

While such an approach has been enormously productive in complicating the oppressor/oppressed model of gender relations, I would submit such a framework remains not only encumbered by the binary terms of resistance and subordination, but is also insufficiently attentive to projects, commitments, and goals that are not necessarily captured by these terms. Notably, the female agent in this analysis seems to stand in for a sometimes repressed, sometimes active feminist consciousness, articulated against the hegemonic male cultural norms of Arab Muslim societies. Even in instances when an explicit *feminist* agency is difficult to locate, there is a tendency to look for expressions and moments of resistance that may suggest a challenge to male domination. When women's actions seem to reinscribe what appear to be "instruments of their own oppression," the social analyst can point to moments of the disruption of, and points of opposition to, male authority that are either located in the interstices of a woman's consciousness (often read as a nascent feminist consciousness) or in the objective effects of the women's actions, however unintended they may be.[15] Agency, in this form of analysis, is understood to be the capacity to realize one's own interests against the weight of custom, tradition, transcendent will, or other obstacles (whether individual or collective). Thus the humanist desire for autonomy and expression of one's self-worth constitute the substrate, the ember that can spark into flame in the form of an act of resistance when conditions permit.[16]

What is seldom problematized in such an analysis is the universality of the desire to be free from relations of subordination and, for women, from structures of male domination, a desire that is central to liberal and progressive thought and presupposed by the concept of resistance it authorizes. This positing of women's agency as consubstantial with resistance to relations of domination, and its concomitant naturalization of freedom as a social ideal, I would argue, is a product of feminism's dual character as both an *analytical* and a *politically prescriptive* project. Despite the many strands and differences within feminism, what accords this tradition an analytical and political coherence is the premise that where society is structured to serve male interests the result will be either a neglect, or a direct suppression of, women's concerns.[17] Feminism, therefore, offers both a *diagnosis* of women's status across cultures as well as a *prescription* for changing the situation of women who are understood to be marginal/subordinate/oppressed.[18] Thus the articulation of conditions of relative freedom that enable women both to formulate and enact self-determined goals and interests remains the object of feminist politics and theorizing. As in the case of liberalism, freedom is normative to feminism: critical scrutiny is applied to those who want to limit women's freedom rather than those who want to extend it.[19]

Feminist discussions about human freedom remain heavily indebted to the distinction liberalism draws between positive and negative liberty. In the liberal tradition negative freedom refers to the absence of external obstacles to self-guided choice and action, whether imposed by the state, corporations, or individuals.[20] Positive freedom, on the other hand, is understood as the capacity to realize an autonomous will, one generally fashioned in accord with the dictates of "universal reason" or "self-interest," and hence unencumbered by the weight of custom, transcendent will, and tradition.[21] While there continues to be considerable debate over the formulation and coherence of these entwined notions,[22] what I want to highlight here is the concept of individual autonomy central to both and the concomitant elements of coercion and consent that are critical to this topography of freedom. It is important to note that the idea of self-realization itself is not an invention of the liberal tradition but existed in premodern history in various forms, such as the platonic notion of self-mastery over one's passions or the more religious notion of realizing oneself through self-transformation present in Buddhism and a variety of mystical traditions including Islam and Christianity. Liberalism's unique contribution is to integrally link the notion of self-fulfillment with individual autonomy insofar as the process of realizing oneself comes to signify the ability to realize the desires of one's "true will."[23] To the degree that autonomy in this tradition of liberalism is a *procedural* principle, and not an ontological or substantive feature of the subject, it delimits the necessary condition for the enactment of the ethics of freedom. Thus, as John Christman argues, even illiberal actions can arguably be tolerated if it is determined that they are undertaken by a freely consenting individual who is acting of her own accord. In other words, it is not the substance of a desire but its "origin that matters in judgments about autonomy."[24]

The concepts of positive and negative freedom, with the attendant requirement of procedural autonomy, provide the ground on which much of the feminist debate unfolds. For example, the positive conception of freedom seems to predominate in projects of feminist historiography (sometimes referred to as "herstory") that seek to capture historically and culturally specific instances of women's self-directed action, unencumbered by patriarchal norms or the will of others.[25] The negative conception of freedom seems to prevail in studies of gender that explore those spaces in women's lives that are independent of men's influence, and possibly coercive presence, treating such spaces as pregnant with possibilities for women's fulfillment or self-realization. Many feminist historians and anthropologists of the Arab Muslim world have thus sought to delimit those conditions and situations in which women seem to autonomously articulate "their own" discourse (such as that of poetry, weaving, cult possession, and so on), at times conferring a potentially liberatory meaning to practices of sex segregation that had traditionally been understood as making women marginal to the public arena of conventional politics.[26]

My intention here is not to question the profound transformation that the liberal discourse of freedom and individual autonomy has enabled in women's lives around the world, but rather to draw attention to the ways in which these liberal presuppositions have become naturalized in the scholarship on gender. It is quite clear that both positive and negative notions of freedom have been used productively to expand the horizon of what constitutes the domain of legitimate feminist practice and debate. For example, in the 1970s, in response to the call by white middle-class feminists to dismantle the institution of the nuclear family, which they believed to be a key source of women's oppression, Native and African American feminists argued that freedom, for them, consisted in being able to form families, since the long history of slavery, genocide, and racism had operated precisely by breaking up their communities and social networks.[27] Such arguments successfully expanded feminist understandings of "self-realization/self-fulfillment" by making considerations of class, race, and ethnicity central, thereby forcing feminists to rethink the concept of individual autonomy in light of other issues.

Since then a number of feminist theorists have launched trenchant critiques of the liberal notion of autonomy from a variety of perspectives.[28] While earlier critics like Nancy Chodorow and Carol Gilligan had drawn attention to the masculinist assumptions underpinning the ideal of autonomy, later scholars such as Seyla Benhabib and Iris Marion Young faulted this ideal for its emphasis on the atomistic, individualized, and bounded characteristics of the self at the expense of its relational qualities formed through social interactions within forms of human community.[29] Consequently, there have been various attempts to redefine autonomy so as to capture the emotional, embodied, and socially embedded character of people, particularly of women.[30] A more radical strain of poststructuralist theory has situated its critique of autonomy within a larger challenge posed to the *illusory* character of the rationalist, self-authorizing, transcendental subject presupposed by Enlightenment thought in general and the liberal tradition in particular. Rational thought, these critics argue, secures its universal scope and authority by performing a necessary exclusion of all that is bodily, feminine, emotional, nonrational, and intersubjective.[31] This exclusion cannot be substantively or conceptually recuperated, however, through recourse to an unproblematic feminine experience, body, or imaginary (*pace* Beauvoir and Irigaray), but must be thought through the very terms of the discourse of metaphysical transcendence that enacts these exclusions.[32]

In what follows I would like to push further in the direction opened by the latter poststructuralist debates. In particular, my argument for uncoupling the notion of self-realization from that of the autonomous will is indebted to poststructuralist critiques of the transcendent subject, voluntarism, and repressive models of power. Yet, as will become clear, my analysis also departs from these frameworks inasmuch as I question the overwhelming tendency within poststructuralist feminist scholarship to conceptualize agency in terms of subversion or resignification of social norms, to locate agency within those operations that resist the dominating and subjectivating modes of power. In other words, the normative political subject of poststructuralist feminist theory often remains a liberatory one whose agency is often conceptualized on the binary model of subordination and subversion. In doing so, this scholarship elides dimensions of human action whose ethical and political status does not map onto the logic of repression and resistance. In order to grasp these modes of action indebted to other reasons and histories, I want to argue that it is crucial to detach the notion of agency from the goals of progressive politics.

It is quite clear that the idea of freedom and liberty as *the* political ideal is relatively new in modern history. Many societies, including Western ones, have flourished with aspirations other than this. Nor, for that matter, does the narrative of individual and collective liberty exhaust the desires with which people live in liberal societies. If we recognize that the desire for freedom from, or subversion of, norms is not an innate desire that motivates all beings at all times, but is also profoundly mediated by cultural and historical conditions, then the question arises: how do we analyze operations of power that construct different kinds of bodies, knowledges, and subjectivities whose trajectories do not follow the entelechy of liberatory politics?

Put simply, my point is this: if the ability to effect change in the world and in oneself is historically and culturally specific (both in terms of what constitutes "change" and the means by which it is effected), then the meaning and sense of agency cannot be fixed in advance but must emerge through an analysis of the particular concepts that enable specific modes of being, responsibility, and effectivity. Viewed in this way, what may appear to be a case of deplorable passivity and docility, from a progressivist point of view, may actually be a form of agency—but one that can be understood only from within the discourses and structures of subordination that create the conditions of its enactment. In this sense, agentive capacity is entailed not only in those acts that resist norms but also in the multiple ways in which one inhabits norms.

It may be argued in response that this kind of challenge to the natural status accorded to the desire for freedom in analyses of gender runs the risk of Orientalizing Arab and Muslim women all over again—repeating the errors of pre-1970s Orientalist scholarship that defined Middle Eastern women as passive, submissive Others, bereft of the enlightened consciousness of their "Western sisters," and hence doomed to lives of servile submission to men. I would contend, however, that to examine the discursive and practical conditions within which women come to cultivate various forms of desire and capacities of ethical action is a radically different project than an Orientalizing one that locates the desire for submission in an ahistorical cultural essence. Indeed, if we accept the notion that all forms of desire are discursively organized (as much of recent feminist scholarship has argued), then it is important to interrogate the practical and conceptual conditions under which different forms of desire emerge, including desire for submission to recognized authority. We cannot treat as natural and imitable only those desires that ensure the emergence of feminist politics.

Consider, for example, the women from the mosque movement that I worked with. The task of realizing piety placed these women in conflict with several structures of authority. Some of these structures were grounded in instituted standards of Islamic orthodoxy, and others in norms of liberal discourse; some were grounded in the authority of parents and male kin, and others in state institutions. Yet the rationale behind these conflicts was not predicated upon, and therefore cannot be understood only by reference to, arguments for gender equality or resistance to male authority. Nor can these women's practices be read as a reinscription of traditional roles, since the women's mosque movement has significantly reconfigured the gendered practice of Islamic pedagogy and the social institution of mosques. One could, of course, argue in response that, the intent of these women notwithstanding, the actual effects of their practices may be analyzed in terms of their role in reinforcing or undermining structures of male domination. While conceding that such an analysis is feasible and has been useful at times, I would nevertheless argue that it remains encumbered by the binary terms of resistance and subordination and ignores projects, discourses, and desires that are not captured by these terms, such as those expressed by the women I worked with.[33]

My argument should be familiar to anthropologists who have long acknowledged that the terms people use to organize their lives are not simply a gloss for universally shared assumptions about the world and one's place in it but are actually constitutive of different forms of personhood, knowledge, and experience.[34] For this reason I have found it necessary, in what follows, to carefully attend to the specific logic of the discourse of piety: a logic that inheres not in the intentionality of the actors but in the relationships that are articulated between words, concepts, and practices that constitute a particular discursive tradition.[35] I would insist, however, that an appeal to understand the coherence of a discursive tradition is neither to justify that tradition nor to argue for some irreducible essentialism or cultural relativism; it is, instead, to take a necessary step toward explaining the force that a discourse commands.

Docility and Agency

In order to elaborate my theoretical approach, let me begin by examining the arguments of Judith Butler, who remains, for many, the preeminent theorist of poststructuralist feminist thought and whose arguments have been central to my own work. Crucial to Butler's analysis are two insights drawn from Michel Foucault, both quite well known by now. Power, according to Foucault, cannot be understood solely on the model of domination as something possessed and deployed by individuals or sovereign agents over others, with a singular intentionality, structure, or location that presides over its rationality and execution. Rather, power is to be understood as a strategic relation of force that permeates life and is productive of new forms of desires, objects, relations, and discourses.[36] Second, the subject, argues Foucault, does not precede power relations, in the form of an individuated consciousness, but is produced through these relations, which form the necessary conditions of its possibility. Central to his formulation is what Foucault calls the paradox of *subjectivation:* the very processes and conditions that secure a subject's subordination are also the means by which she becomes a self-conscious identity and agent. Stated otherwise, one may argue that the set of capacities inhering in a subject—that is, the abilities that define her modes of agency—are not the residue of an undominated self that existed prior to the operations of power but are themselves the products of those operations.[37] Such an understanding of power and subject formation encourages us to conceptualize agency not simply as a synonym for resistance to relations of domination, but as a capacity for action that specific relations of *subordination* create and enable.

Drawing on Foucault's insights, Butler asks a key question: "if power works not merely to dominate or oppress existing subjects, but also forms subjects, what is this formation?" (Butler, PLP, p. 18). By questioning the prediscursive status of the concept of subject, and inquiring instead into the relations of power that produce it, Butler breaks with those feminist analysts who have formulated the issue of personhood in terms of the relative autonomy of the individual from the social. Thus the issue for Butler is not how the social enacts the individual (as it was for generations of feminists), but what are the discursive conditions that sustain the entire metaphysical edifice of contemporary individuality.

Butler's signal contribution to feminist theory lies in her challenge to the sex/gender dichotomy that has served as the ground on which much of feminist debate, at least since the 1940s, has proceeded. For Butler the problem with the sex/gender distinction lies in the assumption that there is a prepresentational matter or sexed body that grounds the cultural inscription of gender. Butler argues not only that there is no prepresentational sex (or material body) that is not already constituted by the system of gender representation but also that gender discourse is *itself* constitutive of materialities it refers to (and is in this sense not purely representational).[38] Butler says,

> To claim that discourse is formative is not to claim that it originates, causes, or exhaustively composes that which it concedes; rather, it is to claim that there is no reference to a pure body which is not at the same time a further formation of that body. In this sense, the linguistic capacity to refer to sexed bodies is not denied, but the very meaning of "referentiality" is altered. In philosophical terms, the constative claim is always to some degree performative.
>
> (BTM, pp. 10–11)

What, then, is the process through which the materiality of the sexed and gendered subject is enacted? To answer this Butler turns not so much to the analysis of institutions and technologies of subject formation, as Foucault did, but to the analysis of language as a system of signification through which subjects are produced and interpolated. In particular, Butler builds upon Derrida's reinterpretation of J. L. Austin's notion of the performative as "that reiterative power of discourse to produce the phenomena that it regulates and constrains" (BTM, p. 2).[39] For Butler the subject in her sexed and gendered materiality is constituted performatively through a reiterated enactment of heterosexual norms, which retroactively produce, on the one hand, "the appearance of gender as an abiding interior depth"[40] and, on the other hand, the putative facticity of sexual difference, which serves to further consolidate the heterosexual imperative. In contrast to a long tradition of feminist scholarship that treated norms as an external social imposition that constrains the individual, Butler forces us to rethink this external-internal opposition by arguing that social norms are the necessary ground through which the subject is realized and comes to enact her agency.

Butler combines the Foucauldian analysis of the subject with psychoanalytic theory, in particular adopting Lacanian notions of foreclosure and abjection to emphasize certain exclusionary operations that she thinks are necessary to subject formation. She argues that the subject is produced simultaneously through a necessary repudiation of identities, forms of subjectivities, and discursive logics, what she calls "a constitutive outside to the subject" (BTM, p. 3), which marks the realm of all that is unspeakable, unsignifiable, and unintelligible from the purview of the subject, but remains, nonetheless, necessary to the subject's self-understanding and formulation.[41] This foreclosure is performatively and reiteratively enacted, in the sense that "the subject who speaks within the sphere of the speakable implicitly reinvokes the foreclosure on which it depends and, thus, depends on it again."[42]

Given Butler's theory of the subject, it is not surprising that her analysis of performativity also informs her conceptualization of agency; indeed, as she says, "the iterability of performativity *is* a theory of agency" (GT [1999],

p. xxiv; emphasis added). To the degree that the stability of social norms is a function of their repeated enactment, agency for Butler is grounded in the essential openness of each iteration and the possibility that it may fail or be reappropriated or resignified for purposes other than the consolidation of norms. Since all social formations are reproduced through a reenactment of norms, this makes these formations vulnerable because each restatement/reenactment can fail. Thus the condition of possibility of each social formation is also "the possibility of its undoing" (Butler, "Further Reflections," p. 14). She explains this point succinctly in regard to sex/gender:

> As a sedimented effect of a reiterative or ritual practice, sex acquires its naturalized effect, and, yet, it is also by virtue of this reiteration that gaps and fissures are opened up as the constitutive instabilities in such constructions, as that which escapes or exceeds the norm. . . . This instability is the *de*constituting possibility in the very process of repetition, the power that undoes the very effects by which "sex" is stabilized, the possibility to put the consolidation of the norms of "sex" into a potentially productive crisis.[43]

(BTM, p. 10)

It is important to note that there are several points on which Butler departs from the notions of agency and resistance that I criticized earlier. To begin with, Butler questions what she calls an "emancipatory model of agency," one that presumes all humans qua humans are "endowed with a will, a freedom, and an intentionality" whose workings are "thwarted by relations of power that are considered external to the subject."[44] In its place Butler locates the possibility of agency within structures of power (rather than outside) and, more important, suggests that the reiterative structure of norms serves not only to *consolidate* a particular regime of discourse/power but also provides the means for its *destabilization*.[45] In other words, there is no possibility of "undoing" social norms that is independent of the "doing" of norms; agency resides, therefore, within this productive reiterability. Butler also resists the impetus to tether the meaning of agency to a predefined teleology of emancipatory politics. As a result, the logic of subversion and resignification cannot be predetermined in Butler's framework because acts of resignification/subversion are, she argues, contingent and fragile, appearing in unpredictable places and behaving in ways that confound our expectations.[46]

I find Butler's critique of humanist conceptions of agency and subject compelling, and, indeed, my arguments in this chapter are manifestly informed by her critique. I have, however, found it productive to argue with certain tensions that characterize Butler's work in order to expand her analytics to a somewhat different, if related, set of problematics. One key tension in Butler's work owes to the fact that, while she emphasizes the ineluctable relationship between the consolidation and destabilization of norms, her discussion of agency tends to focus on those operations of power that resignify and subvert norms. Thus, even though she insists time and again that all acts of subversion are a product of the terms of violence they seek to oppose, Butler's analysis of agency often privileges those moments that "open possibilities for resignifying the terms of violation against their violating aims" (BTM, p. 122) or that provide an occasion "for a radical rearticulation" of the dominant symbolic horizon (p. 23).[47] In other words, the concept of agency in Butler's work is developed primarily in contexts where norms are thrown into question or are subject to resignification.[48]

Clearly Butler's elaboration of the notion of agency should be understood in the specific context of the political interventions in which her work is inserted. The theoretical practice Butler has developed over the last fifteen years is deeply informed by a concern for the violence that heterosexual normativity enacts and the way in which it delimits the possibilities of livable human existence. Her theorization of agency therefore must be understood in its performative dimension: as a political praxis aimed at unsettling dominant discourses of gender and sexuality. As a textual practice situated within the space of the academy, the context of Butler's intervention is not limited to the legal, philosophical, or popular discourses she analyzes but is also constituted by the reception of her work within feminist scholarship. Butler has had to defend herself against the charge, made by a range of feminists, that her work has the effect of undermining any agenda of progressive political and social reform by deconstructing the very conceptions of subject and power that enable it.[49] To counter these claims Butler has continually repositioned her work in relation to the project of articulating a radical democratic politics,[50] and in so doing she has emphasized counterhegemonic modalities of agency.[51] An important consequence of these aspects of Butler's work is that her analysis of the power of norms remains grounded in an agonistic framework, one in which norms suppress and/or are subverted, are reiterated and/or resignified—so that one gets little sense of the work norms perform beyond this register of suppression and subversion within the constitution of the subject.

Norms are not only consolidated and/or subverted, however, but performed, inhabited, and experienced in a variety of ways. This is a point on which I think Butler would not disagree; indeed, in her writings she often reverts to the trope of the "psyche" and the language of psychoanalysis to capture the density of ties through which the individual is attached to the subjectivating power of norms (see, for example, PLP). Butler's exploration of this density often remains, however, subservient, on the one hand, to her overall interest in tracking the possibilities of resistance to the regulating power of normativity[52] and, on the other hand, to her model of performativity, which is primarily conceptualized in terms of a dualistic structure of consolidation/resignification, doing/undoing, of norms.

The Subject of Norms

I would like to push the question of norms further in a direction that I think allows us to deepen the analysis of subject formation and also address the problem of reading agency primarily in terms of resistance to the regularizing impetus of structures of normativity. In particular, I would like to expand Butler's insight that norms are not simply a social imposition on the subject but constitute the very substance of her intimate, valorized interiority. But, in doing so, I want to move away from an agonistic and dualistic framework—one in which norms are conceptualized on the model of doing and undoing, consolidation and subversion—and instead to think about the variety of ways in which norms are lived and inhabited, aspired to, reached for, and consummated. As I will argue below, this in turn requires that we explore the relationship between the immanent form a normative act takes, the model of subjectivity it presupposes (specific articulations of volition, emotion, reason, and bodily expression), and the kinds of authority upon which such an act relies. Let me elaborate by discussing the problems a dualistic conception of norms poses when analyzing the practices of the mosque movement.

Consider, for example, the Islamic virtue of female modesty (al-ihtishām, al-ḥayā') that many Egyptian Muslims uphold and value. Despite a consensus about its importance, there is considerable debate about how this virtue should be lived, and particularly about whether its realization requires the donning of the veil. A majority of the participants in the mosque movement (and the larger piety movement of which the mosque movement is an integral part) argue that the veil is a necessary component of the virtue of modesty because the veil both expresses "true modesty" and is the means through which modesty is acquired. They draw, therefore, an ineluctable relationship between the norm (modesty) and the bodily form it takes (the veil) such that the veiled body becomes the necessary means through which the virtue of modesty is both created *and* expressed. In contrast to this understanding is a position (associated with prominent secularist writers) that argues that the virtue of modesty is no different than any other human attribute—such as moderation or humility: it is a facet of character but does not commit one to any particular expressive repertoire such as donning the veil. Notably, these authors oppose the veil but not the virtue of modesty, which they continue to regard as necessary to appropriate feminine conduct. The veil, in their view, has been invested with an importance that is unwarranted when it comes to judgments about female modesty.

The debate about the veil is only one part of a much larger discussion in Egyptian society wherein political differences between Islamists and secularists, and even among Islamists of various persuasions, are expressed through arguments about ritual performative behavior. The most interesting features of this debate lie not so much in whether the norm of modesty is subverted or enacted but in the radically different ways in which the norm is supposed to be lived and inhabited. Notably, each view posits a very different conceptualization of the relationship between embodied behavior and the virtue or norm of modesty: for the pietists bodily behavior is at the core of the proper realization of the norm; for their opponents it is a contingent and unnecessary element in modesty's enactment.

Some of the questions that follow from this observation are: How do we analyze the work that the body performs in these different conceptualizations of the norm? Is performative behavior differently understood in each of these views and, if so, how? How is the self differently tied to the authority the norm commands in these two imaginaries? Furthermore, what sorts of ethical and political subjects are presupposed by these two imaginaries, and what forms of ethico-political life do they enable or foreclose? These questions cannot be answered as long as we remain within the binary logic of the doing and undoing of norms. They require, instead, that we explode the category of norms into its constituent elements—to examine the immanent form that norms take and to inquire into the attachments their particular morphology generates within the topography of the self. My reason for urging this move has to do with my interest in understanding how different modalities of moral-ethical action contribute to the construction of particular kinds of subjects, subjects whose political anatomy cannot be grasped without applying critical scrutiny to the precise form their embodied actions take.[53]

In what follows I will elaborate upon these points by analyzing an ethnographic example drawn from my fieldwork with the Egyptian women's mosque movement. The ethnographic here stands less as a signature for the "real" and more as a substantiation of my earlier call to tend to the specific workings of disciplinary power that enable particular forms of investments and agency. In the course of this argument I hope to make us rethink the analytical space accorded to embodiment in contemporary feminist debates, with particular attention to the notion of performativity as discussed by Butler.

Cultivating Shyness

Through the course of my fieldwork I had come to know four lower-middle class working women, in their mid to late thirties, who were well tutored and experienced in the art of Islamic piety. Indeed, one may call them virtuosos of piety. In addition to attending mosque lessons they also met as a group to read and discuss issues of Islamic doctrine and Quranic exegesis. Notably, none of these women came from religiously devout families, and in fact some of them had had to wage a struggle against their kin in order to become religiously devout. They told me about their struggles not only with their families but, more important, with themselves in cultivating the desire for greater religious exactitude.

Not unlike other devout women from the mosques I worked with, these women also sought to excel in piety in their day-to-day lives, something they described as the condition of being close to God (variously rendered as *taqar-rab allah* and/or *taqwa*). While piety was achievable through practices that were both devotional as well as worldly in character, it required more than the simple performance of acts: piety also entailed the inculcation of entire dispositions through a simultaneous training of the body, emotions, and reason as sites of discipline until the religious virtues acquired the status of embodied habits.

Among the religious virtues considered important to acquire for pious Muslims in general, and women in particular, is that of modesty or shyness (*al-ḥayā'*), a common topic of discussion among the mosque participants. To practice *al-ḥayā'* means to be diffident, modest, and able to feel and enact shyness. While all the Islamic virtues are gendered (insofar as their measure and standards vary when applied to men and women), this is particularly true of shyness and modesty (*al-ḥayā'*). The struggle involved in cultivating this virtue was brought home to me when, in the course of a discussion about the exegesis of a chapter in the Quran called "The Story" (*Surat al-Qaṣaṣ*), one of the women, Amal, drew our attention to verse 25. This verse is about a woman walking shyly—with *al-ḥayā'*—toward Moses to ask him to approach her father for her hand in marriage. Unlike the other women in the group, Amal was particularly outspoken and confident and would seldom hesitate to assert herself in social situations with men or women. Normally I would not have described her as shy, because I considered shyness to be contradictory to qualities of candidness and self-confidence in a person. Yet, as I was to learn, Amal had learned to be outspoken in a way that was in keeping with Islamic standards of reserve, restraint, and modesty required of pious Muslim women. Here is how the conversation proceeded:

Contemplating the word *istiḥyā'*, which is form ten of the substantive *ḥayā'*,[54] Amal said, "I used to think that, even though shyness was required of us by God, if I acted shyly it would be hypocritical because I didn't actually feel it inside of me. Then, one day, in reading verse (*aya*) twenty-five in *Surat al-Qaṣaṣ* ("The Story") I realized that *al-ḥayā'* was among the good deeds and, given my natural lack of shyness, I had to make or create it first. I realized that making (*ṣana'*) it in yourself is not hypocrisy and that eventually your inside learns to have *al-ḥayā'* too." Here she looked at me and explained the meaning of the word *istiḥyā'*: "It means making oneself shy, even if it means creating it." She continued with her point, "And finally I understood that, once you do this, the sense of shyness (*al-ḥayā'*) eventually imprints itself on your inside." Another friend, Nama, a single woman in her early thirties, who had been sitting and listening, added, "Its just like the veil (*ḥijāb*). In the beginning when you wear it you're embarrassed (*maksūfa*), and don't want to wear it, because people say that you look older and unattractive, that you won't get married and will never find a husband. But you *must* wear the veil, first, because it is God's command (*ḥukm Allah*) and, then, with time, your inside learns to feel shy without the veil, and if you were to take it off your entire being feels uncomfortable (*mish rāḍi*) about it."

To many readers this conversation may exemplify an obsequious deference to social norms that both reflects and reproduces women's subordination. Indeed, Amal's struggle with herself to become shy may appear to be no more than an instance of the internalization of standards of effeminate behavior, one that contributes little to our understanding of agency. Yet if we think of "agency" not simply as a synonym for resistance to social norms but as a modality of action, then this conversation raises some interesting questions about the kind of relationship established between the subject and the norm, between performative behavior and inward disposition. To begin with, what is striking here is that instead of innate human desires eliciting outward forms of conduct, it is the sequence of practices and actions one is engaged in that determines one's desires and emotions. In other words, action does not issue forth from natural feelings but *creates* them. Furthermore, it is through repeated *bodily acts* that one trains one's memory, desire, and intellect to behave according to established standards of conduct. Notably, Amal *does not* regard simulating shyness in the initial stages of her self-cultivation to be hypocritical, as it is in certain liberal conceptions of the self where a dissonance between internal feelings and external expressions would be considered a form of dishonesty or self-betrayal (as captured in the phrase "How can I do something sincerely when my heart is not in it?"). Instead, taking the absence of shyness as a marker of an incomplete learning process, Amal further develops the quality of shyness by synchronizing her outward behavior with her inward motives until the discrepancy between the two is dissolved. This is an example of a mutually constitutive relationship between body learning and body sense—as Nama says, your body literally comes to feel uncomfortable if you do *not* veil.

Second, what is also significant in this program of self-cultivation is that bodily acts—like wearing the veil or conducting oneself modestly in interactions with people (especially men)—do not serve as manipulable masks in a game of public presentation, detachable from an essential interiorized self. Rather they are the *critical markers* of piety as well as the *ineluctable means* by which one trains oneself to be pious. While wearing the veil serves at first as a means to tutor oneself in the attribute of shyness, it is also simultaneously integral to the practice of shyness: one cannot simply discard the veil once a modest deportment has been acquired, because the veil itself is part of what defines that deportment.[55] This is a crucial aspect of the disciplinary program pursued by the participants of the mosque movement, the significance of which is elided when the veil is understood solely in terms of its symbolic value as a marker of women's subordination or Islamic identity.

The complicated relationship between learning, memory, experience, and the self undergirding the model of pedagogy followed by the mosque participants has at times been discussed by scholars through the Latin term *habitus*, meaning an acquired faculty in which the body, mind, and emotions are simultaneously trained to achieve competence at something (such as meditation, dancing, or playing a musical instrument). The term *habitus* has become best known in the social sciences through the work of Pierre Bourdieu, who uses it as a theoretical concept to understand how the structural and class positions of individual subjects come to be embodied as dispositions—largely through unconscious processes.[56] My own work draws upon a longer and richer history of this term, however, one that addresses the centrality of gestural capacities in certain traditions of moral cultivation. Aristotelian in origin and adopted by the three monotheistic traditions,[57] habitus in this older meaning refers to a specific pedagogical process by which moral virtues are acquired through a coordination of outward behavior (e.g., bodily acts, social demeanor) with inward dispositions (e.g., emotional states, thoughts, intentions).[58] Thus habitus in this usage refers to a conscious effort at reorienting desires, brought about by the concordance of inward motives, outward actions, inclinations, and emotional states through the repeated practice of virtuous deeds.[59] As a pedagogical technique necessary for the development of moral virtues, habitus in this sense is not a universal term applicable to all types of knowledges, neither does it necessarily serve as a conceptual bridge between the objective world of social structures and subjective consciousness as it does in Bourdieu's formulation.

This Aristotelian understanding of moral formation influenced a number of Islamic thinkers, foremost among them the eleventh-century theologian Abu Hamid al-Ghazali (d. 1111), but also al-Miskawayh (d. 1030), Ibn Rushd (d. 1198), and Ibn Khaldun (d. 1406). Historian Ira Lapidus draws attention to this genealogy in his analysis of Ibn Khaldun's use of the Arabic term *malaka*.[60] Lapidus argues that although Ibn Khaldun's use of the term *malaka* has often been translated as "habit," its sense is best captured in the Latin term *habitus*, which Lapidus describes as "that inner quality developed as a result of outer practice which makes practice a perfect ability of the soul of the actor."[61] Consider, for example, Ibn Khaldun's remarks in *The Muqadimmah*, which bear remarkable similarity to Aristotle's discussion: "A habit[us] is a firmly rooted quality acquired by doing a certain action and repeating it time after time, until the form of that action is firmly fixed [in one's disposition]. A habit[us] corresponds to the original action after which it was formed."[62] In terms of faith, *malaka*, according to Lapidus, "is the acquisition, from the belief of the heart and the resulting actions, of a quality that has complete control over the heart so that it commands the action of the limbs and makes every activity take place in submissiveness to it to the point that all actions, eventually, become subservient to this affirmation of faith. This is the highest degree of faith. It is perfect faith."[63]

This Aristotelian legacy continues to live within the practices of the contemporary piety movement in Egypt. It is evident in the frequent invocation of Abu Hamid al-Ghazali's spiritual exercises and techniques of moral cultivation, found in popular instruction booklets on how to become pious, and often referred to in ordinary conversations within the Islamic revival.[64] Even though the term *malaka* is not used in these publications and discussions, the role outward behavioral forms play in shaping moral character is clearly indebted to Islamic reformulations of Aristotle's notion of habitus.

Abjection of Female Bodies?

A significant body of literature in feminist theory argues that patriarchal ideologies—whether nationalist, religious, medical, or aesthetic in character—work by objectifying women's bodies and subjecting them to masculinist systems of representation, thereby negating and distorting women's own experience of their corporeality and subjectivity.[65] In this view the virtue of *al-ḥayā'* (shyness or modesty) can be understood as yet another example of the subjection of women's bodies to masculinist or patriarchal valuations, images, and representational logic. A feminist strategy aimed at unsettling such a circumscription would try to expose *al-ḥayā'* for its negative valuation of women, simultaneously bringing to the fore alternative representations and experiences of the feminine body that are denied, submerged, or repressed by its masculinist logic.

A different perspective within feminist theory regards the recuperation of "women's experience" to be an impossible task, since the condition for the possibility of any discourse, or, for that matter, "thought itself," is the rendering of certain materialities and subjectivities as the constitutive outside of the discourse.[66] In this view there is no recuperable ontological "thereness" to this abjected materiality (such as "a feminine experience"), because the abject can only be conceived in relation to hegemonic terms of the discourse, "at and as its most tenuous borders" (Butler, BTM, p. 8). A well-known political intervention arising out of this analytic aims to demonstrate the impossibility of "giving voice" to the subalterity of any abject being—thereby exposing the violence endemic to thought itself. This intervention is famously captured in Gayatri Spivak's rhetorical question, "Can the subaltern speak?"[67]

The analysis I have presented of the practice of *al-ḥayā'* (and the practice of veiling) departs from both these perspectives: I do not regard female subjectivity as that which belies masculinist representations; nor do I see this subjectivity as a sign of the abject materiality that discourse cannot articulate. Rather, I believe that the body's relationship to discourse is variable and that it seldom simply follows either of the paths laid out by these two perspectives within feminist theory. In regard to the feminist argument that privileges the role representations play in securing male domination, it is important to note that even though the concept of al-ḥayā' embeds a masculinist understanding of gendered bodies, far more is at stake in the practice of al-ḥayā' than this framework allows, as is evident from the conversation between Amal and her friend Nama. Crucial to their understanding of al-ḥayā' as an embodied practice is an entire conceptualization of the role the body plays in the making of the self, one in which the outward behavior of the body constitutes both the potentiality and the means through which interiority is realized. A feminist strategy that seeks to unsettle such a conceptualization cannot simply intervene in the system of representation that devalues the feminine body but must also engage the very armature of attachments between outward behavioral forms and the sedimented subjectivity that al-ḥayā' enacts. Representation is only one issue among many in the ethical relationship of the body to the self and others, and it does not by any means determine the form this relationship takes.

Similarly, I remain skeptical of the second feminist framing, in which the corporeal is analyzed on the model of language as the constitutive outside of discourse itself. In this reading it would be possible to read al-ḥayā' as an instantiation of the control a masculinist imaginary must assert over the dangerous supplement femininity signifies in Islamic thought. Such a reading is dissatisfying to me because the relationship it assumes between the body and discourse, one modeled on a linguistic theory of signification, is inadequate to the imaginary of the mosque movement. Various aspects of this argument will become clear below when I address the notion of performativity underlying the Aristotelian model of ethical formation the mosque participants followed. Suffice it to say that the mosque women's practices of modesty and femininity do not signify the abjectness of the feminine within Islamic discourse but articulate a positive and immanent discourse of being in the world. This discourse requires that we carefully examine the *work that bodily practices perform* in creating a subject that is pious in its formation.

Performativity and the Subject

Consider two contrastive views about female modesty that circulate among secular Muslim intellectuals and the piety movement, which I mentioned briefly earlier. The former often criticize the latter for making modesty dependent upon the particularity of attire (such as the veil).[68] Instead, these secular intellectuals propose that the virtue of modesty is a cherished human attribute that is particularly attractive in women but should not mandate the practice of veiling. The veil, they say, was a regional custom in pre-Islamic Arabia that has mistakenly been assigned a divine status. Note that in the view of these secular Muslim intellectuals modesty is not so much an attribute of the body as it is a characteristic of the individual's interiority, which is then expressed in bodily form. In contrast, for the women I worked with this relationship between interiority and exteriority was almost reversed: a modest bodily form (the veiled body) did not simply express the self's interiority but was the means by which it was acquired. Since the mosque participants regarded outward bodily markers to be ineluctable means to the virtue of modesty, the body's precise movements, behaviors, and gestures were all made the object of their efforts to live by the code of modesty.

From certain feminist perspectives the differences between these two perspectives might seem inconsequential since, ultimately, both understandings of modesty have the same effect on the social field: the virtue of modesty itself enshrines various forms of feminine comportment that should be challenged—the veil being only one of them. I would suggest, however, that disagreement about whether or not one should veil seems minor when viewed from a Kantian model of disembodied and universal ethics, but from an Aristotelian point of view (operative among those I worked) the difference between these two understandings of modesty is substantial. In the Aristotelian worldview ethical conduct is not simply a matter of the effect one's behavior produces in the world but depends crucially upon the precise form that behavior takes: both the acquisition and the consummation of ethical virtues devolve upon the proper enactment of prescribed bodily behaviors, gestures, and markers.[69] Thus, an act is judged to be ethical in this tradition not simply because it accomplishes the social objective it is meant to achieve but also because it enacts this objective in the manner and form it is supposed to: an ethical act is, to borrow J. L. Austin's term, "felicitous" only if it achieves its goals in a prescribed behavioral form.[70]

Certain aspects of this Aristotelian model of ethical formation resonate with J. L. Austin's concept of the performative, especially as this concept has been deployed in the analysis of subject formation in Judith Butler's work in *Bodies That Matter* and *Psychic Life of Power*. It is instructive to examine this resonance closely for at least two reasons: one, because such an examination reveals the kinds of questions about bodily performance and subjectivity that are important to foreground in order to understand the force this Aristotelian tradition of ethical formation commands among the mosque participants and, two, because such an examination reveals the kind of analytical labor one needs to perform in order to make the ethnographic particularity of a social formation speak generatively to philosophical concepts—concepts whose anthropological assumptions are often taken for granted.

A performative, which for Austin is primarily a speech act, for Butler includes both bodily and speech acts through which subjects are formed. Butler, in her adoption of Derrida's interpretation of performativity as an iterable practice, formulates a theory of subject formation in which performativity becomes "one of the influential rituals by which subjects are formed and reformulated" (ES, p. 160).[71] Butler is careful to point out the difference between performance as a "bounded act" and performativity, which "consists in a reiteration of norms which precede, constrain, and exceed the performer and in that sense cannot be taken as the fabrication of the performer's 'will' or 'choice'" (BTM, p. 234).[72] In *Excitable Speech* Butler spells out the role bodily performatives play in the constitution of the subject. She argues that "bodily *habitus* constitutes a tacit form of performativity, a citational chain lived and believed at the level of the body" (ES, p. 155) such that the materiality of the subject comes to be enacted through a series of embodied performatives.[73]

As I discussed earlier, Butler's conception of performativity is also at the core of her theory of agency: she claims that the iterable and repetitive character of the performatives makes the structure of norms vulnerable and unstable because the reiteration may fail, be resignified, or be reappropriated for purposes other than the consolidation of norms. This leads Butler to argue: "That no social formation can endure without becoming reinstated, and that every reinstatement puts the 'structure' in question at risk suggests the possibility of its undoing is at once the condition of possibility of the structure itself."[74] In other words, what makes the structure of norms stable—the reiterative character of bodily and speech performatives—is also that which makes the structure susceptible to change and resignification.[75]

Butler's notion of performativity and the labor it enacts in the constitution of the subject may at first glance seem to be a useful way of analyzing the mosque participants' emphasis on embodied virtues in the formation of a pious self. Both views (the mosque participants' and Butler's) suggest that it is through the repeated performance of virtuous practices (norms, in Butler's terms) that the subject's will, desire, intellect, and body come to acquire a particular form. The mosque participants' understanding of virtues may be rendered in Butlerian terms in that they regard virtuous performances not so much as manifestations of their will but more as actions that produce the will in its particularity. In this conception one might say that the pious subject does not precede the performance of normative virtues but is enacted through the performance. Virtuous actions may well be understood as performatives; they enact that which they name: a virtuous self.

Despite these resonances between Butler's notion of performativity and the mosque participants' understanding of virtuous action, it would be a mistake to assume that the logic of piety practices can be so easily accommodated within Butler's theoretical language. Butler herself cautions against a "technological approach" to theory wherein "the theory is articulated on its self-sufficiency, and then shifts register only for the pedagogical purpose of illustrating an already accomplished truth" (CHU, p. 26). Such a perfunctory approach to theory, Butler argues, is inadequate because theoretical formulations always ensue from particular examples and are therefore stained by that particularity; this staining is constitutive and thus raises doubts about the universal applicability of a theoretical formulation. In order to make a particular theoretical formulation travel across cultural and historical specificities, one needs to rethink the structure of assumptions that underlie a theoretical formulation and perform the difficult task of translation and reformulation.[76] If we take this insight seriously, then the question we need to ask of Butler's theorization of performativity is: how does a consideration of the mosque participants' understanding of virtuous action make us rethink the labor performativity enacts in the constitution of the subject?

To address this question I believe it necessary to think through three important dimensions of the articulation of performativity in regard to subject formation: a. the sequencing of the performatives and their interrelationship; b. the place of language in the analysis of performativity; and c. different articulations of the notions of "subversion," "change," or "destabilization" across different models of performativity. One of the crucial differences between Butler's model of the performative and the one implicitly informing the practices of the mosque movement lies in how each performative is related to the ones that follow and precede it. The model of ethical formation followed by the mosque participants emphasizes the sedimented and cumulative character of reiterated performatives, where each performative builds on previous ones and a carefully calibrated system exists by which differences between reiterations are judged in terms of how successfully (or not) the performance has taken root in the body and mind. Thus the mosque participants—no matter how pious they were—exercised great vigilance in scrutinizing themselves to gauge how well (or poorly) their performances had actually taken root in their dispositions (as Amal and Nama did in the conversation described earlier).

Significantly, the question of the disruption of norms is posed differently in the model governing the mosque movement from how it is posed in the model derived from the examples that Butler provides. Not only are the standards by which an action is perceived to have failed or succeeded different, but the practices that *follow* the identification of an act (as successful or failed) are also distinct. Consider, for example, Butler's discussion of drag queens who parody dominant heterosexual norms and in so doing expose "the imitative structure by which hegemonic gender is itself produced and disputes heterosexuality's claim on naturalness and originality" (BTM, p. 125). What is significant here is that as the drag queen becomes more successful in his approximation of heterosexual norms of femininity, the challenge his performance poses to the stability of these norms also increases. The excellence of his performance, in other words, exposes the vulnerability of heterosexual norms and puts their naturalized stability at risk. For the mosque participants, on the other hand, excellence at piety does not put the structure that governs its normativity at risk but rather consolidates it.

Furthermore, when, in Butler's example, a drag queen's performance fails to approximate the ideal of femininity, Butler reads this failure as a sign of the intrinsic inability of the performative structure of heteronormativity to realize its own ideals. In contrast, in the model operative among the mosque participants, a person's failure to enact a virtue successfully is perceived to be the marker of an inadequately formed self, one in which the interiority and exteriority of the person are improperly aligned. The recognition of this disjuncture in turn requires one to undertake a specific series of steps to rectify the situation—steps that build upon the rooted and sedimented character of prior performances of normative virtues. Amal, in the conversation cited above, describes how she followed her initial inability to simulate shyness successfully with repeated acts of shyness that in turn produced the cumulative effect of a shy interiority and disposition. Drag queens may also expend a similar kind of effort in order to better approximate dominant feminine norms, but they take the disjuncture between what is socially performed and what is biologically attributed as necessary to the very structure of their performance. For the mosque participants, in contrast, the relevant disjuncture is that between a religious norm (or ideal) and its actual performance: their actions are aimed precisely at *overcoming* this disjuncture.

One reason these two understandings of performative behavior differ from each other is based in the contrastive conceptions of embodied materiality that underlie them. Butler understands the materiality of the body on the model of language and analyzes the power of bodily performatives in terms of processes of signification whose disruptive potential lies in the indeterminate character of signs. In response to those who charge her with practicing a kind of linguistic reductionism, Butler insists that the body is not reducible to discourse or speech, since "the relationship between speech and the body is that of a chiasmus. Speech is bodily, but the body exceeds the speech it occasions; and speech remains irreducible to the bodily means of its enunciation" (ES, pp. 155–56). So how are we to understand this chiasmus? For Butler the answer lies in formulating a theory of signification that is always operative—whether acknowledged or not—when one tries to speak about this chiasmus, because in speaking one renders discursive what is extra- or nondiscursive (BTM, p. 11). The discursive terms, in turn, become constitutive of the extra-discursive realms of the body because of the formative power of language to constitute that which it represents.[77] Butler remains skeptical of approaches that leave the relationship between discursive and extradiscursive forms of materiality open and untheorized and seeks to demonstrate the power of an analysis that foregrounds the significatory aspects of the body.[78]

It is important to point out here that there are a range of theorists who may agree with Butler about the chiasmatic relationship between the body and discourse but for whom a theory of signification does not quite address a basic problem: how do we develop a vocabulary for thinking conceptually about forms of corporeality that, while efficacious in behavior, do not lend themselves easily to representation, elucidation, and a logic of signs and symbols? For scholars like Talal Asad, William Connolly, Elizabeth Grosz, and Brian Massumi a theory of linguistic signification does not quite apprehend the power that corporeality commands in the making of subjects and objects.[79] These scholars, of course, speak from within a long philosophical tradition that extends from Spinoza to Bergson to Merleau-Ponty to, more recently, Deleuze.

In light of this, a consideration of the mosque participants' understanding of virtuous action raises yet another set of interesting questions regarding Butler's focus on the significatory aspects of bodily performatives. As I mentioned earlier, the mosque participants did not understand the body as a sign of the self's interiority but as a means of developing the self's potentiality. (Potentiality here refers not to a generic human faculty but to the abilities one acquires through specific kinds of embodied training and knowledge.)[80] One might say that for the mosque participants, therefore, the body was not apprehensible through its ability to function as a sign but encompassed an entire manner of being and acting in which the body served as the developable means for the self's consummation. In light of this, it is important to ask whether a theory of embodied performativity that assumes a theory of linguistic signification (as necessary to its articulation) is adequate for analyzing formulations of the body that insist on the inadequacy of the body to function as a sign.

That the mosque participants treat the body as a medium for rather than as a sign of the self also has consequences for how subversion or destabilization might work within such an imaginary. Note that the mosque participants regard both *compliance with* and *rebellion against* norms as dependent upon the teachability of the body—what I have called elsewhere the "docility of the body"—such that both virtuous and unvirtuous dispositions are necessarily learned. This means that the possibility for disrupting the structural stability of norms depends *literally* on retutoring the body rather than on destabilizing the referential structure of the sign or, for that matter, positing an alternative representational logic that challenges masculinist readings of feminine corporeality. Thus anyone interested in reforming this tradition cannot simply assume that resignifying Islamic practices and virtues (like modesty or donning the veil) would change the meaning of these practices for the mosque participants; rather, what is required is a much deeper engagement with the architecture of the self that undergirds a particular mode of living and attachment of which modesty/veiling are a part.

The recalcitrant character of the structure of orthodox Islamic norms contrasts dramatically with the politics of resignification presupposed by Butler's formulation of performativity. Butler argues that the body is knowable through language (even if it is not reducible to language); corporeal politics for her often ensues from those features of signification and reference that destabilize the referential structure. In Butler's conception, insofar as the force of the body is knowable through the system of signification, any challenge to the system comes from interventions in the significatory features of that system. For example, Butler analyzes the reappropriation of the term *queer,* which was historically used as a form of hate speech against lesbians and gays but has now come to serve as a positive term of self-identification. For Butler the appropriation of the term *queer* works by redirecting the force of the reiterative structure of homophobic norms, tethering the term to a different context of valences, meanings, and histories. What is notable for the purpose of my argument here is that it is a change in the referential structure of the sign that destabilizes the normative meaning and force of the term *queer*. In the case of the mosque movement, as I have argued, a change in the referential structure of the system of signs cannot produce the same effect of destabilization. Any attempt to destabilize the normative structure must also take into account the specificity of embodied practices and virtues, and the kind of work they perform on the self, recognizing that any transformation of their meaning requires an engagement with the technical and embodied armature through which these practices are attached to the self.[81]

In conclusion, I would like to clarify the implications of this analytical framework for the manner in which we think about politics, especially in light of some of the questions posed to me when I have presented this essay in public. In pushing at the limits of the analytical project of feminism, I am often asked whether I have lost sight of its politically prescriptive project. Does attention to the ways in which moral agency and norms function within a particular imaginary entail the suspension of critique? What is the "implicit politics" of this essay?

In some ways these questions bespeak the tension that attends the dual character of feminism as both an analytical and political project to the extent that no analytical undertaking is considered enough unless it takes a position vis-à-vis the subordination of women. Marilyn Strathern observed as much when she wrote about the "awkward relationship" between feminism and anthropology. She argued,

> Insofar as the feminist debate is necessarily a politicized one, our common ground or field is thus conceived as the practical contribution that feminist scholarship makes to the solution or dissolution of the problem of women. . . . To present an ethnographic account as authentic ("these are the conditions in this society") cannot avoid being judged for the position it occupies in this particular debate. By failing to take up an explicit feminist position, I have, on occasion, been regarded as not a feminist.
>
> (*Gender of the Gift*, p. 28)

While appreciating Strathern's astute comments about the enterprise of thinking/writing on the double edge of analysis and advocacy, I also think the argument I offer here has repercussions for the way we think about politics. In this essay I have argued that the liberatory goals of feminism should be rethought in light of the fact that the desire for freedom and liberation is a historically situated desire whose motivational force cannot be assumed a priori but needs to be reconsidered in light of other desires, historical projects, and capacities that inhere in a culturally and historically located subject. What follows from this, I would contend, is that in analyzing the problem of politics we must begin with a set of fundamental questions about the conceptual relationship between the body, the self, and moral agency as constituted within different ethical-moral traditions, not holding one particular model to be axiomatic, as often is the case in progressive feminist scholarship. This is particularly germane to the movement I am discussing here since it is organized around self-fashioning and ethical conduct (rather than the transformation of juridical and state institutions), an adequate understanding of which must necessarily address what in other contexts has been called the politics of the body—namely, the constitution of the body within structures of power.

Here Judith Butler's work on power and subject formation is crucial in forcing us to track the question of politics through an analysis of the architecture of the self, the processes (social and technical) through which the self's constituent elements (instincts, desires, emotions, memory) are identified and given coherence. While Butler's attention to embodied politics is often used to explicate how gender inequality works differently in various cultural systems, far less attention is paid to how different modes of affective attachment might parochialize left-liberal assumptions about the constitutive relationship between moral action and embodiment when discussing politics. Women's embodied relationships to the world and themselves, once understood as an enactment of structures of inequality, often serve as the theater in which already known projects, affects, and commitments are played out. Yet, if it is conceded that politics involves more than rational argumentation and evaluation of abstract moral principles, and that political judgments arise from the intersubjective level of being and acting, then it follows that this level must be engaged to think constitutively and critically about what politics is or should be about.

For a scholar of Islam none of these issues can be adequately addressed without encountering the essential tropes through which knowledge about the Muslim world has been organized, key among them the trope of patriarchal violence and Islam's (mis)treatment of women. The veil, more than any other Islamic practice, has become the symbol and evidence of the violence Islam has inflicted upon women. I have seldom presented my arguments in an academic setting, particularly my argument about the veil as a disciplinary practice that constitutes pious subjectivities, without facing a barrage of questions from people demanding to know why I have failed to condemn the patriarchal assumptions behind this practice and the suffering it engenders. I am often struck by my audience's lack of curiosity about what else the veil might perform in the world beyond its violation of women. These exhortations to condemnation are only one indication of how the veil and the commitments it embodies, not to mention other kinds of Islamic practices, have come to be understood through the prism of women's freedom and unfreedom such that to ask a different set of questions about this practice is to lay oneself open to the charge that one is indifferent to women's oppression. The force this coupling of the veil and women's (un)freedom commands is equally manifest in those arguments that endorse or defend the veil on the grounds that it is a product of women's "free choice" and evidence of their "liberation" from the hegemony of Western cultural codes.

What I find most troubling about this framing is the analytical foreclosure it effects and the silence it implicitly condones regarding a whole host of issues—issues that demand attention from scholars who want to think productively about Islamic practices undergirding the contemporary Islamic revival. I understand the political demand feminism imposes to exercise vigilance against culturalist arguments that seem to authorize practices underwriting women's oppression. However, I would submit that our analytical explorations should not be reduced to the requirements of political judgment, in part because the labor that belongs to the field of analysis is different from that required by the demands of political action, both in its temporality and its social impact. It is not that these two modalities of engagement—the political and the analytical—should remain deaf to each other, only that they should not be collapsed into each other.[82] By allowing theoretical inquiry some immunity from the requirements of strategic political action, we leave open the possibility that the task of thinking may proceed in directions not dictated by the logic and pace of immediate political events.

Wendy Brown has written eloquently about what is lost when analysis is subjected to the demands of political attestation, judgment, and action. She argues:

> It is the task of theory . . . to "make meanings slide," while the lifeblood of politics is made up of bids for hegemonic representation that by nature seek to arrest this movement, to fix meaning at the point of the particular political truth—the nonfluid and nonnegotiable representation—that one wishes to prevail. . . . Let us ask what happens when intellectual inquiry is sacrificed to an intensely politicized moment, whether inside or outside an academic institution. What happens when we, out of good and earnest intentions, seek to collapse the distinction between politics and theory, between political bids for hegemonic truth and intellectual inquiry? We do no favor, I think, to politics or to intellectual life by eliminating a productive tension—the way in which politics and theory effectively interrupt each other—in order to consolidate certain political claims as the premise of a program of intellectual inquiry.[83]

I read Wendy Brown here as insisting on the importance of practicing a certain amount of skepticism, a suspension of judgment if you will, toward the normative limits of political discourse. "Intellectual inquiry" here entails pushing against our received assumptions and categories, through which a number of unwieldy problems have been domesticated to customary habits of thought and praxis.

This argument gains particular salience in the current political climate, defined by the events of September 11, 2001, and the subsequent war of terror that the United States government has unleashed on the Muslim world. The longstanding demand that feminists stand witness to the patriarchal ills of Islam has now been enlisted in the service of one of the most unabashed imperial projects of our time. Consider, for example, how the Feminist Majority's international campaign against the Taliban regime was an essential element in the Bush administration's attempt to establish legitimacy for the bombing of Afghanistan—aptly called "Operation Enduring Freedom."[84] It was the burka-clad body of the Afghan woman—and *not* the destruction wrought by twenty years of war funded by the United States through one of the largest covert operations in American history—that served as the primary referent in the Feminist Majority's vast mobilization against the Taliban regime (and later the Bush administration's war). While the denial of education to Afghan women and the restrictions imposed on their movements were often noted, it was this visual image of the burka more than anything else that condensed and organized knowledge about Afghanistan and its women, as if this alone could provide an adequate understanding of their suffering. The inadequacy of this knowledge has today become strikingly evident as reports from Afghanistan increasingly suggest that the lives of Afghan women have not improved since the ouster of the Taliban and that, if anything, life on the streets has become less safe than it was under the old regime because of conditions of increased sociopolitical instability.[85] We need to entertain the possibility that had there been some analytical complexity added to the picture that organizations such as the Feminist Majority presented of Afghan women's situation under Taliban rule, had the need for historical reflection not been hijacked by the need for immediate political action, then feminism might have been less recruitable to this imperial project.

The ethical questions that imperial projects of this proportion pose for feminist scholars and activists are also relevant to the more sedate context of the women's mosque movement that has been the focus of this essay. To the degree that feminism is a politically prescriptive project, it requires the remaking of sensibilities and commitments of women whose lives contrast with feminism's emancipatory visions. Many feminists, who would oppose the use of military force, would have little difficulty supporting projects of social reform aimed at transforming the attachments, commitments, and sensibilities of the kind that undergird the practices of the women I worked with, so that these women may be allowed to live a more enlightened existence. Indeed, my own history of involvement in feminist politics attests to an unwavering belief in projects of reform aimed at rendering certain life forms provisional if not extinct. But the questions that I have come to ask myself, which I would like to pose to the reader as well, are: Do my political visions ever run up against the responsibility I incur for the destruction of life forms so that "unenlightened" women may be taught to live more freely? Do I even fully comprehend the forms of life that I want so passionately to remake? Would an intimate knowledge of life worlds that are distinct from mine ever bring me to question my own certainty about what I prescribe as a superior way of life for others?

It was in the course of the encounter between my own objections to the piety movement and the texture of the lives of the women I worked with that the political and the ethical converged for me again in a personal sense. In the course of conducting fieldwork with this movement, I came to recognize that politically responsible scholarship entails not simply being faithful to the desires and aspirations of "my informants" and urging my audience to "understand and respect" the diversity of desires that characterizes our world today. Nor is it enough to reveal the assumptions of my own or my fellow scholars' biases and (in)tolerances. As someone who has come to believe, along with a number of other feminists, that the political project of feminism is not predetermined but needs to be continually negotiated within specific contexts, the questions I have come to ask myself again and again are: What do we mean when we as feminists say that gender equality is the central principle of our analysis and politics? How does my enmeshment within the thick texture of my informants' lives affect my openness to this question? Are we willing to countenance the sometimes violent task of remaking sensibilities, life worlds, and attachments so that women of the kind I worked with may be taught to value the principle of freedom? Furthermore, does a commitment to the ideal of equality in our own lives endow us with the capacity to know that this ideal captures what is or should be fulfilling for everyone else? If it does not, as is surely the case, then I think we need to rethink, with far more humility than we are accustomed to, what feminist politics really means. (Here I want to be clear that my comments are not directed at "Western feminists" alone, but also include "Third World" feminists and all those who are located somewhere within this polarized terrain, since these questions implicate all of us, given the liberatory impetus of the feminist tradition.)

As to the question whether my framework calls for the suspension of critique in regard to the patriarchal character of the mosque movement, my response is that I urge no such stance. But what I do urge is an expansion of a normative understanding of critique, one that is quite prevalent among many progressives and feminists (among whom I have often included myself). Criticism, in this view, is about successfully demolishing your opponent's position and exposing the implausibility of her argument and its logical inconsistencies. This, I would submit, is a limited and weak understanding of the notion of critique. Critique, I believe, is most powerful when it leaves open the possibility that we might also be remade in the process of engaging another's worldview, that we might come to learn things that we did not already know before we undertook the engagement. This requires that we occasionally turn the critical gaze upon ourselves, leaving open the possibility that we may be remade through an encounter.

The questions I have posed above about politics should not be seen as a call for the abandonment of struggle against what we consider to be unjust practices in the situated context of our own lives or as an advocacy for the pious lifestyles of the women I worked with. To do so would be only to mirror the teleological certainty that characterizes some of the versions of progressive liberalism that I criticized earlier. Rather, my suggestion is that we leave open the possibility that our political and analytical certainties might be transformed in the process of exploring nonliberal movements of the kind I studied, that the lives of the women with whom I worked might have something to teach us beyond what we can learn from the circumscribed social scientific exercise of "understanding and translation." If there is a normative political position that underlies this essay, it is to urge that we—my readers and myself—embark upon an inquiry in which we do not assume that the political positions we uphold will necessarily be vindicated, or provide the ground for our theoretical analysis, but instead hold open the possibility that we may come to ask of politics a whole series of questions that seemed settled when we first embarked upon the inquiry. It asks us to consider that perhaps we do not always know *what* we oppose and that a political vision at times has to admit its own finitude to even comprehend what it has sought to oppose. This is not a question that can be directly attributed to Butler's work per se, but is rather one that, as I said at the outset, could not have been pursued without the channels of thought and inquiry that she has opened for many.

NOTES

1. This dilemma seems to be further compounded by the fact that women's partici-pation in the Islamic movement in a number of countries (like Iran, Egypt, Indo-nesia, and Malaysia) is not limited to the poor and middle classes (classes often considered to have a "natural affinity" for religion), but also from the upper- and middle-income strata.

2. There are three important strands that comprise the Islamic revival in Egypt: state-oriented political groups and parties, militant Islamists (whose presence has declined since the 1980s), and a network of socioreligious nonprofit orga-nizations that provide charitable services to the poor and perform the work of proselytization. The women's mosque movement is an important subset of this network of socioreligious organizations and draws upon the same discourse of piety (referred to as *da'wa*). For an analysis of the historical and institutional re-lationship between the nonprofit organizations and the women's mosque move-ment, see Saba Mahmood, *Politics of Piety: The Islamic Revival and the Feminist Subject* (Princeton: Princeton University Press, 2005), chapter 2.

3. This sensibility has a palpable public presence in Egypt, manifest in the vast proliferation of neighborhood mosques and other institutions of Islamic learn-ing and social welfare, in a dramatic increase in attendance at mosques by both women and men, and in marked displays of religious sociability. Examples of the latter include the adoption of the veil (*ḥijāb*), a brisk consumption and produc-tion of religious media and literature, and a growing circle of intellectuals who write and comment upon contemporary affairs in the popular press from a self-described Islamic point of view. Neighborhood mosques have come to serve as the organizational center for many of these activities.

4. My research is based on two years of fieldwork (1995–1997) conducted in five different mosques from a range of socioeconomic backgrounds in Cairo, Egypt. In addition, I also carried out participant observation among the leaders and par-ticipants of the mosque movement in the context of their daily lives. This was supplemented with a yearlong study with a sheikh from the Islamic University of al-Azhar on issues of Islamic jurisprudence and religious practice.

5. In addition to Butler's *Gender Trouble*, see also Chandra Mohanty, "Under West-ern Eyes: Feminist Scholarship and Colonialist Discourses," in *Third World Women and the Politics of Feminism*, ed. Chandra Mohanty, Ann Russo, and Lourdes Torres (Bloomington: Indiana University Press), pp. 51–80; Michelle

Rosaldo, "Moral/Analytic Dilemmas Posed by the Intersection of Feminism and Social Science," in *Social Science as Moral Inquiry*, ed. Norma Haan, Robert N. Bellah, Paul Rabinow, and William M. Sullivan (New York: Columbia University Press, 1983), pp. 76–95; Marilyn Strathern, "An Awkward Relationship: The Case of Feminism and Anthropology," *Signs* 12, no. 2 (Winter 1987): 276–92; and Strathern, *Gender of the Gift: Problems with Women and Problems with Society in Melanesia* (Berkeley and Los Angeles: University of California Press, 1988).

6. Mosques have played a critical role in the Islamic revival in Egypt: since the 1970s there has been an unprecedented increase in the establishment of mosques by local neighborhoods and nongovernmental organizations, many of which provide a range of social services to the Cairene, especially the poor, such as medical, welfare, and educational services. Given the program of economic liberalization pursued by the Egyptian government since the 1970s and the concomitant decline in state-provided social services, these mosques fill a critical lacuna for many Egyptians.

7. Currently there are hardly any neighborhoods in this city of eleven million inhabitants where women do not offer religious lessons to each other. The attendance at these gatherings varies between ten to five hundred women, depending on the popularity of the woman teacher. The movement continues to be informally organized by women and has no organizational center that oversees its coordination.

8. This is in contrast, for example, to a movement among women in the Islamic republic of Iran aimed at the reinterpretation of sacred texts so as to derive a more equitable model of relations between Muslim women and men; see Haleh Afshar, *Islam and Feminisms: An Iranian Case Study* (New York: St. Martin's, 1998); and Afsaneh Najmabadi, "Feminism in an Islamic Republic: 'Years of Hardship, Years of Growth,'" in *Islam, Gender, and Social Change*, ed. Yvonne Yazbeck Haddad and John L. Esposito (New York: Oxford University Press, 1998), pp. 59–84.

9. For recent studies of the Islamic movement in Egypt, see Charles Hirschkind, "Civic Virtue and Religious Reason: An Islamic Counterpublic," *Cultural Anthropology* 16, no. 1 (2001): 3–34; and "The Ethics of Listening: Cassette-Sermon Audition in Contemporary Egypt," *American Ethnologist* 28, no. 3 (2001): 623–49; Mahmood, *Politics of Piety*; Armando Salvatore, *Islam and the Political Discourse of Modernity* (Reading, UK: Ithaca, 1997); and Gregory Starrett, *Putting Islam to Work: Education, Politics, and Religious Transformation in Egypt* (Berkeley and Los Angeles: University of California Press, 1998).

10. Piety here refers more to one's practical (and thus "secular") conduct than to inward spiritual states as the term connotes in the English Puritan tradition.

11. Secularism is commonly thought of as the domain of real life emancipated from the ideological restrictions of religion. As Talal Asad has argued in *Formations of the Secular: Christianity, Islam, Modernity* (Stanford: Stanford University Press, 2003), however, it was precisely the positing of the opposition between a secular domain and a religious one (in which the former comes to be seen as the ground from which the latter emerges) that provided the basis for a modern normative conception not only of religion but of politics as well. This juxtaposition of secular and religious domains has been facilitated through the displacement of

religious authority from the realms of the state and its institutions of law. To say that a society is secular does not mean that "religion" is banished from its politics, law, and forms of association. Rather, religion is admitted into these domains on the condition that it take particular forms; when it departs from these forms it confronts a set of regulatory barriers. The banning of the veil as a proper form of attire for girls and women in Turkey and France is a case in point.

12.　In 1996 the Egyptian parliament passed a law that aims to nationalize a majority of the neighborhood mosques, and the Ministry of Religious Affairs now requires all women and men who want to preach in mosques to enroll in a two-year state-run program regardless of their prior training in religious affairs ("Wazīr al-Auqāf al-maṣri lil-Ḥayāt: mu'assasāt al-Azhar tu'ayyid tanzīm al-khaṭāba," al-Ḥayāt, January 25, 1997, p. 7). In addition, women's mosque lessons are regularly recorded and monitored by state employees. The government continues to suspend lessons delivered by women mosque teachers for making remarks critical of the state. For an analysis of the kind of politics the piety movement has made possible, see Mahmood, Politics of Piety, chapters 2 and 4.

13.　In the Muslim context, see, for example, Janice Boddy, Wombs and Alien Spirits: Women, Men, and the Zār Cult in Northern Sudan (Madison: University of Wisconsin Press, 1989); Mary Hegland, "Flagellation and Fundamentalism: (Trans)forming Meaning, Identity, and Gender Through Pakistani Women's Rituals of Mourning," American Ethnologist 25, no. 2 (1998): 240–66; Arlene MacLeod, Accommodating Protest: Working Women, the New Veiling and Change in Cairo (New York: Columbia University Press, 1991); and Azam Torab, "Piety as Gendered Agency: A Study of Jalaseh Ritual Discourse in an Urban Neighborhood in Iran," Journal of the Royal Anthropological Institute 2, no. 2 (1996): 235–52. For a similar argument made in the context of Christian evangelical movements, see Elizabeth Brusco, The Reformation of Machismo: Evangelical Conversion and Gender in Colombia (Austin: University of Texas Press, 1995); and Judith Stacey, Brave New Families: Stories of Domestic Upheaval in Late Twentieth-Century America (New York: Basic, 1991).

14.　For a review of this scholarship on the Middle East, see Lila Abu-Lughod, "Anthropology's Orient: The Boundaries of Theory on the Arab World," in Theory, Politics, and the Arab World: Critical Responses, ed. H. Sharabi (New York: Routledge, 1990), pp. 81–131.

15.　Consider, for example, Janice Boddy's rich ethnographic work on women's zār cult in northern Sudan, which uses Islamic idioms and spirit mediums. In analyzing the practices of these women, Boddy argued that the women she studied "use perhaps unconsciously, perhaps strategically, what we in the West might prefer to consider instruments of their oppression as means to assert their value both collectively, through the ceremonies they organize and stage, and individually, in the context of their marriages, so insisting on their dynamic complementarity with men. This in itself is a means of resisting and setting limits to domination"; Wombs and Alien Spirits, p. 345; emphasis added.

16.　Aspects of this argument may also be found in a number of anthropological works on women in the Arab world, such as Susan Davis, Patience and Power: Women's

Lives in a Moroccan Village (Cambridge: Schenkman, 1983); Daisy Dwyer, *Images and Self-Images: Male and Female in Morocco* (New York: Columbia University Press, 1978); Evelyn Early, *Baladi Women of Cairo: Playing with an Egg and a Stone* (Boulder: Rienner, 1993); MacLeod, *Accomodating Protest;* and Unni Wikan, *Behind the Veil in Arabia: Women in Oman* (Chicago: University of Chicago Press, 1991).

17. Despite the debates within feminism, this is a premise that is shared across various feminist political positions including radical, socialist, liberal, and psychoanalytical, and marks the domain of feminist discourse. Even in the case of Marxist and socialist feminists who argue that women's subordination is determined by social relations of economic production, there is at least an acknowledgment of the inherent tension between women's interests and those of the larger society dominated and shaped by men. See Nancy Hartsock, *Money, Sex, Power* (New York: Longman 1983); and Catherine MacKinnon, *Toward a Feminist Theory of the State* (Cambridge: Harvard University Press, 1989). For an anthropological argument about the universal character of gender inequality, see Sylvia Yanagisako and Jane Collier, eds., *Gender and Kinship: Essays Toward a Unified Analysis* (Stanford: Stanford University Press, 1987).

18. On this see Strathern, *The Gender of the Gift*, pp. 26–28.

19. John Stuart Mill, a central figure in the liberal and feminist tradition, for example, argued, "The burden of proof is supposed to be with those who are against liberty; who contend for any restriction or prohibition. . . . The *a priori* assumption is in favor of freedom"; John Stuart Mill, *On Liberty and Other Essays*, ed. John Gray (New York: Oxford University Press, 1991 [1859]), p. 472.

20. Within classical political philosophy this notion (identified with the thought of Bentham and Hobbes) finds its most direct application in debates about the proper role of state intervention in the protected sphere of the private lives of individuals. This is also the ground on which feminists have debated the appropriateness of antipornographic legislation proposed by a number of feminists; see, for example, Sandra Bartky, *Femininity and Domination: Studies in the Phenomenology of Oppression* (New York: Routledge, 1990); Catherine MacKinnon, *Only Words* (Cambridge: Harvard University Press, 1993); Gayle Rubin, "Thinking Sex: Notes for a Radical Theory of the Politics of Sexuality," in *Pleasure and Danger: Exploring Female Sexuality*, ed. C. Vance (Boston: Routledge and Kegan Paul, 1984), pp. 267–319; Samois Collective, *Coming to Power: Writings and Graphics on Lesbian S/M* (Boston: Alyson, 1987).

21. See Isaiah Berlin, *Four Essays on Liberty* (Oxford: Oxford University Press, 1969); Thomas Hill Green, *Lectures on the Principles of Politica Obligation, and Other Writings*, ed. P. Harris and J. Morrow (Cambridge: Cambridge University Press, 1986); Avital Simhony, "Beyond Negative and Positive Freedom: T. H. Green's View of Freedom," *Political Theory* 21, no. 1 (1993): 28–54; and Charles Taylor, "What's Wrong with Negative Liberty?" in *Philosophy and the Human Sciences: Philosophical Papers* 2 (Cambridge: Cambridge University Press, 1985), pp. 211–29.

22. See Ian Hunt, "Freedom and Its Conditions," *Australasian Philosophy* 69, no. 3 (1991): 288–301; Gerald MacCallum, "Negative and Positive Freedom,"

Philosophical Review 76, no. 3 (1967): 312–34; Simhony, "Beyond Negative and Positive Freedom"; and David West, "Spinoza on Positive Freedom," *Political Studies* 41, no. 2 (1993): 284–96.

23. The slippery character of the human will formed in accord with reason and self-interest is itself a point of much discussion among a range of liberal thinkers such as Hobbes, Spinoza, Hegel, Rousseau, and Freud. See Thomas Heller, Morton Sosna, and David Wellbery, eds., *Reconstructing Individualism: Autonomy, Individuality, and the Self in Western Thought* (Stanford: Stanford University Press, 1986); and Charles Taylor, *Sources of the Self: The Making of Modern Identity* (Cambridge: Harvard University Press, 1989). During the twentieth century, within liberal societies the disciplines of psychoanalysis and psychology have played a crucial role in determining what the "true inner" self really is and what its concomitant needs and desires should be. See, e.g., Ian Hacking, *Rewriting the Soul: Multiple Personality and the Sciences of Memory* (Princeton: Princeton University Press, 1995); and Nikolas Rose, *Inventing Our Selves: Psychology, Power, and Personhood* (Cambridge: Cambridge University Press, 1998).

24. John Christman, "Liberalism and Individual Positive Freedom," *Ethics* 101 (1991): 359. This longstanding liberal principle has generated a number of paradoxes in history. For example, the British tolerated acts of sati (widow burning) in colonial India, despite their official opposition to the practice, in those cases where the officials could determine that the widow was not coerced but went "willingly to the pyre." For an excellent discussion of this debate, see Lata Mani, *Contentious Traditions: The Debate on Sati in Colonial India* (Berkeley: University of California Press, 1998). Similarly, some critics of sadomasochism in the United States argue that the practice may be tolerated on the condition that it is undertaken by consenting adults who have a "choice" in the matter and is not the result of "coercion."

25. For an illuminating discussion of the historiographical project of "herstory," see Joan Scott, *Gender and the Politics of History* (New York: Columbia University Press, 1988), pp. 15–27.

26. See Leila Ahmed, "Western Ethnocentrism and Perceptions of the Harem," *Feminist Studies* 8, no. 3 (1982): 521–34; and Wikan, *Behind the Veil.*

27. See, for example, Beth Brant, ed., *A Gathering of Spirit: Writing and Art by North American Indian Women* (Rockland, ME: Sinister Wisdom, 1984); Patricia Hill Collins, *Black Feminist Thought: Knowledge, Consciousness, and the Politics of Empowerment* (New York: Routledge, 1991); Angela Davis, *Women, Race, and Class* (New York: Vintage, 1983); Audre Lorde, *Sister Outsider: Essays and Speeches* (Trumansburg: Crossing, 1984). Similarly, "A Black Feminist Statement" by the Combahee River Collective rejected the appeal for lesbian separatism made by white feminists on the grounds that the history of racial oppression required black women to make alliances with male members of their communities in order to continue fighting against institutionalized racism. See Gloria Hull, Patricia Bell-Scott, and Barbara Smith, eds., *All the Women Are White, All the Blacks Are Men, But Some of Us Are Brave: Black Women's Studies* (New York: Feminist, 1982).

28. For an interesting discussion of the contradictions generated by the privileged position accorded to the concept of autonomy in feminist theory, see Parveen Adams and Jeff Minson, "The 'Subject' of Feminism," in *m/f* 2 (1978): 43–61.

29. Nancy Chodorow, *The Reproduction of Mothering: Psychoanalysis and the Sociology of Gender* (Berkeley: University of California Press, 1978); Carol Gilligan, *In a Different Voice: Psychological Theory and Women's Development* (Cambridge: Harvard University Press, 1982); Seyla Benhabib, *Situating the Self: Gender, Community, and Postmodernism in Contemporary Ethics* (New York: Routledge, 1992); Iris Marion Young, *Justice and the Politics of Difference* (Princeton: Princeton University Press, 1990).

30. Suad Joseph, ed., *Intimate Selving in Arab Families: Gender, Self, and Identity* (Syracuse: Syracuse University Press, 1999); Marilyn Friedman, "Autonomy and Social Relationships: Rethinking the Feminist Critique," in *Feminists Rethink the Self*, ed. D. T. Meyers (Boulder: Westview, 1997), pp. 40–61; Marilyn Friedman, *Autonomy, Gender, Politics* (New York: Oxford University Press, 2003); Jennifer Nedelsky, "Reconceiving Autonomy: Sources, Thoughts, and Possibilities," *Yale Journal of Law and Feminism* 1, no. 1 (1989): 7–36.

31. In addition to Butler's *Gender Trouble*, see Moira Gatens, *Imaginary Bodies: Ethics, Power, and Corporeality* (London: Routledge, 1996); and Elizabeth Grosz, *Volatile Bodies: Toward a Corporeal Feminism* (Bloomington: Indiana University Press, 1994).

32. For an excellent discussion of this point in the scholarship on feminist ethics, see Claire Colebrook, "Feminism and Autonomy: The Crisis of the Self-Authoring Subject," in *Body and Society* 3, no. 2 (1997): 21–41.

33. Studies on the resurgent popularity of the veil in urban Egypt since the 1980s provide excellent examples of these problems. The proliferation of such studies reflects scholars' surprise that, contrary to their expectations, so many "modern Egyptian women" have returned to wearing the veil. Some of these studies offer functionalist explanations, citing a variety of reasons why women take on the veil voluntarily (for example, the veil makes it easy for women to avoid sexual harassment on public transportation, lowers the cost of attire for working women, and so on). Other studies identify the veil as a symbol of resistance to the commodification of women's bodies in imported Western media and, more generally, to the hegemony of Western values. While these studies have made important contributions, it is surprising that their authors have paid so little attention to Islamic virtues of female modesty or piety, especially given that many of the women who have taken up the veil frame their decision precisely in these terms. Instead, analysts often explain the motivations of veiled women in terms of standard models of sociological causality (such as social protest, economic necessity, anomie, or utilitarian strategy), while concepts like morality, divinity, and virtue are accorded the status of the phantom imaginings of the hegemonized. See Fadwa El Guindi, "Veiling Infitah with Muslim Ethic: Egypt's Contemporary Islamic Movement," *Social Problems* 28, no. 4 (1981): 465–85; Valerie Hoffman-Ladd, "Polemics on the Modesty and Segregation of Women in Contemporary Egypt," *International Journal of Middle East Studies* 19 (1987): 23–50; MacLeod, *Accommodating*

Protest; Sherifa Zuhur, *Revealing Reveiling: Islamist Gender Ideology in Contemporary Egypt* (Albany: State University Press of New York, 1992).

34. For an excellent exploration of the use of language in the cultural construction of personhood, see Steven Caton, *"Peaks of Yemen I Summon": Poetry as Cultural Practice in a North Yemeni Tribe* (Berkeley: University of California Press, 1990); Webb Keane, "From Fetishism to Sincerity: On Agency, the Speaking Subject, and Their Historicity in the Context of Religious Conversion," *Comparative Studies in Society and History* 39, no. 4 (1997): 674–93; Rosaldo, "Moral/Analytic Dilemmas." Also see Marilyn Strathern's critique of Western conceptions of "society and culture" that feminist deconstructivist approaches assume in analyzing gender relations in non-Western societies in *Reproducing the Future: Essays on Anthropology, Kinship, and the New Reproductive Technologies* (New York: Routledge, 1992).

35. The concept "discursive tradition" is from Talal Asad, "The Idea of an Anthropology of Islam," *Occasional Papers Series* (Washington, DC: Center for Contemporary Arab Studies, Georgetown University, 1986). See my discussion of the relevance of this concept to my overall argument in Mahmood, *Politics of Piety*, chapter 3.

36. Michel Foucault, *The History of Sexuality: An Introduction*, trans. Robert Hurley (New York: Pantheon, 1978); and his "Truth and Power," in *Power/Knowledge: Selected Interviews and Other Writings* 1972–1977, ed. and trans. Colin Gordon (New York: Pantheon, 1980), pp. 109–33.

37. See Foucault, "Truth and Power"; and "The Subject and Power," in *Michel Foucault: Beyond Structuralism and Hermeneutics*, ed. Hubert Dreyfus and Paul Rabinow (Chicago: University of Chicago Press, 1983), pp. 208–26. An important aspect of Foucault's analytics of power is his focus on what he called its "techniques," the various mechanisms and strategies through which power comes to be exercised at its point of application on subjects and objects. Butler differs from Foucault in this respect in that her work is not so much an exploration of techniques as of issues of representation, interpellation, and psychic manifestations. Over time, Butler has articulated her differences with Foucault in various places; see, for example, *Bodies That Matter: On the Discursive Limits of "Sex"* (BTM), p. 248, n. 19; *The Psychic Life of Power: Theories in Subjection* (PLP), pp. 83–105; *Gender Trouble: Feminism and the Subversion of Identity*, 10th anniversary ed. (GT [1999]), pp. 119–41; and Butler and William Connolly, "Politics, Power, and Ethics," http://muse.jhu.edu/journals/theory_and_event/v004/4.2butler.html.

38. Feminist philosophers Elizabeth Grosz and Moira Gatens, influenced by the work of Gilles Deleuze, make a similar critique of the problematic distinction between materiality and representation underpinning the sex/gender dichotomy. See Gatens, *Imaginary Bodies*; and Grosz, *Volatile Bodies*. While they resemble Butler in their rejection of any simple appeal to a prerepresentational body, or a feminine ontology, as the foundation for articulating feminist politics, they differ from Butler in that they accord the body a force that can affect systems of representation in terms other than those of the system itself. For an interesting discussion of the differences between these theorists, see Claire Colebrook, "From

Radical Representations to Corporeal Becomings: The Feminist Philosophy of Lloyd, Grosz, and Gatens," *Hypatia* 15, no 2 (2000): 76–93.

39. Whereas for Austin the performative derives its force from the conventions that govern a speech act, for Derrida this force must be understood in terms of the iterable character of all signs; see Jacques Derrida, "Signature Event Context," in *Limited Inc.* (Evanston, IL: Northwestern University Press, 1988), pp. 1–23. For an interesting critique of Derrida's reading of Austin, see Stanley Cavell, "What Did Derrida Want of Austin?" in *Philosophical Passages: Wittgenstein, Emerson, Austin, Derrida* (Oxford: Blackwell, 1995), pp. 42–65.

40. Butler, "Further Reflections," p. 14.

41. For Butler's discussion of how Foucauldian conceptions of power and the subject may be productively combined with the work of Freud and Lacan, see PLP, pp. 83–105.

42. Butler, *Excitable Speech* (ES), pp. 139–40.

43. Butler's analysis of the production of sexed/gendered subjects is built upon a general theory of subject formation, one she makes more explicit in her later writings. See ES, PLP, and, with Ernesto Laclau, and Slavoj Žižek, *Contingency, Hegemony, Universality* (CHU).

44. Butler, Seyla Benhabib, Drucilla Cornell, and Nancy Fraser, *Feminist Contentions* (FC), p. 136.

45. Echoing Foucault, Butler argues, "The paradox of subjectivation (*assujetissement*) is precisely that the subject who would resist such norms is itself enabled, if not produced, by such norms. Although this constitutive constraint does not foreclose the possibility of agency, it does locate agency as a reiterative or rearticulatory practice, immanent to power, and not a relation of external opposition to power" (BTM, p. 15).

46. See Butler's treatment of this topic in "Gender Is Burning," in BTM, pp. 121–40; and in "Doing Justice to Someone."

47. For example, in discussing the question of agency, Butler writes, "an account of iterability of the subject . . . shows how agency may well consist in opposing and transforming the social terms by which it is spawned" (PLP, p. 29). Note the equivalence drawn here between agency and the ability of performatives to oppose normative structures. Such oft-repeated statements stand in tension with her own cautionary phrases, in this case within the same text, when she admonishes the reader that agency should not be conceptualized as "always and only opposed to power" (PLP, p. 17).

48. Amy Hollywood suggests that Butler inherits her valorization of resignification-the propensity of utterances and speech acts to break from their prior significations from Derrida. But whereas Derrida, Hollywood argues, remains ethically and politically neutral toward this characteristic of language and signs, Butler often reads resignification as politically positive. See Hollywood's essay in this volume.

49. See, for example, Susan Bordo, *Unbearable Weight: Feminism, Western Culture, and the Body* (Berkeley and Los Angeles: University of California Press, 1993); and the exchange in FC.

50. For Butler's most recent engagement with this project, see CHU. It is clear from this text that while Butler is uncomfortable, more so than her interlocutors, with a universalist theory of radical change, she remains interested in theorizing about conditions conducive to creating the possibility of radical democratic politics.

51. Consider, for example, the following statement by Butler in which she immediately qualifies her objection to a subject-centered theory of agency with the reassurance that her objections do not foreclose the possibility of resistance to subjection: "If . . . subjectivation is bound up with subjection . . . then it will not do to invoke a notion of the subject as the ground of agency, since the subject is itself produced through operations of power that delimit in advance what the aims and expanse of agency will be. It does not follow from this insight, however, that we are all always already trapped, and that there is no point of resistance to regulation or to the form of subjection that regulation takes" (CHU, p. 151).

52. Butler argues, for example, that Foucault's notion of subjectivation can be productively supplemented with certain reformulations of psychoanalytic theory. For Butler the force of this supplementation seems to reside, however, in its ability to address the "problem of locating or accounting for resistance: Where does resistance to or in disciplinary subject formation take place? Does [Foucault's] reduction of the psychoanalytically rich notion of the psyche to that of the imprisoning soul [in *Discipline and Punish*] eliminate the possibility of resistance to normalization and to subject formation, a resistance that emerges precisely from the incommensurability between psyche and subject?" (PLP, p. 87).

53. My analysis of the work different conceptions and practices of norm perform in the constitution of the subject draws heavily upon Foucault's later work on ethics. See Michel Foucault, *The Use of Pleasure*, vol. 2 of *The History of Sexuality*, trans. Robert Hurley (New York: Vintage, 1990); and Foucault, *Ethics: Subjectivity, and Truth*: vol. 1 of *Essential Works of Foucault, 1954–1984*, ed. Paul Rabinow, trans. Robert Hurley et al. (New York: New, 1997). For my elaboration of this approach to understanding Islamist politics, see Mahmood, *Politics of Piety*, especially chapters 1 and 4.

54. Most Arabic verbs are based on a triconsonantal root from which ten verbal forms (and sometimes fifteen) are derived.

55. This concept can perhaps be illuminated by analogy to two different models of dieting: an older model, in which the practice of dieting is understood to be a temporary and instrumental solution to the problem of weight gain, and a more contemporary model in which dieting is understood to be synonymous with a healthy and nutritious lifestyle. The second model presupposes an ethical relationship between oneself and the rest of the world and in this sense is similar to what Foucault called "practices of the care of the self." The differences between the two models point to the fact that it does not mean much to simply note that systems of power mark their truth on human bodies through disciplines of self-formation. In order to understand the force these disciplines command, one needs to explicate the conceptual relationship articulated between different aspects of the body and the particular notion of the self that animates distinct disciplinary regimes.

56. Pierre Bourdieu, *Outline of a Theory of Practice*, trans. Richard Nice (Cambridge: Cambridge University Press, 1977).

57. See "Nicomachean Ethics," in *The Basic Works of Aristotle,* ed. Richard McKeon (New York: Random House, 1941), particularly pp. 592–93.

58. For the emphasis placed in the Aristotelian tradition on the conscious training of various human faculties and assiduous discipline in the cultivation of habitus, see Cary Nederman, "Nature, Ethics, and the Doctrine of 'Habitus': Aristotelian Moral Psychology in the Twelfth Century" in *Traditio* 45 (1989–1990): 87–110. For Bourdieu habitus is primarily imbibed through unconscious processes. See, for a fuller discussion of this point, Mahmood, *Politics of Piety*, chapter 4.

59. In retaining the distinction between inward motives and outward behavior, so often invoked by the mosque participants, I do not mean to suggest that it is an appropriate description of reality or an analytical principle. Instead, I am interested in understanding the different kinds of relationships posited between body/mind, body/soul, inner/outer when such distinctions are used in a tradition of thought. For example, the body/soul distinction as used by Plato suggested a metaphysical primacy of the soul over the body. Aristotle reworked this relationship, seeing the two as an inseparable unity whereby the soul became the form of the body's matter. The women I worked with seemed to regard the body almost as the material enactment of the soul whereby the latter was a condition of the former.

60. See O. N. Leaman, "Malaka," in *The Encyclopedia of Islam*, CD-ROM, version 1.0 (Leiden: Brill, 1999) for a discussion of the term *malaka* in the Islamic tradition.

61. Ira Lapidus, "Knowledge, Virtue, and Action: The Classical Muslim Conception of *Adab* and the Nature of Religious Fulfillment in Islam," in *Moral Conduct and Authority: The Place of Adab in South Asian Islam*, ed. Barbara Daly Metcalf (Berkeley: University of California Press, 1984), p. 54.

62. Ibn Khaldun, *The Muqaddimah: An Introduction to History*, trans. Franz Rosenthal (New York: Pantheon, 1958), p. 346.

63. Lapidus, "Knowledge, Virtue, and Action," pp. 55–56.

64. See Ahmed Farid, *al-Baḥar al-rā'iq* (Alexandria: Dār al-imān, 1990); and Farid, *Tazkiyyat al-nufūs* (Alexandria: Dār al 'aqida lil-turāth, 1993) as well as Said Hawwa, *al-Mustakhlas fi tazkiyat al-anfus* (Cairo: Dār al-salām, 1995). While A. H. al-Ghazali was critical of the neo-Platonist influence on Islam (Majid Fakhry, *A History of Islamic Philosophy* [New York: Columbia University Press, 1983], pp. 217–33), his ethical thought retained a distinctly Aristotelian influence. On this point, see Mohamed Ahmed Sherif, *Ghazali's Theory of Virtue* (Albany: State University of New York Press, 1975); and the introduction by T. J. Winter in Abu Hamid al-Ghazali, *On Disciplining the Soul (kitāb riyadat al-nafs) and on Breaking the Two Desires (kitāb kasr al-shahwatayn)*, in *The Revival of the Religious Sciences (ihyā 'ulūm al-dīn)*, books 22 and 23, trans. T. J. Winter (Cambridge: Islamic Texts Society, 1995), pp. xv–xcii. For al-Ghazali's seminal work on practices of moral self-cultivation, see A. H. Ghazali, *The Recitation and Interpretation of the Qurān: al-Ghazāli's Theory*, trans. M. Abul Quasem (London: KPI, 1984); A. H. Ghazali, *Inner Dimensions of Islamic Worship*, trans. M. Holland (Leicester: Islamic Foundation, 1992); and Ghazali, *On Disciplining the Soul*.

65. Bordo, *Unbearable Weight;* Nilüfer Göle, *The Forbidden Modern: Civilization and Veiling* (Ann Arbor University of Michigan Press, 1996); Mani, *Contentious Traditions;* Emily Martin, *The Woman in the Body: A Cultural Analysis of Reproduction* (Boston: Beacon, 1987).

66. Claire Colebrook, "Incorporeality: The Ghostly Body of Metaphysics," *Body and Society* 6, no. 2 (2000): 35.

67. Gayatri Spivak, "Can the Subaltern Speak?" in *Marxism and the Interpretation of Culture*, ed. Cary Nelson and Lawrence Grossberg (Urbana: University of Illinois Press, 1988), pp. 271–313.

68. For an argument between these two groups about the veil and the virtue of modesty, see the exchange between the then mufti of Egypt, Sayyid Tantawi and the prominent intellectual Muhammed Said Ashmawi, who has been a leading voice for "Islamic liberalism" in the Arab world. See Muhammed Said Ashmawi, "Fatwa al-ḥijāb ghair shar'iya," *Rūz al-Yūsuf,* August 8, 1994, p. 28; and "al-Ḥijāb laisa farīda," *Rūz al-Yūsuf,* June 13, 1994, p. 22; Muhammed Sayyid Tantawi, "Bal al-ḥijāb farīda Islāmiya," *Rūz al-Yūsuf,* June 27, 1994, p. 68.

69. For further discussion of this point, see Mahmood, *Politics of Piety*, chapters 1 and 4.

70. J. L. Austin, *How to Do Things with Words*, ed. J. O. Urmson and Marina Sbisà (Cambridge: Harvard University Press, 1994).

71. For Derrida's interpretation of performativity, see Jacques Derrida, "Signature Event Context," in *Limited Inc.* (Evanston, IL: Northwestern University Press, 1988), pp. 1–23.

72. An important aspect of Butler's formulation of performativity is its relationship to concepts in psychoanalytic theory. On this relationship, see the chapter "Critically Queer" in BTM, pp. 223–42.

73. See Amy Hollywood's excellent discussion of Butler's analysis of embodied performativity, and its relationship to the concept of ritual elsewhere, in this volume.

74. Butler, "Further Reflections," p. 14.

75. While Butler remains indebted to Derrida in this formulation, she also departs from him by placing a stronger emphasis on the historically sedimented quality of performatives. See ES, pp. 147–50.

76. Butler argues this point eloquently: "no assertion of universality takes place apart from a cultural norm, and, given the array of contesting norms that constitute the international field, no assertion can be made without at once requiring a cultural translation. Without translation, the very concept of universality cannot cross the linguistic borders it claims, in principle, to be able to cross. Or we might put it another way: without translation, the only way the assertion of universality can cross a border is through colonial and expansionist logic" (CUH, p. 35).

77. Note that, to the degree that Butler calls attention to the formative power of discourse, her work posits a strong critique of a representational model of language. Her objections are twofold: one, that this model incorrectly presupposes that language is anterior to the object it represents, when it in fact constitutes the object as well; two, that this model presumes a relationship of exteriority between language and power, when, in essence, language is not simply a tool for power but is itself a form of power. On these points, see Butler's critique of Bourdieu's

representational theory of language in Butler, PLP; also see Butler and Connolly, "Politics, Power, and Ethics."

78. In response to a question posed by William Connolly about the nondiscursive character of bodily practices, Butler argues: "To focus on linguistic practice here and non-linguistic practice there, and to claim that both are important is still not to focus on the relation between them. It is that relation that I think we still do not know how to think. . . . It will not be easy to say that power backs language when one form that power takes is language. Similarly, it will not be possible to look at non-discursive practices when it turns out that our very way of delimiting and conceptualizing the practice depends on the formative power of a certain conceptual discourse. We are in each of these cases caught in a chiasmus relation, one in which the terms to be related also partake of one another, but do not collapse into one another" (Butler and Connolly, "Politics, Power, and Ethics").

79. Talal Asad, *Genealogies of Religion: Discipline and Reasons of Power in Christianity and Islam* (Baltimore: Johns Hopkins University Press, 1993); William Connolly, *Why I Am Not a Secularist* (Minneapolis: University of Minnesota Press, 1999); Grosz, *Volatile Bodies*; Brian Massumi, *Parables for the Virtual: Movement, Affect, Sensation* (Durham: Duke University Press, 2002).

80. For a discussion of this Aristotelian conception of potentiality, see Giorgio Agamben, *Potentialities: Collected Essays in Philosophy*, ed. and trans. Daniel Heller-Roazen (Stanford: Stanford University Press, 1999).

81. For the kinds of questions that are opened up with regard to agency and gender by the framework I propose here, see Mahmood, *Politics of Piety*, chapter 5; for suggestions on what it means to explore questions of embodiment in regard to the formation of the subject, see chapter 3.

82. The distinction between these two forms of human labor, as Judith Butler points out, goes back to at least Aristotle, who argues that "theoretical wisdom" is not the same as "practical wisdom" since each are oriented toward different ends: the former pursues what Aristotle calls "happiness" and the latter "virtue" (CUH, pp. 264–66). For contemporary reformulations of this argument, see Wendy Brown's discussion of the work of Benedetto Croce, Maurice Merleau-Ponty, and Michel Foucault in Wendy Brown, *Politics Out of History* (Princeton: Princeton University Press, 2001), pp. 40–44.

83. Brown, *Politics Out of History*, p. 41.

84. On this, see Charles Hirschkind and Saba Mahmood, "Feminism, the Taliban, and Politics of Counter-Insurgency," *Anthropological Quarterly* 75, no. 2 (2002): 339–54.

85. See Amnesty International, Afghanistan: "No One Listens to Us and No One Treats Us as Human Beings": Justice Denied to Women, Amnesty International reports, AI Index: ASA (11/023/2003) on-line at http://www.web.amnesty.org/library/index/engasa110232003; Anna Badkhen, "Afghan Women still Shrouded in Oppression: Widespread Abuse, Restrictions on Freedom Continue Almost Year After Fall of Taliban," *San Francisco Chronicle*, October 14, 2002; and Human Rights Watch, "We Want to Live as Humans": Repression of Women and Girls in Western Afghanistan, Human Rights Watch reports, vol. 14, no. 11 (C), available online at http://www.hrw.org/reports/2002/afghnwmn1202.

THEORIZING BODIES

8. "JUDITH BUTLER" IN MY HANDS

REBECCA SCHNEIDER

"**J**UDITH BUTLER," LIKE most of us who write, gives titles to her works. This is handy. Titles allow us to cite others and to cite ourselves. The title of an essay Butler published in *Qui Parle* in 1997 is "'How Can I Deny That These Hands and This Body Are Mine?'" To cite her title, I have to indicate that her title is itself a citation by encasing it in the proper layering of grammatical indicators. Butler's title cites Descartes. The original question about denial belongs, it seems, to him, as he did not indicate otherwise. And Butler lets us know to whom her sedimentation of grammatical indication refers, saying, on the second page, "The name of this paper that I have already begun, but not yet begun, is: 'How can I deny that these hands and this body are mine?'" She goes on to situate her citation as well as to suggest that citation is, by virtue of repetition, both located and loose. Any citation indicates that, as utterances, the uttered might emanate from the reader as well as the citing writer: "These are, of course, Descartes' words, but they could be ours or, indeed, mine, given the dilemmas posed by contemporary constructivism" (p. 3). Or given, one might simply say, quotation marks.

Of course, one of the dilemmas posed by contemporary constructivism concerns the degree to which utterances, re-uttered, like rituals (re)enacted, become one or undo one. That is, utterances bring one into subjecthood, even as, by virtue of citation and the necessary repetitions of language, utterances bring one out of an identity that could be called discretely or entirely "one" or "mine." As Butler's essay "How Can I Deny . . . '" makes clear, simply on the level of citation, this dilemma of "contemporary constructivism" is hardly a contemporary dilemma at all. Butler cites Descartes, but she might have cited Aristotle's claim that mimesis becomes us.

I toyed with titling the essay I sit here writing (as I am sitting by a fire, dressed in black, in my living room), "'How Can I Deny That These Hands and This Body Are Mine?'" (The reader might pause to notice the quotation marks.) Perhaps I will have decided against it. In order to cite my essay citing Butler citing Descartes, a future writer who also has not yet begun her essay (though her fire may already be lit) would have to increase the quotation marks to the point of unintelligibility. Perhaps I will have made this choice. I still can, I suppose, as the fire still seems to burn and as sleep continues to elude me. As I am still clothed. As there appears to be time at hand. We'll have to wait and see, I suppose, what I decide—if writing is ever fully decided or fully a writer's decision. If writing, that is, ever "takes place" once an essay passes through a writer's hands into the hands of others.

But let us step back a moment. In the essay "'How Can I Deny. . . '" Butler sets a scene for her reader well before that reader takes the sheet in her hand to turn to page 2 and the acknowledgment of the citation recited above. The scene on the opening page is "a sleepless night last year" in which Butler, in her "living room," has turned on her TV to find Elizabeth Fox-Genovese arguing against "certain radical strains in feminist thinking." What were those strains? Fox-Genovese was apparently particularly critical of the view that the difference between the sexes might be discursively fabricated, as if difference were not real or as if difference were "all a matter of language." The discerning reader will guess that Butler's essay will be at pains to ask for deeper reflection on Fox-Genovese's dismissal of these "certain radical strains."

Agreeing that the language of constructivism can indeed risk "a certain form of linguisticism," Butler argues that Fox-Genovese may be overestimating the risk of linguisticism by assuming that "what is constructed by language is therefore also language, that the object of linguistic construction is nothing other than language itself" ("How Can I Deny?" p. 3). This is arguably a common misreading of poststructuralist discourse generally, which is often accused of engaging in a "textualism" aimed at doing away with the body and replacing "it" with language. Butler is sympathetic with this criticism, which "sometimes" seems to fit:

The language of discursive construction takes various forms in contemporary scholarship, and sometimes it does seem as if the body is created ex nihilo from the

resources of discourse. To claim, for instance, that the body is fabricated in discourse is not only to figure discourse as a fabricating kind of activity, but to sidestep
the important questions of "in what way" and "to what extent."

("'How Can I Deny?'" p. 2)

The questions of "in what way" and "to what extent" prompts Butler to consider less the "line" between text and body (like some absolute difference
Fox-Genovese might draw between the sexes ["'How Can I Deny?'" p. 3])
than the tangle or weave of their interconstitution—a weave necessarily full
of holes, overlaps, and blindspots at chiasmatic crossings. Butler patiently
points out, as she has in so many of her writings, the sometimes agonizing
interdependencies of "texts" and "bodies" by which both—body and text—
define and exceed the limits of each other in a tangle of complicity that is
(like doubt) less an opposition than a weave of "fabrication" and matter. In
her book of the same year, *Excitable Speech*, the tangle might be figured as
composed in "call and response" as she takes up, in that work, the vocal
weave of hail and acknowledgment in Althusser's analysis of interpellation
as subject formation.[1] In "'How Can I Deny . . . '" she explores the interconstitution of language and body by turning to and working through Descartes,
taking up the body of his *Meditations* and siting (or tracing) the figure of his
physical body as it, necessarily if paradoxically, is given to appear both as
hallucinatory and as fact. Descartes' body appears *in and in relation to* his
text, both through that text and as its condition. In this way Butler figures
Descartes as a proto-phenomenologist (p. 13).

What I hope to read here, in and through this essay I am writing, is the
tangled place of writing, reading, and performance in Butler's approach to
the body and text. I am, I will say, an advocate of the tangle; I want less to
disentangle than to read the crossing of threads in the interest of call and
response between text and body, body and text. This essay will begin with a
close reading of several moments in "'How Can I Deny That These Hands
and This Body Are Mine?'" I will use that essay to set up the problem of the
body as given to be spectral—as well as blind and unknowing—in Butler's
work. I will then offer a brief examination of some tropes of vision, blindness,
and the body as they are found in Western performance history to suggest
that Butler's approach to the body as blind and blindspot is hounded by a
particular Western architectonic of (theatrical) perspective that continues to
play out in much work on performativity in literary theory. I will perform a
close reading of Butler's reading of Toni Morrison's reading of a folk parable
about reading—an exercise in repetition and mimesis—toward rethinking
repetition and mimesis as *at hand* not only in live performance but in text and
its reception as well. I will close by briefly turning to some feminist "ritual"
performance artists who might be read to resist the thrall to the scandalized,

unknowing, and blind body that Butler both beckons and denies. Ironically, I sit before this fire far more comfortable with Butler's adopted question about denial ("'How Can I Deny?'") than with the ritual artists' *refusals to deny* to which I turn at the close. But comfort may not, in the end, be the goal.

How Can I Deny That These Hands and This Body Are Yours?

Let us return to Butler, so many years ago when identity politics was not politically incorrect, sleepless in her living room, ruminating on Fox-Genovese and the problem of the body in fabrication. Butler has just written, on page 2, that, although discourse may be a "fabricating kind of activity," it does not necessarily follow that the body is entirely composed of cloth. My wordplay with fabric here is to bring into this discussion the place—even the placedness—of a reader. My hope is that the mention of fabric will remind us that Roland Barthes situated writing as a "fabric of quotation" when arguing for the place of the reader (in whose hands a text such as *The Meditations* will come to lie). Barthes positioned the reader as a kind of writer—making sense of writing by, in effect, rewriting through reading. Barthes suggested that meaning is as much fabricated in the hands (or embodied act) of the reader as in the text read. Fabric, as a trope, is apparently handy in this regard. It suggests a weave—a back and forth—a crossing of threads. Fabric is thus somehow suited not only to the cross-stitch of utterance that is citation but to reading writing, and writing about reading.

Why fabric? Why not a "picture" of quotation? An "image" of quotation? A "screen" of quotation? Of course, the place of "fabric" is also elemental in Descartes, as the most famous passage in the *Meditations* is the setting of the scene for the entrance of Descartes' doubt: "I am here, seated by the fire, attired in a dressing gown, having this paper in my hands and other similar matters." When Descartes comes to illustrate his doubt—providing Butler with her title "'How Can I Deny . . . '"—he does so through the possibility that he is deluded by a dream. But he is careful to note the irony that the proof of the dream *as dream* would be the *physical act* of dreaming—a reliance on matter to situate delusion: "Truly, how frequently nocturnal rest persuades me of such usual things—that I am here, that I am dressed in a robe, that I am sitting by the fire—when, however, the clothes having been taken off, I am lying between the sheets!"[2] The fabric, on or off—the thick matter of a purple winter robe or the thinner aspect of (paper?) sheets—is the *matter* given to situate *both* the body's verity *and* its propensity for delusion in a tangle or weave that, ultimately, will make verity dependent on delusion, and delusion or deception an indication of veracity, or *being*.

Butler phrases this tangle in the following way:

What happens in the course of Descartes' fabulous trajectory of doubt is that the very language through which he calls the body into question ends by asserting the body as a condition of his own writing. Thus the body that comes into question as an "object" that may be doubted surfaces in the text as a figural precondition of his writing.

("How Can I Deny?" p. 6)

I cite this passage not to settle on it but to examine, more closely, Butler's next move. She asks, "But what is the status of Cartesian doubt, understood as something which takes place in writing, in a writing that we read and which, in reading, we are compelled to re-perform?" (ibid.). In this question Butler moves from writing to reading and then from reading to performance, or, perhaps oddly, "re-performance"—a reperformance that is in some way "compelled." However, the essay will not take up reading and how reading compels reperformance and what reperformance might mean in the context of doubt, denial, the body, and the paper in hand. Rather, Butler will draw a line immediately back to writing (through Derrida) to argue that Cartesian doubt, as a method, is a method of *writing*:

But what is the status of Cartesian doubt, understood as something which takes place in writing, in a writing that we read and which, in reading, we are compelled to re-perform? Derrida raises the question of whether the Cartesian "I" is compatible with the method of doubt, if that method is understood as transposable, one that anyone might perform. A method must be repeatable or iterable; intuition (or self-inspection) requires the singularity of the mind under inspection. How can a method be made compatible with the requirements of introspection? Although Descartes' meditative method is an introspective one, in which he seeks in an unmediated fashion to know himself, it is also one that is written, and which is apparently performed in the very temporality of writing.

("How Can I Deny?" p. 6)

Interestingly, the reperformance we are in some way *compelled* to undertake when reading becomes, in her next sentence, qua Derrida, a writing "anyone *might* perform." The compelled reperformance—was it one of reading or of writing or of doubting or of dressing in a gown before a fire or TV? The compelled reperformance simply disappears *as we read*, and writing as *future possibility* (anyone might perform) takes its place.

What happened to the "reperformance" of writing at the juncture of reading? The compelled reperformance of reading (that, by reading, I write or rewrite or in some other way *act*) is occluded in favor of the "anyone might perform" of writing—a future possibility, a deferred or later date. There seems to be a slight sleight of hand at work here. What happened to Butler's reperformance? How did reading slip seamlessly into writing, compulsion into deferral and possibility?

That compulsion and deferral (and possibility) might be the same things is something to consider. But that reading and writing are the same things is not necessarily a claim Butler would be eager to make. Rather reperformance seems to suggest the instability of the copula that might appear to bind reading and writing as language acts. Reperformance has an air of the body about it—an air of practice, of making, of doing, or taking on. Derrida himself, through whom Butler jumps in this excerpt from reading to writing, posits the limits of claiming that reading is writing and writing is reading in the preface to "Plato's Pharmacy." He writes, "If reading and writing are one, as is easily thought these days, if reading *is* writing, this oneness designates neither undifferentiated (con)fusion nor identity at perfect rest; the *is* that couples reading with writing must rip apart."[3] With the word *must* we are (again) compelled toward a fissure that is also a unity (like a veracious delusion) between reading and writing. Into that fissure might fit, for Derrida, a body (or a hand). Or, at least, into the fissure a body is in some way compelled. The fissure houses the compulsion to *catch our fingers* in the "game" or "play" (*Dissemination,* p. 64). Thus Derrida playfully scoffs at any attempt to read or even "look at a text without touching it, without laying a hand on the 'object,' without risking—which is the only chance of entering into the game, by getting a few fingers caught—the addition of some new thread" (*Dissemination,* p. 63).

To my reading, Butler moves from writing to reading to reperformance, only to drop reading and performance like some inconsequential robe. She will drop the purple plush to crawl between the sheets and, ignoring reading, will not, in this text, wrestle with the fact that the sheets are, necessarily, already (even then) in my hands. It is at this juncture that writing takes precedence in her weave, as if writing were, at the end of the day, the privileged mode if not the singular mode that *matters*—and, in a gloriously paradoxical weave indebted to Derrida as much as to Descartes, writing *matters* because it renders spectral. Here, before the fire of this text, it is as if reading—futured bodies, futured hands (and the tempting reference to reperforming)—is ultimately to be rendered immaterial by writing as though the very lure to remember the ghost will force us to forget that it is always a matter of the living, *in your hands.*

Now, to be sure, the body does not entirely disappear in Butler's account. As we have noted above, she is keen to remind us that discourse may fabricate the body, but the body is not entirely fabricated by discourse. And yet the way in which the body *matters* in her response to Fox-Genovese is, ultimately, as the figure of unknowability. She writes:

Although the body depends on language to be known, the body also exceeds every possible linguistic effort of capture. It would be tempting to conclude that this means that the body exists outside of language, that it has an ontology separable from any linguistic one, and that we might be able to describe this separable ontology.

But this is where I would hesitate, perhaps permanently, for as we begin that description of what is outside of language, the chiasm appears: we have already contaminated, though not contained, the very body we seek to establish in its ontological purity. The body escapes its linguistic grasp, but so too does it escape the subsequent effort to determine ontologically that very escape.

("How Can I Deny?" p. 2)

Certainly, we can agree with Butler: the body can not be entirely captured in language, even as it can not entirely escape. But is the supposition that language entirely governs the body's knowability (or ability to know) necessarily to deny other modes of knowability than written language—modes of knowability that might pertain to the body as a mode of knowing and expressing—a mode that takes part in writing and reading without necessarily being "ontologically pure"? If language is an operation of surrogacy par excellence (and therefore not "ontologically pure"), then is not the body, too, an "operation of surrogacy" of sorts? Is it not only capable of, but necessarily engaged in, operations of surrogacy—of reperformance—that are, though not necessarily of verbal or textual language, still *bodily*? Might this other mode of knowability be embodied operations of reperformance so casually dismissed by Butler? For Butler the reason the body does not entirely disappear is that writing depends upon it as its condition, even if writing renders the body spectral: "the effort to excise the body fails because the body returns, spectrally, as a figural dimension of the text" ("How Can I Deny?" p. 14). At the close of the essay she offers the following:

There is no doubt that a hand writes Descartes' text, a hand figured within that text as appearing at a distance from the one who looks upon it and asks after its reality. The hand is reflexively spectralized in the course of the writing it performs. It undoes its reality precisely at the moment in which it acts, or rather, becomes undone precisely by the traces of the act of writing it performs.

("How Can I Deny?" pp. 17–18)

What I want to explore here is whether the "return" of the body is necessarily a spectral return. Certainly Descartes' hand is rendered spectral. But is the spectral return the only return that takes place, given that "the body" in the scene of writing is not only the writers' absent physicality, now rendered figural, but the literal body of a reader compelled by the precondition that is writing's readability, to reperform? As the mimetic opening of Butler's "'How Can I Deny . . . '" suggests, she is given to reperform Descartes, and it is this mimetic operation that cannot be entirely contained within the text but is, I am suggesting, never entirely spectral either. It is mimesis that escapes— messy as mimesis is—as much as the writer's absented body escapes, and to the degree that mimesis escapes, or refuses to be contained, the reader's body is . . . at hand.

Let us recall: Butler, like Descartes, can't sleep. So, she goes to her living room and turns on the TV where, like some shimmering shadow cast by a fire, she encounters Fox-Genovese's televisual body. She narrates the encounter thus:

> I became aware of being, as it were, a sleepless body in the world accused, at least obliquely, with having made the body less rather than more relevant. Indeed, I was not altogether sure that the bad dream from which I had awoken some hours earlier was not in some sense being further played out on the screen. Was I waking or was I dreaming?
>
> ("'How Can I Deny?'" p. 1)

Though she doesn't mention whether she is wearing a robe, this nocturnal angst is a direct reperformance (in writing) of Descartes' famous night bout with doubt (though interestingly Butler calls her doubt "paranoia"). The question for this essay now becomes, what is the status of reperformance in Butler's insistence on the body's inevitable spectrality?

Let us think about Butler's sentence on being compelled to reperform. What can this mean? Of course, it can easily refer to the performative operations of language generally—about which she has written profusely and eloquently. That words are conventions born of surrogacy and dependent on repetition, and that in reading and writing one repeats the operation of surrogacy, or is compelled to repeat it, is the condition of iterability. The act of "performance" and its relationship to performativity (operations of language that have "effect" in the world, if we use Austin as guide) is of course very interesting here. That reading compels one to reperform might mean that one, in reading, is compelled to reenact the operation of surrogacy by which meaning is remade (and by which meaning, in any exact or identical measure, escapes). This compulsion to enact the operation of surrogacy suggests that text, then, might be considered a script—a play script—given to utterance or, simply, pitched toward a reader whom it then compels to (re)perform.

If the author's body is rendered spectral, does that have to mean that "the body" is always already vanished? The body, instead, is in the place of hands—as it is in Descartes' text as well as, later, in Derrida's. Decartes writes of "having this paper in my hands." So what does it serve to claim that "the body" is spectralized by text if, as Derrida plays it, the "risk" is in the touch of writing by reading?

I could be accused of romancing the reading body here. I'm certainly romancing the notion that the body's "return" is not only or purely spectral and that the "figuration" of Descartes' now spectral body may compel (or at least invite) a body double. I'm suggesting a return that might be more like a crossing, an inhabitation, a possession, a re-placement, a reenactment—as your body in the place of mine (or mine in the place of yours). This is perhaps the "compelling" aspect of reperformance. This is to think through Descartes' "paper in my hands," as it passes through or returns in the hands of Butler, and Butler's paper in my hands, and—now—my sheets in yours. This is an operation of transmission that figures the body not simply as given to be figural in text but as a return that can never be entirely or purely "spectralized" ("'How Can I Deny?'" p. 17). Of course, the specter is a figure of return, but is return always a *spectral* figure? Or is there rather here a chiasmatic tangle that doesn't banish performance to disappearance but asks about the ways in which the body remains to take up, to resist, to reperform in and through difference?[4] This is, perhaps, the paradox of mimesis—and the tangle between bodies (as much as between words) caught in the compulsion to "reperform."

Histories of Theaters, Reperformed

In its vision this chorus beholds its lord and master Dionysus and is therefore eternally the serving chorus: it sees how the god suffers and glorifies himself and therefore does not itself *act*.
    —Nietzsche, *Birth of Tragedy*, p. 65

It is worth taking a moment to discuss the mimetic and its paradoxes in the context of theater history. My aim in this section is to briefly explore the theatrical backdrop to the "visual bias" that couples with a textual bias to render the body spectral and/or blind in much contemporary cultural constructivism. The distinction between "theater" and "ritual" as we have historicized it is, I will suggest, of great interest, and not unrelated to recent attempts, Butler's included, to parse performance and performativity. Throughout, the mimetic body remains oddly messy—indeed scandalous—and the linkage of the body to both blindness and scandal (when not spectral) is worth closer examination. I will turn, now, to considering the question of text "in hand" by turning to theater history and then back to Butler to ask whether or not Butler's claims about bodies and knowability are limited by a particular architecture of vision and blindness inherited, at least in part, from Western habits of theater and ritual. The following may seem like a lengthy digression, but the reader will, I hope, appreciate the relation to the topic at hand.

Bodies engaged in mimesis are bodies in time passing—in time, passing. As is often repeated: to mime is to copy, to translate, to represent, to repeat. To repeat suggests a space between objects or ideas, as a space between firsts and seconds. That any second, or double, or "next" might be identical to the first, or to the one before or beside, becomes almost moot. Sameness between one and another is, in the paradox of mimesis, the same only by virtue of difference: the one is not the other, even as, twinned, the other is not *not* the one.

Because it is difference that enables the simulacra of sameness in mimeticism, difference can be argued to exist at the core of any repetition.[5] Yet difference, fundamental to the mimetic, is often read as servicing the "sameness" of resemblance in that we read the mimetic for its uncanny ability to, as Elin Diamond put it, "pattern difference into sameness."[6] It is the irony of mimetic repetition that the inverse can also be said to be true—sameness is patterned into difference.[7] As Diamond makes clear, emphasis on sameness or difference is a matter of "reading," and reading is, as Barthes made clear, a matter of accessing a cross-hatch fabric of quotation. Still, it is because difference is fundamental to the mimetic that even the least verisimilitude can be mimetic—can appear to harbor some quality of "same." I can mimic an object, a character, an idea. I can repeat an axiom, an image, a cliché, a tradition. I can repeat myself.[8] Indeed, if we take this far enough we will reach the conclusion that I cannot not repeat and we will be sounding the discourse of the "theater" of everyday life.

To repeat: to repeat suggests a space between objects or ideas, as a space between firsts and seconds. Space between presents the possibility of passage, an interval, a moment—or, to borrow a word from the bible of naturalist theater, a beat. Bodies engaged in mimesis, or twice-behaved behavior, can be said to be bodies in passage, retracing a beat, reperforming, and attempting to pass. In some forms of theater the visual is not the primary signature of passing, as it is, generally, in European-derived theater traditions in the West. Still in thrall to perspectivalism and naturalism, the majority of Euro-American theater and filmic practice continues to romance the visual as the privileged corridor between a one and its mimetic other, an original and a second, the acted and the actor, until, for moments if not for hours, the other passes for the one, or the one passes for the other, and we are transfixed. Not insignificantly, we have chosen to mark this passing by a double negative. In the theater, as opposed to much religious ritual, one achieves "suspension of disbelief" rather than, strictly speaking, "belief." Or so the common saying goes. Rather than achieving belief (Marlon Brando *is* Stanley and Stanley *does* rape Vivien Leigh who *is* Blanche), we achieve a facsimile, an almost but not quite. Not belief, but not not belief. Not doubt, but not not doubt. The magical negative and its double is the magic of repetition as (double) negation. Double negation is disavowed affirmation: closeted (belief).[9]

In this fecund soup of the double negative, where things are but are not (or where things are not, but are [not not])—where, perhaps, I can not deny that my hand is not not yours—mimesis makes all things wet and slippery: the seeming original slips in and out of the ostensible copy. Butler mimes/ cites Descartes, whose text is illuminated through that mimicry, coming, in a sense, after her reperformance—a performance that slips around and through something we imagine as original (Descartes' original text). Slippery, mimesis always gets away from us if we search for precision—especially if we seek an origin. The First Copy, like a first second, is an oxymoron par excellence. Mimesis "itself" can have no origin, no discrete being—it *passes* from hand to hand. This is different than saying that mimesis has no history—Benjamin, in "On the Mimetic Faculty," makes it clear that it does.[10] Nevertheless, a linear narrative history of the mimetic faculty will be ultimately troubled if it reaches, with a teleological drive, for a root.

The effort to locate origins of representational practice in a distant human past raises deliciously murky questions because of the paradoxical project of articulating original copies—like "first" bodies or singular authors. If our mimetic faculty defines us—if we are, with Aristotle, mimetic creatures at base, and if, with Benjamin, the mimetic plays a "decisive role" in all of our "higher functions" ("Mimetic Faculty," p. 333)—then perhaps our capacities to generate copies precede anything that might be located as authentic *human* practice. The first *truly* human would have to have been the first being "aping" human. The copy would have had to precede the original as well as follow it. The original would copy the copy, the copy would be the original, and The Theater would have to have staged the invention of an everyday life beyond its frame.

Mimesis, like the body, makes messes of fine distinctions.

And theater scholars have long wrestled with this mess. In the effort to orient ourselves and our Western theatrical practices with a narrative history, theater historians have often labored under the effort to distinguish theater as an art from the mess of mimesis generally and from ritual particularly. If the attempt to chart an origin of mimesis, and to distinguish theater from reperformance generally, is a troubled project (as suggested above), theater historians could ask: What are the origins of theater *art*? The way that question has historically been answered has had profound effect on our ways of thinking about performativity and operations of surrogacy in general.

The question of theater's origins in the West has often been grounded through the distinguishing of theater as an art not only from everyday mimetic "aping" but from (religious) ritual as a practice. It is no surprise that efforts to find an origin of theater *art* distinct from ritual *acts* have celebrated Ancient Greece, where historians have reveled in the first full-fledged dramatic texts, relegating the religious ritual significance of Greek theatrical competition somewhat to the sidelines, something to be sloughed off in the progression of "civilization." The primacy of text to theater art, versus the primacy of bodily practice to shamanic and religious ritual, begins, in such historicizing, to find cultural articulation.[11] Bodies in *art* theater could be read retroactively to service "original" texts—written play texts and, ultimately, their now discrete human authors. Declaring an Original in the form of a great author's work, theater historians could parse a morass of a "prehistorical" mimesis that, linked to the slippages of the acting body, threatened historical linearity and the status of distinct or recouperable origins. Despite the fact that theater is repetitive (re)enactment across bodies in time, with difference as a modus operandi, the importance of bodies and of repetition could be veiled through the sacralizing of ostensible "sameness" in the function of origin, text, and author.[12] Segregating text (here in the form of drama) from embodied ritual practice, theater historians could use Greek drama to isolate "art" from the mess of live bodily repetition. In this way we could rescue text from the slippery body, the passing of texts through hands and mouths, and ignore the ways in which the live body, refusing to be spectralized, returns to trouble absolute boundaries between sameness and difference. Isolating text and spectralizing bodies, Sophocles' *Antigone* could remain *Sophocles' Antigone,* stretched across time in pure originality and ultimately untouched (undirtied? unburied?) by the variant bodies of players, the whims of directors, or the frisky fingers of readers such as Judith Butler.[13]

If the emergence of play texts is one reason we have rooted theater history in ancient Greece, it is arguably not the only reason. Just as compelling is the argument that theater history took root in ancient Greece because it is there that we could recognize, retroactively, a signature of Western aesthetics: side by side with the emergence of theater *text* we find a practice enacted in an architectural crucible for *vision*—a particular cultural vision that could be read (retroactively) to aid in the distinction of "art" from embodied ritual practice. As the Nietzsche epigraph to this section suggests, we could find in Greece a formula for vision that parses seeing from acting, or witnessing from taking action. Seeing, the chorus does not act. The equation retroactively secured onto the Greek stage could become: he who sees does not act and he who acts does not see.

Meaning "a place for viewing," the *theatron* provided a space delineated for particular visual form, even as textuality was emerging as elemental. Some, like Kaja Silverman, claim that the "specular" has *always* been "constitutive of human subjectivity." Silverman writes that "ever since the inception of cave drawing, it has been via images that we see and are seen."[14] However, such a claim invites pause when we consider the wide range of cultural and historical orientations to imagery that might have constituted said subjectivity. We can certainly debate the assumption that "specularity" was in any way solely constitutive of the practice that accompanied the image on the cave wall. If Silverman wants to make the cave wall the earliest cinema, Richard Schechner has claimed the same wall for interactive performance and embodied ritual, emphasizing the evidence that cave drawings bear the marks of finger rubbings, suggesting that the "images" were ritually rubbed and touched, taken in hand, stroked or otherwise tactilely "fondled" by participants who might not neatly fall under the rubric of spectators.[15]

If the cave wall may have been handled, the *theatron* (on the other hand) was not an arena for tactile engagement. This theater was a man-made cave marked "look but don't touch" and might therefore be claimed as the earliest display case if it were not already assigned as the font of theater proper. There, Bacchic bodies began to be "represented" rather than rubbed, touched, engaged, inhabited, or ritually possessed. An a-tactile visuality, in tandem with the emergence of textual drama, has retroactively offered historians a glass behind which to display a theater/ritual distinction. In the ways we've charted our histories, the institution of theater art could be (arguably falsely) distinguished from "primitive" ritual when disembodied vision took place as a primary mode of reception: *as a ritual participant became spectator, imagined as a nonacting, nontouching viewer, determined foremost as one who sees and hears but does not, in the same moment, act.*

That vision was spatially organized is important. We might say that (disembodied) vision as cultural trope took place—arranged into a cultural formation that, with the retrospections of the Renaissance and neoclassicism, would develop into perspective, a model of vision to which we are arguably "habituated" to this day.[16] Even if actual practice in ancient Greece can not be so neatly binarized into rigid bicamerality, the retrospection of history could recognize the *theatron* as a prototype (especially when viewed backward through Roman revisions) of the proscenium arch—marking a foundational separation of an actor, one who acts, from the audience and chorus, those who view. The *theatron* could thus be read as a space that instituted reception as distanced from action and action as blinded to reception. He who sees does not act; he who acts does not see. The audience, by this model, does not act. Similarly, the actor does not see—he, through the vehicle of "character," agrees not to see his future, though it is the very scripted future the audience has come to watch played out. At least the actor pretends not to see. He agrees to be blinded, just as the audience agrees not to act. The ancient *theatron*—even if by virtue of historical misreading—became an incubatory model for the later extremes of perspectival viewing by which a live theatergoer is habitually rendered spectral—she becomes a spectator not acknowledged as participant, not countenanced by the scene, but ritually disembodied before a scene of an acting body rendered blind.

Here, then, we find the institution of active blindness and disembodied viewing written in stone in the architecture of the *theatron* that divides disembodied seer from embodied performance (and, given that the architecture of the Athenian Assembly—the Pnyx—mirrored the *theatron*, we might say that rhetoric contains this "architectural" posture as well). The separation of embodied action and disembodied vision could aid theater historians to craft a distinction between theater art and ritual practice. The distinction between art and ritual enabled the designation of other cultural performance forms, not based on the Western model of specularity, as ritualistic and therefore as "exotic" or "primitive."[17] That is, other cultural modes of performance could be labeled primitive by virtue of their tactility, a tactility read as rituality— "rituality" being understood as embodied repetitive practice, not consonant with the model of atactile, display case vision. Any practice retaining traces of nonocularcentric exchange, or habits of tactile embodied knowing (such as, perhaps, the Indian notion of *rasa*, based on a concept of taste more than on sight, and most certainly traditional Oceanic and African performance forms based on interactivity and nonbicameral participation), could be read as ritualistic and, by extension, that which "civilization" had, for better or worse, sloughed off. Following predictably on this, many twentieth-century theater discontents, bemoaning the alienation of specularity, sought to reinvest theater with "ritual" efficacy by staging a body marked for visceral impact—a primal body—challenging the vision-marked divide between the stage and the house through invoking a tactile embodiedness understood, often, as linked to "primitive" rituality.[18]

Theater as art, then, came to be understood as marked by a vision that institutes a blind, demarcating if not completely separating viewer and viewed. This blind, as cultural practice, disavows active seeing and sighted action but also removes the present moment of reciprocal exigency between viewer and viewed in favor of the specular appearance of theatrical and rhetorical *presence* (and its inverse, ostensible spectator absence or invisibility). The blind, designating a viewing spectator who does not act, also disavows mutual creativity—an avowed "active" role on the part of those in the position of spectator. Such a disavowal props the status of the "original" author (as discussed above relative to the mess of mimesis) or, today, the status of the auteur and his "totally original" production.

I am curious about the degree to which we continue to tote habitual baggage of a one-way ocularcentrism that separates spectator (spectral or disembodied viewer) from actor (embodied but blind), as well as reader from writer, in our approaches not only to theatrical performance but also to discursive performativity. If theater historians had labored to distinguish theater performance from ritual practice, theorists of performativity have more recently labored to parse performativity and performance, remixing the terms *theater* and *ritual*. What interests me here is the degree to which the remix retains the above-articulated Western performance paradigm of disembodied vision/blinded actor.

Double Blinds: Performance and Performativity

For over twenty years now, in the mix of anthropology and theater studies that produced the appellation *performance studies*, theater and ritual have no longer been the distinct entities traditional theater historians had labored to produce. Lately, and coming more from literary critical and philosophical circles, the pressure for distinction has shifted to the difference between performance and performativity. In an effort to redress the ebullient misreading for the theatrical that occurred in the wake of *Gender Trouble*, Judith Butler underscored in her later work an important distinction between theatrical embodied performance and discursive performativity, saying succinctly in *Bodies That Matter* that the "reduction of performativity to performance would be a mistake" (p. 234).[19] As Jon McKenzie writes, if in *Gender Trouble* Butler "sought to theorize performativity *via* performance [in "Critically Queer"], she also emphasized performativity *contra* performance."[20] For Butler, theater and the social rituals she read through Victor Turner in *Gender Trouble* are both willed performance, or conscious performing. In this formation then, *both* theater and ritual participate in the "blind" that once distinguished theater performance from ritual. Now, with a resurrection of J. L. Austin, we find, importantly, that conscious performance and ritual acts veil, blind, or "conceal" their dependence on the profound conventionality of discursive performatives in order to institute an appearance of presence. If performance, ritual and theatrical, is consciously embodied, performatives are discursive and somehow unconscious. They are not willed (not staged), but blindly deployed as we participate in that great stream of repetition by which any word we use is ghosted by a historicity not completely accessible to us and by which we can never be certain of that word's future signification. According to Butler's formulation, unlike performance (willed in ritual and theater), performativity is in excess of any fully conscious manipulation.

> Performativity is . . . not a singular "act," for it is always a reiteration of a norm or set of norms, and to the extent that it acquires an act-like status in the present, it conceals or dissimulates the conventions of which it is a repetition. Moreover, *this act is not primarily theatrical;* indeed its apparent theatricality is produced to the extent that its historicity remains dissimulated (and, conversely, its theatricality gains a certain inevitability given the impossibility of a full disclosure of its historicity).
>
> (BTM, pp. 12–13)

This quotation underscores the move by which performativity comes to signify the repetition of conventional norms that necessarily deny any act a singular presentness, and performance comes to mean dissimulation of that historicity in the effort to make a bogus presentness appear singular—or "totally original." Of course, provocatively, the two now distinct terms (*performance* and *performativity*) remain impossibly tangled in and dependent upon each other.

For Butler, conscious performance conceals discursive performativity by utilizing blinds, like scrims, in the interest of mounting a present-moment-ness of an act that disavows its historicity—that attempts to *pass* as that which it repeats, closeting the space between firsts and seconds described above. Such a performance act, in ritual and theater, thus both institutes and manipulates blindness. Performativity, on the other hand, is the discursive conventionality that is concealed and manipulated by performance. Thus we are concerned with a double blinding. To say that theatrical performance, or social ritual, conceals performativity even as it performs is in essence to say that "conscious" theater and ritual conceals, or blinds its participants, to the very blindness within which it necessarily operates.

This vision-bound analysis of performance and discourse as engaged in concealment, blinds, and veils is in keeping with the Western "origins" of theater by which performance, through privileging blinds and disembodied vision, supposedly came to be separated from ritual. And yet here, quite rightly, we reencounter the notion of ritual in the suggestion that willed performance engages in, is invested in, *rituals* of blinding, of veiling, in order to, precisely, distinguish itself from ritual.

Blindness Takes Place: Butler in My Hands

I find Butler's distinction between performance and performatives compelling and deeply important. My question is directed now to the reiteration of blindness (which is to say tropes of vision) as seemingly essential, if not foundational, to discursive exchange in general. Even a cursory study of non-Western performance practices shows that "vision" is not always the privileged mode of reception. Such a study also almost immediately shows that a spectator-participant need not always be separated as "he who sees but does not act."[21] In the dominant Western model of theatrical performance, however, a blinded actor does not avow a future he agrees, in the space of performance, not to see. The actor agrees to act *as if* that future were unknown, though to the degree that he is "faithful to" the text, that future is decidedly determined.[22] The inactive spectator (or the spectator whose vision is rendered distinct from an act, as the Nietzsche epigraph suggests) is strangely situated as noncomplicit in the scene he observes. In the course of Western theater, as the chorus eventually disappears, the place of the spectator is increasingly disembodied. If this Western theater model (one that, with the Renaissance reenactment of Vitruvius's Roman reenactment of the Greek theater, will birth perspective), a model hinging on blinded bodies and disembodied seers who remark the body as blind, is applied unproblematically to discursive exchange and ritual *in general*, what modes of knowing are disavowed? That is, if this Euro-cultural inheritance of acting blind in a limited architecture of reception is given to be universal, what is occluded— what denied?

To probe this question I turn now to a parable Butler cites in *Excitable Speech*.[23] Through this parable Butler places in my hands not only her text (referred to as language) but that which she marks text to repeatedly blind— a body. My question becomes: what to do with the blinded author, and the spectralized body, when she is, as she has been placed, in my hands? When her language blinding the body is in my hands, do I re-cite? Am I compelled to reperform the ritual blinding and the ritual spectralizing of the participant body? Or can I do something else with my hands? Let me explain.

In *Excitable Speech* Butler addresses the problem of threatening language. She eloquently explores the ways in which speech is "always in some ways out of our control"—finding in that lack of control the promise of agency by which threatening speech can be counterappropriated in a "ritual chain of resignification" (p. 14). The key to this lack of control is, in Butler's text, the slippery slope of the body as instrument and address of speech. The speaking body is always in "excess" of that which it iterates, as is the body which speech addresses—a body that cannot be fully fixed by language even as language interpellates the body for social constitution. And yet, as if to try and *fix* this lack of bodily fixity, Butler articulates that lack by rendering the body blind, or blinding the body, fixing it as the "sign of unknowingness" (ES, p. 10).

Toward that end Butler recites a parable offered elsewhere by Toni Morrison.[24] In the recited parable young kids play a mean joke on a wise old blind woman. They ask the blind woman to guess whether a bird they hold in their hands is living or dead. The blind woman responds by what Butler cites as "refusing and displacing the question" (ES, p. 6). The blind woman says: "I don't know . . . but what I do know is that it is in your hands. It is in your hands" (Morrison, *Lecture*, p. 30; quoted by Butler, ibid.).

Morrison reads the blind woman as a writer and the bird as language. For Butler, Morrison's analogy suggests that writing is blind, for "it cannot know the hands into which it will fall, how it will be read and used, or the ultimate sources from which it is derived" (ES, p. 8). Butler argues that the children's question is cruel "not because it is certain that they have killed the bird, but because the use of language to force the choice from the blind woman is itself a seizing hold of language, one whose force is drawn from the conjectured destruction of the bird" (ES, p. 9). Since we have established that the blind woman is a writer and the bird is language, the bird in the hands of these threatening children might be the writing of the blind writer herself—the language she has manipulated that is now, much like a book, in their hands.

There is the odd moment in reading this parable and Butler's explication—a moment not countenanced within the text but strangely necessary to it—a moment that invites bodily knowledge and is disturbingly of the present moment, even as the status of any articulable presentness is troubled, importantly, by Butler's theories of performativity. That is the moment when the reader is palpably aware that the writer's text is decidedly—*literally*—in her hands. This moment, which the parable enables, makes apparent the thorny question of language's "scandalous" relationship to bodies, as it is precisely the reader's body that is invited into the space of the text by the invocation of the bodily instrument of language itself: It's in your hands. It's in your hands. Butler, after Shoshana Felman, would mark such a moment as one of "excess"—that which language can not foresee, the bodily ingredient and bodily instrument to which language is necessarily blind. Indeed, in *Excitable Speech* Butler invokes Felman's "scandal" to reiterate that "the body is the blindspot of speech, that which acts in excess of what is said, but which also acts in and through what is said" (ES, p. 11).

Felman's scandalous body is extremely important. The speaking body, and here the reading body, destroys, as Butler notes, the metaphysical dichotomy between the mental and the physical, between matter and language—that mind/body split which, I might add, looks significantly like the *theatron*'s division between disembodied seer and blind embodied actor. What results in this breakdown of the mind/body split, however, is not some recuperated unity, some essentialized singularity, but rather, for Felman, a productive site of scandal at the base of the structural division, like some Benjaminian flash of insight in a moment of danger.

Butler turns to Felman after explicating the parable in order to remind her reader that speech acts *are* bodily acts, "hands" are involved. And yet here a curious reversal occurs—much like the moment when "reperformance" disappears from her text on Descartes. Just as bodily knowledge appears to be avowed by the blind woman's invocation of in-handedness, Butler uses Felman to remind us that the body, involved, is involved specifically *as a blind(spot)*. She resubsumes bodily knowledge into the tropic primacy of disembodied vision. Just as bodily knowledge is invoked in the parable, Butler remarks the bodily as essentially excessive, that which can not be countenanced by the very language that enabled it. While this is the key to Butler's notions of agency—that agency is achieved in the space between language as instituting and language as failing to fix—nevertheless the fixedness of bodily *blindness* or *unknowingness* as the linguistic signature of that space bears troubling. Interestingly, unlike Butler and Felman, Morrison never suggests that language is blind to the body or that the body is in excess of language. For Morrison there is an agency in the *doing* of language. Indeed, alarmingly, the body is the one thing the blind writer appears to see: "I don't know . . . but what I do know is that it is in your hands. It is in your hands" (Morrison, *Lecture*, p. 30; quoted in Butler, ES, p. 6).

In the parable the blind woman's reference to in-handedness, tactile knowing, is for Butler a "refusal and a displacement" of the children's question. But can we read this parable differently? I would submit that the blind woman's refusal does not refuse the children's question. And it is not even clear that the woman regards the children's challenge as "threatening." Rather, the blind woman refuses that which the question seems to assume—vision as the only means of knowing. The reference to in-handedness is not a displacement—but rather a re-placement, off of the paradigm of vision and its assumptions of blindness-to-the-bodily and onto the potentiality or presentness of tactility. If bodily tactility is scandalous, perhaps it is only scandalous relative to our habitual denials of the body as a means of knowingness—that is, not relative to some foundational or essentially scandalizing body. Read in this way, the violence in this parable's exchange between readers and writer becomes the ritual of denial—the reading children's denial that the body could very well touch and know if the body could be avowed as *belonging to the scene*. Here the refusal of the question, or the rendering rhetorical of the question, rests in the hands of the children, who apparently do not offer the bird to the writer to touch, to take in hand. They choose to script the body, again, as blindspot and assume that the blind writer will have no way to "see." Perhaps the force of the parable is to render their assumption . . . shortsighted.

Can we speak of Butler's blind(spot)ed body as *taking place*? Of course, it takes place in language, through a repetitive blinding or disavowing the possibility of bodily knowingness, as Butler remarks the blindspotted body as "the *sign* of unknowingness" (ES, p. 10). This is reminiscent of the *theatron*: the disembodied spectator, agreeing not to act, agreeing not to be countenanced or embodied within the scene/seen as participant, views the embodied actor agreeing not to see (if Oedipus is indeed the prototype that modernism has made of him, then this blinding is ritually literalized on stage).

Butler implicitly erases her own body from the space of the text, even as she has invoked it.[25] It is as if the blind(ed) woman were saying: It's out of my hands. It's out of my hands. I am, in and through the author/ity of my language, blind to the body. I am, through text, disembodied or "spectralized." And this, I think, is not the gist of Morrison's recitation of the parable.

Indeed, near the conclusion of her own explication of the parable Morrison imagines the children chastising the blind woman for not redressing the space between them. Morrison has the children ask: "Why didn't you reach out, touch us with your soft fingers, delay the sound bite, the lesson until you knew who we were?" In the end it is clear that without literally crossing the space, without the literal softness of fingers, the blind writer had nevertheless touched the children with a letteral tactility born of a language that avows *in-handedness as knowing,* a language passing from hand to hand, mouth to mouth, and (as Morrison unpacks in another story in her text) even seeing eye to seeing eye (Morrison, *Lecture,* p. 30).[26] Thus she offers a model of exchange that, unlike the *theatron* of performance, is not based on blinded body/disembodied vision.

How, then, to handle Butler's text? Her language, gestically blindspotting even while figurally placing her body, sleepless, in her "living room"—her writing fulsomely reperforming the conviction that her body will be rendered spectral and unknowing—is in my hands. It's in my hands—and it's in yours—in time, passing. If I chose only to emphasize a spectralized body of the author, what other possibilities of embodiedness do I blind? Must I blind you, reader, even as my own body (my fingers on this keyboard) passes? Or is passing rather more resistant to linear time than we are habituated to imagine? Can I resite? Can my hands become you, your hands become me, in an exchange rendered coauthorship—like the complicit work of riffing in jazz—undoing the singular seat of the Dead Author, the Forefather, and making room for lots of bodies, lots of risky fingers, in play? Can the emphasis on in-handedness, on reading as an act of passing, and of passing on, find resonance?[27] Why should I deny that these hands and these bodies are ours?

Epilogue: "Hold It"

With Butler in hand, I return to the question of distinction between ritual and performance raised earlier in this essay. While this epilogue does not offer answers, it suggests, I hope, an avenue for future inquiry.

Reading our habits of performance as nested in ritual blindings is imperative. To do so, however, we might attempt to retain a sense in which ritual need not automatically be subsumed into ocularcentrist habits of knowing. If we read for embodied practice, then the blinding ocularcentrism of Western approaches to performance and discursivity becomes a *ritual* ocularcentrism, something we repeatedly reenact. The effort is not so much to get us to *see* ourselves blinding the body and relegating it as unknowing again and again (we all read *Oedipus* in junior high) but to avow the bodily in-handedness of that ritual repetition and to recognize it as central to our cultural habits of exchange (we all read *Oedipus* in junior high): we are in the habit of doing it to ourselves.

Felman is right. We blind the body to preserve a site for scandal. The body, and its messy unlocatability, its indiscretions, is alive with the potential of counter- and cross-mimesis. But however necessary scandal may be as one means to interrupt our habits of viewing, we need to critically interrogate our thrall to ritual execcation. We need to trouble the coupling of scandal as always already a matter of the scandalous body. Can we imagine a body without burdening it with the necessity of scandal? Does repeatedly scandalizing the body bear a gendered history worth interrogating?

As a parting gesture, necessarily brief, I want to turn to feminist ritual artists who complicate the model of disembodied vision by producing work that refuses to refuse the body as knowing and thus refuses the body as repetitive "sign of unknowingness."

The claim that the body is always already the blindspot of speech is a functional claim. As discussed above, blindspotting is what grants the body, for Felman, the potential to disruptive scandal. Similarly, blindspotting and the inability to "fix" the body in knowledge is what holds, for Butler, the promise of potential and constant resignification. As opposed to this promise of the blindspot, cultural feminist ritual artists, also interested in disruption and resignification, proposed an alternative means. In the 1960s and 1970s such artists often made explicit a body that refused to unproblematically repeat its signification both as blindspot and as scandal (thus, ironically but predictably, provoking scandal). The important point is that the scandal of feminist ritual art, often expressed across the body as a stage, lay less in the body itself than in the artists' insistence that the body need not operate as scandalous. The scandal, then, was less their bodies than their denial of the body as scandal.[28] This is not an end to "scandal" as a mode of questioning the prerogatives and fixities of language, but it is an unmooring of the site of scandal from its delimitation to a body repetitively marked as blind sign of unknowingness.

In the 1960s and 1970s, artists such as Mary Beth Edelson and Carolee Schneemann—facing the fact of their nonadmittance into the art world by virtue of their gender—suggested that blindspotting the body, producing a disembodied seer and a blinded object, is a model to which we are habituated. Rather than saying that the body *is* the blindspot of speech, they suggested that the body is ritually blinded by cultural habits of reception—rituals that can be rearranged. Their work suggests that we are culturally habituated to a body that we repeatedly iterate as unknowing, repeatedly iterate as blind—unable to "see back." These artists used their bodies as site of their artwork, and they often used the word *ritual* to try and wrest their work away from the prerogatives of the vision machine (and its gendered dynamics) that determined the artist and art spectator as disembodied subjects and the art-work as blind object.[29]

Because work such as Schneeman's and Edelman's was often libidinous, incorporating naked and desiring female bodies as active agents—as *makers* of art rather than solely as displays or products of a masculinized artist—their work produced scandal in a variety of circles (the title of the seventies and eighties feminist art collective and journal *Heresies*, of which Edelson was a founding member, suggests an awareness of that production). The scandal in such work (especially in terms of its reception by the broader art estab-lishment) had to do not only with the wielding of the body as vehicle of "knowing," but with its collapse of the distinction between ritual and art per-formance. Such work brought art under the embodied participant umbrella of ritual—suggesting bodily investment where art has been more comfort-able with disembodied disinterest. Across the twentieth century art perfor-mance has seen a number of collapses in distinction at the level of the frame: between art and life, between art and porn, between art and kitsch, between art and commodity.

The collapse of the frames distinguishing art and ritual, however, espe-cially when articulated by feminist artists, raised issues that still have not been fully addressed. Edelson reads the photographs that resulted from her art rituals as part of the "play" or transformation of her body in ritual con-text. This suggests that the body is not primarily rendered spectral in her work but, like ritual, reperformed. Here, perhaps, she approaches the body as rather resiliently given to enactment, passage (not only passing away but passing through and passing as), transformation, and "play." While Edelson relied on Nietzsche for the sense of play she courts, we might recall, as well, Derrida's invocation of fingers as necessarily putting text (or image or body) *in play*.[30] The ways in which Edelson and Schneeman (and many others, such as Hannah Wilke) often marked or caressed or otherwise explicitly "touched up" photographic images resonates here. It would be interesting to theorize the ways in which Edelson's overtly "touched" or "handled" photographs are deeply connected to her naming of her work as "ritual" art. Her late seventies work was certainly pitched toward a feminist sacrality she imagined as dis-tinct from the "scandal" that the desiring female body marked within patri-archy. While we might go along with Jill Dolan's critique of cultural feminist ritual art production as essentialist, we might also, with Diana Fuss, read for the habitual (and tiring) scandal to patriarchy at the heart of *feminist* essen-tialism. We might ask whether the scandal provoked by feminist essentialists was not, in some part, a refusal to *be scandalized* by the body or, for that mat-ter, necessarily spectralized.[31] Interestingly, Edelson wrote of her *Body Works* series of rituals that the photographs make "a political statement that says I am, and I am my body, and [perhaps most disconcertingly] I am not going away" (*Seven Cycles,* p. 17).

It is this *not going away*—or better, it is the question of the status and mode of return through tactile reperformance and its compulsions that has been the central concern of this essay. We continue to struggle with the difficulty of avowing embodiment (especially as concerns text) and acknowledging the ways in which the body is not always already spectral but (re)living the mess of mimesis. Quotation marks, scratched beyond neat, textual legibility, lodge in bodies where text is *in hand* and where I can not so much deny that these hands and this body are mine as acknowledge that they pass (touch) yours.

I will close with a gesture culled from the final lines of *Death of the Last Black Man in the Whole Entire World,* a play by Suzan-Lori Parks (1995). Performance theorists Harry Elam Jr. and Alice Rayner have suggested that this play is more ritual ceremony than aesthetic performance, despite its frame of "theater art." They argue that Parks's work is linked to ritual because her work makes explicit the ways in which theater is composed in repetition of tactile signifiers—bodied words.[32] One might suggest that all theater, like ritual, consists of bodied words, tactile signifiers, gestic acts. But one might also remember that, in thrall to "original" authors, we are in the habit of disavowing the basis of theater in embodiment and repetition—in reperformance—a reperformance that includes the supposedly disembodied spectator in the house as well as the actors "consciously performing" on the stage. Indeed the "bodied" words that conclude Parks's provocative play can mean both "stop it" and "take it up," and they resound in syncopated time with the words of Morrison's "blind" writer as she says: "It is in your hands. It is in your hands."

Parks:

"Hold it. Hold it. Hold it. Hold it. Hold it. Hold it. Hold it."

NOTES

1. Judith Butler, *Excitable Speech: Politics of the Performative* (ES).
2. Rene Descartes, *Meditations,* trans. George Heffernan (Notre Dame, IN: University of Notre Dame Press 1992), p. 89.
3. Jaques Derrida, *Dissemination,* trans. Barbara Johnson (Chicago: University of Chicago Press, 1981), pp. 63–64.
4. See Rebecca Schneider, "Performance Remains," *Performance Research* 6, no. 2 (2001): 100–8.

5. Portions of this section are taken from an earlier version of this essay. See Re-
    becca Schneider, "Taking the Blind in Hand," *Contemporary Theatre Review* 10,
    no. 3 (2000): 23–38.

6. Elin Diamond, *Unmaking Mimesis: Essays on Feminism and Theater* (New York:
    Routledge, 1997), p. iii. Deleuze distinguishes the specificity of repetition, found-
    ed on difference, from the generality of resemblance based in sameness.

7. See Hal Foster on this point in his readings of Andy Warhol's serial "Death in
    America" images, Hal Foster, *The Return of the Real* (Cambridge: MIT Press,
    1996), pp. 127–68.

8. On twice-behaved behavior, see Richard Schechner, *Between Theater and An-
    thropology* (Philadelphia: University of Pennsylvania Press, 1985), pp. 35–116.

9. Schechner claims this double negative as "performance consciousness" and reads
    it as a cultural universal (*Between Theater,* p. 6). While this may in part be true,
    it appears to me that the particular "not/not not" of the "suspension of disbelief"
    model has Euro-American overtones that deserve noting. Are dominant contem-
    porary Western cultural models of reception more comfortable with "disbelief"
    regarding representation than with approaching representational practices for
    the ways in which habits of "suspending disbelief," often in the name of "enter-
    tainment," become a model of belief itself?

10. Walter Benjamin, "On the Mimetic Faculty," in *Reflections*, ed. Peter Demetz
    (New York: Schocken, 1986), pp. 333–36.

11. This mode of charting theatrical history is now, among theater historians,
    generally outmoded, but its effect lingers, and most undergraduates (trained
    in reading dramatic texts as the privileged site of theater) come to introduc-
    tory classes with these assumptions in place. An example of a theater history
    textbook that attempted to parse theater from the more primordial "ritual" to
    narrate theater as evolutionary Progress is Kenneth Macgowan and William
    Melnitz's *The Living Stage: A History of World Theatre* (New York: Prentice
    Hall, 1955). Strains remain of the notion that the "abysmal savage" (ibid., p. 2)
    or unsophisticated rube was "merely" engaged in ritual until "highly civilized
    men" invent dramatic text in Greece (p. 21). Oscar Brockett first published his
    History of Theatre in 1968, but comparing a paragraph from 1982 (the fourth
    edition) with one from 2003 (the ninth edition) is telling, as one sees the ru-
    brics ritual, theater, and performativity slip and slide. Brockett is not as *overtly*
    text-centric as his predecessors, but what is alarming is that the link between
    the primitive and contemporary "unsophisticated" culture remains. From 1982:
    "Theatrical and dramatic elements are present in every society, no matter how
    complex or unsophisticated it is. These elements are as evident in our own
    political campaigns, parades, sports events, religious services, and children's
    make-believe as they are in the dances and ceremonies of primitive peoples.
    Nevertheless, most participants do not consider such activities to be primarily
    theatrical, even when they make use of spectacle, dialogue, and conflict. Con-
    sequently, it is usual to acknowledge a distinction between *the theater as a form
    of art* and *the incidental use of theatrical elements in other activities.* . . . It would
    be impossible to construct a coherent history of all the theatrical devices found
    in humanities diverse undertaking through the ages. Therefore, this book is

primarily about the theater as an institution"; Oscar G. Brockett, *History of the Theatre,* 4th ed. (Boston: Allyn and Bacon, 1982), p.1. From 2003: "Performative elements (including dramatic and theatrical) are present in every society, no matter how complex or unsophisticated the culture may be. These elements are as evident in our own political campaigns, parades, sports events, religious services, and children's make-believe as they are in the dances and rituals of primitive peoples. Nevertheless, most participants do not consider such activities to be primarily theatrical, even when spectacle, dialogue, and conflict play large roles. Consequently, it is usual to acknowledge a distinction between *theater* (as a form of art and entertainment) and the presence of *theatrical* or *performative elements* . . . It would be virtually impossible to construct a coherent history of all the human activities that through the ages have made use of performative conventions. Therefore, this book is primarily about the theater as an autonomous activity"; Oscar G. Brockett, *History of the Theatre,* 9th ed. (Boston: Allyn and Bacon, 2003), p.1.

12. See Michel Foucault, "What Is an Author?" in *Language, Countermemory, Practice* (Ithaca: Cornell University Press, 1977) , pp. 113–38.

13. See Butler, *Antigone's Claim* (AC).

14. Kaja Silverman, *The Threshold of the Visible World* (New York: Routledge, 1996), p. 195.This claim is surprising, given Silverman's efforts to negotiate a reading for the tactile, or the "proprioceptive self," in the early chapters of her book.

15. Richard Schechner, *Performance Theory* (New York: Routledge, 1988), pp. 69–70.

16. See Erwin Panovsky, *Perspective as Symbolic Form*, trans. Christopher S. Wood (New York: Zone, 1991), p. 34; and Hubert Damisch, *The Origin of Perspective*, trans. John Goodman (Cambridge: MIT Press, 1995), pp. 22–41.

17. Felicia Hughes-Freeland has discussed the tendency to designate as "ritual" *any* social practice that appears bizarre and exotic; "Introduction," *Ritual, Performance, Media* (New York: Routledge, 1998), pp.1-28. The more recent attempt to read ritual as "performance" is, interestingly, in part an attempt to redress, with postcolonial hindsight, that exoticism. See Edward L. Schieffelin, "Problematizing Performance" (ibid., pp. 104–207) on anthropology's move away from a symbolic to a "performance" approach to ritual. Theater scholars trained in performance studies similarly attempt to approach performance and theater *as* ritual. I will discuss this in greater depth later in this essay as regards literary criticism's move to "performativity."

18. Christopher Innes reads the entire modernist avant-garde as marked by an idealization of the primitive and a search for rituality. See his *Avant-Garde Theatre* (New York: Routledge, 1993). See also Rebecca Schneider, *The Explicit Body in Performance* (New York: Routledge, 1997), pp.126–52.

19. Judith Butler, *Gender Trouble: Feminism and the Subversion of Identity* (GT); *Bodies That Matter* (BTM).

20. Jon McKenzie, "Genre Trouble: (The) Butler Did It," in *Ends of Performance*, ed. Peggy Phelan and Jill Lane (New York: New York University Press, 1988), p. 225.

21. The literature is far too voluminous to cite. By way of example, see Margaret Thompson Drewal, *Yoruban Ritual* (Bloomington: Indiana University Press, 1992), pp. 1–28.

22. I am arguing that the actor, playing out a drama, is agreeing to act as if he does not know, can not see, the outcome of his drama. This is certainly the case in nineteenth- and twentieth-century naturalisms, however it is problematic to suggest that the kernel of such acting might be found in ancient Greece, where masks, declarative oratory, and certainly broad if not hieroglyphic gesture could not be more distinct from "fourth wall" drama. Still, in the structural separation of spectacle from spectator, and in the dramas themselves, "vision" was gaining a tropic centrality. Sophocles' Oedipus trilogy is only the most obvious example. See Butler on this blindness, AC, p. 5.

23. Butler, *Excitable Speech: Politics of the Performative* (ES).

24. Toni Morrison, *Lecture and Speech of Acceptance, Upon the Award of the Nobel Prize for Literature, Delivered in Stockholm on the Seventh of December, Nineteen Hundred and Ninety-Three* (New York : Knopf, 1994).

25. The objection may be raised that in *Excitable Speech* (unlike in "'How Can I Deny'") Butler never refers to the body directly as *her* body. This is true; her indirectness has the effect of the blind she directs. If "the writer" is given to be blind, and the body is given as the blindspot of writing, can we not then infer that this blindspot is the writer's body—or at least that the blindspot is in relation to that body as well as any future body that takes the text in hand?

26. For a useful engagement of some of these issues facing bodies as contained (and extruded), remembered and disavowed, in texts over time, see Carolyn Dinshaw, *Getting Medieval: Sexualities and Communities, Pre- and Postmodern* (Durham: Duke University Press, 1999), pp. 1–54.

27. See Schneider, *The Explicit Body*.

28. I wrote at the opening of this essay that I feel far more comfortable with Butler's adopted question about denial ("'How Can I Deny That These Hands and This Body Are Mine?'" *Qui Parle* 11, no. 1 [1997]: 1–20) than with the ritual artists' *refusals to deny* their bodies—refusal to disappear their bodies—to which I now turn. On the force and discomfort of the "refusal to deny" or the "refusal to perform a denial" see, ironically, Butler, AC, p. 8. I say ironically because Antigone's refusal, which Butler appears to admire, is to deny an act concerning a body doomed to wander the earth as a specter. Antigone seeks to cover the "exposed body" of her brother (AC, p. 53). But, in covering that body (as if in a robe), she is also acknowledging it as his *and* as hers—not relegating it only to *spectral* return. Butler reads Antigone's refusal through Sophocles' play (AC, 83, n. 2). And yet Butler forgets, throughout, that that text *is a play,* pitched *toward play* and an "aberrant future" (AC, p. 82) in mimetic repetition—in the mouths and in the hands of *bodies* ritually reperforming the refusals to deny. Does she forget? Or is she, as she says of Lacan regarding Antigone, simply "manifesting her own blindness" (AC, p. 53)?

29. See Carolee Schneeman, *More Than Meat Joy* (New Paltz, NY: McPherson, 1997), Mary Beth Edelson, *Seven Cycles: Public Rituals* (New York: Seven Cycles, 1980) and *Shapeshifter: Seven Mediums* (Edelson, 1990). See also the more recent collection *The Art of Mary Beth Edelson* (New York: Seven Cycles, 2002), also authored by the artist.

30. Edelson, *The Art of Mary Beth Edelson*, p. 65.

31. Jill Dolan, *The Feminist Spectator as Critic* (Ann Arbor: UMI Research, 1988); Diana Fuss, *Essentially Speaking* (New York: Routledge,1989), p. 7. The "spectral" word is Butler's—as is its necessity ("'How Can I Deny,'" p. 18).

32. Harry Elam Jr. and Alice Rayner, "Unfinished Business: Reconfiguring History in Suzan-Lori Parks's *The Death of the Last Black Man in the Whole Entire World*," *Theater Journal* 46, no. 4 (1994): 447–62.

9. PERFORMATIVITY, CITATIONALITY, RITUALIZATION

AMY HOLLYWOOD

I N *Bodies That Matter* Judith Butler responds to her critics, those for whom *Gender Trouble*'s account of performative subjectivity threatens to dissolve the gendered subject into language and/or marks a return of liberal humanist conceptions of a voluntarist self who freely chooses her or his identity.[1] These critiques are contradictory in ways symptomatic of central theoretical dualisms Butler continually deconstructs in her work.[2] Characteristically, her response to her critics takes the form of an interrogation of the concept of materiality to which many of them appeal and an articulation of the extremely complex relationships between the "materiality of the body" and "the performativity of gender."[3] According to Butler, neither materiality nor sex are given, but rather "the materiality of sex is constructed through a ritualized repetition of norms" (BTM, p. x). She argues that performativity is a kind of "citational practice" by which sexed and gendered subjects are continuously constituted.[4] The gaps and fissures in that citational process—the ways in which repetition both repeats the same and differs and defers from it—mark the multiple sites on/in which the contestation of regulatory norms occurs. Butler grounds resistance not in bodies or materialities external to systems of regulatory discourses and norms but in the processes of resignification through which body subjects are themselves constituted.

Given some of the responses to *Bodies That Matter*, I am not sure that those who thought *Gender Trouble* dissolved the body and the subject into language have been convinced by Butler's reformulation and careful articulation of the discursive practices formative of materiality, bodies, and subjects.[5] Against these continued critiques, I would place Butler's assertion that

> there is no reference to a pure body which is not at the same time a further formation of that body. In this sense, the linguistic capacity to refer to sexed bodies is not denied, but the very meaning of "referentiality" is altered. In philosophical terms, the constative claim is always to some degree performative.
>
> (BTM, pp. 10–11)

Yet I think that Butler's recent focus on linguistic practices (narrowly construed) and psychoanalytic accounts of subject formation might usefully be supplemented with attention to the other bodily practices through which subjects are constituted.[6] Whereas *Gender Trouble* clearly understands "words, acts, gestures, and desires" as performative,[7] Butler's reliance on Austinean notions of performativity allows many critics to miss her crucial claim that acts signify. *Bodies That Matter* makes extensive use of Lacanian psychoanalytic theory, in which language serves as the master trope for signification. As a result, Butler seems even more deeply invested in the primacy of language as formative of subjectivity. In *Excitable Speech* Butler ostensibly returns to an analysis of the constitutive role of bodily practices, particularly in her discussion of Pierre Bourdieu's account of the habitus. Yet the language of her text tends, as I will show, to conflate bodily practices with speech acts (themselves understood as one form of bodily practice).[8] Because Butler's primary concern in *Bodies That Matter* and *Excitable Speech* is with linguistic performativity, she does not clearly articulate how actions as well as language signify.[9]

Here I will return to and supplement Butler's account of repeated actions as performative of gender,[10] extending her analysis from gender to the subject and demonstrating that the subject is formed not only through the linguistic citation of norms[11] but also by the body subject's encounters with other bodies in the world and by its practical or bodily citations (this would include ritual acts and bodily practices like those analyzed by Marcel Mauss, Pierre Bourdieu, and Talal Asad—modes of walking, standing, and sitting, sleeping and eating, giving birth, nursing, healing, etc.).[12] I will argue that these encounters, insofar as they are constitutive of subjectivity, are best characterized as sharing in certain structural features of signification; yet signification is not solely linguistic. Attention to how bodily practices and rituals signify and to how they constitute subjects may work against dematerializing readings of Butler's texts. Performative actions, like linguistic performatives, constitute that to which they refer.

In order to understand why readings of Butler so easily slide from a bodily to a linguistic understanding of the performative, and, at the same time, to clarify how speech acts and ritual actions signify, I will begin with Butler's reformulation of materiality as materialization and her identification of this process with ritual (BTM, p. x; see also pp. 10, 95, 126, 185). Following J. L. Austin in *How to Do Things with Words* and Jacques Derrida in "Signature, Event, Context," Butler's accounts of performativity and citationality—of the ways in which language acts—rely on an at first barely articulated analogy with ritual action (actions that signify, according to some ritual theorists).[13] Butler expands the role of "ritual" in her account of the performative in *Excitable Speech*, going so far as to argue that speech acts are themselves rituals, a move rendered ironic by the fact that some ritual theorists now understand rituals as speech acts.[14] Ritual serves to ballast her account of the force of the performative without itself being explicitly defined or theorized.[15] What I want to do here is explore the use of the term *ritual* within the work of Butler, Austin, and Derrida to demonstrate the ways in which all three lean their accounts of the force of the performative on ritual. I will ask why this is so, suggest what they mean by the term, and explore the significance of their work for the understanding of ritual. I will argue that Derrida's understanding of the structures of signification offers useful suggestions for a theory of ritualization—and, by extension, of subject formation and materialization—grounded in the performative.[16] The result will be both a better reading of Butler and a new account of ritual and bodily actions as performative.

Ritual Matters

In *Bodies That Matter* Butler describes the process of materialization as a "ritualized repetition of norms" (p. x). She goes on to claim that

> as a sedimented effect of a reiterative or ritual practice, sex acquires its naturalized effect, and, yet, it is also by virtue of this reiteration that gaps and fissures are opened up as the constitutive instabilities in such constructions, as that which escapes or exceeds the norm, as that which cannot be wholly defined or fixed by the repetitive labor of that norm.

> (p. 10)

Here *ritual* is interchangeable with *reiterative,* suggesting that the term serves only to highlight the repetitive nature of those practices and citations through which the sexed body is formed.[17] This is important for Butler because it is the temporality of citationality that allows for the slippage between norms and their instantiation; resistance occurs in the space and time interval demanded by repetition.

Later in *Bodies That Matter* Butler introduces the notion of constraint in proximity to that of ritual, further suggesting that ritual has to do not only with repeated practices but also with power;

> performativity cannot be understood outside of a process of iterability, a regularized and constrained repetition of norms. And this repetition is not performed *by* a subject; this repetition is what enables a subject and constitutes the temporal conditions for the subject. This iterability implies that "performance" is not a singular "act" or event, but a ritualized production, a ritual reiterated under and through constraint, under and through force of prohibition and taboo, with the threat of ostracism and even death controlling and compelling the shape of the production, but not, I will insist, determining it fully in advance.[18]
>
> (BTM, p. 95)

One might read ritual in this passage as again marking the repeated nature of the "performance" of gender (as opposed to a singular act or event); it is the reiterative nature of the practice that opens the door to resistance and ensures that the repetition of norms is not fully determinative of body subjects. Yet the passage also suggests an association between "ritualized production" and "a *regularized and constrained* repetition of norms" (my emphasis), leading us to ask about the precise relationships between ritual, constraint, and power. In other words, if the performative has the power to act, where does that power or, to use Austin's and Derrida's language, force come from? Does it come from outside the speech act? Or is it, rather, internal to that performance?

Butler takes up the question of the force of the performative in *Excitable Speech*. Here she posits a disjunction between Pierre Bourdieu's work on the performative and that of Jacques Derrida.[19] For Bourdieu force is located within the social context, understood as outside of the utterance itself; "authority comes to language from outside."[20] Butler reads Derrida, conversely, as claiming that the force of the performative is a structural condition of language and marks the decontextualization necessary to iterability (ES, p. 147). The antithesis Butler sets up between Bourdieu and Derrida (one implicitly operating in Bourdieu's text) is crucially tied to the concept of ritual. According to Butler, Derrida transforms ritual completely into linguistic iterability.[21] As a result "the socially complex notion of ritual . . . is rendered void of all social meanings; its repetitive function is abstracted from its social operation and established as an inherent structural feature of any and all marks" (ES, pp. 150–51). Bourdieu, in contrast, locates the power or force of the performative in convention or ritual and so in social institutions outside of the domain of language and thus closed to the changes made possible by iterability. By denying the temporality of performativity, Bourdieu renders it a fully determinative and determined linguistic practice.

Butler responds to this dilemma by tying the force of the performative neither to the structure of the sign nor to extralinguistic social institutions but rather to the body (of the speaker).[22] She locates the force of the performative in the chiasmatic relationship between speech and the body; "speech is bodily, but the body exceeds the speech it occasions; and speech remains irreducible to the bodily means of its enunciation" (ES, pp. 155–56). Furthermore, Butler argues that the body is itself constituted of and by speech acts. To facilitate this move, she appeals to Bourdieu's notion of the habitus, the set of bodily dispositions or embodied practices through which cultures maintain a sense of their own obviousness.[23] As Butler argues, the habitus is "formed, but it is also *formative*: it is in this sense that the bodily *habitus* constitutes a tacit form of performativity, a citational chain lived and believed at the level of the body" (ES, p. 155). The habitus is the embodied result of the reiteration of norms; it is the result of (or is itself?) a subjectivity constructed through the repetition of the discourses and practices into which we are born and called into subjectivity.[24]

To clarify the relationship between the force of the performative and the body, Butler points to the importance of the body lying behind the threat of hate speech. The language of the body itself, in fact, is part of the speech act and determines (how) its force (is read? i.e., as threat, joke, citation). Asked why speech and the body should be given precedence when anonymous hate mail is potentially as hurtful as spoken utterances, Butler suggests that even if "performatives cannot always be retethered to their moment of utterance . . . they carry the mnemic trace of the body in the force that they exercise" (ES, p. 159). In other words, hate mail threatens insofar as it carries the trace of the addresser's body and the body of the addressee is then marked by the force of the utterance.[25] There seems to be a certain circularity to Butler's argument, however, for the force of the utterance derives from the speaking body, yet in the absence of the speaking body the force of the utterance on the body of the addressee points to the speaking body. Perhaps the materiality of hate mail and of language itself effects this movement from the body of the addressee to that of the speaker.

Butler goes on to argue that the body "is not simply the sedimentation of speech acts by which it has been constituted" (ES, p. 155). She points here to the chiasmatic relationship between speech and the body in which neither is fully contained by or reducible to the other. She is thus able to argue that the body both provides and resists the force of speech. Whereas in Butler's Derridean account of signification iteration provides the "break" necessary to resistance, the body protects against the overgeneralization of this break feared by Bourdieu. Yet I am not clear why, in Butler's analysis of the relationship between the body and the performative, the body is understood as produced only by *speech* acts, particularly given Bourdieu's (and, as we will see, Mauss's) concern for the day-to-day bodily practices that make up the habitus. Perhaps Butler understands those bodily practices formative of subjectivity, now interpreted as themselves signifying chains insofar as they are citational, as speech acts.[26] Yet I think it is important to distinguish meaningful action from language that acts, particularly given the need to clarify *how* action means and language acts and the specificity of these different operations.

Butler argues, finally, that the performative should be rethought as a social ritual, "as one of the very 'modalities of practices [that] are powerful and hard to resist precisely because they are silent and insidious, insistent and insinuating'" (ES, p. 159, citing Bourdieu). Of course, speech acts are not generally silent—although perhaps the conventions on which they depend are—pointing to a disanalogy between the performative and those bodily practices constitutive of the habitus. More important, if, as Butler argues, the performative needs to be read as "ritual practice" and "one of the influential rituals by which subjects are formed and reformulated" (ES, p. 160), then we need a more clearly articulated theory of ritual to make sense of the performative and its force. According to Butler, speech acts are like rituals in their bodiliness, their constraining power (derived from that bodiliness), and their iterability. Yet we derive this account of ritual from Butler's analysis of speech acts as constitutive of subjectivity. Within Butler's account the particularity of bodily practices and rituals are quickly subsumed into that of the speech act, suggesting that ritual remains an untheorized ballast for the force of language. She uses Bourdieu's account of the habitus as a way to show that bodily practices shape the subject, only to identify those practices with speech acts. Although I think Butler means to say that bodily practices themselves signify, this crucial point remains unarticulated.

From Speech Acts to Ritual Meaning

To understand why Butler leans her conception of the performative on the relatively untheorized notion of ritual, and to unpack further what ritual means in the context of these discussions, I would like to examine some of her sources. The proximity of ritual to the performative has its roots in the work of J. L. Austin,[27] for whom certain ritual utterances served as prime examples of the performative (W, p. 5) and the infelicities that plague it (W, pp. 18–19). In his preliminary isolation of the performative Austin differentiates it from what he calls constative utterances. Constatives are statements that describe situations or states of affairs and therefore are either true or false. Yet there are also grammatically unexceptional statements that do not describe situations or states of affairs and so cannot be taken as true or false;

many such statements, however, are not nonsense. They therefore require explanation and classification. Austin argues that such statements "do" something rather than "say" something. His examples include speech acts drawn from the realm of what, in "ordinary language," we often refer to as rituals:

> Examples:
> (E. a.) 'I do (sc. take this woman to be my lawful wedded wife)'—as uttered in the course of the marriage ceremony.
> (E. b.) 'I name this ship the *Queen Elizabeth*'—as uttered when smashing the bottle against the stem.
> (E. c.) 'I give and bequeath my watch to my brother'—as occurring in a will.
> (E. d.) 'I bet you sixpence it will rain tomorrow.' (W, p. 5)

In all but the final example Austin makes clear that the context is essential to the phrase performing an action (ultimately, it will be crucial for the final example too, as an actor making a promise during the performance of a play is not considered to have made a promise—although she is still performing).

It is in large part the social context of the performative that gives rise to the numerous possibilities for "misfiring." Austin offers a preliminary schematization of the conditions necessary for a happy or felicitous speech act performance, dividing them into three categories, A, B, and Gamma. A and B concern the procedures and conventions necessary for the adequate performance of a speech act:

> (A. 1) There must exist an accepted conventional procedure having a certain conventional effect, that procedure to include the uttering of certain words by certain persons in certain circumstances, and further,
> (A. 2) the particular person and circumstances in a given case must be appropriate for the invocation of the particular procedure invoked.
> (B. 1) The procedure must be executed by all participants both correctly and
> (B. 2) completely.

Gamma, in contrast, is concerned with the speaker and his or her relation to what is spoken.

> (Gamma. 1) Where, as often, the procedure is designed for use by persons having certain thoughts and feelings, or for the inauguration of certain consequential conduct on the part of any participant, then a person participating in and so invoking the procedure must in fact have those thoughts or feelings, and the participants must intend so to conduct themselves, and further
> (Gamma. 2) must actually so conduct themselves subsequently.
> (W, pp. 14–15)

These conditions are not all of the same type, for failure to meet conditions A and B lead to the misfiring of the performative (it does not, in fact, take place), while failure to meet conditions Gamma, the conditions of intentionality, constitutes an abuse of the performative, which has, nonetheless, taken place. (I have made a promise but been insincere or made a promise and failed to live up to it.)

Only conditions A and B seem, at first sight, relevant to our exploration of the role of ritual and convention in the analysis of performative speech acts; in elaborating the failures marked by A and B, Austin makes the analogy between performatives and ritual explicit. Austin argues that because a statement must be made by the correct person, to the correct persons, and in the correct circumstances for the action to be completed, there are innumerable possibilities for failed performatives. He claims, furthermore, that this "infelicity is an ill to which *all* acts are heir which have the general character of ritual or ceremonial, all *conventional* acts" (W, pp. 18–19). This suggests that ritual, ceremonial, or conventional acts, whether linguistic or not, are marked by constraints with regard to the social context in which they occur. These constraints, moreover, are the source of the happy or unhappy performance of a speech act and hence, by implication, of its *force*.[28]

The move from conditions A and B listed above to the problem of intentionality is, arguably, one away from the understanding of the performative as tied to ritual.[29] Yet as Austin moves on in his discussion of the performative he increasingly focuses on the issue of intentionality and the role of the assumed sovereign "I" who enacts. At a loss in his attempt to find a grammatical or semantic marker by means of which the performative can be readily distinguished from the constative, Austin argues in lecture 5 that if a certain reduction can be effected on an utterance it is shown to have performative force. The operation involves determining whether an utterance can be rendered as an explicit performative, one in which a verb (of the proper sort) appears in the first-person present indicative. (In this way, one could argue, Austin, like Butler, attempts to tether the performative to the body or to demonstrate the ways in which the performative always bears the trace of the body. Derrida, as we will see, conflates this move with claims to intentionality.) Not all statements in this form are performative, nor do all performatives appear in this form, but all performatives can be *reduced* to this form. It is the appropriate grammatical form for the performative, according to Austin, because "actions can only be performed by persons, and obviously in our cases the utterer must be the performer" and since the speech is an act, the person "must be doing something" (W, p. 60). In those cases where the "I" is not explicit in the performative, moreover, she or he is always referred to either "*by his being the person who does* the uttering" or "*by his appending his signature*" (W, p. 60). There is necessarily an "I" behind the performative who somehow serves as the "utterance-*origin*" and hence as the source of the performative's force.

There is a tension, then, between Austin's claim that it is the conventionality of the speech act, like the conventionality of ritual, that gives force to the utterance and his suggestion that the utterance source, the speaking or signing "I," is the locus of force.[30] In "Signature, Event, Context" Derrida exploits this ambiguity in Austin's texts to argue for a "general theory" of the mark in which its force is tied to a conventionality not of external circumstances but of the mark itself.[31] For Derrida all language takes on the character of the performative and of ritual (rather than ritual being reduced to language, as Butler claims). In making this argument Derrida associates Austin's attempt to tie the force of the performative to the speaking subject with his interest in intentionality as a condition for the correct use of the performative. Although this slide might not be entirely justified (and we might, with Felman and Butler, more usefully tie the force of the performative to the body of the speaker and hence to that which often escapes conscious intentionality), it is suggestive of the ways in which subsequent readings of Austin's text have attempted to delimit the performative and protect against the erosion of the constative effected within it.[32]

Having cited Austin's claim that the possibilities for misfiring that haunt the performative are also endemic to all "ritual or ceremonial, all *conventional* acts" (W, pp. 18–19), Derrida goes on to locate the specificity of Austin's claims and make his own generalization:

> Austin seems to consider only the conventionality that forms the *circumstances* of the statement, its contextual surroundings, and not a certain intrinsic conventionality of that which constitutes locution itself, that is, everything that might quickly be summarized under the problematic heading of the "arbitrariness of the sign"; which extends, aggravates, and radicalizes the difficult. Ritual is not eventuality, but, as iterability, is a structural character of every mark.
>
> (SEC, pp. 323–24)

Ritual as iterability, Derrida claims, is what marks the sign as communicative and performative. Key for Derrida, as for Butler, is the iterability or repeatability of the sign; it is this reiterative structure, the fact that the sign is the same and yet also differs and defers (both from possible referents and from other signs), that marks its force (and its power of signification). Butler argues that for Derrida the force of the performative lies in its "decontextualization"; because the mark must be repeated in order to signify, it is always both tied to and divorced from its original context of utterance. This separation, according to Butler, provides the performative's force. Yet I think that this is to forget that iterability is always marked by similarity as well as difference. The force of the mark, on my account, is twofold. It derives from that which is the same in the mark and from that which differs; force is therefore subject to multiple deployments.

Butler argues that Derrida is interested in ritual only insofar as it serves as a useful analogy for his account of language as iteration. I would like to follow out a version of that argument here, yet ultimately I will argue that more can be derived from Derrida's deployment of ritual than he himself may have intended. Embedded within Austin's notion of ritual is the understanding of social context and external constraints as intrinsic to the felicitous operation of its performance. Derrida reads Austin as equating context with intentionality (A and B, with Gamma);[33] it is in this light that Derrida points to the impossibility of ever fully determining context: "For a context to be exhaustively determinable, in the sense demanded by Austin, it at least would be necessary for the conscious intention to be totally present and actually transparent to itself and others, since it is a determining focal point of the context" (SEC, p. 326). Yet arguably this is precisely what is not required for ritual or conventional actions. Within ritual action the intentionality of the players is often unimportant to the force of the utterance. By focusing on Austin's sovereign "I" as the focal point for contextualization rather than on the question of who is speaking to whom and in what circumstances, in arguing that a condition of the mark is the absence of an empirical addressee, and in emphasizing the structure of the mark over its semantic content, Derrida, as Butler argues, seems to "evacuate the social" from the realm of language and its utterance.[34]

Yet as Butler shows, Derrida never argues that the context is unimportant to determining the meaning and force of an utterance, only that this context can never be fully determined and thus the speaking subject can not have full control of her meanings. Moreover, the question of force and constraint is crucial to Derrida and is intimately related to the iterative structure of signification (which, I will argue, can occur through both linguistic marks and action). He suggests that in providing a more general theory of language (as writing), a generalizing movement eschewed by Austin, he is able to show the way in which what seems external to the operation of the performative is also internal to it (and, I think, constitutive of those very social institutions in which Bourdieu wants to locate the force of performatives and ritual). Derrida here points to Austin's exclusion of the citation from his account of performative and constative speech acts. For Austin the performance of an utterance in a play or the recitation of a poem is a parasitic or abnormal use of language, dependent on the more primary "ordinary language" he wishes to analyze. (At issue here, it should be noted, is the question of intentionality, sincerity, and other aspects of the Gamma criteria.) For Derrida citationality is iterability—rather than being a secondary parasite, it marks the structural conditions for signification itself. The risk of citationality—that the performative cannot be tied to an intending subject—is a risk endemic to signification itself. By clinging to intentionality as a necessary condition for determining the total context in which performative and constative uses of language can be distinguished, Derrida argues, Austin misses the primacy of citationality and the structural inability of any context ever to be fully determined (see SEC, p. 310).

For Derrida, then, the force of the utterance lies within the structure of language as iteration. This force, as I have suggested, can work in multiple (possibly endless) ways. In a concise summation of much of his early work on writing and difference, Derrida suggests the duplicity of the force of signification.

> Deconstruction does not consist in passing from one concept to another, but in overturning and displacing a conceptual order, as well as the nonconceptual order with which the conceptual order is articulated. For example, writing, as a classical concept, carries with it predicates which have been subordinated, excluded, or held in reserve by forces and according to necessities to be analyzed. It is these predicates (I have mentioned some) whose force of generality, generalization, and generativity find themselves liberated, grafted onto a "new" concept of writing which also corresponds to whatever always has *resisted* the former organization of forces, which always has constituted the *remainder* irreducible to the dominant force which organized the—to say it quickly—logocentric hierarchy. To leave to this new concept the old name of writing is to maintain the structure of the graft, the transition and indispensable adherence to an effective *intervention* in the constituted historic field. And it is also to give their chance and their force, their power of *communication*, to everything played out in the operations of deconstruction.
>
> (SEC, pp. 329–30)

I cannot unpack these lines fully without an analysis of the context of its utterance. It serves my purposes here, however, simply by showing that force works for Derrida in at least two ways. On the one hand, force is the result of a tethering of the mark to the same, its repetition of that which has come before; yet on the other hand, deconstruction attempts to exploit the fact that to be repeated the mark must always also differ and defer from that which it cites (although, as I will show, the ends toward which this break is deployed are open). Derrida's analysis of the structural conditions of the mark and the deconstructive reversal of speech and writing, presence and absence, ordinary language and citationality mark a redeployment of the force of the mark toward new ends.[35]

Butler argues that in evacuating the social context from the performative Derrida denies the historicity of language. Yet for Derrida historicity is not only the repetition of the *same*. Against hermeneutic claims Derrida insists that history is never a fully recuperable presence or materiality but rather is change, rupture, and break (the *repetition* of the same and hence always different). Paradoxically, the force of this rupture or of the break constitutive of history is what enables the fiction of a universal, disembodied, self-present subject. Derrida refigures or resignifies this break and its consequences not to reinstall a new universalizing authority (as Bourdieu, for example, suggests) but rather to mark the alterity of history in and by writing. The universal subject is always a contextual one, regardless of whether that context is erased through a "false break" that attempts to make generalization a total and radical decontextualization (what Butler claims Derrida himself does). The generality of the mark makes it reiterable and generative, yet this generality always requires a context. The attempt to escape contextualization in general (to claim a universality untethered to any context) is a reification of one determined context at the expense of new ones.

The invocation of ritual, as it is outlined by Austin, suggests that constraint comes not from within the sign but is maintained by forces external to it—either convention or the conscious intention of the speaker. If, then, the apt performance of ritual, like that of speech acts, depends on who is speaking to whom and in what context, there might seem to be something external to the ritual itself that determines this delimited context for applicability and provides the force of its action (this is what Bourdieu, in particular, will argue). Derrida claims, conversely, that Austin ultimately tries to reduce the source of performative force and the "total context" in which performativity can be discerned to the speaking subject. We might read Austin more generously as claiming that the force of the perlocutionary utterance (which requires the proper outcome follow from it in order to be performative) is dependent on the speaking subject and that of the illocutionary (in which the saying, in the right conditions, *is* the performance) on convention. Yet even the illocutionary always has a signatory—the one authorized to use this form of conventional speech. This leads to the question of who or what authorizes the signatory, again taking us to convention and determining contexts external to the speech act itself. Against both these moves Derrida argues for the primacy of citationality and therefore the inability ever fully to determine context. In doing so, moreover, he suggests how the process of iteration is itself constitutive of those social conventions through which performatives derive their force. For Derrida the outside is constituted by the inside and the inside by the outside.

I think it is important to remember that, just as Butler's aim in *Excitable Speech* is not to give a full account of the habitus as constitutive of the subject, Derrida is not interested in elaborating a theory of ritual in SEC but rather in giving a general account of signification. Yet if we accept the claim that ritual is signifying action, Derrida's account of the sign has implications for ritual theory. In *Excitable Speech* Butler is primarily interested in the linguistic character of signification and so at times seems in danger of conflating signification with language and hence reading Derrida as reducing ritual to language. This runs parallel to the error made by those ritual theorists who claim that ritual is meaningless. They assume that meaning necessitates reference (of a particular sort); when attempts to understand ritual actions as referring to some other reality break down, the claim is made that rituals do not signify.[36] In providing an account of signification not dependent on this kind of reference, Derrida offers a way to reformulate ritual as meaningful without claiming that it refers to independently existing external realities. Rather, social realities are constituted by ritual action. (Hence the move to say that rituals are performative—their meanings are not primarily constative but generated by the action itself.) Rather than reducing the social complexity of ritual, then, I believe that Derrida's analysis is suggestive for understanding ritual as meaningful action, particularly when brought together with Bourdieu's and Butler's attention to the body as speaker and ritual actor. For Derrida the signifying and constitutive force of the performative is a function of its reiterative structure (both as a repetition of the same and as the break) and as its effect.[37] The very contexts in which the performative operates are themselves products of performative utterances and acts, subverting the distinction between utterance and context on which Austin's analysis (at least provisionally) depends. Ritual can be understood in the same way, for just as speech acts mean as well as do, rituals are meaningful actions. For Derrida force would lie within the reiterative structure of ritual (as repetition and break) and as an effect of ritual rather than solely outside ritual as that which enables its performance.

In *Bodies That Matter* Butler takes up Derrida's emphasis on ritual as repetition, an iterability that is always marked by differance, yet she also suggests that ritual is a "regularized and constrained repetition of norms." At this point it is not clear whether Butler follows Derrida in placing the force of the performative or of citationality within the process of reiteration or whether she wishes to maintain an outside—a social world untouched by the constitutive force of the performative—from which these constraints emanate. The latter seems an unlikely position for Butler to hold given her other philosophical commitments. In *Excitable Speech* she argues that the force of the performative lies neither fully outside nor within the performative but is tied to the body who speaks (and who is addressed?). I think that this move places Butler closer to Derrida's position than she herself acknowledges, for emphasis on the chiasmatic relationship of speech and the body functions in ways analogous to Derrida's critique of claims to full contextualization. Speech is of the body, and the body speaks and is constituted, according to Butler, by speech acts, yet neither can be fully reduced to the other. Similarly, when Derrida argues against Austin that the citation is not a secondary example of the performative but the revelation of its very structure, of its force and its risk, Derrida does not simply exchange externally for internally generated constraints. Rather, he deconstructs the very opposition between external and internal as he describes the performative's constitutive force and the possibility of its failure. Materialization and subjectification are processes in which body subjects are constituted; the possibilities for resistance lie in the endless possibilities for misfiring that structure the performative itself (although the misfiring of particular performatives will depend in large part on the contexts—constituted by hosts of other performatives—in which they occur).

This clearly coincides with Butler's understanding of the possibilities for resistance in *Bodies That Matter*. Her account of the chiasmatic relationship between body and speech in *Excitable Speech*, however, at times leads to another reading, one that claims resistance is grounded in the body insofar as it is irreducible to speech acts. This move might suggest that Butler has come to distrust her own deconstructive impulses and wishes to reinstall "the body itself" as site of resistance. This reading is clearly in tension with Butler's account of the body as constituted through the performative repetition of norms that makes up the habitus (although Butler, as I have shown, is unclear about the relationship between speech acts and ritual actions in this process and tends to conflate ritual with speech acts). Butler suggests the irreducibility of the body to speech in order to create a space for resistance to the social and discursive norms through which subjects are constituted—a resistance she believes is foreclosed by Bourdieu's assertion that the formation of the body by these norms is completely effective. What should be emphasized here is not the irreducibility of the body to speech (as if we could get to that body somehow) but rather an account of bodily practices as themselves performative acts subject to the same misfiring and slippages Austin and Derrida locate in speech acts and signification in general.[38] Recent ritual theory similarly argues that outside and inside are indeterminable and that, as Butler argues, "social positions are themselves constructed through a more tacit operation of performativity" (ES, p. 156). As Derrida and Butler suggest, it is the process of ritualization that constitutes social beings, social worlds, and the constraints through which identities are maintained and differences enunciated.

From Ritual to Ritualization

Ritual, understood as a specific kind of action or as action opposed to thought, is conceptually articulated within the modern Western study of religion, for which Protestant Christianity is hegemonic.[39] Talal Asad uses entries in the *Encyclopedia Britannica* to argue for a fairly recent change in the understanding of ritual. Whereas the entries from 1771 to 1852 define ritual as a book containing the script for religious ceremonies, in the new entry for 1910 ritual is universalized and attention shifts from the script to the action itself. As Asad explains,

> [a] crucial part of every religion, ritual is now regarded as a type of routine behavior that symbolizes or expresses something and, as such, relates differentially to individual consciousness and social organization. That is to say, it is no longer a *script* for regulating practice but a type of practice that is interpretable as standing for some further *verbally definable*, but tacit, event.[40]

Crucial to this move is the claim that rituals as expressive serve some psychological or sociological function—they symbolize meanings that have their real field of operation within the realm of the mind or the social group. For Asad the move is one from text to "behavior, which is itself *likened* to a text," a text to be read by the anthropologist or historian of religion.[41]

To this conception of ritual as symbolic action Asad opposes an understanding of "rites as apt performances" and "disciplinary practices," a view he argues can be seen in medieval Christian conceptions of the monastic life.[42] Through an analysis of aspects of medieval monasticism Asad argues that injunctions for the monastic life prescribe actions and rites "directed at forming and reforming Christian dispositions."[43] Asad's understanding of ritual as "disciplinary practice" is indebted to the work of Michel Foucault and to that of the sociologist Marcel Mauss. To undermine further the modern distinction between symbolic and technical actions, he makes use of Mauss's conception of bodily techniques. According to Mauss, "the body is man's first and most natural instrument. Or more accurately, not to speak of instruments, man's first and most natural technical object, and at the same time technical means, is his body."[44] It is through bodily practices that subjectivities are formed, virtues inculcated, and beliefs embodied. Mauss introduced the notion of the habitus to describe the "techniques and work of collective and individual practical reason" that shape embodied experience.[45]

Unlike Mauss, Asad wishes to assimilate ritual, at least outside the modern Western context, with bodily practices. Mauss, on the contrary, is interested in those bodily practices that are, he argues, shaped by cultural as well as biological and psychological factors yet do not stand clearly within the realm of formalized, ritual, or ceremonial activity. His analysis begins with the problem of what to do with those miscellaneous phenomena such as gait, athletic styles, manners of sleeping and eating, clothing, birth and nursing patterns that are marked by cultural styles yet do not seem to warrant the designation of ritual. Asad suggests that outside of the modern Western context these kinds of regulated bodily activities are continuous with the more constrained activities of what we would call the ritual life.[46] Thus there is no clearly marked differentiation between symbolic and technical activities;

the distinction is instead between those activities (or aspects of activities) in which bodies are the objects and means of transformation and those in which other tools are employed to other ends.

Asad's assumption of the continuity between bodily practices and ritual actions is congruent with Catherine Bell's argument that historians of religion and anthropologists might usefully move away from a concept of ritual to one of ritualization. Bell refuses to define ritual as a static entity.

> Ritualization is fundamentally a way of doing things to trigger the perception that these practices are special. A great deal of strategy is employed simply in the degree to which some activities are ritualized and therein differentiated from other acts. While formalization and periodization appear to be common techniques for ritualization, they are not intrinsic to "ritual" per se; some ritualized practices distinguish themselves by their deliberate informality, although usually in contrast to a known tradition or style of ritualization. Hence, ritual acts must be understood within a semantic framework whereby the significance of an action is dependent upon its place and relationship within a context of all other ways of acting: what it echoes, what it inverts, what it alludes to, what it denies.[47]

Although the formalization of actions—their limitation to certain times, places, contexts, ritual agents—is one of the techniques used to mark off some practices as having a special significance within the life of the community, Bell insists that the ways in which ritualization occurs are specific to individual groups and communities; in other words, ritualization works and must be understood contextually (even if the total context can never be fully determined).

Bell also argues that ritualization, in giving special significance to certain practices, does so not because these actions refer to or symbolize meanings external to them but rather because social subjects and their relations are engendered through the bodily practices of ritual life. Against common functionalist theories of ritual, which understand it as an attempt to forge social solidarity, to resolve conflicts within the community, or to transmit shared beliefs, Bell argues that ritual involves the "production of ritualized agents, persons who have an instinctive knowledge of these schemes embedded in their bodies, in their sense of reality, and in their understanding of how to act in ways that both maintain and qualify the complex microrelations of power."[48] To questions about the relationship between ritualization and power, then, Bell argues that power and its dispositions are generated and regulated through rituals themselves rather than lying outside them as that which constrains or otherwise marks these activities off as special.

Bell's account of ritualization, then, can be rendered consonant with the understanding of ritual we have drawn out of Derrida's reading of Austin. For both Bell and Derrida ritual is like language not because it is a text whose symbolic meanings must be uncovered or deciphered but because rituals are actions that generate meanings in the specific context of other sets of meaningful actions and discourses. Meaning is generated through the iteration and differentiation of signs. Signs refer to other signs within the signifying chain rather than to external realities. Although linguistic signs can and do refer to extralinguistic realities as well as to other signs (a question Derrida seemed to be concerned with in his more recent work on names), in the realm of signifying actions (such as bodily practices and rituals), the distinction between signifying chain and external reality is more difficult to maintain. In other words, ritual actions are—not surprisingly—more like performative speech acts than they are like constatives. Meanings are constitutive and generate that to which they refer.[49]

Methodologically, Bell stresses the importance of the total context to understanding what counts as a ritual within a particular community, whereas Derrida emphasizes our inability ever fully to delimit the context and thereby to fix the meanings or ritualized nature of any activity. (This may give rise to the very un-Derridean tendency, in Bell's work, to separate the performers of an action from the action and its effects. In my Derridean account the two are inseparable, for actions themselves constitute performers.) Through repetition, the movement whereby actions or marks are repeated in another time and place, subjectivities and relations between them are generated. The openness of Bell's understanding of ritualization might usefully be augmented by a crucial insight from Derrida, for repetition (at some level) is the one constraint on ritualization—the one bit of formalization that is constitutive of the process of ritualization itself.[50] This also suggests the aspect of ritualization that establishes continuity between bodily practices and more fully ritualized activities, for both depend on iteration and hence generate meanings and constitute realities. The meaning is the constituted reality, thereby rendering ritual actions more like illocutions (in which the doing or saying, in the right conditions, is the performance) than like perlocutions (in which the proper outcome must follow from the saying or doing for it to be counted a performative). The habitus, in the sense used by Bourdieu and Butler, is made up of bodily practices and rituals (and the distinction between the two is itself a fluid one).

Bell's conception of ritualization and its relationship to power is directly influenced by the work of Foucault, particularly his reconceptualization of power. This helps explain the agreement between her analysis of the ambiguities of subjectivization and that of Butler. Against those theories of ritual which see it as the field in which the power of an elite is wielded and maintained over the populace,[51] Bell argues that ritualization involves the (often very unequal) circulation of power among all the players within the ritual field.[52]

Ritual mastery, that sense of ritual which is at least a basic social mastery of the schemes and strategies of ritualization, means not only that ritualization is the appropriation of a social body but that the social body in turn is able to appropriate a field of action structured in great measure by others. The circulation of this phenomenon is intrinsic to it.[53]

Like other discursive formations generative of subjectivity, ritual is productive of the subject and marks the possibility of that subject's resistance to the very norms and rituals through which it is constituted (see ES, p. 5). Against those theorists who stress the conservative nature of ritual, Bell argues that ritual mastery "experiences itself as relatively empowered, not as conditioned or molded."[54] In a similar way, Margaret Thomson Drewal argues that ritual involves repetition, but always (as does all repetition) repetition with a difference (it has to occur in a different time and place in order for it to be repetition). The room opened for improvisation (which differs in different ritualizations) within the ritual space marks it as a site of both domination and resistance.[55]

Austin argues that the right conditions are necessary for the successful performance of an illocutionary speech act; absent those conditions, the performative misfires and does not, strictly speaking, take place. Derrida and Butler, together with ritual theorists like Asad, Bell, and Drewal, help us to think about the misfiring of the performative in new ways. In changed conditions performatives constitute new kinds of subjects and of communities. Seen in this way, misfiring looks less like a danger than a possibility, one that opens room for improvisation and resistance within the very authoritarian structures of child rearing, education, and religion in which subjects are constituted. We neither freely chose ourselves and our communities, nor are the worlds into which we are born absolutely determinative and authoritarian ones in which no new meanings can be performed. Instead, subjects and communities are created and sustained by the complex interplay of sameness and difference constitutive of repetition itself.

NOTES

1. Butler, *Gender Trouble: Feminism and the Subversion of Identity* (GT) and *Bodies That Matter: On the Discursive Limits of "Sex"* (BTM). For one version of these arguments, see Susan Bordo, *Unbearable Weight: Feminism, Western Culture, and the Body* (Berkeley: University of California Press, 1993), pp. 289–95.

2. One of the problems is the grammatical injunction that there be a subject who either acts or who is fully determined and acted on. See BTM and *The Psychic Life of Power: Theories of Subjection* (PLP).

3. Butler interrogates the concept of materiality without, however, differentiating

between different modes of materiality. For this point, my thanks to Saba Mahmood. For an insightful challenge to the liberatory conception of the subject operating within Butler's work, see Saba Mahmood, "Feminist Theory, Embodiment, and the Docile Agent: Some Reflections on the Egyptian Islamic Revival," *Cultural Anthropology* 16 (2001): 202–35. See also her essay in this volume.

4. One problem with the term *performativity*, as Butler shows in BTM and ES, is the implication, when the theatrical meaning of the term comes to the fore, that the subject intentionally performs. For J. L. Austin theatrical performance implies utterance without intentionality (or without the intention seemingly indicated by the words spoken). Ritual theorists Caroline Humphrey and James Laidlaw argue that rituals are actions in which apt performance does not depend on intentionality. The example I think of here is the consecrated priest who performs sacraments without belief or right intention, yet the sacrament is still said to be aptly performed. I would argue that in this case intentionality is objective and communal rather than individual. The point to note is that there are distinctions between theatrical and ritual performance, although we might finally want to put them on a continuum rather than opposing them. See Caroline Humphrey and James Laidlaw, *The Archetypal Actions of Ritual: A Theory of Ritual Illustrated by the Jain Rite of Worship* (Oxford: Clarendon, 1994); and Stanley Tambiah, "A Performance Approach to Ritual," in *Culture, Thought, and Social Action* (Cambridge: Harvard University Press, 1985), pp. 132–34.

5. See, for example Jacquelyn Zita's review in *Signs* 21 (1996): 786–95; and Caroline Walker Bynum, "Why All The Fuss About the Body? A Medievalist's Perspective," *Critical Inquiry* 22 (1995): 1–33.

6. Butler claims in *Feminist Contentions* that *Gender Trouble* does not give an account of the formation of the subject but only of the gendering of the subject. *Bodies That Matter* then might be taken as extending this discussion to the sexed body. Yet I think that all of these theories have implications for a more general account of subjectivity, one toward which Butler herself continually moves. See Butler, Benhabib, Cornell, and Fraser, *Feminist Contentions: A Philosophical Exchange* (FC), p. 133.

7. Butler, GT, p. 136.

8. See Butler, *Excitable Speech: A Politics of the Performative* (ES).

9. I will use signification here as an umbrella term for that which both constatives and performatives do. Insofar as they can be strictly separated, constatives have meaning and can be true or false, whereas performatives have force and can be efficacious or not efficacious, felicitous or infelicitous. Despite the complexity of twentieth-century theories of meaning and reference, meaning ultimately seems to depend on reference to something outside of or beyond the utterance itself (even if it be something as illusive as "the truth or falsity of the utterance"). An efficacious performative, on the other hand, constitutes that to which it refers. On twentieth-century philosophies, both analytic and continental, of meaning, reference, signification, and performativity, see Benjamin Lee, *Talking Heads: Language, Metalanguage, and the Semiotics of Subjectivity* (Durham: Duke University Press, 1997). Most important for my argument here, Lee describes Austin's discovery "that language cannot be understood without looking for the interplay

between indexicality and meta-indexicality, between signs whose interpretation is tied to the moment of speaking and signs that represent such signs"; ibid., p. 11. Attention to this distinction will be necessary for a more complete account of ritual and bodily practices as performative.

10. Similarly, Butler argues in *Gender Trouble* that gender itself is "the repeated stylization of the body, a set of repeated acts within a highly rigid regulatory frame that congeal over time to produce the appearance of substance, of a natural sort of being" (GT, p. 33).

11. As Butler shows, psychoanalysis offers a useful analysis of some of these norms, particularly as they deal with sexual difference and sexuality. For her arguments about the importance of psychoanalysis to contemporary political theory, see BTM, pp. 12–16; and PLP, pp. 1–30, 83–105, and 114.

12. Psychoanalysis deals with this too, although arguably thinkers like Freud and Kristeva more fully than Lacan. Butler is most interested in the movement between psychic and material bodies. See BTM, pp. 72–88.

13. See, for example, Edmund Leach, "Ritual," in *International Encyclopedia of the Social Sciences* (New York: Macmillan, 1966). The distinction is, of course, too simple and like that made between performative and constative utterances, ultimately breaks down.

14. This has occurred, I think, because of the problems involved in understanding just how ritual actions signify. See note 4.

15. While Austin leans his conception of the speech act on an untheorized conception of ritual, ritual theorists have turned to Austin's and Searle's account of the performative in order to explain ritual. This is the outcome of the tendency to understand ritual as expressive or symbolic action. Given the bankruptcy of symbolic accounts of ritual, and under pressure to come to an understanding of how the parallel between language and action might operate, Stanley Tambiah and others argue that like illocutions and perlocutions, rituals are not constative but performative. They do not mean, but act. See, for example, Tambiah, "Performance Approach," p. 128. Lawson and McCauley point to other theorists, like Benjamin Ray, who use speech act theory to deal only with the linguistic component of ritual. As Lawson and McCauley argue, any good theory of ritual must deal with its multimedia character. This is precisely what Tambiah attempts to do by playing on the multiple meanings of performance. See E. Thomas Lawson and Robert McCauley, *Rethinking Ritual: Connecting Cognition and Culture* (New York: Cambridge, 1990), pp. 51–54. Although I agree that rituals are not referential in normally conceived ways, they are intentional (in the sense of having an end or aim—although that end may not always be the one toward which the actor understands herself as moving) and hence cognitive.

16. I would like, in a longer study, to articulate these theoretical insights through a brief analysis of the changing shape of Christian baptism, a subject of some discussion in Butler insofar as it has to do with naming (BTM, pp. 213–18). In early Christianity and some parts of Protestant Christianity the importance of bodily practices to the ritual of baptism make it inexplicable in Butler's purely linguistic terms.

17. Butler uses ritual the same way in *Gender Trouble*: "As in other ritual social dramas, the action of gender requires a performance that is *repeated*" (GT, p. 140). Although it is not clear if repetition is all there is to ritual, it is clearly a key ingredient.

18. The claim that repetition is not performed by the subject but constitutes the subject is also important, although it leads one to ask *who* or *what* performs. As I will argue below, Butler's point is that in ritual the performance is itself constitutive of the performer.

19. See Pierre Bourdieu, *Language and Symbolic Power*, trans. Gino Raymond and Matthew Adamson (Cambridge: Harvard University Press, 1991).

20. Ibid., p. 109. Cited by Butler, ES, p. 146.

21. I think it is possible to read Derrida more generously here, for although he understands ritual in terms of iterability, this is not necessarily to reduce it to language in the narrow sense. Since for Derrida social meanings are generated by iteration, we can extend this to iterated actions as well as linguistic signs (hence to ritual as well as language).

22. Butler argued in a response to this paper that she ties the force of the performative not to the body of the speaker but through that body to the conventions governing violence. Yet this position seems in danger of returning to the problems represented for Butler by Bourdieu. Shoshana Felman's analysis of the performative is crucial here. See Shoshana Felman, *The Literary Speech Act: Don Juan with J. L. Austin, or Seduction in Two Languages,* trans. Catherine Porter (Ithaca: Cornell University Press, 1983).

23. See Pierre Bourdieu, *Outline of Theory of Practice*, trans. Richard Nice (Cambridge: Cambridge University Press, 1977). Butler calls them rituals (ES, p. 152), although Bourdieu does not.

24. Butler is closer to Catherine Bell's emphasis on ritualization as a form of practice than to Humphrey and Laidlow's insistence that ritualization involves action. For Humphrey and Laidlow ritual is intentional (and hence involves action), but with intentionality divorced from the individual. See Catherine Bell, *Ritual Theory, Ritual Practice* (Oxford: Oxford University Press, 1992); Humphrey and Laidlow, *Archetypal Actions*.

25. One might also argue that it is: insofar as hate mail points to a veiled but still material and bodily threat it carries this destructive force. The veiling of the body behind the threat, in fact, makes it all the more potent because its specific parameters are unknown. This suggests that the tie to the body is crucial and yet can perhaps work more effectively when hidden or veiled and hence only loosely tethered to its utterance through writing and the unsigned text.

26. If bodily practices are speech acts insofar as they are citational, moreover, we are back with Derrida's position in which what makes ritual and language signify *and* act is iteration.

27. See J. L. Austin, *How to Do Things with Words*, ed. J. O. Urmson and Marina Sbisà (Cambridge: Harvard University Press, 1962). Hereafter cited as W.

28. *Force* is Austin's term (W, p. 1).

29. Austin later denies that "purely polite conventional ritual phrases" should be included among performatives (W, p. 84).

30. Austin makes this even more confusing when he goes on to claim that illocution-ary acts are conventional whereas perlocutionary acts are not. This suggests that in illocutionary acts the force of the utterance derives from convention whereas in perlocutionary acts it derives from the speaker, yet Austin never goes so far as to make this claim. Moreover, he goes on in lecture 10 to raise a host of difficul-ties about our ability easily to distinguish illocutionary and perlocutionary acts (see W, p. 121).

31. See Jacques Derrida, "Signature, Event, Context," *Margins of Philosophy*, trans. Alan Bass (Chicago: University of Chicago Press, 1982), pp. 307–30. Hereafter cited as SEC. The essay, it should be noted, was performed in the context of a con-ference on "Communication" presided over by Paul Ricoeur (hermeneutics haunts the piece and is the other pole of reflection on language that runs through it).

32. See in particular the work of John Searle and the debates between Searle and Derrida. John Searle, *Speech Acts* (Cambridge: Cambridge University Press, 1969); John Searle, *Intentionality* (Cambridge: Cambridge University Press, 1983); John Searle, "Reiterating the Differences," *Glyph* 1 (1977): 198–208; and Jacques Derrida, *Limited Inc.* (Evanston: Northwestern University Press, 1988).

33. Stanley Cavell contests this reading. See his "What Did Derrida Want of Austin?" in *Philosophical Passages: The Bucknell Lectures in Literary Theory* (Cambridge: Blackwell, 1995), pp. 42–65.

34. This is Butler's phrase. She focuses on the third of these problems, which is her reading of Bourdieu's implicit critique of Derrida (ES, pp. 149–50).

35. Nancy Fraser argues that Butler tends to conflate the break and resignification with critique and positive political change. This valorization of the break is in-herited, I think, from Derrida. My reading of Derrida suggests that he, while celebrating deconstruction's break with previous significations, also suggests the political and ethical neutrality of the break as such. See Butler et al., FC, pp. 67–68.

36. Often the fact that participants give so many divergent interpretations of the same ritual actions is taken to be a problem for "symbolic" or "expressive" ac-counts of ritual. Yet the existence of multiple meanings or interpretations of a ritual does not mean that it has no meaning, any more than the possibility of multiple interpretations of a text mean it is nonsensical. For this mistake, see Humphrey and Laidlaw, *Archetypal Actions*. A similar problem occurs if the self-referentiality of ritual is taken as grounds for claiming it is without meaning. For the mistake, see Fritz Staal, "The Meaningless of Ritual," *Numen* 26 (1979): 2–22. Lawson and McCauley offer an account of self-reflexive holism to counter these claims; see Lawson and McCauley, *Rethinking Religion*, pp. 137–69.

37. Austin begins by making a clear distinction between constative and performative speech, only to have the distinction blur in the course of his exposition. Finally, what he has described is different ways in which utterances operate, not two radically different forms of utterance. Similarly, ritual actions are both consta-tive and performative—they both signify and do things—although as constitutive acts the performative comes to the fore.

38. Once again I think that the confusion in Butler's account stems from her empha-sis on speech acts and inattention to the other bodily practices through which

subjects are constituted. More attention is given to such issues, however, in *Gender Trouble*.

39. See Talal Asad, *Genealogies of Religion: Discipline and Reasons of Power in Christianity and Islam* (Baltimore: Johns Hopkins University Press, 1993), especially chapters 2, 3, and 4; and Bell, *Ritual Theory, Ritual Practice*.

40. Asad, *Genealogies*, p. 57.

41. Ibid., p. 58. For Asad this reduction of action to textuality is problematic in that it reduces action to discourse. Yet to see action as meaningful does not necessarily mean to engage in western imperialist anthropological enterprises, as Asad seems sometimes to suggest. (See his critique of Geertz.) On the contrary, the problem with the expressivist conception of ritual seems to me to be not the claim that actions *mean* as well as *do things* but rather the insistence on reading the "discourse of actions" in terms of psychology or sociology. It is the search for hidden, symbolic meanings that is the problem, for it obscures the semantics of ritual action itself. On this issue see Daniel Sperber, *Rethinking Symbolism*, trans. A. Morton (Cambridge: Cambridge University Press, 1975); and Lawson and McCauley, *Rethinking Religion*, pp. 37–41.

42. Asad argues that rites as apt performances presume "a code" but claims that it is a regulatory as opposed to a semantic code. See Asad, *Genealogies*, p. 62.

43. Ibid., p. 131.

44. Marcel Mauss, *Sociology and Psychology: Essays*, trans. B. Brewster (London: Routledge and Kegan Paul, 1979), p. 104.

45. Ibid., p. 101.

46. Asad uses *The Rule of Benedict* to make this claim, which he doesn't make as explicit as I have here.

47. Bell, *Ritual Theory, Ritual Practice*, p. 220.

48. Ibid., p. 221.

49. Do rituals and bodily practices then constitute the object of belief as well as its subject? And if so, can we distinguish between fictions and other kinds of realities?

50. Of course, every account of ritual I have ever read includes some discussion of repetition, at the very least as an identificatory criterion. Derrida's work enables us to see what is at stake in ritual repetition and how it is tied to ritual force and meaning. See Jonathan Z. Smith on the power of routinization. Jonathan Z. Smith, "The Bare Facts of Ritual," in *Imagining Religion: From Babylon to Jonestown* (Chicago: University of Chicago Press, 1982), pp. 53–65.

51. See, for example, Bourdieu, *Outline*; and Maurice Bloch, *Ritual, History, and Power: Selected Papers in Anthropology* (London: Athlone, 1989). For more nuanced historicized accounts, see Bruce Lincoln, *Discourse and the Construction of Society: Comparative Studies of Myth, Ritual, and Classification* (Oxford: Oxford University Press, 1989), pp. 53–74; Lincoln, *Authority: Construction and Corrosion* (Chicago: University of Chicago Press, 1994); and Michel de Certeau, *The Practice of Everyday Life*, trans. Steven Rendall (Berkeley: University of California Press, 1984).

52. Bruce Lincoln makes a useful distinction between authority, persuasion, and force. Persuasion and force are potentialities implied by authority, "but once actualized and rendered explicit they signal—indeed, they are, at least temporarily—its negation" (Lincoln, *Authority*, p. 6). If we understand authority as that which is generated through ritual (in keeping with Lincoln's fluid account of authority and my own of the generative capacities of bodily practice and ritual), then ritual actions mark the participants' complicity in legitimizing authority. However, as with hate speech as analyzed by Butler, the force of the speaker's body (or of the state or army or other body that legitimates this authority) always implicitly stands behind authoritative discourse.

53. Bell, *Ritual Theory, Ritual Practice*, p. 215.

54. Ibid., p. 210.

55. Margaret Thomson Drewal, *Yoruba Ritual: Performers, Play, Agency* (Bloomington: Indiana University Press, 1992), pp. 1–11.

AFTERWORD
JUDITH BUTLER

I AM PLEASED FOR this opportunity to respond in general terms to these very provocative papers and to try, within reason, to explain something of my intellectual relation to religion. I fear that I cannot possibly do either of these very well, so I will offer some fragments of understanding and hope that they address the concerns and challenges raised by these very probing and challenging papers.

Most of the papers collected here respond to my work prior to the publication of *Precarious Life: Powers of Mourning and Violence* and the recent articles I have written regarding contemporary politics, Jewish self-criticism, and criticisms of Zionism.[1] There are a few other publications, some recent, that deal directly with religious issues not mentioned here: "Merleau-Ponty and the Touch of Malebranche"[2] and "Kierkegaard's Speculative Despair."[3] I have also written on ethics in my most recent book, *Giving an Account of Oneself*[4] and approached several ethical quandaries in *Undoing Gender*. Currently, I am working on Walter Benjamin's "A Critique of Violence"[5] and some of his other early writings that link the concept of the messianic to the "rhythms of transience" and the prospect of the obliteration of all traces of guilt. I consider this view as an important corrective to the juridification of the subject, typified in that essay by the fate of Niobe. I am also interested, in this regard, in the possibility of a left messianism, pre- and post-Zionist, that has for the most part been left out of contemporary understandings of Jewish thought. My work on this topic emerged from a seminar I offered at Berkeley on "Violence and Ethics in Jewish Philosophy," the general subject of my current research.

My response will be composed of three sections: the first considers "Judaism" and my relation to it in general terms; the second is a "response to my readers" trying to focus on key terms that prompted some trouble for contributors to this text; the third is "Papal Postscript." In 2004 then Cardinal Ratzinger published some remarks on gender theory and the family, and I would like to consider briefly what is at stake for the pope in reading gender theory and engaging with new gender politics.

Judaism

Let me begin by offering a context for the intellectual engagement that I have had with religion. The first point would have to be that intellectual engagement itself became possible for me first in the context of classes I took as part of an extracurricular Jewish education in my early teens. At that point, around 1970, I was moved by the political radicalism of those who were slightly older than me and I was also very claimed by the sermons that my rabbi, Daniel Silver, gave at the synagogue I attended in Cleveland, Ohio. In fact, I used to skip the religious classes in order to sit in the back of the sanctuary to hear his lectures. I remember several such sermons, but one in particular was particularly striking, since he began by considering the difference between Hebraism and Hellenism in Erich Auerbach's *Mimesis*.[6] He also spoke on Freud, obsession, purification, grief, and community, all issues that became for me part of a philosophical trajectory formed within a religious context.

Because I regularly missed Hebrew class for reasons unknown, I was expelled from the religious classroom and forced to take a tutorial with the rabbi as a punishment. Little did my teachers know that this was, in fact, my most ardent wish. When asked by the rabbi what I wanted to study in this tutorial, I proposed three topics: 1. why was Spinoza excommunicated from the Jewish community? 2. what is existential theology? and, 3. can one show that German Idealism was in any way responsible for the rise of Nazism in Germany? These questions form the beginning of what I would call "intellectual engagement" for me, at least one that took place within the context of a pedagogical relation, however vexed that relation was in its initial form.

I offer this autobiographical vignette in order to suggest that, prior to any questions of gender or sexuality, there were for me questions regarding the

Jewish community, its history of persecution, its methods of expelling its own, its relation to violence, and the question of what of theology could remain after the Nazi death camps. For the existential theologians (Tillich, Buber, Niebuhr, Jaspers) religious questions followed from an acceptance of human finitude, and there was no theological debate on whether or not God exists. I see now that most of religious studies also sets this question aside. The idea that God had died or had himself (*sic*) been annihilated in the course of the twentieth century was a particular conviction for postwar Ashkenazi Jews. And since the same Shoah that seemed to destroy the belief in God—or through which, alternatively, God vanished—made it imperative for the Jews to cohere as a community that would survive and mourn the loss of those who did not, it seemed to me that Judaism could only be a kind of existential theology. The questions that one poses, as it were, after the death of God are no less religious than those posed before this ostensible event. Whether one sought meaning or an alternative to meaning, asked about nihilism or whether ethical relationality bears a religious significance or whether the subject is self-made or grounded in a set of relations that precede and exceed its knowing, these questions were all made possible against the background of a religious horizon, even if no theology could be built upon such inquiry.

Somewhere in the midst of this early education I came to understand as well that textual interpretation was at the heart of these life and death questions. To know how to live, one had to know how to read, and one had to be able to develop an interpretation of what one read. There was a tacit hermeneutics at work in these early efforts at reading. And it was only later when I went to study with Hans-Georg Gadamer at Heidelberg that I came to understand how firmly rooted contemporary hermeneutics was in biblical interpretation, especially in the early versions of hermeneutics found in Dilthey and Schleiermacher. For Gadamer the text, in being read, was given new life and new temporality. His reading of Walter Benjamin in *Truth and Method* incited me.[7] And it resonated with what I had understood from my Jewish education. The Talmud worked slightly differently, but I understood that the text was precisely "living" to the extent that it remained interpretable, and that something of the text was extended and augmented with every interpretation.

The Bible was particularly important precisely because it gave rise to quandaries, to problems of interpretation and, hence, to communities of interpreters defined by their quarreling and their differences. These had to be close readings not because the "intentions" of some vanished God had to be discerned. There were no such intentions. The text contained, as it were, so many marks of that vanishing, and the abandoned reader was left with the fragments of an indecipherable world the code to which had been permanently lost. Later, Kafka became the writer for me, Edmund Jabès the poet, and both Freud and Benjamin crucial theoretical allies, and I suppose it is safe to say that they remain so. One could thus become very Jewish in the absence of God without precisely becoming secular. That negation of God formed a historical horizon within which thought began and within which it would suffer its own foundering time and again. God survived as a lost thought. There was and is little for me of Nietzschean joy or Deleuzian affirmation in any of this, but neither is there a turn to unalloyed mourning. There is, as it were, mourning with others and living with others, and this question of the Other, a mandate to attend to the precariousness of life, and not just Jewish life. These views had little to do with Zionism but did hold out for a sense of Judaism as diasporic, in the world, intermixed with the non-Jew, and building an ethic and politics on the basis of that proximate and constitutive encounter with alterity.

I was not interested in defining Jewish identity, but rather in seeing how a framework of Jewish values could be brought to bear on the field of ethics and politics. The formation of the Jewish subject against the background of the Nazi holocaust has become a standard way of narrating the emergence of twentieth-century Jewish identity. My own formation would seem to confirm that Ashkenazi trajectory, given that my family is from Hungary, Poland, and Russia, and nearly all the Hungarians were destroyed in the camps. My subsequent education was premised on this very graphic and personal loss as the defining event, even the groundwork for an ethic of solidarity, antiracism, and public mourning. As important as this historical framework is to understand contemporary Jewish ethics, it is equally important to remember that Mizrachim and Sephardim, who together compose nearly half the Israeli population, come from non-European sources as diverse as Iraq, Spain, and North Africa. Mizrachim are Arab Jews whose very existence puts into crisis the prevailing framework in which there are Arabs on one side of a divide and Jews on the other. Regardless of the way that Mizrachim vote in Israeli elections, they produce a demographic and historiographical problem for an Ashkenazi narrative of the founding of the state of Israel that fails to understand the complex and interconstitutive cultural relations between Jewish and Arab cultural traditions. I would also suggest that, philosophically, the question of the Arab Jew opens up the question of the "Other" who is at the heart of identity, the one who can only be expelled or occupied at the expense of oneself. Politically, this question opens the way to a nonidentitarian sense of Jewishness, one whose responsiveness to the Other is essential to who one "is."

Edward Said seemed to refer to this other trajectory for Jewish ethics when he wrote of Freud's relation to Jewishness in *Freud and the Non-European*.[8] There he finds, for instance, a reference to the unhoused and diasporic character of Jewish life, one that aligns it "in our age of vast population transfers"

with "refugees, exiles, expatriates and immigrants" and that he further characterizes as "the diasporic, wandering, unresolved, cosmopolitan consciousness of someone who is both inside and outside his or her community" (p.
53). The non-European from the Jewish point of view, he writes, is essential
to the meaning of Judaism, and we might well understand that Said, in writing this book, makes himself essential to the understanding of what Judaism
is yet to become. What he affirms in Freud's embrace of Moses as the non-
European Egyptian who becomes the founder of the Jews is the challenge it
poses for thinking identity along more complex lines. For Said, it

> refuses to resolve identity into some of the nationalist or religious herds in which
> so many people want so desperately to run. More bold is Freud's profound exem-
> plification of the insight that even for the most definable, the most identifiable, the
> most stubborn communal identity—for him, this was the Jewish identity—there are
> inherent limits that prevent it from being fully incorporated into one, and only one,
> Identity. . . . In other words, identity cannot be thought or worked through itself
> alone; it cannot constitute or even imagine itself without that radical originary break
> or flaw which will not be repressed, because Moses was Egyptian, and therefore
> always outside the identity inside which so many have stood, and suffered—and
> later, perhaps, triumphed.
>
> (pp. 53–54)

Remarkable here is that what Said finds at the site of Judaism's origin is
precisely an impurity, a mixing with otherness, which turns out to be constitutive of what it is to be a Jew.[9] "The strength of this thought," he tells
us, "is that it can be articulated in and speak to other besieged identities as
well . . . as a troubling, disabling, destabilizing secular wound" (p. 54). He
asks whether we might continue to think this thought of two peoples, diasporic, living together, where the diasporic, understood as a way of attaining
identity only with and through the other, becomes the basis for a certain
binationalism. "Can [this thought] aspire to the condition of a politics of
diasporic life? Can it ever become the not-so-precarious foundation in the
land of Jews and Palestinians of a bi-national state in which Israel and Pales-
tine are parts, rather than antagonists of each other's history and underlying
reality" (p. 55)? Is it, I might add, precisely through a politics that affirms the
irresolution of identity that binationalism first becomes thinkable?
    I have elaborated above on the relationship of Judaism to the origin of my
thinking to explain as well some of the recent turns in my thinking about
contemporary politics, post-Zionism, and the risks of Jewish self-critique
as well as the ethical and political injunction to move beyond the ethos of
nationalism and a narrow politics of identity. Of course, autobiographies are
only logical, if they ever are, in retrospect. But let me suggest that the begin-

nings of this ethical and political framework were there in the question of Spinoza's expulsion from the Jewish communities. He apparently maintained beliefs that were considered not in accord with prevailing rabbinic standards (such as angels and miracles), and he would not alter them in order to keep his place in the community. His expulsion draws the line between what is speakable and unspeakable in his community at that time. As a result, it shows how the community defines itself through establishing what shall remain unspeakable. In contemporary political life an analogy suggests itself when those who criticize Israel are considered antisemitic. Specifically, if a Jew criticizes Israel publicly or queries whether the current form of the state is a justified or auspicious one, is a Jew therefore speaking against the Jews? This conclusion can only be true if a given stand on the state of Israel is (or has become) definitive of Judaism. My view is that it must be possible to openly debate this question without suffering expulsion from the community or being attacked as "antisemitic" for voicing a dissenting view on the contemporary organization of the state apparatus in what is called Israel. Open debate characterized the Talmudic struggles over interpretation that formed my earliest intellectual engagements with Judaism. In this sense my dissenting voice draws upon a Jewish tradition that has enduring value and so does not act against the Jewish people but mobilizes an alternative framework for the voicing of dissent.

Response to the Authors in this Volume

The essays in this volume try to make sense of a series of writings that I published primarily between 1990 and 2000. I am, fortunately or not, a living author, and this means that I am always in the process of restaging and finding new experimental possibilities for prior positions. I suppose that this does make me into a "process philosopher" of a certain stripe. I'm aware of resonances among my various writings, but I do not intend them to follow upon one another systematically or to amount to a single, comprehensive "position." They are, for me, various experimental forays. Indeed, part of what being a "living" author means, as I understand it, is to be always underway, revising one's stand or approaching the same thematic from another angle with a different set of questions. In this way I cannot quite "stand" for "my work" as an evolving totality. My sense is that this very notion of "one's work" belongs to another century and perhaps also another gender (how many of us, by virtue of various divisions of labor, write episodically, discontinuously?). My own inconsistencies may well be due to a failure to go back and try to reconcile various claims with each other. I confess, however, that my failure to go back and perform such a reckoning is what permits me to write and to think something new. This might actually be a kind of principled forgetful-ness about my prior deeds. Of course, a reader may or may not find such a procedure (or lack thereof) acceptable, but, for me, it is what allows me to continue to write. It also makes me into someone who has a difficult time giving a coherent account of what I have thought and how I have revised myself and what my current positions now mean in relation to the previous ones. This is the work that others may wish to do, and I am grateful for the illuminations they offer me and readers of my work. But it is not precisely my work, and cannot be, since that form of heightened reflexivity would doubt-less stop me from moving forward. So I live with a certain inability to reckon myself with myself or, rather, that inability permits me to live.

That said, here are several points about key terms, italicized for the reader below, and what I might have meant by them, offered within the framework of that forgetfulness and nonunity that appears to be my authorial self:

1. *Drag* was a way of exemplifying how reality-effects can be plausibly produced through reiterated performances, but it was never meant to be the primary example or norm for gender subversion. Of course, it makes sense that it was taken up that way, but it has never had that particular place for me. It was meant to elucidate a structure that is at work in everyday performances of gender, and so to make this reiterative production of reality-effects legible as a repeated practice in so-called ordinary social life. Most important was the idea that "reality" is given to certain kinds of gender appearances over others, and that those who are transgendered are regularly debased and pathologized for "not being real." The point is that the ontological field is mobilized by power relations, and that what we come to regard and affirm as "real" or "unreal" can and does undergo critical change depending on social mobilizations of various kinds.

2. It is interesting to consider that *abjection,* a term that I worked with mainly, if not exclusively, in *Bodies That Matter,* might in certain contexts be considered "liberatory." I am not sure that abjection is as key to every account of subject formation as it is in the first part of *Bodies That Matter.* If virtue in some ascetic discourses requires abjection, and if it is regularly linked with the male sex, then it would seem that there may be ways of denaturalizing that link and recasting abjection as a critique of virtue. These are wonderfully interesting insights, and my only question would be: what is it, finally, to identify a practice as "liberatory?" As Mrozik shows, these matters are highly contextual, and we have to ask: liberated from what and in the direction of what? If the account we give is historical, then what might appear liberating in one context can give rise to different account of oppression in another. Surely the overcoming of "abjection" in full is not possible for any subject, but the values accorded to this complex condition shift historically.

3. It seems important to return to origin stories to see how the story of the emergence of the human installs a gendered norm as the logical presupposition of human-ness. If the narrative sequence is necessary, then a logical relation is also entailed. And so origin stories are not just variable tales but ways of building a sensical notion of the human. If it can be shown that the origin story admits to a certain possibility of gender prior to sexual difference (i.e., Adam is not a sexually differentiated being, as Stone points out), then a counternormativity is at work in the very story that is supposed to install the necessity of sexual difference. This is a very exhilarating argument. Similarly, the practice of ordination required that one, in a communal setting, partake of the body of Christ, where one meaning of this "partaking" is to stand in the place of a man and to establish continuity with his morphological sex. It is, of course, interesting to note both how this kind of argument precludes women from ordination (unless a certain "trans" assumption is allowed), but also requires that the "partaking" remain at a symbolic level and so not become literalized as homosexual erotic feasting, as it were.

4. I am interested in the way that Hutchins describes the expansion of the self toward a more ethically capacious position, a motion of the self that constitutes an opening of the future. That this is, even parenthetically, identified as the "motion of the holy" suggests a redescription of the holy that locates a certain transcendence as a feature of the self. That the holy might be a kind of motion and that the self might be said to be composed of that motion strikes me as a post-Aristotelian way of coming to terms with that which is at once "in" the self and "exceeds" the self. This paradox points to the failure to ground the self in itself, something that Amy Hollywood has pointed out as the religious background of some poststructuralist thinking.[10]

In Judaism what is affirmed as the sacred is precisely that which cannot be fully captured by any appearance, certainly no visual icon. There are no idols that might represent the sacred, and, for this reason, the infinite is precisely that which cannot appear. How is it, then, that we might understand this motion of the self as that which can only appear indirectly in its effects, precisely in its altered capacity to respond to others, their suffering, the demand to self-alteration they place upon us, the ethical obligations that are addressed to us in various ways? If this motion can only appear indirectly, then there will have to be a hermeneutics that comes to bear upon this encounter, one that would know and mark its inability to capture what it seeks to know.

5. *Critique*, in Foucault's sense, involves calling into question the necessity of a given grid of intelligibility, a given regime of representability. The operation of critique cannot work through a straightforward language of representation, since critique interrogates the constraints on representability that are historical and changeable. To interrogate those constraints is to ask

how the orchestration of reality works such that it does not always show a trace of its own working. It is at those moments in which a grid of intelligibility seeks to *enforce* its own necessity that it displays its contingent and forcible character and solicits the transformative potential of critique.

6. There are perhaps two responses to Schneider's close reading of my troubled relation to the body.

a. Toni Morrison's vignette relayed in *Excitable Speech* about the blind woman who tells the taunting children that "the bird is in your hand" is a complex tale, and it can easily give rise to different interpretations. In my view the blind woman cannot see the hands that hold the bird, but she knows that they are there. When she says that the bird is in their hands, she says that the responsibility for the precarious life of that bird is the responsibility of those children. Important here is the context of impending cruelty, the admonition that the blind woman delivers, but also the assignation of responsibility that comes through her speech. She neither sees nor touches that bird, but the "hand" figures in her language as the instrument of care and cruelty, posing the question of whether their touch will be fatal or life-giving. What is interesting here is the way that words can function as "hands" insofar as they also have the power to wound. Whether we can attribute a physical capacity to injure to words is, of course, controversial. It would be as wrong to say that words do not wound as it would be to say that words are the exact equivalent of a physical blow. The vignette relays this difficulty.

b. When Descartes asks whether *these* hands are his own, he is, of course, not blind, but rather seduced by the effects of the plural pronoun. If my hands can become *these* hands, then a separation can be effected between these hands and what belongs to me. The grammar induces a skepticism about what is his own. He sees the empirical hands, and he touches those hands, and he touches with those hands. His question is only possible on the condition that he suspends belief in the empirical reality that he sees, that is, in empiricism more generally and the proofs furnished by the tactile and visible world. Because Descartes is not blind, but only doubts what he sees, he turns against his own capacity to see in a way that is nearly impossible to imagine. Descartes' self-blinding is no model for any of us, but a kind of madness, an estrangement from bodily truths that happens, in part, because of the language he uses. The words do not furnish the body. So though the phrase "these hands" appears to refer to his own hands, the phrase points, but does not quite deliver. One ought not to derive from Descartes' predicament a generalized scene of writing. Rather, Descartes is haunted by the spectral return of his body in various tormenting external figures that bear his own disowned corporeality. If we think, though, that we might counter Cartesian madness through a simple return to the body, to an "owning" that is secure, something about language makes that less than certain.

In the first instance, the "hands" both figure a kind of responsibility in the face of a choice to be cruel or not; in the second, they figure a disowned bodily limb that returns in spectral form. In neither case are they purely literal, but in neither are they purely not. In the same way, I am perhaps in my reader's hands, but also, emphatically, over here, *and not*.

7. Although *subversion* is sometimes considered a kind of tactic that a subject deliberately instrumentalizes for an explicit purpose at hand, I am not sure that it must carry that meaning. If it did have that meaning, subversion would be nothing other than an instrumentality deployed by an autonomous will. What would we make of those kinds of subversions that happen unwittingly? When Foucault points out that the discourse that pathologizes homosexuality at the end of the nineteenth century inadvertently produced the possibility of an emancipatory political discourse for homosexuals, he is pointing out a subversive trajectory of power that is not reducible to intention or will. Similarly, in *Gender Trouble* and elsewhere, it would seem that subversion happens not only or exclusively as a "tactic" mobilized by an intention but also as a strategy without intention, one that follows from reversals and proliferations of discourse and power in their convergence. Even when there is agency, it is a vexed one, since one is mired in the discourse that makes one's agency possible and so never fully distanced from it as an instrumental relation would imply. This is the meaning of the paradox of subjection, since one depends upon that very norm to be formed as a subject and an agent even as one struggles against the conditions of one's own formation.

I think it would be difficult to find the term *resistance* in my work. I think it is probably used no more than four (4) times and, in my view, implies an exteriority to power that, in *Gender Trouble* at least, subversion did not. *Subversion* was the preferred term because it communicates something of the mire from which political agency emerges, and *resistance* tends to convey the purity and oppositional character of a stance. And though Foucault claimed that where there is power, there is resistance, I could not find any resources in myself to believe that he was, in that instance, right. If I am in part the object that I oppose, then I am mired from the start. No less than my own ontology is at stake when I engage in the kind of critique that I do. There is no "uprooting" of myself from such formative norms without a full destruction of myself. This is why agency is a vexed affair, and *resistance* does not seem the right word for this kind of struggle.

So if I am asked to accept the claim that there is no subverting of a norm without inhabiting that norm, then I fully agree. It is part of what is meant when I say that the norm that forms the subject is also the one that is subject to revision or alteration or critique. If such a norm is part of one's formation, it inhabits one from the start and reconstitutes it as a result.

I am not sure that one opposes the norms by which one is formed and sustained in order to maximize one's freedom. I can see that the framework that opposes freedom to unfreedom, valorizing the former and debunking the latter, misses other kinds of cultural relations—fealty, piety—that may be at work in a given ethical practice. This point seems to be a crucial corrective to some feminist theorizing, especially on Islam. If one considers Saba Mahmood's fine analysis, then we can see that she is tracing the development of schools of interpretation within the mosque movement in which women actively offer modes of interpretation that at once conform to Quranic law and innovate precisely on the question of what it means to conform, how best to conform, and how to reconcile such conformity with secular demands that emerge from the workplace and wider market realities.[11] They are simultaneously conforming to and restaging that doctrine, "working the norm," and thus making it generate new possibilities. They are also, clearly, in and through their own speech acts, claiming the enunciative position of interpreting the law: this can be at once an act of conformity and something new. Do these not constitute something like "new possibilities" that are produced through practical reiterations of faith, both interpretive and ritualistic, that are not fully predictable in advance? Is there not a difference between an innovation that works with the norm and a "transcendence" of the norm that works in the name of emancipation and "freedom?"

8. The theory of *performativity* in *Gender Trouble* was written without reference to J. L. Austin. I understood something of what Derrida was doing with the term, especially in his writings on Kafka, and I then turned to Bourdieu, but Austin came later, forming the focus of my concerns in *Excitable Speech*.

Although in the transition from *Gender Trouble* to *Bodies That Matter* some scholars worried that *performativity* seemed to slide from being a dimension of bodily acting to a dimension of language, I want to suggest that it is at once a bodily act and a speech act. I tried to make this clear in my afterword to Shoshana Felman's *The Scandal of the Speaking Body*: "As bodily, the speech act loses its claim to sovereignty in a different way than it does when recast as writing. The speech act 'says' more than it can ever intend or know" (p. 114); and, "when the body speaks, it fails to fulfill the claims made on behalf of consciousness. But the body is not 'outside' the speech act. At once the organ of speech, the very organic condition of speech, and the vehicle of speech, the body signifies the organic conditions for verbalization" (pp. 116–17); and, "the mouth is the precise place of mediation between language and the body" (p. 117).[12]

I think it would be wrong, as Hollywood suggests, to say that, in my view, the body is produced by speech acts. How would that exactly work? Does someone *say*, "let there be this new body there" and then a new body arrives in the world? No, there are several convergent factors, including felicitous reproductive methods, that "produce" a human body, any body.

The question at issue is rather something like the following: how does a body saturated with social norms and conventions bear those structures, give current and future life to those social realities? Note from the outset that there is a passive impression ("saturated") and an active re-inhabiting ("bear," "give life"). The body enters into institutional life from the start and has that life impressed upon it, registers that impression through a passivity that is never completely unalloyed.[13] After all, that impression is registered through a kind of responsiveness. The response to those social meanings involves a reiteration of their force—precisely a kind of inhabiting of what is impressed upon one from the start. If this reiteration can be called a "ritual," then this is the case only because rituals are, by definition, shared and social. Indeed, in the same way that Foucault would shift the structuralist emphasis on "structures" to a social emphasis on "norms," so "ritual" has the benefit of adding a social dimension to Derridean "iterability." Speech acts are not the same as the iterability of language—indeed, discourses can reiterate without any verbal enunciation. And speech acts do not unilaterally produce a body; indeed, they often bespeak a body that in some ways eludes intentionality. Speech acts also can be ways in which a social residue is reanimated, but they are only one set of ways.

Importantly, Bourdieu's notion of the "body as belief" considered in *Excitable Speech* offers us a way to see how norms are taken up and lived through a kind of prethetic adherence. Similarly, if one says that the performativity of gender relies upon the credible or plausible reiteration of reality-effects, then it would seem that "belief" is essential to the living of the body within its social context. The context does not simply surround this body, but saturates it. And though to say the "body is saturated" is to privilege a passive construction, it is crucial to add that the body "adheres" to its saturation. This may be the paradoxical structure of "inhabiting" one's social body, since social conventions and norms (without which ritual cannot be thought) are impressed upon one as the condition of existence itself and yet actively inhabited and orchestrated, giving rise to an "agency" that is always less than intentional.

Papal Postscript

In Ratzinger's 2004 "Letter to the Bishops of the Catholic Church in the Collaboration of Men and Women in the Church and the World,"[14] he takes on two approaches to women's issues. The first, he maintains, sustains an oppositional relationship to men. The second is one that he characterizes with the following language:

In order to avoid the domination of one sex or the other, their differences tend to be denied, viewed as mere effects of historical and cultural conditioning. In this perspective, physical difference, termed sex, is minimized, while the purely cultural element, termed gender, is emphasized to the maximum and held to be primary. The obscuring of the difference or duality of the sexes has enormous consequences on a variety of levels. This theory of the human person, intended to promote prospects for equality of women through liberation from biological determinism, has in reality inspired ideologies which, for example, call into question the family, in its natural two-parent structure of mother and father, and make homosexuality and heterosexuality virtually equivalent, in a new model of polymorphous sexuality.

He goes further to suggest that this second approach to women's issues is rooted in a motivation understood as "the human attempt to be freed from one's biological conditioning. According to this perspective, human nature in itself does not possess characteristics in an absolute manner: all persons can and ought to constitute themselves as they like, since they are free from every predetermination linked to their essential constitution."

It is difficult to know how best to respond to a document that constitutes part of a papal encyclical. Ratzinger formulates his criticism of this paraphrased position within doctrinal terms, so if one wants to argue with it, one would either have to argue against the doctrine or show that the doctrine or other Catholic religious sources can yield an alternative point of view. I am, then, caught at this moment, since it seems important to try and engage this position, given its enormous authority throughout the world. It is my sense that religionists might well try to take on this and other more recent documents[15] that seek not only to target feminism but also lesbian and gay life, transgendered embodiment, gay marriage, and the scope of legitimate human sexuality. Of course, many progressive secularists would simply say that "this is the Pope! What do you expect?" and debunk the arguments that way. And then there may well be Catholic responses that seek to alter doctrine in the Church, offering theological arguments that seek to temper or expand Ratzinger's positions here. I would like to position myself in neither way, but what way is then left? Ratzinger characterizes positions here, without citation, so whereas it appears that he may have read some of them, he is not beholden to any textual evidence in making his claims. The scripture, of course, is cited, but the positions that defy or threaten scripture are clearly not (as far as my research has yielded).[16]

Ratzinger goes on to make clear how the doctrine of sexual difference he defends is rooted in the story of Genesis, a story that establishes the "truth" of men and women. His opposition to gay marriage, which seeks to "destroy" that truth, is thus linked with his implicit creationism. One could simply reply by saying, yes, the truth of man and woman that you outline is no truth at all and we seek to destroy it in order to give rise to a more humane and radical set of gender practices. But to speak this way is simply to reiterate the cultural divide that makes no analysis possible. Perhaps one needs to start with the status of the story, of Genesis itself, and to see what other readings are possible. Perhaps one needs to ask which biology Ratzinger actually accepts, and whether the biological theories he supports are ones that consider homosexuality to be a benign part of human sexual variation. It seems that his remark that social constructionists seek to deny and transcend biological differences commits him to a theological reading of social construction, since that "transcendence" is, presumably, what is to be sought for the "sacralization" of sexuality in terms of its transcendent function. Can it be shown that the biological differences to which he refers are actually consonant with the transcendent meanings he reserves for heterosexual sexuality in the service of reproduction? In addition to finding out which biological account Ratzinger has in mind, it would be important to understand whether the social practices he seeks to curb, including civil unions for same-sex partners, are either prescribed or proscribed by any ostensible biological function. The point is not to deny biology and to embrace a voluntaristic self-making but to ask whether and how biology and social practice are understood in relation to one another.

If religionists are to engage and challenge the papal authority within its own terms, they will have to offer ways of thinking through the relationship of embodiment and transcendence; biology and social practice and process; the meanings of justice, love, and equality; and the revisable character of papal authority itself. That I cannot quite engage this issue is perhaps a sign of how badly we need religionists to do so within the terms that can make it more difficult for this papal authority to legitimate itself without contest. And if those who debunk this authority in the name of a smug secularism simply choose to turn the other way, than this quite forceful and reactionary machinery is left free to have its way in demeaning the sexual and gendered lives of those who already struggle against unjust restrictions and abjected sexualities within the social and political world. If there is a social site in which sexuality is imbued with paralyzing judgments, it is doubtless in and through the papal pulpit. And, because it is a site of power, it must be engaged critically and insistently until open and sustained conflict on the place and meaning of religious authority of this kind yields hope for intimate associations and gendered practices that have not always been accorded "dignity" within society. Let a thousand conflicts of interpretation bloom, I say! And I say this not because pluralism alone will ease our minds but because the proliferation of possible interpretations may well lead to the subversion of an authority that grounds itself in what may not be questioned. In such a world, questions, loud and clear, remain intrinsic goods.

Berkeley, August 2005

NOTES

1.   The final two chapters of *Precarious Life* are particularly relevant to Jewish issues: "The Charge of Anti-Semitism: Jews, Israel, and the Risks of Public Critique" (originally published in the *London Review of Books*, August 1993) and "Precarious Life," which works with a Levinasian conception of "the face" to consider differential forms of humanization in the recent U.S. wars against Afghanistan and Iraq.

2.   Judith Butler, "Merleau-Ponty and the Touch of Malebranche" in *The Cambridge Companion to Merleau-Ponty*, ed. Taylor Carmen and Mark B. N. Hansen (Cambridge: Cambridge University Press, 2005), pp. 181–205.

3.   Judith Butler, "Kierkegaard's Speculative Despair" in *The Age of German Idealism, The History of Philosophy,* ed. Robert C. Solomon and Kathleen V. Higgins, vol. 6 (New York: Routledge, 1993), pp. 363–95. This article includes a consideration of the paradoxical language of faith and an extended reading of *Fear and Trembling* in relation to the "trembling" of Hegel's bondman in the *Phenomenology of Spirit.*

4.   Judith Butler, *Giving an Account of Oneself* (GAO).

5.   In Walter Benjamin, *Reflections: Essays, Aphorisms, Autobiographical Writings*, ed. Peter Dementz, trans. Edmund Jephcott (New York: Schocken, 1978).

6.   Erich Auerbach, *Mimesis: The Representation of Reality in Western Literature*, trans. Willard R. Trask (Princeton: Princeton University Press, 1968).

7.   Hans-Georg Gadamer, *Truth and Method*, trans. Joel Weinsheimer and Donald G. Marshall (New York: Continuum/Seabury, 1975).

8.   Edward Said, *Freud and the Non-European* (New York: Verso, 2003).

9.   See also Bonnie Honig, *Democracy and the Foreigner* (Princeton: Princeton University Press, 2003).

10.   See Amy Hollywood, *Sensible Ecstasy: Mysticism, Sexual Difference, and the Demands of History* (Chicago: University of Chicago Press, 2002).

11.   See also Saba Mahmood, *The Politics of Piety: The Islamic Revival and the Feminist Subject* (Princeton: Princeton University Press, 2004).

12.   Judith Butler, "Afterword," in Shoshana Felman, *The Scandal of the Speaking Body: Don Juan with J. L. Austin, or Seduction in Two Languages* (Stanford: Stanford University Press, 2002), pp. 113–24.

13.   I consider this relation of passivity and activity in two chapters devoted to Emmanuel Levinas and Jean Laplanche in GAO. Also, in "Merleau-Ponty and the Touch of Malebranche," I suggest that Merleau-Ponty rewrites psychoanalysis as a seventeenth-century theology (one based on the idea that sentience is itself a result of being "touched" by God) at the same time that he offers a tactile account of phenomenology. Merleau-Ponty writes that "it must be possible to recognize the origin of a principle of passivity in freedom." This last essay might also be interesting to read in light of Rebecca Schneider's remarks. I write there: "our inability to ground ourselves is based on the fact that we are animated by others into whose hands we are born and, hopefully, sustained. We are always, in some way, done to as we are doing ... touched in the act of touching" (p. 203).

14.   See "Letter to the Bishops of the Catholic Church in the Collaboration of Men

and Women in the Church and the World," July 31, 2004, http://www.vatican.va/roman_curia/congregations/cfaith/documents/rc_con_cfaith_doc_20040731_collaboration-en.html.

15. Cardinal Joseph Ratzinger, "Family, Marriage and 'de facto' Unions," The Pontifical Council for the Family, July 26, 2000, http://www.vatican.va/roman_curia/pontifical_councils/family/documents/rc_pc_family_doc_20001109_de-facto-unions_en.html.

16. Several European media identified my work as targeted by Ratzinger's letter, but I have found no direct citations in what he has written. See, for example, on the Internet: "Vatican Fires Volley in Sex War," *Agence France-Presse,* August 1, 2004, http://www.edicom.ch/news/international/040731143133.sa.shtml; Martin Reichert, "Sein Kreuz mit den Frauen," *Die Tagezeitung*, July 31, 2004 http://www.taz.de/pt/2004/07/31/a0222.nf//text.

SELECTED BIBLIOGRAPHY

BOOKS BY JUDITH BUTLER

AC   *Antigone's Claim: Kinship Between Life and Death.* New York: Columbia University Press, 2000.

BTM *Bodies That Matter: On the Discursive Limits of "Sex."* New York: Routledge, 1993.

ES   *Excitable Speech: A Politics of the Performative.* New York: Routledge, 1997.

GAO *Giving an Account of Oneself.* New York: Fordham University Press, 2005.

GT   *Gender Trouble: Feminism and the Subversion of Identity.* New York: Routledge, 1990.

GT (1999)
    Gender Trouble: Feminism and the Subversion of Identity. 10th anniversary edition. New York: Routledge, 1999.

PL   *Precarious Life: The Powers of Mourning and Violence.* New York: Verso, 2004.

PLP *The Psychic Life of Power: Theories in Subjection.* Stanford: Stanford University Press, 1997.

UG   *Undoing Gender.* New York: Routledge, 2004.

CHU *Contingency, Hegemony, Universality: Contemporary Dialogues on the Left.* With Ernesto Laclau and Slavoj Žižek. London: Verso, 2000.

FC   *Feminist Contentions: A Philosophical Exchange.* With Seyla Benhabib, Drucilla Cornell, and Nancy Fraser. New York: Routledge, 1995.

ARTICLES AND ESSAYS BY JUDITH BUTLER

"Afterword." In Shoshana Felman. *The Scandal of the Speaking Body: Don Juan with J. L. Austin, or Seduction in Two Languages.* Stanford: Stanford University Press, 2002. Pp. 113–24.

"Against Proper Objects." "More Gender Trouble: Feminism Meets Queer Theory." *Differences: A Journal of Feminist Cultural Studies* 6, nos. 2 and 3 (Summer-Fall 1994): 1–26.

"Contingent Foundations: Feminism and the Question of 'Postmodernism.'" In *Feminists Theorize the Political.* Ed. Judith Butler and Joan W. Scott. New York: Routledge, 1992. Pp. 3–21.

"Doing Justice to Someone: Sex Reassignment and Allegories of Transsexuality." *GLQ: A Journal of Lesbian and Gay Studies* 7, no. 4 (2001): 621–36; revised in UG.

"Ethical Ambivalence." In *The Turn to Ethics.* Ed. Marjorie Garber, Beatrice Hanssen, and Rebecca Walkowitz. New York: Routledge, 2000. Pp. 15–46.

"Further Reflections on Conversations of Our Time." *Diacritics* 27, no. 1 (1997): 13–15.

"Gender as Performance." In *A Critical Sense: Interviews with Intellectuals.* Ed. Peter Osborne. New York: Routledge, 1996. Pp. 109–26; first published in *Radical Philosophy* 67 (Summer 1994).

"Gender Trouble, Feminist Theory and Psychoanalytic Discourse." In *Feminism/Postmodernism.* Ed. Linda J. Nicholson. New York: Routledge, 1990. Pp. 324–40.

"'How Can I Deny That These Hands and This Body Are Mine?'" *Qui Parle* 11, no. 1 (1997): 1–20.

"Imitation and Gender Insubordination." In *Inside/Outside: Lesbian Theories, Gay Theories.* Ed. Diana Fuss. New York: Routledge, 1991. Pp. 13–31.

"Is Kinship Always Already Heterosexual?" *Differences: A Journal of Feminist Cultural Studies* 13, no. 1 (Spring 2002): 14–44; reprinted in UG.

"Kierkegaard's Speculative Despair." In *The Age of German Idealism.* Ed. Robert Solomon and Kathleen Higgens. London: Routledge, 1993. Pp. 363–95.

"Merleau-Ponty and the Touch of Malebranche." In *The Cambridge Companion to Merleau-Ponty.* Ed. Taylor Carmen and Mark B. N. Hansen. Cambridge: Cambridge University Press, 2005. Pp. 181–205.

"Performative Acts and Gender Constitution: An Essay in Phenomenology and Feminist Theory." In *Performing Feminisms: Feminisms: Feminist Critical Theory and Theatre.* Ed. Sue-Ellen Case. Baltimore: Johns Hopkins University Press, 1990. Pp. 270–82.

"Performativity's Social Magic." In *Bourdieu: A Critical Reader.* Ed. Richard Shusterman. Oxford: Blackwell, 1999. Pp. 113–28.

"Politics, Power, and Ethics: A Discussion Between Judith Butler and William Connolly." With William Connolly. *Theory and Event* 24, no. 2 (2000). http://muse.jhu.edu/journals/theory_and_event/v004/4.2butler.html

"Reflections on Germany." In *Queer Theory and the Jewish Question.* Ed. Daniel Boyarin, Daniel Itzkovitz, Ann Pellegrini. New York: Columbia University Press, 2003. Pp. 385–402.

"Subjects of Sex/Gender/Desire." In *Feminism and Politics.* Ed. Anne Phillips. New York: Oxford University Press, 1998. Pp. 273–91.

"Variations on Sex and Gender: Beauvoir, Wittig, and Foucault." In *Feminism as Critique: On the Politics of Gender*. Ed. Seyla Benhabib and Drucilla Cornell. Minneapolis: University of Minnesota Press, 1987. Pp. 128–142.

"What Is Critique? An Essay on Foucault's Virtue." In *The Political*. Ed. David Ingram. Oxford: Blackwell, 2002. Pp. 212–28.

SECONDARY SOURCES IN RELIGIOUS STUDIES

Althaus-Reid, Marcella. *The Queer God*. New York: Routledge, 2003.

Beal, Timothy. *The Book of Hiding: Gender, Ethnicity, Annihilation, and Esther*. New York: Routledge, 1997.

Boyarin, Daniel, Daniel Itzkovitz, and Ann Pellegrini, eds. *Queer Theory and the Jewish Question*. New York: Columbia University Press, 2003.

Brooten, Bernadette. *Love Between Women: Early Christian Responses to Female Homoeroticism*. Chicago: University of Chicago Press, 1996.

Daniell, Anne. "The Spiritual Body: Incarnations of Pauline and Butlerian Embodiment Themes for Constructive Theologizing Toward the Parousia." *Journal of Feminist Studies in Religion* 16, no. 1 (Spring 2000): 5–21.

Fulkerson, Mary McClintock. "Church Documents on Human Sexuality and the Authority of Scripture." *Interpretation* 49, no. 1 (January 1995): 46–59.

—— "Gender—Being It or Doing It? The Church, Homosexuality, and the Politics of Identity." In *Que(e)rying Religion: A Critical Anthology*. Ed. Gary David Comstock and Susan E. Henking. New York: Continuum, 1997. Pp. 188–201.

Goss, Robert E., and Mona West. *Take Back the Word: A Queer Reading of the Bible*. Cleveland: Pilgrim, 2000.

Gottschall, Marilyn. "The Ethical Implications of the Deconstruction of Gender." *Journal of the American Academy of Religion* 70, no. 2 (June 2002): 279–99.

Jakobsen, Janet R., and Ann Pellegrini. *Love the Sin: Sexual Regulation and the Limits of Religious Tolerance*. New York: New York University Press, 2003.

Keller, Mary. *The Hammer and the Flute: Women, Power, and Spirit Possession*. Baltimore: Johns Hopkins University Press, 2002.

Rudy, Kathy. *Sex and the Church: Gender, Homosexuality, and the Transformation of Christian Ethics*. Boston: Beacon, 1997.

Stone, Ken. *Queer Commentary and the Hebrew Bible*. Cleveland: Pilgrim and Sheffield Academic, 2001.

Ward, Graham. "Theology and Masculinity." *Journal of Men's Studies* 7, no. 2 (1999): 281.

CONTRIBUTORS

EDITORS

ELLEN T. ARMOUR is R.A. Webb Associate Professor of Religious Studies at Rhodes College. She is the author of *Deconstruction, Feminist Theology, and the Problem of Difference: Subverting the Race/Gender Divide* (Chicago: University of Chicago Press, 1999) and is currently working on a book on religion and postmodernism.

SUSAN M. ST. VILLE is formerly assistant professor and director of gender studies at Notre Dame University. She is currently a licensed clinical social worker practicing in the Chicago area. She is coeditor of *Transfigurations: Feminist Theology and the French Feminists* (Minneapolis: Fortress, 1993).

CONTRIBUTORS

KAREN TRIMBLE ALLIAUME is assistant professor in the Department of Theology and director of the Women's Studies Program at Lewis University in Romeoville, Illinois. She is completing a book manuscript, with the working title "Re(as)sembling Christ: Feminist Christology, Identity Politics, and the Imagination of Christian Communities," for publication.

AMY HOLLYWOOD is Elizabeth H. Monrad Professor of Christian Studies at Harvard Divinity School. She is the author of *Sensible Ecstasy: Mysticism, Sexual Difference, and the Demands of History* (Chicago: University of Chicago Press, 2002).

TERESA J. HORNSBY is assistant professor of religious studies and director of the Women and Gender Studies Program at Drury University in Springfield, Montana. She is the author of a number of essays on feminist and queer issues in biblical studies.

CHRISTINA K. HUTCHINS teaches process theology at Pacific School of Religion, and her essays and poems have been published in *Theology and Sexuality*, the *Journal of Feminist Studies of Religion*, *Frontiers*, *North American Review*, and in anthologies including *God, Literature and Process Thought* (Burlington, VT: Ashgate 2002).

SABA MAHMOOD is assistant professor of anthropology at the University of California, Berkeley. She is the author of *Politics of Piety: The Islamic Revival and the Feminist Subject* (Princeton: Princeton University Press, 2004).

SUSANNE MROZIK is assistant professor of religion at Mount Holyoke College and has published a number of articles on Buddhist ethics in the *Journal of Buddhist Ethics* and the *Journal of Religious Ethics*.

CLAUDIA SCHIPPERT is assistant professor of humanities and director of the Religious Studies Program at the University of Central Florida in Orlando, Florida. Recent publications include "Containing Uncertainty: Sexual Values and Citizenship" (*Journal of Homosexuality*) and "Sporting Heroic Bodies in a Christian Nation-at-War" (*Journal of Religion and Popular Culture*).

REBECCA SCHNEIDER is head of the M.A. and Ph.D. programs in theater and performance studies at Brown University. She is the author of *The Explicit Body in Performance* (New York: Routledge, 1997), "Hello Dolly Well Hello Dolly: The Double and Its Theatre" (*Psychoanalysis and Performance*), and "Solo Solo Solo" in *After Criticism: New Responses to Art and Performance* (Malden, MA: Blackwell, 2005), pp. 23–47.

KEN STONE is associate professor of Hebrew Bible at the Chicago Theological Seminary. His most recent book is *Practicing Safer Texts: Food, Sex, and Bible in Queer Perspective* (London: Clark/Continuum, 2005).

INDEX